Congressional Procedures
and the
Policy Process

SECOND EDITION

Congressional Procedures
and the
Policy Process

SECOND EDITION

Walter J. Oleszek

CQ Press, a division of
Congressional Quarterly Inc.
1414 22nd Street N.W., Washington, D.C. 20037

Politics and Public Policy Series

Advisory Editor

Robert L. Peabody

Johns Hopkins University

Copyright © 1984 Congressional Quarterly Inc.

Printed in the United States of America

Library of Congress Cataloging in Publication Data

Oleszek, Walter J.
    Congressional procedures and the policy process

    Bibliography: p.

    Includes index.

    1. United States. Congress. I. Title.
JK1096.043 1984   328.73   83-20860
ISBN 0-87187-281-1

For Janet,

Mark, and Eric

Table of Contents

Tables

Illustrations

Foreword

In his insightful preface to *Jefferson's Manual,* still incorporated in the rules of the House of Representatives, Thomas Jefferson, then serving as vice president, observed:

> It is much more natural that there be a rule to go by than what that rule is; that there may be a uniformity of proceedings in business not subject to the caprice of the specter or captiousness of the members.*

In *Congressional Procedures and the Policy Process,* now in its second edition, Walter J. Oleszek operates from the basic assumptions "that Congress matters and that its rules and procedures are important." Through countless examples and illustrations, he shows just how the rules, procedures, and traditions of Congress affect the course and content of legislation.

For more than 15 years, Dr. Oleszek has been both a close observer of and a participant in the congressional scene. After receiving his Ph.D. from the State University of New York at Albany in 1968, he joined the staff of the Congressional Research Service of the Library of Congress. He participated as a key staff member on the House Select Committee on Committees (1973-1974), chaired by Rep. Richard W. Bolling of Missouri; the Senate Select Committee on the Committee System (1976-1977), chaired by Illinois Sen. Adlai E. Stevenson, III; and the House Select Committee on Committees (1979-1980), chaired by Rep. Jerry M. Patterson. With Roger H. Davidson, Dr. Oleszek is the coauthor of two other books, *Congress against Itself* (1977) and *Congress and Its Members* (1981).

Working closely with members of Congress and committees on a day-to-day basis, Dr. Oleszek is eminently qualified to explain how bills originate, how they move through the committees to the floor, and what is similar and what is different about floor deliberations in the 435-member House as compared to the 100-member Senate. Throughout his book he pays special attention to the strategic impact of rules and reforms on legislative outcomes.

The book's presentation is clear and concise. It is a book from which students and citizens in general can learn in an interesting way just how floor debate is managed in each chamber and how "prolonged debate" (the filibuster) inhibiting the flow of legislation is dealt with in the Senate.

Congressional Procedures and the Policy Process has the further virtue of incorporating the many changes in the rules and procedures of Congress since the first edition (1978).

Robert L. Peabody

Constitution, Jefferson's Manual, and Rules of the House of Representatives, 93d Cong., 2d sess., H. Doc. 416 (Washington, D.C.: U.S. Government Printing Office, 1975), 119-120.

Preface

My objective in this book is to examine how the contemporary Congress makes laws and how its rules and procedures shape public policy. Although the legislative branch has always been a source of interest to scholars and journalists, the interplay of rules, precedents, pressures, and strategies has received less attention. This book describes the procedural route taken by most major legislation from its introduction to final passage and presidential action.

In Chapters 1 and 2 I also look at the constitutional role assigned to Congress, the key participants on Capitol Hill, and some of the social, economic, and political forces that influence decision making. Chapter 3 examines the increasingly important congressional budget process, and Chapter 10 surveys Congress's efforts to oversee the implementation of the laws. The emphasis throughout is on the use of the rules for strategic purposes — to expedite or delay legislation, to secure enactment, or to bring about the defeat of bills.

The major theme of *Congressional Procedures and the Policy Process* is that rules and procedures are important: They have a significant effect on domestic and foreign policy, and they are the object of continuous scrutiny by members of Congress and interested outsiders. I have included numerous examples of this interaction between rules and policy making. These examples will, I trust, convey some sense of the congressional atmosphere.

Finally, this book implicitly addresses the question of why Congress is not the efficient, streamlined, disciplined body some people want it to be. Congress's procedural rules encourage deliberation, collegial decision making, dissent, openness, participation, and accessibility. These facts of congressional life make coalition politics a necessity at every stage of the process, and they underscore the importance of bargaining and accommodation. They are not, however, qualities that encourage quick decisions or tidy organizational patterns.

In this volume I emphasize the rules and procedures most significant to congressional lawmaking. I do not attempt to survey every detail of the parliamentary procedures used by Congress.

Congress is truly a dynamic institution. That is the principal reason for preparing a second edition of this book. The House and Senate periodically employ new procedures in response to changing circumstances. Each chamber also modifies or discards established routines to strengthen its policy-making capabilities, enhance its oversight of administrative activities, and augment its representational responsibilities. The aim of the second edition is to spotlight for readers significant congressional developments since the first edition was published in 1978.

I am grateful to the numerous individuals who contributed to this book by offering constructive criticisms and suggestions at every stage of preparation. I am deeply indebted to my editor at CQ Press, my colleagues at the Congressional Research Service of the Library of Congress, and scores of senators and representatives, legislative staff aides, scholars, and political commentators for their insights on Congress. Any faults and shortcomings of this book are mine, however.

My editor at Congressional Quarterly, Michael D. Wormser, deserves my special and grateful thanks for shepherding this manuscript to final publication. Just like a "floor manager," he artfully circumvented dead ends and pitfalls and contributed significantly and creatively to the end result. I gladly acknowledge his thoughtful suggestions for improving the manuscript.

I am also deeply in debt to Walter Kravitz, a former colleague at the Congressional Research Service, who, with James M. Enelow, read the entire manuscript with great care and suggested numerous improvements and clarifications. A storehouse of knowledge about the workings of Congress, Mr. Kravitz extended himself to polish the book and to further educate me about legislative procedures. I consider myself fortunate to have worked over the years with such a knowledgeable and considerate colleague.

My thanks, too, must go to David R. Tarr, director of CQ's Book Department, and Joanne D. Daniels, director of CQ Press, for their encouragement and support throughout this project. My deep appreciation also goes to Robert L. Peabody, advisory editor for this book, for his support in the initial conception of this study.

Whatever understanding of the legislative process I may have comes in no small part from my colleagues at the Congressional Research Service. That institution, I should note, bears no responsibility whatsoever for the views or interpretations expressed within these pages. In particular, three CRS colleagues were tremendously helpful to me at every stage of the book's progress: Roger H. Davidson, Louis Fisher, and Robert Keith. These highly capable colleagues never failed to offer astute advice and suggestions, particularly on Chapter 3 dealing with the congressional budget process. Many other associates at CRS offered valuable assistance by clarifying issues or answering questions. These include Mildred Amer, Stanley Bach, Richard Beth, Judy Carlile, Edward Davis, Frederick Kaiser, Ronald Moe, Daniel Mulhollan, Clark Norton, Paul Rundquist, and Richard Sachs.

In addition, my sincere thanks go to the administrative leaders of CRS, especially Director Gilbert Gude, and Frederick Pauls, chief of the Government Division, for encouraging CRS employees — on their own time, of course — to teach, write, and stay abreast of the issues of the day.

There are several others who have provided valuable aid throughout my more than 15 years on Capitol Hill. I want to acknowledge that my understanding of how Congress works stems in part from the answers to the scores of questions that I put to the House and Senate parliamentarians. As the premier experts on congressional procedures, I am under heavy obligation to them for all their kind assistance.

Finally, I dedicate the second edition of this book to my wife, Janet, and my two sons, Mark and Eric. Fortunate, indeed, am I to have such warm, loving, and helpful partners.

Walter J. Oleszek

1

Congress and Lawmaking

"In republican government," wrote James Madison, "the legislative authority necessarily predominates." [1] And Madison, among others, tried to ensure that in the new United States government, Congress *would* emerge as the central policy-making authority.

Lawmaking is Congress's most basic response to the entire range of national concerns, from agriculture to housing, environment to national defense, health to the economy. The process by which Congress transforms an idea into national policy is the subject of this book. This process is complicated and variable, but it is governed by rules, procedures, precedents, and customs, and is open to the use of some generally predictable strategies and tactics.

Members of Congress have major responsibilities other than lawmaking — to represent their constituents and to review the implementation of laws. All these functions are integral parts of the congressional process.

This first chapter examines the constitutional foundation of congressional policy making, the functions of rules and procedures in organizations, the interaction of rules (formal and informal) and policy making in the congressional context, and the important features of congressional decision making.

The Constitutional Context

Congress's central role in policy making can be traced to the writers of the Constitution. Madison, Hamilton, and the others developed a political system that established Congress as the lawmaking body and set out its relationship with the other branches of government and with the people. Several familiar basic principles underlie the specific provisions of the Constitution. These include limited government, separation of powers, checks and balances, and federalism. Each principle continues to shape lawmaking today despite the enormous changes that have transformed and enlarged the role of government in American society.

1

Limited Government

The framers of the Constitution wanted a strong and effective national government, but at the same time they wanted to avoid concentrating too much power in the central government lest it threaten personal and property rights. Limitation of government, the framers believed, could be achieved by dividing power among three branches of national government and between the nation and the states. The division of power assured both policy conflicts and cooperation because it made officials in the several branches responsive to different constituencies, responsibilities, and perceptions of the public welfare.

The framers believed that the "accumulation of all powers, legislative, executive, and judiciary, in the same hands may justly be pronounced the very definition of tyranny." [2] As men of practical political experience, they had witnessed firsthand the abuses of King George III and his royal governors. They also wanted to avoid the possible "elective despotism" of their own state legislatures.[3] Wary of excessive authority in either an executive or legislative body, the framers also were familiar with the works of influential political theorists, particularly Locke and Montesquieu, who stressed such concepts as the separation of powers, checks and balances, and popular control of government.

Separation of Powers

The framers combined their practical experience with a theoretical outlook and established three independent branches of national government, none having a monopoly of governing power. Their objective was twofold. First, the separation of powers was designed to restrain the power of any one branch. Second, it was meant to ensure that cooperation would be necessary for effective government.

The framers held a strong bias in favor of lawmaking by representative assemblies, and so viewed Congress as the prime national policy maker. The Constitution names Congress the first branch of government, assigns it "all legislative power," and grants it explicit and implied responsibilities. Almost half the words of the Constitution (Article I) are devoted to the legislative branch, enumerating the many specific powers of Congress.

In sharp contrast, Articles II and III, creating the executive and judicial branches, describe only briefly the framework and duties of these governmental units. Although separation of powers implies that Congress "enacts" the laws, the president "executes" them, and the Supreme Court "interprets" them, such a rigid division of labor was not intended by the framers. They did grant certain unique responsibilities to each branch and ensured their separateness by, for example, prohibiting any officer from serving in more than one branch simultaneously.

Checks and Balances

An essential corollary of separation of powers is checks and balances. The framers of the Constitution realized that individuals in each branch might seek to aggrandize power at the expense of the other branches. Inevitably, conflicts would develop. In particular, the Constitution provides an open invitation to struggles for power by Congress and the president.

To restrain each branch, the framers devised a system of checks and balances. Congress's own legislative power was effectively "checked" by establishing a bicameral body consisting of the House of Representatives and the Senate. The laws Congress passes may be vetoed by the president. Treaties and high-level presidential appointments require the approval of the Senate. And many decisions and actions of Congress and the president are subject to review by the federal judiciary.

Checks and balances have a dual effect; they encourage cooperation and accommodation among the branches, and they introduced the potential for conflict. And since 1789 Congress and the president have indeed cooperated with each other *and* protected their own powers. Each branch depends in various ways on the other. When conflicts occur, they are resolved most frequently by negotiation, bargaining and compromise.

Federalism

Just as the three branches check each other, the state and federal governments also are countervailing forces. This division of power is another way to curb and control governing power. While the term "federalism" (like separation of powers or checks and balances) is not mentioned in the Constitution, the framers understood that federalism was a plan of government acceptable to the 13 original states. The "supremacy" clause of the Constitution made certain that the states would not pass unconstitutional laws; however, powers not granted to Congress remained with the states.

Federalism has infused "localism" into congressional proceedings. As a representative institution, Congress and its members respond to the needs and interests of states and congressional districts. The nation's diversity is given ample expression in Congress by legislators whose tenure rests on the continued support of their constituents.

Thus, the Constitution outlines a complicated system. Power is divided among the branches and between levels of government, and popular opinion is reflected differently in each. Both Congress and the president, each with different constituencies, terms of office, and times of election, can claim to represent majority sentiment on national issues. Given each branch's independence, formidable powers, different perspectives on many issues, and intricate mix of formal and informal relationships, it is apparent that important national policies reflect the judgment of both the legislative and executive branches and the views of pressure groups and influential persons.

Congress: An Independent Policy Maker

Much has been written about the growth of executive power in the twentieth century and the diminished role of Congress, but in fact there has been a dynamic, not static, pattern of activity between the legislative and

Major Sources of House and Senate Rules

U.S. Constitution. Article I, Section 5, states: "Each House may determine the Rules of Its Proceedings." In addition, other procedures of Congress are addressed, such as quorums, adjournments, and roll calls.

Standing Rules. The formal rules of the House are contained in the *Constitution, Jefferson's Manual* and the *Rules of the House of Representatives*. For the Senate, its rules are in the *Senate Manual Containing the Standing Rules, Orders, Laws, and Resolutions Affecting the Business of the United States Senate*. Each chamber prints its rule book biennially as a House or Senate document.

Precedents. Each chamber, particular the larger House, has scores of precedents, or "unwritten law," based upon past rulings of the Chair. The modern precedents of the Senate are compiled in one volume prepared by Floyd M. Riddick, parliamentarian emeritus. It is revised and updated periodically, printed as a Senate document, and entitled *Senate Procedure, Precedents and Practices*. House precedents are contained in several sources. Precedents from 1789 to 1936 are found in 11 volumes: *Hinds' Precedents of the House of Representatives* (from 1789 to 1907) and *Cannon's Precedents of the House of Representatives* (from 1908 to 1936). Precedents from 1936 through 1973 can be found in the multivolume series (not yet complete) entitled *Deschler's Precedents of the United States House of Representatives*. Hinds, Cannon, and Deschler were parliamentarians of the House. Further, the precedents now are updated every two years and published as *Procedure in the U.S. House of Representatives*. It is prepared by the House parliamentarian.

Statutory Rules. There are many public laws whose provisions have the force of congressional rules. Notable examples include the Legislative Reorganization Act of 1946 (PL 79-601), the Legislative Reorganization Act of 1970 (PL 91-510), and the Congressional Budget and Impoundment Control Act of 1974 (PL 93-344).

Jefferson's Manual. When Thomas Jefferson was vice president (1797-1801) he prepared a manual of parliamentary procedure for the Senate. Ironically, the House in 1837 made it a formal part of its rules, but the Senate did not grant it such status. The provisions of his manual "govern the House in all cases to which they are applicable and in which they are not inconsistent with the standing rules and orders of the House."

Party Rules. Each of the two major political parties has its own set of party rules. Some of these party regulations directly affect legislative procedure. The House Democratic Caucus, for example, has a provision that affects the Speaker's use of the suspension of the rules procedure.

Informal Practices and Customs. Each chamber develops its own informal traditions and customs. They can be uncovered by examining such sources as the *Congressional Record* — the substantially verbatim account of House and Senate floor debate, scholarly accounts, and other studies of Congress. Several committees and party groups also prepare manuals of legislative procedure and practice.

executive branches. First one and then the other may be perceived as the predominant branch, and various periods are characterized as times of "congressional government" or "presidential government." [4] Such descriptions often underestimate the other branch's strategic importance, however. President John F. Kennedy, who served during a period regarded by some observers as one of presidential resurgence, observed that Congress "looks more powerful sitting here than it did when I was there." From his position in the White House, he looked at the collective power of Congress and found it "substantial." [5]

In short, the American political system is largely congressional *and* presidential government.

The strength and independence of Congress contrast sharply with the position of legislatures in other democratic countries. In most, policy making is concentrated in the hands of a prime minister and cabinet who are normally elected members of the legislature and are leaders of the majority party. As a result, the policy of the prime minister and his cabinet typically is approved by the legislature, with voting divided strictly along party lines. Conversely, if a prime minister loses a "vote of confidence" in parliament, he or she is expected to resign, and a general election is held to choose a successor government.

The U.S. Congress, by contrast, is elected separately from the president and has independent policy-making authority. As a result, a study of policy making in the United States requires a separate examination of the congressional process.

Functions of Rules and Procedures

Any decision-making body, Congress included, needs a set of rules, procedures, and conventions, formal and informal, in order to function. *(See box, p. 4.)*

In the case of Congress, the Constitution authorizes the House and Senate to formulate their own rules of procedure and also prescribes some basic procedures for both houses, such as the presidential veto process. Thomas Jefferson, who as vice president compiled the first parliamentary manual for the United States Senate, emphasized the importance of rules to any legislative body.

> It is much more material that there should be a rule to go by, than what the rule is; that there may be uniformity of proceeding in business not subject to the caprice of the Speaker or captiousness of the members. It is very material that order, decency, and regularity be preserved in a dignified public body. [6]

Rules and procedures in an organization serve many functions. Among them are to provide stability, legitimize decisions, divide responsibilities, reduce conflict, and distribute power. Each of these functions will be illustrated by examples drawn from a college or university setting and by parallel functions in Congress.

5

Stability

Rules provide stability and predictability in personal and organizational affairs. Individuals and institutions can conduct their day-to-day business without having to debate procedure. Universities, for example, have specific requirements for bachelor's, master's, and doctorate degrees. Students know that if they are to progress from one degree to the next they must comply with rules and requirements. Daily or weekly changes in those requirements would cause chaos on any campus. Similarly, legislators need not decide each day who can speak on the floor, offer amendments, or close debate. Such matters are governed by regularized procedures that continue from one Congress to the next and afford similar rights and privileges to every member.

To be sure, House and Senate rules change in response to new circumstances, needs, and demands. The history of Congress is reflected in the evolution of the House and Senate rules. Increases in the size of the House in the nineteenth century, for instance, produced limitations on debate for individual representatives. Explained Senate Democratic leader Robert C. Byrd, W.Va., about Senate proceedings:

> The day-to-day functioning of the Senate has given rise to a set of traditions, rules, and practices with a life and history all its own. The body of principles and procedures governing many Senatorial obligations and routines . . . is not so much the result of reasoned deliberations as the fruit of jousting and adjusting to circumstances in which the Senate found itself from time to time.[7]

Legitimacy

Students typically receive final course grades that are based on their classroom performance, examinations, and term papers. They accept the professors' evaluations if they believe in their fairness and legitimacy. If professors suddenly decided to use students' political opinions as the basis for final grades, there would be a storm of protest against such arbitrary procedures. In a similar fashion, members of Congress and citizens accept legislative decisions when they believe the decisions have been approved according to orderly and fair procedures.

Division of Labor

Any university requires a division of labor if it is to carry out its tasks effectively and responsibly, and rules establish the various jurisdictions. Hence there are history, chemistry, and art departments; admissions officers and bursars; and food service and physical plant managers, all with specialized assignments. For Congress, committees are the heart of its legislative process. They provide the division of labor and specialization that Congress needs to handle about 15,000 measures that are introduced biennially, and to review the administration of scores of federal programs. Like specialized bodies in many organizations, committees do not make final policy decisions but initiate recommendations that are forwarded to their respective chambers.

The jurisdiction, or policy mandate, of Congress's standing (permanent) committees is outlined in the House and Senate rules. Legislation generally is referred to the committee that has authority over the subject matter. As a result, the rules generally determine which committee, and thus which members and their staffs, will exercise significant influence over a particular issue such as defense, taxes, health, or education. Sen. Edward M. Kennedy, D-Mass., won assignment to the Armed Services Committee in 1983 (even though he became one of its most junior members) to gain greater influence and credibility in debating the critical issues of war and peace.

Rules also prescribe the standards committees are expected to observe during their policy deliberations. These rules also allocate staff resources to committees and subcommittees.

Conflict Resolution

Rules reduce conflicts among members and units of organizations by distinguishing appropriate actions and behavior from the inappropriate. For example, universities have procedures by which students may drop or add classes. There are discussions with faculty advisers, completion of appropriate paperwork, and the approval of a dean. Students who informally attempt to drop or add classes may encounter conflicts with their professors as well as sanctions from the dean's office. Most of the conflicts can be avoided by observance of established procedures. Similarly, congressional rules reduce conflict by, for example, establishing procedures to fill vacancies on committees when several members are competing for the same position.

As Rep. Clarence A. Cannon, D-Mo. (1923-64), a former House parliamentarian and subsequently the chairman of the Appropriations Committee, explained:

> The time of the House is too valuable, the scope of its enactments too far-reaching, and the constantly increasing pressure of its business too great to justify lengthy and perhaps acrimonious discussion of questions of procedure which have been authoritatively decided in former sessions.[8]

Distribution of Power

A major consequence of rules is that they generally distribute power in any organization. Rules, therefore, often are a source of conflict themselves. During the 1960s, many campuses witnessed struggles among students, faculty, and administrators involving the curriculum. The charge of irrelevance in course work was a frequent criticism of many students. As a result, the "rules of the game" for curriculum development were changed on many campuses. Students, junior faculty, and even community groups became involved in reshaping the structure and content of the educational program.

Like universities, Congress distributes power according to its rules and customs. Informal party rules, for example, establish a hierarchy of leadership positions in both chambers. And House and Senate rules accord prerogatives to congressional committee chairmen that are unavailable to noncommittee leaders. Rules, therefore, are not neutral devices. They help to shore up the more powerful members and influence the attainment of member goals such as winning reelection, gaining internal influence, or winning congressional passage of legislation. Thus, attempts to change the rules almost invariably are efforts to redistribute power.

In recent years, House rules have been amended to strengthen the Speaker's authority to limit opportunities for members to delay floor proceedings. When the 98th Congress (1983-85) convened, the Democratic majority in the House enacted a package of rules changes designed to "protect the majority of the Members against the enthronement of some minority." One of these changes permitted the Speaker to declare that the House is in the Committee of the Whole. Previously, a House vote was required for such action. *(Details, see Chapter 6.)* To Democrats, such changes improved the efficiency of House operations. But Republicans had another view: "The rules changes are plainly designed to reduce the role of the minority." [9]

Rules and Policy Making in Congress

Rules play similar, but not identical, roles in most complex organizations. Congress has its own characteristics that affect the functions of the rules. First, members of Congress owe their positions to the electorate, not to their congressional peers or to influential congressional leaders. No one in Congress has authority over the other members comparable to that of university presidents and tenured faculty over junior faculty or to that of a corporation president over lower-level executives. Members cannot be fired except by their constituency. And each member has equal voting power in committees and on the floor of the House or Senate.

The rules of Congress, unlike those of many organizations, are especially sensitive to the rights of minorities, including the minority party, ideological minorities, and individual members. Skillful use of the rules enables the minority to check majority action by delaying, defeating, or reshaping legislation. Intensity often counts as much as numbers — an apathetic majority may find it difficult to prevail over a well-organized minority. Except in the few instances when extraordinary majorities are needed, such as overriding presidential vetoes (a two-thirds vote), Senate ratification of treaties (two-thirds), and ending extended debate (a filibuster) in the Senate (three-fifths), the rules of the House and Senate require a simple majority to decide public policies.

Congress also is different from other organizations in its degree of responsiveness to external groups and pressures. The legislative branch is not as self-contained an institution as a university or a corporation. Congress is involved with every significant national and international issue. Its agenda compels members to respond to changing constituent interests and needs.

Congress also is subject to numerous other influences, particularly the president, pressure groups, political parties, and state and local officials.

Finally, Congress is a collegial, not a hierarchical, body. Power does not flow from the top down, as in a corporation, but in practically every direction. There is only minimal centralized authority at the top; congressional policies are not "announced" but are "made" by shifting coalitions that vary from issue to issue. Congress's deliberations are more accessible to the public than those of perhaps any other kind of organization. These are some of the characteristics that set Congress apart from other bodies. Inevitably these differences affect the decision-making process.

Procedure and Policy

Legislative procedures and policy making are inextricably linked in at least four ways.

First, procedures affect policy outcomes. Congress processes legislation by complex rules and procedures that permeate the institution. Some matters are only gently brushed by the rules, while others become locked in their grip. Major civil rights legislation, for example, failed for decades to win congressional approval because southern senators used their chamber's rules and procedures to kill or modify such measures.

Congressional procedures are employed to define, restrict, or expand the policy options available to members during floor debate. They may prevent consideration of certain issues or presage policy outcomes. The House, for instance, often considers controversial measures under procedures that shape its decision making. These procedures sometimes even name the representatives who may offer amendments to legislation (prohibiting others from doing so); require that the amendments be printed in advance in the *Congressional Record*; forbid other members from proposing changes in the policy proposals; and specify the exact order in which these previously printed amendments can be offered on the floor. In short, such tightly structured procedures enhance the policy influence of certain members, committees, or party leaders; facilitate expeditious treatment of issues; grant priority to some policy alternatives but not others; and determine, in general, the overall character of policy decisions.

A second point is that very often policy decisions are expressed as procedural moves. Representatives and senators, on various occasions, prefer not to make clear-cut decisions on certain complex and far-reaching public issues. Should a major weapons system be continued or curtailed? Should the nation's energy production needs take precedence over environmental concerns? Should financial assistance for the elderly be reduced and priority given to aiding disadvantaged children? On questions like these, members may be "cross-pressured" — the president may exert influence one way while constituent interests dictate another approach. Legislators sometimes lack adequate information to make informed judgments. They may be reluctant to oppose powerful pressure groups. Or they may feel that an issue does not lend itself to a simple "yes" or "no" vote.

As a result, legislators employ various procedural devices to handle knotty problems. A matter may be postponed on the ground of insufficient study in committee. Congress may direct an agency to prepare a detailed report before an issue is considered. Or a measure may be "tabled" by the House or Senate, a procedural vote that effectively defeats a proposal without rendering a clear judgment on its substance.

Third, the nature of the policy can determine the use of certain procedures. The House and Senate generally consider noncontroversial measures under expeditious procedures, whereas controversial proposals normally involve lengthy deliberation. Extraordinary circumstances might prompt Congress to invoke rarely used practices to enact legislation with dispatch. For example, during the severe winter weather of 1977 President Jimmy Carter urged Congress to approve quickly a law granting him authority to order transfers of natural gas to states hard hit by gas shortages. On January 26, 1977, the measure was introduced in the Senate. To speed the bill's passage, the Senate employed a seldom-used procedure that brought the measure immediately to the floor for debate, bypassing the usual committee stage entirely.[10] Moreover, under pressure from its leadership, the Senate rejected all substantive amendments and passed the measure by a 91-2 vote after two days of debate. As national issues change, some procedures become nearly extinct while others are used more and more frequently to meet new needs.

Finally, policy outcomes are more likely to be influenced by members with procedural expertise. Members who are skilled parliamentarians are better prepared to gain approval of their proposals than those who are only vaguely familiar with the rules. Just as carpenters and lawyers must learn their trade, members of Congress need to understand the rules if they expect to perform effectively. Congressional procedures are confusing to members. "To table, to refer to committee, to amend — so many things come up," declared Sen. S. I. Hayakawa, R-Calif. (1977-83). "You don't know whether you are coming or going." [11] House Speaker John W. McCormack of Massachusetts once advised House newcomers:

> Learn the rules and understand the precedents and procedures of the House. The congressman who knows how the House operates will soon be recognized for his parliamentary skills — and his prestige will rise among his colleagues, no matter what his party.[12]

Members who know the rules will always have the potential to shape legislation to their ends and to become key figures in coalitions trying to pass or defeat legislation. Some members even become parliamentary "watchdogs" or use "guerrilla warfare" tactics to harass the opposition. Those who do not understand the rules reduce their proficiency and influence as legislators.

Members also learn the rules so they can better circumvent them for their own political and policy ends. There is, in brief, conventional and unconventional lawmaking. Conventional lawmaking involves the traditional parliamentary pathway of committee hearings, markups, and reports; floor consideration; conference committee deliberations; House and Senate approval of the conference reports; and presidential signature or veto. *(See chart, p. 13.)*

Unconventional lawmaking traverses a circuitous procedural route. A classic example involved the 1982 tax increase fashioned by Senate Finance Committee Chairman Robert Dole, R-Kan., and signed into law by President Reagan.

Despite the constitutional requirement that the House must initiate revenue-raising measures, it was plain to members of both chambers that the Senate initiated the nearly $100 billion tax bill. To be sure, there was technical compliance with the Constitution. The GOP-led Senate took a minor House-passed tax bill (HR 4961) and added its tax package to it. Then the Democratic-controlled House voted to go directly to conference with the Senate and thus avoid taking any political blame for a tax increase during an election year — and in a recession to boot. As a result, there were no House committee hearings, or a committee report, on the Senate's product; nor was there any House floor debate — except on the conference report — on one of the largest tax increases in American history.[13]

Precedents and Folkways

Congress is regulated not only by formal rules, but by informal ones that influence legislative procedure and member behavior. Two types of informal rules are precedents and "folkways." Precedents, the accumulated past decisions on matters of procedure, represent a blend of the formal and informal. They are the "common law" of Congress and govern many procedures not explicitly covered in the formal rules. As a noted House parliamentarian wrote, the great majority of the "rules of all parliamentary bodies are unwritten law; they spring up by precedent and custom; these precedents and customs are this day the chief law of both Houses of Congress." [14] For example, formal rules prescribe the order of business in the House and Senate, but precedents permit variations through the unanimous consent of the members. The rulings of the Speaker of the House and presiding officer of the Senate form a large body of precedents. They are given formal status by the parliamentarians in each chamber and then become part of the accepted rules and procedures.

Folkways, on the other hand, are unwritten norms of behavior that members are expected to observe. "Without these folkways," concluded a scholar, "the Senate could hardly operate with its present organization and rules." [15] Several of the more important are "legislative work" (members should concentrate on congressional duties and not be publicity seekers), "courtesy" (members should be solicitous toward their colleagues and avoid personal attacks on them), and "specialization" (members should master a few policy areas and not try to impress their colleagues as a "jack of all trades"). Those who abide by these and other norms, which can change over time, are rewarded with increased influence in the policy process, for example, by being appointed to prestigious committees. Conversely, legislators who persistently violate Congress's informal customs are apt to see legislation they support blocked in committee or on the floor. Congressional decision making, then, is shaped by each chamber's formal and informal structure of rules, precedents, and traditions.

Congressional Decision Making

The congressional decision-making process is constantly evolving, but it has certain enduring features that affect consideration of all legislation. The first is the decentralized power structure of Congress, characterized by numerous specialized committees and a weak central party leadership. A second feature is the existence of multiple decision points for every piece of legislation. The many decision points mean that at each step of a bill's progress a majority coalition must be formed to move the measure along. This leads to the third important feature of the process: the frequent need for bargaining and compromise at every juncture in order to form a winning coalition. And finally, each Congress has only a two-year life cycle in which to pass legislation once it has been introduced. The pressure of time is an ever-present force underlying the process.

Decentralized Power Structure

Congress's decentralized character reflects both political and structural realities. Politically, legislators owe their reelection to voters in widely differing states and localities; structurally, the legislative branch has an elaborate division of labor to help it manage its immense workload. Responsibility for specific subject areas is dispersed among numerous committees and subcommittees (more than 300 in the two chambers).

Structural decentralization means that policy making is subject to various disintegrative processes. Broad issues are divided into smaller subissues for consideration by the committees. Overlapping and fragmented committee responsibilities can impede the development of comprehensive and coordinated national policies. Many House committees, for example, consider some aspect of energy policy.[16] Jurisdictional controversies occur as committees fight to protect their "turf." Finally, committees develop special relationships with pressure groups, executive agencies, and scores of other interested participants. These alliances, often called "subgovernments," "issue networks," or "sloppy large hexagons," dominate numerous policy areas. Committees, then, become advocates of policies and not simply impartial instruments of the House or Senate.[17]

In theory, political parties are supposed to provide the cohesive force to balance the centrifugal influences of a fragmented committee system. For the most part, the reality is much different. Parties serve to organize their members and elect the formal leaders of Congress. From time to time, Democrats and Republicans meet in policy committees and caucuses to discuss policy issues. Neither party, however, commands the consistent

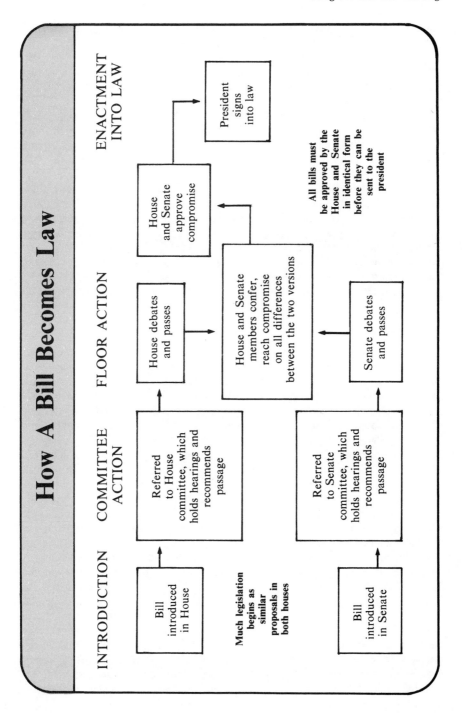

How A Bill Becomes Law

support of all its members. There is too great a spread of ideological convictions within each party. Too many countervailing pressures (constituency, individual conscience, career considerations, or committee loyalty) also influence the actions of representatives and senators. As a result, public policies usually are enacted because diverse elements of both parties temporarily coalesce to achieve common goals.

The absence of disciplined parties, in or out of Congress, underscores the difficult and delicate role of congressional party leaders. They cannot dictate policy because they lack the means to force agreement among competing party factions or autonomous committees and subcommittees. A number of legislators are not particularly dependent on their state or local parties for reelection. This means that party leaders cannot count on automatic party support but must rely heavily on their skills as bargainers and negotiators to influence legislative decisions. In addition, the power and style of any party leader depend on several factors, some outside the leader's control. Among them are personality, intellectual and political talent, the leader's view of the job, the size of the majority or minority party in the chamber, whether the White House is controlled by the opposition party, the expectations of colleagues, and the institutional complexion of the House or Senate during a particular historical era.

Multiple Decision Points

Although Congress can on occasion act quickly, normally legislation has to work its way slowly through multiple decision points. One congressional report identified more than 100 specific steps that might mark a "bill's progress through the Congress from introduction to possible enactment into law." [18] After a bill is introduced, it usually is referred to committee and then frequently to a subcommittee. The views of executive departments and agencies often are solicited. Hearings are held and reports on the bill are issued by the subcommittee and full committee. The bill then is "reported out" of the full committee and scheduled for consideration by the entire membership. After floor debate and final action in one chamber, the same steps generally are repeated in the other house. At any point in this sequential process, the bill is subject to delay, defeat, or modification. "It is very easy to defeat a bill in Congress," President Kennedy once noted. "It is much more difficult to pass one." [19]

The diagram on page 13 outlines the major procedural steps in how a bill becomes law. Congressional procedures require bills to overcome numerous hurdles. At each stage, measures and procedures must receive majority approval. All along the procedural route, therefore, strategically located committees, groups, or individuals can delay, block, or change proposals if they can form majority coalitions. Bargaining may be necessary at each juncture in order to build the majority coalition that advances the bill to the next step in the legislative process. Thus, advocates of a piece of legislation must attract not just one majority but several successive majorities at each of the critical intersections along the legislative route.

Bargaining and Coalition Building

There are three principal forms of bargaining used to build majority coalitions: logrolling, compromise, and nonlegislative favors.

Logrolling is an exchange of voting support on different bills by different members of Congress. It is an effective means of coalition building because members rarely are equally concerned about all the measures before Congress. For example, representatives A, B, and C strongly support a bill that increases government aid to farmers. A, B, and C are indifferent toward a second bill that increases the minimum wage, which is strongly supported by representatives D, E, and F. Because D, E, and F do not have strong feelings about the farm bill, a bargain is struck: A, B, and C agree to vote for the minimum wage bill, and D, E, and F agree to vote for the farm bill. Thus both bills are helped on their way past the key decision points at which A, B, C, D, E, and F have influence.

Logrolling may be either explicit or implicit. A, B, and C may have negotiated directly with D, E, and F. Alternatively, A, B, and C may have voted for the minimum wage bill, letting it be known through the press or in other informal ways that they anticipate similar treatment on the farm bill from D, E, and F. The expectation is that D, E, and F will honor the tacit agreement since at a later date they may again need the support of A, B, and C.

Compromise, unlike logrolling, builds coalitions through negotiation over the *content* of legislation. Each side agrees to modify policy goals on a given bill in a way that generally is acceptable to the other. A middle ground often is found — particularly with bills involving money. A, B, and C, for example, support a $50 million education bill; D, E, and F want to increase the funding to $100 million. The six meet and compromise on a $75 million bill they all can support.

Note the distinction between logrolling and compromise. In the logrolling example, the participants did not modify their objectives on the bills that mattered to them; each side traded voting support on a bill that meant little in return for support on a bill in which they were keenly interested. In a compromise, both sides modify their positions.

Nonlegislative favors are useful because policy goals are only one of the many objectives of members of Congress. Other objectives include assignment to a prestigious committee, getting reelected, running for higher office, obtaining larger office space and staff, or even being selected to attend a conference abroad. The wide variety of these nonpolicy objectives creates numerous bargaining opportunities — particularly for party leaders, who can dispense many favors — from which coalitions can be built. As Senate majority leader from 1955 to 1961, Lyndon B. Johnson of Texas was known for his skill in using his powers to satisfy the personal needs of senators in order to build support for legislation Johnson wanted.

> For Johnson, each one of these assignments contained a potential opportunity for bargaining, for creating obligations, provided that he knew his fellow senators well enough to determine which invitations would matter the

most to whom. If he knew that the wife of the senator from Idaho had been dreaming of a trip to Paris for ten years, or that the advisers to another senator had warned him about his slipping popularity with Italian voters, Johnson could increase the potential usefulness of assignments to the Parliamentary Conference in Paris or to the dedication of the cemeteries in Italy.[20]

In this way, Johnson made his colleagues understand that there was a debt to be repaid.

The Congressional Cycle

Every bill introduced in Congress faces the two-year deadline of the congressional term. (The term of the 98th Congress, elected in November 1982, began at noon on January 3, 1983, and expires at noon on January 3, 1985.) Legislation introduced must be passed by both the House and the Senate in identical form within the two-year term in order to become law. And Congress normally adjourns prior to the end of the two-year term; thus bills usually have less than two full years. Bills that have not completed the required procedural journey prior to final adjournment of a Congress automatically die and must be reintroduced in a new Congress. Inaction or postponement at any stage of the process can mean the defeat of a bill. This book repeatedly focuses on the various delaying and expediting tactics available to members during the legislative process.

Many measures considered by Congress come up in cycles. Much of Congress's annual agenda is filled with legislation required each year to continue and finance the activities of federal agencies and programs. Generally, this kind of legislation appears regularly on the congressional agenda at about the same time each year. Other legislation comes up for renewal every few years.

Often, there are emergencies that demand immediate attention. Other issues become timely because public interest has focused on them; consumer product safety, environmental protection, and the energy shortage in the 1970s are examples of such issues.

Complex legislation often is introduced early because it takes longer to process than a simple bill. A disproportionately large number of major bills are enacted during the last few weeks of a Congress. Compromises that were not possible in July can be made in December. By this time — with the two-year term about to expire — the pressures on members of the House and Senate are intense, and lawmaking can become frantic and furious.

It is a time when legislators pass dozens of bills without debate or recorded votes, a time when a canny legislator can slip in special favors for the folks back home or for special-interest lobbyists roaming Capitol corridors.[21]

Finally, many ideas require years or even decades of germination before they are enacted into law. Controversial proposals — reintroduced in successive Congresses — may need a four, six, or eight-year period before they win enactment. Many of the 1960s policies of Presidents Kennedy and

Johnson, for example, first were considered during the Congresses of the 1950s.

Summary

Rules and procedures affect what Congress does and how it does it. They define the steps by which bills become law, decentralize authority among numerous specialized committees, distribute power among members, and permit orderly consideration of policies. Above all, the rules and organization of Congress create numerous decision points through which legislation must pass in order to become law. As a result, congressional decision making presents many opportunities for members to defeat bills they oppose. Proponents, by contrast, must win at every step of the way. At each procedural stage, they must assemble a majority coalition. Throughout the legislative process, time is a critical factor as members maneuver to enact or defeat legislation under the pressure of numerous scheduling deadlines and the two-year period of each Congress.

In Chapter 1, an overall view of the congressional process has been presented. In Chapter 2, the focus shifts to the organizational setting and political environment of Congress to examine differences between the House and Senate; the leadership structure in Congress; pressures exerted on Congress by the executive branch, interest groups, and public opinion; and the extensive overhaul of congressional procedures realized during the past decade.

Chapter 3 examines Congress's budget process, which shapes much of the legislative decision making.

Chapter 4 turns to the initial steps of the legislative process — the introduction and referral of bills to House and Senate committees, and committee action on bills. Chapter 5 explains how legislation that has emerged from committee is scheduled for floor action in the House. Chapter 6 then examines floor action in the House. In Chapter 7 the spotlight is put on the Senate, with a discussion of how legislation is scheduled in that chamber. Senate floor action is the subject of Chapter 8.

Chapter 9 describes how House-Senate differences are reconciled when each chamber passes a different version of the same bill. Chapter 10, "Legislative Oversight," discusses how Congress monitors the implementation of the laws it has passed.

The final chapter reexamines the legislative process, pulling together the major themes of this book.

Notes

1. Benjamin Fletcher Wright, ed., *The Federalist By Alexander Hamilton, James Madison, and John Jay* (Cambridge, Mass.: The Belknap Press of Harvard University Press, 1961), 356 (Federalist No. 51).
2. Paul L. Ford, ed., *The Federalist, A Commentary on the Constitution of the United States by Alexander Hamilton, James Madison and John Jay* (New

York: Henry Holt & Co., 1898), 319 (Federalist No. 47). James Madison wrote this commentary on "Separation of the Departments of Power."

3. Thomas Jefferson, "Notes on Virginia" in *Free Government in the Making,* ed. Alpheus Thomas Mason (New York: Oxford University Press, 1965), 164.

4. See Woodrow Wilson, *Congressional Government* (Boston: Chapman Publishers, 1885) and James MacGregor Burns, *Presidential Government* (Boston: Houghton Mifflin Co., 1966).

5. Donald Bruce Johnson and Jack L. Walker, eds., "President John Kennedy Discusses the Presidency," in *The Dynamics of the American Presidency* (New York: John Wiley & Sons, 1964), 144.

6. *Constitution, Jefferson's Manual, and Rules of the House of Representatives,* 97th Cong., 2d sess., H. Doc. No. 97-271, 113-114.

7. U.S., Congress, Senate, *Congressional Record,* daily ed., April 8, 1981, S3615.

8. Clarence Cannon, *Cannon's Procedure in the House of Representatives,* 86th Cong., 1st sess., H. Doc. No. 122, iii.

9. U.S., Congress, House, *Congressional Record,* daily ed., January 3, 1983, H5-H22.

10. U.S., Congress, *Congressional Record,* January 26, 1977, 2320-2327. Majority Leader Robert C. Byrd requested and received the unanimous consent of the Senate to bypass the committee stage and place the measure directly on the calendar for immediate floor consideration. For important bills, this is an unusual procedure.

11. *Los Angeles Times,* part I, Feb. 7, 1977, 5.

12. U.S., Congress, *Congressional Record,* March 9, 1976, 5909.

13. For a discussion of the House decision to send the tax bill to conference, see *Congressional Record,* daily ed., July 28, 1982, H4776-H4788. Several House members brought suit in federal district court challenging the constitutionality of the tax bill. The U.S. District Court for the District of Columbia dismissed the case because House plaintiffs lacked standing, and their grievance was with the House. See *Congressional Record,* daily ed., December 20, 1982, E5362-E5364, and January 27, 1983, S374.

14. Quoted in *Deschler's Precedents of the United States House of Representatives,* vol. 1, 94th Cong., 2d sess., H. Doc. No. 94-661, iv.

15. Donald Matthews, *U.S. Senators and Their World* (Chapel Hill, N.C.: University of North Carolina Press, 1960), Chapter 5. Several of the folkways described by Matthews have undergone considerable change. For example, the norm of "apprenticeship," specifying that new members should be seen and not heard, has all but disappeared in both chambers. See Norman J. Ornstein, Robert L. Peabody, and David W. Rohde, "The Contemporary Senate: Into the 1980s," in *Congress Reconsidered,* 2d. ed., ed. Lawrence C. Dodd and Bruce I Oppenheimer (Washington, D.C.: CQ Press, 1981), 16-19.

16. During the 96th Congress (1979-1981), a House reorganization panel found that there were 83 committees and subcommittees in the House alone that exercised some jurisdiction over energy issues. See *Final Report of the Select Committee on Committees, U.S. House of Representatives,* 96th Cong., 2d sess., H. Rept. No. 96-866, 334-355.

17. Roger H. Davidson and Walter J. Oleszek, *Congress against Itself* (Bloomington, Ind.: Indiana University Press, 1977), and Roger H. Davidson, "Breaking Up Those 'Cozy Triangles': An Impossible Dream?" in *Legislative Reform and Public Policy,* ed. Susan Welch and John G. Peters (New York: Praeger Publishers, 1977), 30-53; Hugh Heclo, "Issue Networks and the Executive

Establishment," in *The New American Political System*, ed. Anthony King (Washington, D.C.: American Enterprise Institute for Public Policy Research, 1978), 87-124; and Charles O. Jones, *The United States Congress, People, Place, and Policy* (Homewood, Ill.: The Dorsey Press, 1982), 360. "Sloppy large hexagons," a phrase coined by Professor Jones, refers to the broad number of participants that shape policy issues.

18. *The Bill Status System for the United States House of Representatives.* Committee on House Administration, July 1, 1975, 19.
19. "President John Kennedy Discusses the Presidency," *The Dynamics of the American Presidency,* 144.
20. Doris Kearns, *Lyndon Johnson and the American Dream* (New York: Harper & Row, 1976), 119.
21. *Los Angeles Times,* part I, October 6, 1982, 1.

2

The Congressional Environment

Congress is an independent policy maker. This does not mean that it is impermeable to outside influences; nor does it mean that each member operates independently of every other member. Rather, there is a tangled, multifaceted relationship between Congress and the other governmental and nongovernmental forces. Similarly, there are complicated internal hierarchies and networks that affect the way Congress goes about its business. This chapter will focus on some of the conditions that mold the congressional environment, including the bicameral nature of Congress, the key actors in the congressional leadership, the outside pressures on Congress, and the procedural changes that swept through the House and Senate during the past decade.

The House and Senate Compared

The "House and Senate are naturally unlike," observed Woodrow Wilson.[1] Each chamber has its own rules, precedents, and customs; different terms of office; varying constitutional responsibilities; and differing constituencies. "We are constituted differently, we serve different purposes in the representative system, we operate differently, why should [the House and Senate] not have different rules," Oregon Senator Wayne Morse (1945-69) once commented.[2] Table 2-1 (p. 22) lists the major differences between the chambers.

Probably the three most important differences between the two chambers are: 1) the House is more than four times the size of the Senate, 2) senators represent a broader constituency than do representatives, and 3) senators serve longer terms of office. These differences affect the way the two houses operate in a number of ways.

Complexity of the Rules

Certainly the factor of size explains much about why the two chambers differ. Because it is larger, the House is a more structured body than the Senate. The restraints imposed on representatives by rules and precedents

Table 2-1 Major Differences Between the House and Senate

House	Senate
Larger (435)	Smaller (100)
Shorter term of office (2 years)	Longer term of office (6 years)
More procedural restraints on members	Fewer procedural restraints on members
Narrower constituency	Broader, more varied, constituency
Policy specialists	Policy generalists
Less press and media coverage	More press and media coverage
Power less evenly distributed	Power more evenly distributed
Less prestigious	More prestigious
More expeditious in floor debate	Less expeditious in floor debate
Less reliance on staff	More reliance on staff

are far more severe than those affecting senators. More than 400 pages are needed to describe the House rules for the 98th Congress, and its precedents from 1789 to 1936 are contained in 11 huge volumes; those from 1936 forward are recorded in the multivolumed *Deschler's Precedents*. In contrast, the Senate's rules are contained in 90 pages and its precedents in one volume.

Whereas Senate rules maximize freedom of expression, House rules "show a constant subordination of the individual to the necessities of the whole House as the voice of the national will." [3] Furthermore, House and Senate rules differ fundamentally in their basic purpose. House rules are designed to permit a determined majority to work its will. Senate rules, on the other hand, are intended to slow down, or even defer, action on legislation by granting inordinate parliamentary power (through the filibuster, for example) to individual members and determined minorities.

The Senate, as a result, is more personal and individualistic than the House. It functions to a large extent by unanimous consent, in effect adjusting or disregarding its rules as it goes along. It is not uncommon for votes on a bill to be rescheduled or delayed until an interested senator can be present. Senate party leaders are careful to consult all senators who have expressed an interest in the pending legislation. In the House, the leadership can only consult key members — usually committee leaders — about upcoming floor action.

Policy 'Incubation'

Incubation entails "keeping a proposal alive, while it picks up support, or waits for a better climate, or while the problem to which it is addressed grows." [4] Both houses fulfill this role, but it is promoted in the Senate particularly because of that body's flexible rules, more varied constituent pressures on senators, and greater press and media coverage. As the chamber of greater prestige, lesser complexity, longer term of office, and smaller size, the Senate is simply easier for the media to cover than the House.[5] As a result, the Senate is comparatively less concerned than the House with the technical perfection of legislation and more involved with cultivating national constituencies, formulating questions for national debate, and gaining general public support for policy proposals. The policy-generating role is particularly characteristic of senators with presidential ambitions, who need to capture both headlines and national constituencies.[6]

Specialists vs. Generalists

Another difference between the chambers is that representatives tend to be known as subject matter "specialists" while senators tend to be "generalists." "If the Senate has been the nation's great forum," a representative said, then the "House has been its workshop." [7] Indeed its greater work force and division of labor facilitate policy specialization in the House. "Senators do not specialize as intensively or as exclusively in their committee work as House members do" because senators must spread their "efforts over a greater span of subjects than the average representative." [8] During the 98th Congress (1983-85), for example, the average senator served on 11 committees and subcommittees compared to six for the average representative.

One reason for the specialist-generalist distinction is that senators represent a broader constituency than House members. This compels the former to generalize as they attempt to be conversant on numerous national and international issues that affect their state. With their six-year term, senators are less vulnerable to immediate constituency pressures. Therefore, they can afford to be more cosmopolitan in their viewpoints than House members. Journalists, too, tend to expect senators, more than representatives, to have an informed opinion on almost every important public issue.

A result of the generalist role is greater reliance by senators on knowledgeable personal and committee staff aides for advice in decision making. A House member, on the other hand, is more likely to be an expert himself on particular policy issues. If not, he often relies on informed colleagues rather than staff aides for advice on legislation. "House members rely most heavily upon their colleagues for all information," one study concluded, while senators "will often turn to other sources, especially their own staffs, for their immediate information needs." [9] Consequently, Senate staff aides generally have more influence over the laws and programs of the nation than do their counterparts in the House.

Distribution of Power

Another difference between the two chambers is that power to influence policy is more evenly distributed in the Senate than in the House. While it is true that House procedural changes in the 1970s created additional committee leadership opportunities for junior representatives, it still is easier for junior senators to exert influence over significant policy issues. Every senator of the majority party typically chairs at least one committee or subcommittee (the average in 1982 was 2.3 chairmanships). "All of a sudden I'm making a difference," declared John Heinz, R-Pa., soon after his election to the Senate. He had spent five years in the House. "You have more say, more of an input. You're more intimately involved with the executive branch. Your vote, you feel, counts for much more." [10] Unlike the average representative, senators can readily exercise initiative in legislation and oversight, get floor amendments incorporated in legislation reported from committees on which they are not members, influence the scheduling of bills and, in general, participate more widely and equally in all Senate and party activities.

Similarities

There are many similarities between the House and Senate. Both chambers are essentially equal in power and share similar responsibilities in lawmaking, oversight, and representation. Both have heavy workloads, decentralized committee and party structures, and somewhat parallel committee jurisdictions. The roles and responsibilities of one chamber interact with those of the other. House and Senate party leaders often work together to coordinate action on legislation. Cooperation generally is made easier when both houses are controlled by the same party.

In recent years, the two chambers have become more similar in some unexpected areas. Today's House members appear to be more dependent on staff than were their colleagues of a decade ago. And many senators, like House members, prepare to run for reelection almost immediately after being sworn into office. A few weeks after being elected in November 1982, Sen. Pete Wilson, R-Calif., hired a campaign consulting group to help prepare for his 1988 reelection.[11] "Senators start raising their [campaign] war chests sometimes three or four years before their reelection date," observed Sen. Thomas F. Eagleton, D-Mo.[12]

Leadership Structure of Congress

In both the House and Senate, the party leadership is crucial to the smooth functioning of the legislative process. Leaders help to organize orderly consideration of legislative proposals, promote party support for or against legislation, attempt to reconcile differences that threaten to disrupt the chambers, plan strategy on important bills, consult with the president, and publicize legislative achievements. *(Leadership structure of Congress, see box, p. 27.)*

In the House, the formal leadership consists of the Speaker, who is both the chamber's presiding officer and the leader of the majority party; the majority and minority leaders; whips from each party; assistants to the whips; and various partisan (Democratic and Republican) committees that assist with party strategy, legislative scheduling, and the assignment of party members to the legislative committees.

In the Senate, there is no party official comparable to the Speaker. Under the Constitution, the vice president of the United States assumes the post of president of the Senate, and in his absence the president pro tempore or, more commonly, a temporary presiding officer presides; none of these individuals, however, has political power comparable to that of the Speaker. The Senate also has majority and minority leaders, whips, assistant whips, and party committees.

The leadership structures in both houses have great influence over the course a bill may take; few important bills become law without the support of the majority leadership.

The significance of leadership pressures on members of Congress was summed up succinctly years ago by Speaker Sam Rayburn of Texas, who advised members that "to get along, you have to go along." [13] Rayburn's advice is no longer as relevant as it once was, but the rules and customs of both houses still place significant resources in the hands of the leaders to give them the ability to work their will.

Party leaders may offer tangible incentives to influence the course of legislation. These include influencing committee assignments, sharing media attention with colleagues, raising money and campaigning for colleagues, selecting members to serve on special committees or panels, intervening with the White House, or mobilizing support or opposition to policy proposals.

A less tangible type of influence is the leadership's expression of approval and personal friendliness toward the party faithful, and coolness toward party defectors. Party leaders in the House, for example, "are in good position to influence the attitude of the House toward a member early in his career by telling other members what they think of him. There are also visible ways, such as the Speaker's selection of members to preside over the House or over the Committee of the Whole, by which party leaders indicate the younger members whom they regard highly." [14]

Most party leaders have been eager to dispense favors to members (both of their own party and even of the opposition party) so as to create a stack of IOUs that can be called upon in the event of expected close votes on important measures. Leaders usually rely on tact and persuasion rather than threats or harsh criticism to win members' support.

Speaker of the House

Former Speaker Thomas B. Reed of Maine once called that office "the embodiment of the House, its power and dignity," and it is treated as such by the members.[15] Associated with the prestige and dignity of the office are numerous powers that enable the Speaker to play a central role in the legislative process.

The position of the Speaker is established by the Constitution, but until the early nineteenth century the Speaker had little real power. Henry Clay was reportedly the first really influential Speaker (1811-14, 1815-20, 1823-25). The power of the office reached its peak in the early 1900s, under a series of Speakers who extended and sometimes abused the prerogatives of the office. Drastic reform of the rules came about as a result of the 1910 "revolt" against Speaker Joseph G. Cannon, who was stripped of his authority to sit on the House Rules Committee, to appoint committee members, and to control all floor action.

Modern Speakers achieve their influence largely through personal prestige, mastery of the art of persuasion, legislative expertise, and the support of the members. The Speaker's primary formal powers are presiding over the House, deciding points of order, referring bills and resolutions to the appropriate House committees, scheduling legislation for floor action, and appointing House members to select, joint, and House-Senate conference committees. Although the Speaker may participate in debate he does so rarely, and usually only when his remarks may affect the outcome of a crucial vote. He also may vote, but most recent Speakers seldom vote except to break a tie. (Speaker Thomas P. O'Neill, Jr., D-Mass., in 1981 voted six times, an unusually high number.)

Although the Constitution does not specify that the Speaker must be a member of the House, no nonmember has ever been elected to the post. It has become common practice to elect the majority leader as Speaker when an opening occurs. Since the Civil War, neither party has ousted a sitting Speaker as long as his party remained in the majority. As Randall Ripley has observed, "In general, the Speaker retains leadership status in his party as long as he remains in the House." [16]

Majority and Minority Leaders

Both the majority and minority parties of the House and Senate appoint officials to shape and direct strategy on the floor. These officials, elected by their respective party caucuses, try to hold together their parties' loose alliances in hopes of shaping them into voting majorities to pass or defeat bills and amendments. Majority leaders have considerable influence over the scheduling of bills. The majority leader in the House ranks just below the Speaker in importance. In the Senate, the majority leader is the most influential officer because neither the vice president nor the president pro tempore holds substantive powers over the chamber's proceedings. Like the Speaker, the majority and minority leaders in both chambers receive larger salaries than other members as well as additional staff resources and other perquisites.

Duties of the House majority and minority leaders are not spelled out in the standing rules of the House, nor is official provision made for the offices (except through specific appropriations). In practice, the majority leader's job has been to formulate the party's legislative program in cooperation with the Speaker and other party leaders, steer the program through the House, work to ensure that committee chairmen take action on bills deemed of importance to the party, and help to establish the legislative agenda.

Everyday duties of the minority leader correspond to those of the majority leader, except that the minority leader has no authority over scheduling legislation. The minority leader speaks for his party and acts as field general on the floor. It is the minority leader's duty to consult ranking minority members of House committees and encourage them to follow

Congressional Leadership

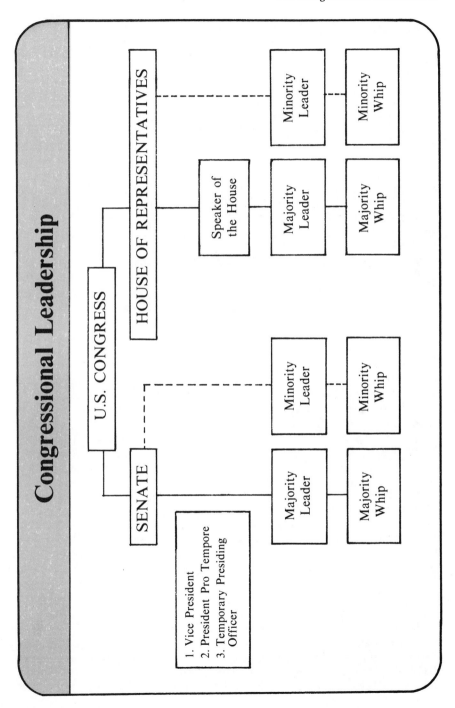

agreed upon party positions. If the occupant of the White House is of the minority party, that party's leader in the House probably will be the president's spokesman. "It's a dual role," House Minority Leader Robert H. Michel, R-Ill., has noted. "On each decision, [the leader's job] makes you look at things from two perspectives — your own district's and the President's." [17]

The functions of the Senate majority leader are similar to those of his counterpart in the House. He can nominate members to party committees, influence the election of party officers, affect the assignment of members to committees, and appoint ad hoc party task forces to study and recommend substantive or procedural reforms. Traditionally, the "primary role of the majority leader remains similar to that at its inception, namely, to program and to expedite the flow of his party's legislation." [18] And not only is his party's legislative initiatives involved; all Senate floor business essentially is scheduled by the majority leader in consultation with the minority leadership. Scheduling, perhaps, is the bedrock on which the majority leader's fundamental authority rests. The majority leader is aided in controlling scheduling by many parliamentary and procedural precedents, such as the priority given him (and the minority leader) when he seeks recognition on the floor, and the ability to set the times and dates the Senate recesses (or adjourns) and reconvenes. These informal prerogatives can be useful in deciding what tactics to employ against filibusters, for instance.

If used aggressively by the majority leader, scheduling, discussed in Chapter 7, can be transformed from a largely procedural responsibility to one with significant programmatic and political overtones. Legislation can be scheduled to suit party or White House interests; to facilitate comprehensive policy making through the sequential consideration of related topics; to expedite policies supported by the leadership; or to coordinate House-Senate decision making.

With the aid of the majority whip, the majority leader also is responsible for securing the attendance of party colleagues during important floor sessions and ascertaining in advance how senators are likely to vote on issues. Measures may be scheduled to maximize attendance by the bill's supporters and minimize attendance by the opponents. The leadership expends a great deal of effort to ensure that senators backing a measure favored by the party are on hand for important votes.

Occupying center stage in the Senate, the majority leader is best positioned institutionally to know the status of legislation, when a bill probably will be scheduled, how intensely committed are its supporters and opponents, what strategies are being formulated to pass or defeat it, and under what conditions the president will intervene to help secure the measure's enactment or defeat. A knowledgeable majority leader is in a good position to guide and advise his colleagues.

The minority leader in the Senate has important responsibilities, too. These include summarizing minority criticism of the majority party's legislation, mobilizing support for minority party positions, and acting as Senate spokesman for the president if both are of the same party.

Whips

Each party in the House and Senate appoints a whip and usually a number of assistant whips to aid the floor leader in implementing the party's legislative program. The principal jobs of the whips are to aid the party leadership in developing a program; transmit information to party members; check attendance before key votes; conduct counts of party members for and against major bills; assist the leaders in interpreting the counts and developing strategy; build coalitions to pass amendments and bills; oversee floor activity generally; and publicize the party's accomplishments.[19] In sum, their "first function is gathering intelligence, knowing where the votes are," observed House Majority Leader Jim Wright, D-Texas. "Their second function is persuasion, producing the votes." [20]

Congressional parties have expanded their whip structure over the years. In addition to the whip, House Democrats have a chief deputy whip, four deputy whips, 13 at-large whips, and 23 zone whips. House Republicans and Senate Democrats have somewhat similar whip organizations. In recent years only Senate Republicans have chosen not to appoint assistant whips. Their control of the Senate (since 1981) ensures that a Republican leader is always on the floor and thus able to protect the party's interests.

The increase in the number of whips reflects the important changes that have taken place in the House and Senate, particularly the diffusion of authority among subcommittees and the election of more and more independent-minded members. Such developments have made the task of leadership more difficult, precipitating the whip expansion. Additional whips provide greater geographical, ideological, and seniority balance in the party leadership structure.

Party Caucuses

Over the years, both parties have relied periodically on caucuses of party members (called "conferences" by Republicans in both houses and by Senate Democrats) to adopt party positions on legislation, elect party leaders, approve committee assignments, and, on rare occasions, discipline party members. After relative inactivity during much of the twentieth century, party caucuses emerged in the late 1960s as important bodies. Caucuses now meet regularly to consider substantive and procedural matters. During the Reagan presidency, for example, the House Democratic Caucus appointed numerous task forces to formulate a party agenda for the 1980s and to highlight how Democrats differed from Republicans.

Party Committees

The parties have their own committees in each chamber to assist the party leadership and deal with related business. Steering committees recommend the order in which measures should be taken up and help with floor tactics, while policy committees research proposed legislation and recommend party positions. The two functions may be combined in a single committee, as happened in 1973 when the House Democratic Caucus voted to create a new Democratic Steering and Policy Committee, chaired by the Speaker, to give added coherence to the party's legislative strategy. In 1974 the committee was given the responsibility of assigning Democrats to House committees. Since then, the committee has evolved in other ways. As one account explained:

> Since he became Speaker in 1977, O'Neill has slowly developed the Steering Committee's role beyond its original power of committee assignment. In the past two years, the panel — which includes 30 House Democrats, 18 of them members of the leadership or O'Neill appointees — has received frequent briefings from outside experts. Its new function [of serving as a sounding board for policy proposals] could make it the driving force for preparing and selling the party's legislative package.[21]

Congressional Leaders and the President

For the most part, congressional leaders have sought to cooperate with a president of their own political party and to defeat or amend programs put forth by a president belonging to the opposing party. When President Reagan took office in 1981, for example, Majority Leader Howard H. Baker, Jr., R-Tenn., "quickly decided to mobilize the Senate into an instrument of the presidential party. Rather than establish an independent power center, Baker decided to cast his lot with the White House, helping to push the president's program through the Senate but also informing the president of the things that mattered to his colleagues."[22] As Baker expressed it, "I am the President's spear carrier in the Senate."[23]

Over the years, there have been several important instances in which congressional leaders have resisted the program of a president of their own party or have developed their own legislative program and imposed it on the White House. Cases in which a party's congressional leadership has cooperated in a substantial way with an opposing party's president are less frequent and have been limited mainly to national defense and foreign policy issues. One notable exception occurred during the later years of the Eisenhower administration. In describing his relationship with Senate Majority Leader Johnson, a Democrat, President Dwight D. Eisenhower said, "We had our differences . . . yet when put in perspective, he was far more often helpful than obstructive. . . ."[24] More recently, President Reagan in 1982 succeeded in gaining the help of Speaker O'Neill to win passage of a major income tax hike.

Other Groups

In addition to the party leadership, there are numerous informal groupings of senators and representatives that play a significant role in the legislative process. During the 98th Congress, there were more than 80 informal groups, many of them bipartisan and bicameral, serving multiple purposes: information clearinghouses, mobilizers of interests and votes on specific issues, and contact points for executive officials.[25] By definition, the groups operate outside the regular structure of Congress, and their impact on congressional procedures frequently is hard to discern. Underlying all of these groups are the bonds of mutual interests and personal friendship that play such a large part in the functioning of Congress. Many of these groups were formed to represent specific interests, such as the Rural Caucus and the Congressional Black Caucus. Other informal groups, such as the House Democratic Study Group and the House Republican Wednesday Group, focus in part on procedural issues. Still other groups are composed of members who have similar outlooks on certain issues, such as the Members of Congress for Peace Through Law.

Pressures on Members

In making their legislative decisions, members of Congress are influenced by numerous pressures — from their constituents, the White House, the news media, lobbyists and organized interest groups, and their own party leadership and colleagues on Capitol Hill. These pressures are a central feature of the congressional environment; they affect the formal procedures and rules of Congress. All of these pressures are present in varying degrees at every step of the legislative process. The interests and influence of groups and individuals outside Congress have a considerable impact on the fate of legislation. This section highlights some of the major influences on members.

The Executive Branch

The executive branch constitutes one of the most important sources of external pressure exerted on Congress. As noted in Chapter 1, there is an ongoing institutional struggle between the executive and legislative branches. Sometimes the rivalry is seen as no more than a means by which members of Congress develop public stature by demonstrating their ability to thwart the president's objectives. British political scientist Harold Laski subscribed to such a view when he wrote, "There can be no doubt that in its own eyes, Congress establishes its prestige when it either refuses to let the president have his own way, or compels him to compromise with it." [26]

Many of the president's legislative functions and activities are not mentioned in the Constitution. For example, the president is able to influence congressional action through the manipulation of patronage, the allocation of federal funds and projects that may be vital to the reelection of certain members of Congress, and the handling of constituents' cases in which senators and representatives are interested. As leader of the Democratic or Republican Party, the president is his party's chief election campaigner. As the leading political figure, the president occupies a strategic position for promoting broad coalitions of social groups and interests. The president also has ready access to the news media for promoting his administration's policies and commanding headlines.

The president's role as legislative leader, however, derives from the Constitution. While the Constitution vests "all legislative powers" in Congress, it also directs the president to "give to the Congress information of the state of the union and recommend to their consideration such measures as he shall judge necessary and expedient." This function has been broadened over the years. The president presents to Congress each year, in addition to his State of the Union message, two other general statements of presidential aims: an economic report, including proposals directed to the maintenance of maximum employment, and a budget message outlining his appropriations requests and policy proposals. And during a typical session, the president transmits to Congress scores of other legislative proposals, some on his own initiative or that of his cabinet officials and others in conformity with various statutes.

Another legislative vehicle for presidential leadership is the constitutional power to veto acts passed by Congress or to threaten to veto them. Presidents also find their office a "bully pulpit," as President Theodore Roosevelt said, from which to make direct appeals to public opinion through television, radio, and the press. Even in the early days of the Republic, presidents reached out to the people, often successfully, to build support for their legislative programs.

To enhance the prospects for securing a good working relationship with Congress, presidents in recent years have established congressional liaison offices in the White House to keep tabs on legislative activities on Capitol Hill and to lobby on behalf of administration policies. In addition, all federal departments now have their own congressional liaison team. There are scores of executive branch officials charged with handling the administration's relations with Congress.

The Media

Of all the pressures on Congress, none is such a two-way proposition as the relationship between legislators and the media.

While senators and representatives must contend with the peculiarities of the news-gathering business, such as deadlines and limited space or time to describe events, and with constant media scrutiny of their actions, they also must rely on news organizations to inform the public of their legislative interests and accomplishments. At the same time, reporters must depend to some extent on "inside" information from members, a condition that makes many of them reluctant to displease their sources lest the pipeline of information be shut off.

But Congress basically is an open organization. Information flows freely on Capitol Hill and secrets rarely remain secret for long. It has always been the case that an enterprising reporter usually could find out what was newsworthy. And in the 1970s rules and procedural changes opened to the public and the media more activities of Congress. In 1979 cable television stations began gavel-to-gavel, nationwide coverage of House floor proceedings. Pressure has mounted in the Senate to permit similar radio and television coverage of its floor activities.

This new openness has created pressures on members that, although present before, were less intense. Members' actions are subject to closer scrutiny by the media and by constituents as well as by political opponents and interest groups. Proclaimed one House member:

[W]hile open markup sessions do have advantages with which I cannot disagree, they also tend to exacerbate the consideration of complex, controversial issues. I can think of several instances during the committee's deliberations where sound tax reform decisions were later weakened upon reconsideration. I attribute several of these reversals to pressures brought to bear by the present open meeting policy.[27]

Conversely, members' fears of changing their positions once they have been expressed in public can make more difficult the process of arriving at necessary compromises.

Most members of the House and Senate are skilled in public relations and realize that almost every Capitol Hill reporter must file stories every day. That the legislators seek to benefit from this situation is indicated by the stacks of press releases and background statements that almost always inundate both the House and Senate press galleries. A 1973 study of Congress and the press concluded: "Regardless of the occasional hostility and suspicion between them, the working relationship of newsmen and legislators is fundamental to the democratic process; to be a congressman is to work with the press."[28] Or as CBS Evening News anchorman Walter Cronkite once put it: "Politics and media are inseparable. It is only the politicians and the media that are incompatible."[29]

Constituent Pressures

Although there are many pressures competing for influence on Capitol Hill, it is still the constituents, not the president or the party or the congressional leadership, who grant and can take away a member's job.[30] A member who is popular back home can defy all three in a way unthinkable in a country like Great Britain, where the leadership of the legislature, the executive, and the party are the same.

The extent to which a member of Congress seeks to follow the wishes of his constituents is determined to a considerable extent by the issue at stake. Few members would actively oppose construction in their district of a dam or post office wanted by most constituents. Few, if any, would follow locally popular policies that they were convinced would seriously endanger the nation. Between these extremes lies a wide spectrum of different blends of pressure from constituents and from conscience. But it is in this gray area that members must make most of their decisions.

Constituent opinion may set clear limits beyond which the member is unlikely to trespass. That opinion, however, probably is reflected differently among the lawmaker's several constituencies.

"Each member of Congress," wrote Richard F. Fenno, Jr., "perceives four concentric constituencies: geographic (the district itself), reelection (the voters), primary (strong supporters), and personal (close friends)."[31]

Relationships among the several constituencies can shape members' policy decisions. A representative from a farm district who seeks reelection is not likely to push policies designed to lower the price of foods grown by those who elect him. But on most questions the member has great leeway.

The composition of a particular constituency may have more effect on the kinds of issues the member takes up in Congress than the member's ideological preferences. Thus a representative from a district with a large ethnic minority might become a champion of immigration reform, and a senator from a Western state might concentrate on natural resources policies. The committees on which senators and representatives seek membership often are determined by the type of constituency served.

Washington Lobbyists

Of all the pressures on Congress, none receives such widespread publicity and yet is so dimly understood as the role of Washington-based lobbyists and the groups they represent. The popular image of an agent for special interests who buys members' votes is a vast oversimplification.

Lobbyists and lobby groups play an active part in the modern legislative process. The corps of Washington lobbyists has grown markedly since the 1930s, in line with the expansion of federal authority into new areas and with the huge increase in federal spending. The federal government has become a tremendous force in the life of the nation, and the number of fields in which changes in federal policy may spell success or failure for special interest groups has been greatly enlarged. Thus commercial and industrial interests, labor unions, ethnic and racial groups, professional organizations, citizen groups and representatives of foreign interests — all from time to time and some continuously — have sought by one method or another to exert pressure on Congress to attain their legislative goals.

Pressure groups, whether operating at the grass-roots level to influence public opinion or through direct contacts with members of Congress, perform some important and indispensable functions. These include helping to inform both Congress and the public about problems and issues, stimulating public debate, opening a path to Congress for the wronged and needy, and making known to Congress the practical aspects of proposed legislation: whom it would help, whom it would hurt, who is for it and who is against it. The spinoff from this process is considerable technical information produced by research on legislative proposals.

Many observers of Congress point out, however, that interest groups may, in pursuing their own objectives, lead the legislature into decisions that benefit a particular pressure group but do not necessarily serve other segments of the public. A group's power to influence legislation often is based less on its arguments than on the size of its membership, the amount of financial and manpower resources it can commit to legislative lobbying campaigns and the astuteness of the organization's representatives.

In recent years there has been a significant increase in the number of political action committees (PACs) — from 608 in 1974 to 3,371 in 1982.

Balancing Public and Private Pressures

Rep. Dennis E. Eckart was racing off the other day to spend the weekend in his Ohio district. When his four-year-old son, Eddie, spied the suitcase in his hand, the boy asked why he was going.

"To talk to people," replied Eckart.

"There are people here, Daddy," Eddie replied.

Eckart, a Democrat, tells that story with some sadness. But he is a 33-year-old, second-term member of the House with high ambition and a new district, thanks to redistricting. So he goes back to Ohio many weekends, leaving his wife and son in suburban Virginia, and he knows he is paying a price for his political success.

"If you ask my son what I do for a living, he says campaigning," Eckart said with a wry laugh. "It's tough, extremely tough, to balance all the demands on you, and still be a father, a husband, a son, an uncle, a brother and a godfather."

This balancing act described by Eckart has always been a problem on Capitol Hill. The conflicts between a lawmaker's public and private lives were highlighted by the decision of the House in July 1983 to censure two members who engaged in sexual relations with teen-aged pages.

For most members of Congress, the conflicts are far less dramatic, much more on the order of Eckart's concern for his son. But all members share the strains and stresses of serving in what Rep. Newt Gingrich, R-Ga., calls "the most human institution in the Federal Government."

Indeed, some members have either forgotten, or never felt, the conflicting pressures described by Eckart. "I so completely submerged my private life into my public life, and I did so at such an early age, that I can't tell where one stops and the other starts," said Rep. Guy Vander Jagt, a Michigan Republican.

Still, the balancing act between public and private lives bothers most members. One of their biggest complaints is that even simple joys become "events," played out in the glaring eye of public notice.

Absent parents are an inevitable part of congressional life. Rep. Les AuCoin, an Oregon Democrat, says that in many congressional families "too many kids are almost strangers to their parents."

Time is the most precious commodity in any lawmaker's life, and its scarcity afflicts many congressional marriages. Eckart says he feels like a "guided missile," directed by his staff through remote control to attend this hearing or that fund-raiser. And that sort of life, he adds, "places added stress on any marriage. I can say that without equivocation." Eckart's wife, Sandy, left her job, her home, and her family to move to Washington with him, and she often feels left out of his work. "She's almost stopped calling and asking if I'll be home for dinner," Eckart said.

Source: Adapted from Steven V. Roberts, "Tales of Two Lives: One Public, the Other Private," *New York Times,* July 28, 1983, A20.

PACs are legal entities created by interest groups to raise and contribute money to election campaigns. With the rising costs of congressional campaigns, many members have become concerned about the influence of PAC money on legislative decisions. One House member even revised his vote-gathering techniques because of the money-politics connection.

> I go out on the floor and say to a member, "I need your help on this bill," and often he will say, "I can't do that, I got $5,000 from a special interest." So I no longer lobby [other] Congressmen, I lobby the lobbyists to lobby the Congressmen.[32]

To be sure, other legislators emphasize the value of PACs as voluntary organizations that encourage and strengthen citizen participation in the electoral and legislative processes.

Congress in Flux

The Congress of the 1980s is markedly different from that of two decades earlier. Sweeping changes have influenced the lawmaking process and the distribution of power. They have affected Congress's responsiveness to national problems and its policy-making capabilities.

The first steps toward a revitalized Congress came in the late 1960s and early 1970s, induced by external events and internal institutional pressures. Of fundamental importance were the two overriding issues of the period: the Vietnam War and the Watergate scandal. Both forced Congress to examine itself and reflect on whether it had the tools, and the will, to handle those crises and others that might arise in the future. Meanwhile, the House and Senate membership was changing dramatically: More than three-fourths of the seats in each chamber changed hands between the 1970 and 1982 elections. Many of the new members came to Congress determined to revitalize the institution and restore it to a position equal with that of the presidency. Rules were revised and procedures rewritten as Congress prepared to exert greater influence in governing the nation.

The first major reform of this period was the Legislative Reorganization Act of 1970 (PL 91-510). Under that measure, much of the secrecy surrounding members' actions and positions on issues and legislation, particularly in the House, was peeled off. All roll-call votes taken in the committees — where the vast majority of legislation is formulated — were required to be made public. For the first time, House members' positions on important floor amendments were individually recorded and printed in the *Congressional Record* in the same manner as senators' on roll-call votes. Previously, House members had voted in virtual anonymity by voice votes or nonrecorded teller votes, and often many did not vote at all.[33] *(Details of House voting changes, see Chapter 6.)*

The 1970 act was the precursor of further changes that made Congress a more open institution. The House in 1973 and the Senate in 1975 decided to hold most of their committee bill-drafting sessions, called markups, in public. And House-Senate conference committees, which reconcile differences in legislation passed by the two chambers, formally were opened to the public in 1975. Conference negotiators traditionally had met behind closed doors.

Indeed, by the end of 1975 both chambers had stripped away most vestiges of the secrecy that had cloaked their committee proceedings. Recall, too, that the House in 1979 began to televise its floor sessions. These actions meant that the media, and therefore most citizens, had access to information about the actions of members of Congress that formerly was difficult to obtain. Special interest organizations, from labor unions to corporations, generally had easy access to such information in the past through their continual contacts with legislators, and the pressures on members accordingly were one-sided. The new work-in-the-open requirements were designed to give citizens and less powerful organizations more influence on legislative proceedings.

Congress also took steps to provide committees and members' offices with computers and modern technology. Capitol Hill today abounds with word processing systems, data banks, and computer terminals that permit committees, members, and staff aides to retrieve information on such things as the current status of all bills on which they have a particular interest. By "enhancing its information sources and analyzing capacity, Congress has curbed the erosion of its power to the executive." [34] Further, computerization has equalized relations between junior members, who know how to "tap and use new information sources," and the expert senior members.

Besides computerizing its operations and opening up more of its proceedings to public scrutiny, Congress made fundamental changes in its power structure. One of these changes involved seniority — status (and thus power) based on length of service. Until the 1970s there had been few concerted or successful attacks on a system that tended to reward members' electoral longevity with favorable committee assignments and powerful committee chairmanships. Beginning about 1970, however, newly elected members and reformers in both houses, aided by outside interest groups, started to chip away at the system. They revived long-dormant party units, such as the caucuses, to bring about numerous procedural changes. By 1975 both chambers had decided to require their committee chairmen to stand for reelection by their party colleagues at the beginning of each Congress; that year, House Democrats unseated three committee chairmen. House Democrats now also choose the chairmen of the 13 Appropriations subcommittees; in 1977 they ousted the Military Construction Subcommittee chairman.

During this period, additional staff assistance and new positions of responsibility were provided junior members, whose input largely had been lost in the past. In 1973 the House Democratic Caucus drew up a subcommittee "bill of rights" that curbed the chairmen's powers, provided that subcommittees would have defined jurisdictions, guaranteed each subcommittee an adequate budget, and required chairmen to refer most measures to subcommittees within two weeks. The changes affecting House and Senate committee chairmen are considered more fully in Chapter 4.

Paradoxically, House and Senate leaders and caucuses gained new authority despite the general trend toward further decentralization. The Speaker, for example, became chairman of the Democratic committee in the House that assigns party members to standing committees, and he was given the authority to appoint the Democratic members of the Rules Committee, including the chairman. House rules were changed to strengthen the Speaker's control of floor action and to reduce opportunities for dilatory tactics. The Speaker now can postpone action on certain issues, such as approval of the *Journal* (the official record of House proceedings), and thwart attempts of members to force time-consuming votes on such routine matters.

The problem of concentrated power was somewhat different in the Senate, whose relatively smaller size allowed more members to have responsible committee positions. As part of the 1970 Legislative Reorganization Act and the 1977 Committee System Reorganization Amendments, limits were placed on the number of committees and subcommittees on which senators could serve.

The unique problem faced by the Senate involved the filibuster, under which bills could be talked to death; the related cloture rule (Rule XXII) required a two-thirds majority of senators voting to end a filibuster. This stiff requirement gave considerable power to a minority of senators — one-third plus one — who could prevent the majority from bringing a bill to a final vote.

The Senate in 1975 took steps to restrict the filibuster as the major method of obstructing legislation by lowering the number of votes needed for cloture to a "constitutional majority" of three-fifths of the Senate membership — 60 votes if there are no vacancies. The old two-thirds requirement still applies, however, on proposals to change the Senate's rules. In 1979 the Senate further tightened Rule XXII to deal with so-called post-cloture filibusters. *(Details, see Chapter 8.)*

Institutionally, one of the basic changes the 94th Congress made was the creation of a congressional budget control system designed to bring order out of the prevailing chaos in the appropriations process. The new law, the 1974 Congressional Budget and Impoundment Control Act, was intended to give Congress much greater influence in deciding the fundamental governmental issue of who gets how much money and for what purpose. And just as important was the goal of forcing Congress to make spending decisions affecting the federal government in a rational framework that related total revenues to expenditures — something that Congress had never really done before. *(Details, see Chapter 3.)*

These, then, are the highlights of several important changes Congress made in its power structure and procedures in the 1970s. There have been numerous explanations as to why they came about. Certainly the perceived erosion of Congress's power relative to the president's — a process that had occurred over several decades — stimulated and influenced congressional reorganization efforts. The decline of congressional control over the power of the purse and over war-making decisions, particularly under Presidents Lyndon B. Johnson and Richard M. Nixon, provoked the national legislature to strengthen itself in both areas by passing the 1974 budget act and the 1973 War Powers Resolution.

Another factor was public disenchantment with Congress. Many members believed it imperative for Congress to "put its house in order" if public confidence in the legislative branch was to be restored. In 1977 both the House and Senate enacted strong codes of ethics in response to public distrust of legislators.

The large influx of new members during the late 1960s and 1970s also contributed to the legislative resurgence. By the start of the 98th Congress more than half of all representatives and senators had begun their service in 1975 or later. With little stake in the status quo, the new members supported institutional changes that would enhance their power.[35]

Finally, there were members and groups within Congress who worked with outside interests, such as Common Cause and other public interest lobby groups, to modernize Congress's organization and procedures. In the House, for example, the Democratic Study Group provided much of the organization, ideas and votes needed to bring about numerous procedural changes.

A principal result of the past decade's changes has been to reinforce the decentralized tendencies of Congress. Power has been dispersed further throughout Congress's components — committees, subcommittees, caucuses, party committees, the leadership, and informal groups — rather than concentrated in a relatively few individuals such as committee chairmen and party leaders. This development affects legislative-executive relations as well. "The [old] seniority system is gone," observed one U.S. representative. "Before, the president had a chain of command to work with and through, but it has disappeared. Now, no one can deliver the votes." [36] In short, the changes of the past decade have greatly increased the need for bargaining and coalition building.

Summary

This chapter has discussed the general environment in which members of Congress operate, the many influences — both internal and external — on congressional procedures and decision making, including the party leadership and outside pressures — from the executive branch, members' constituents, the news media, and lobbying groups. It also has reviewed the procedural and structural reforms undertaken by Congress itself during the 1970s. Finally, the chapter has highlighted some of the similarities and differences in the House and Senate that affect the operations of the national legislature. This chapter completes a preliminary overview of Congress.

Chapter 3 turns to a detailed discussion of the congressional budget process. The power of the purse is one of Congress's fundamental constitutional prerogatives. The 1974 budget act has become a major integrating mechanism in an institution that thrives on fragmented authority. Congress's budgetary process imposes a web of relationships upon committees and members that affects action on almost all public policy. To examine the budget process at this stage should aid in understanding the fundamental thrust of the remaining chapters, which discuss what typically happens to bills as they follow the lawmaking route.

Notes

1. Woodrow Wilson, *Constitutional Government in the United States* (New York: Columbia University Press, 1911), 87.
2. U.S., Congress, *Congressional Record,* February 7, 1967, 2838.
3. Asher C. Hinds, *Hinds' Precedents of the House of Representatives,* Vol. I, v.
4. Nelson W. Polsby, "Policy Analysis and Congress," *Public Policy* (Fall 1969): 67.
5. Michael Green, "Obstacles to Reform: Nobody Covers the House," *Washington Monthly*, June 1970, 62-70.
6. See Robert L. Peabody, Norman J. Ornstein, and David W. Rohde, "The United States Senate as a Presidential Incubator: Many Are Called but Few Are Chosen," *Political Science Quarterly* (Summer 1976): 236-258.
7. Charles Clapp, *The Congressman* (Garden City, N.Y.: Doubleday, 1963), 39.
8. Richard F. Fenno, Jr., *Congressmen in Committees* (Boston: Little, Brown & Co., 1973), 172.
9. Norman J. Ornstein, "Legislative Behavior and Legislative Structure: A Comparative Look at House and Senate Resource Utilization," in *Legislative Staffing,* ed. James J. Heaphey and Alan B. Balutis (New York: John Wiley & Sons, 1975), 175.
10. *New York Times,* March 8, 1977, 16. Rep. Paul Simon, D-Ill., explained why he planned to run for the Senate in 1984: "If you are a generalist by nature, which I am, the Senate is a better forum. In the House, you are restricted by your committee. But in the Senate, you're not tied down. You have a lot more room to exert influence." See *Chicago Tribune,* July 21, 1983, 9.
11. *Los Angeles Times,* part I, November 28, 1982, 33.
12. Ibid., January 27, 1983, 12.
13. Richard W. Bolling, *House Out of Order* (E. P. Dutton, 1965), 48.
14. Randall B. Ripley, *Party Leaders in the House of Representatives,* (Washington, D.C.: The Brookings Institution, 1967), 7.
15. U.S. Congress, *Congressional Record,* March 3, 1893, 2614.
16. Ripley, *Party Leaders in the House,* 13.
17. *Chicago Tribune,* August 16, 1982, 2.
18. Robert L. Peabody, *Leadership in Congress* (Boston: Little, Brown & Co., 1976), 336.
19. Lawrence C. Dodd, "The Expanded Roles of the House Democratic Whip System: The 93rd and 94th Congresses," *Congressional Studies,* 27-56. See also Dodd and Terry Sullivan, "Majority Party Leadership and Partisan Vote Gathering: The House Democratic Whip System," in *Understanding Congressional Leadership,* ed. Frank H. Mackaman, (Washington, D.C.: CQ Press, 1981), 227-260.
20. *New York Times,* November 18, 1977, A18.

21. Richard E. Cohen, "House Democrats No Longer Can Use the Excuse That They Lack the Votes," *National Journal,* January 22, 1983, 155.
22. Allen Schick, "How the Budget Was Won and Lost," in *President and Congress, Assessing Reagan's First Year,* ed. Norman J. Ornstein (Washington, D.C.: American Enterprise Institute for Public Policy Research, 1982), 18.
23. U.S., Congress. Senate, *Congressional Record,* daily ed., 98th Cong., 1st sess., July 28, 1983, S11029.
24. Dwight D. Eisenhower, *Waging the Peace, 1956-1961* (Garden City, N.Y.: Doubleday, 1965), 593.
25. See Arthur G. Stevens, Jr., Daniel P. Mulhollan, and Paul S. Rundquist, "U.S. Congressional Structure and Representation: The Role of Informa! Groups," *Legislative Studies Quarterly* (August 1981): 415-438; Burdett A. Loomis, "Congressional Caucuses and the Politics of Representation," in *Congress Reconsidered,* 2d ed., ed. Lawrence C. Dodd and Bruce I. Oppenheimer, (Washington, D.C.: CQ Press, 1981), 204-220; and Susan Webb Hammond, Arthur G. Stevens Jr., and Daniel P. Mulhollan, "Congressional Caucuses: Legislators as Lobbyists," in *Interest Group Politics,* ed. Allan J. Cigler and Burdett A. Loomis, (Washington, D.C.: CQ Press, 1983), 275-297.
26. Harold J. Laski, *The American Presidency: An Interpretation* (New York: Harper & Bros., 1940), 116.
27. U.S., Congress, *Congressional Record,* December 3, 1979, 38285.
28. Delmar D. Dunn, "Symbiosis: Congress and the Press," in *To Be A Congressman: The Promise and the Power* (Washington: Acropolis Books, 1973), 50.
29. Doris A. Graber, *Mass Media and American Politics* (Washington, D.C.: CQ Press, 1980), 193. Also see Dom Bonafede, "The Washington Press — Competing For Power With the Federal Government;" "The Washington Press — An Interpreter Or a Participant in Policy Making?;" and "The Washington Press — It Magnifies the President's Flaws and Blemishes," *National Journal,* April 17, 24, and May 1, 1982, 664-674, 716-721, and 767-771.
30. For a valuable discussion of constituent pressures, see David Mayhew, *The Electoral Connection* (New Haven: Yale University Press, 1974).
31. Richard F. Fenno, Jr., *Home Style* (Boston: Little, Brown & Co., 1978), 27. Also see Glenn R. Parker, "Cycles in Congressional District Attention," *Journal of Politics* (May 1980): 540-548; and Diana Evans Yiannakis, "House Members' Communication Styles: Newsletters and Press Releases," *Journal of Politics,* (November 1982): 1049-1071.
32. Mark Green, "On the Hill, All the Votes Money Can Buy: Political Pac-Man," *New Republic,* December 13, 1982, 19. See also Herbert E. Alexander, *Financing Politics,* 2d ed. (Washington, D.C.: CQ Press, 1980); Michael Malbin, "Of Mountains and Molehills: PACs, Campaigns, and Public Policy, in *Parties, Interest Groups, and Campaign Finance Laws,* ed. Michael Malbin (Washington, D.C.: American Enterprise Institute for Public Policy Research, 1980); and the *Washington Post* series on lobbying, July 31-Aug. 2, 1983.
33. The *Congressional Record* is issued each day that Congress is in session. It contains, according to law, "substantially a verbatim report of proceedings." Members may edit a transcript of their remarks or may, with permission, "revise and extend" them. Until March 1, 1978, members could insert speeches in the Record as if they had been delivered on the floor. A House rule now requires a "bullet" (a black dot) to precede and follow any material added so that it is distinguishable from what was actually said on the floor. Page citations to the *Congressional Record* that contain a page number preceded by "H" or "S" refer

to the daily edition, not the bound volumes.

34. Stephen Frantzich, "Communications and Congress," in *The Communications Revolution in Politics,* Proceedings of the Academy of Political Science, vol. 34, no. 4, New York, 1982, 95.

35. Noteworthy, too, has been the large number of voluntary retirements among House members. Just as seats have become safer than ever, House incumbents are choosing to leave Congress in greater numbers than before. See Joseph Cooper and William West, "Voluntary Retirement, Incumbency, and the Modern House," *Political Science Quarterly* (Summer 1981): 279-300; and John R. Hibbing, "Voluntary Retirement from the House in the Twentieth Century," *Journal of Politics* (November 1982): 1020-1034. Also see Peter Swenson, "The Influence of Recruitment On the Structure of Power In the U.S. House, 1870-1940," *Legislative Studies Quarterly* (February 1982): 7-36.

36. Dom Bonafede, "Carter and Congress — It Seems That If Something Can Go Wrong, It Will," *National Journal,* November 12, 1977, 1759.

3

The Congressional Budget Process

The Framers of the Constitution deliberately lodged the power of the purse in Congress. Only Congress can authorize the government to collect taxes, borrow money, and make expenditures. The executive branch can spend funds only for the purposes and in the amounts specified by Congress. As Article I, Section 9, proclaims: "No Money shall be drawn from the Treasury, but in Consequence of Appropriations made by Law."

These words have not been amended since they were written into the Constitution. But the Framers would wonder about the effectiveness of the congressional purse strings today when over 75 percent of federal expenditures is relatively uncontrollable under existing law. This means that the national government is required to spend money automatically for certain purposes because of laws previously enacted by Congress. "Uncontrollables" include interest on the public debt (the debt currently is over $1 trillion); entitlements (laws that require benefit payments to all eligible individuals, such as Social Security, Medicare, and black lung benefits programs); and contract obligations that must be paid when due (the Defense Department's procurement arrangements with the Lockheed Corporation, for example).

A consequence of uncontrollables is clear. On the day the 98th Congress convened (January 3, 1983), it could have adjourned the session immediately, without passing any laws, and spending by the federal government for 1984 still would have been in the range of $500 billion. Further, spending each year thereafter would continue — and increase — because many federal programs are indexed to the cost of living. The chairman of the House Budget Committee, James R. Jones, D-Okla., dubbed this fiscal situation the "automatic pilot theory of government." [1]

Congress, of course, can convert uncontrollables into controllables by changing the basic law that authorizes automatic funding without regular legislative review. But there are serious political risks for members who want to subject uncontrollables to annual budgetary scrutiny. The elderly, for example, are sensitive to any changes in Social Security and have the clout to quickly mobilize against legislators who arouse their ire.

Congress chooses to place programs in the uncontrollable category for a variety of reasons. Stability, certainty, and preferred status are among the values that accrue to such programs. Retired persons, for instance, would have "to live under a great deal of financial uncertainty" if Congress subjected Social Security to annual review.[2]

Impact of Budgetary Decisions

Budgetary decisions of Congress, in short, profoundly affect the taxpaying electorate, the economy, and the volume and variety of federal programs and activities. The federal budget itself (prepared annually by the president as directed by the Budget and Accounting Act of 1921) reflects key choices among competing national priorities and identifies where the nation has been, where it is now, and where the administration plans to make future fiscal as well as policy commitments.

It is hardly surprising that Congress devotes a large percentage of its time to spending and taxing issues. This is particularly true during periods of fiscal scarcity and economic hardship, when the pressure and competition for funds are greatest.

Steps in the Budget Process

In broad terms, federal budgeting is composed of four phases:

- Preparation and submission of the budget by the president to Congress.
- Congressional action on the president's budget proposals.
- Execution of budget-related laws by federal departments and agencies.
- Audits of agency spending.

The first and third steps are controlled primarily by the executive branch; the fourth is conducted largely by the General Accounting Office (GAO), a legislative support agency of Congress. The focus of this chapter is on the second stage, the basic elements and features of Congress's procedures in considering the budget.

Authorization-Appropriations Process

Fundamental to the congressional budget process is the distinction between authorizations and appropriations. This two-step, sequential procedure works as follows: Congress first passes an authorization bill that establishes or continues an agency or program and provides it with the legal authority to operate. Authorizations may be for one or more years, and such legislation may recommend funding levels for programs and agencies. They also make in order later consideration of appropriations.

Authorization bills must be approved in identical form by each house and then submitted to the president for his signature or veto. Before any money can be withdrawn from the Treasury, however, a separate appropriations bill must be enacted. Examples of authorization and appropriations laws are illustrated on page 65.

Today, much of the federal government is funded through the annual

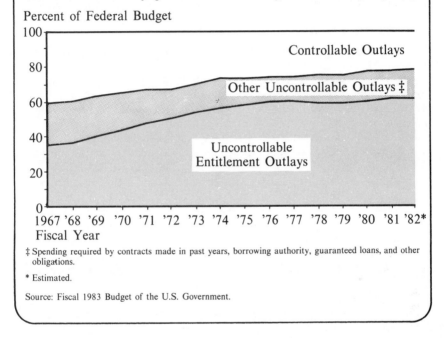

Congress's Shrinking Power Over Outlays

More than three-fourths of all federal government spending is outside the immediate control of Congress. The chart below shows, in the shaded area, the percent of total federal spending that the government is committed by law to undertake. These outlays can be controlled only if Congress changes the basic law that authorizes the expenditures. Most uncontrollable expenditures arise from entitlement programs such as Social Security, Medicare, and welfare spending.

Percent of Federal Budget

Controllable Outlays

Other Uncontrollable Outlays ‡

Uncontrollable Entitlement Outlays

1967 '68 '69 '70 '71 '72 '73 '74 '75 '76 '77 '78 '79 '80 '81 '82*
Fiscal Year

‡ Spending required by contracts made in past years, borrowing authority, guaranteed loans, and other obligations.

* Estimated.

Source: Fiscal 1983 Budget of the U.S. Government.

enactment of 13 general appropriations bills. Roughly one-half of federal spending each year is subject to the congressional authorization-appropriations process. The other half gets its legal basis from laws that provide spending authority automatically, such as the entitlement programs just referred to. *(Details, see 'Backdoor' Spending, p. 54.)*

Appropriations approved by Congress provide "budget authority;" this allows government agencies to make financial commitments up to a specified amount that eventually result in the spending of dollars. As one budget analyst explains it:

> Congress does not directly control the level of federal spending that will occur in a particular year. Rather, it grants the executive branch authority (referred to as *budget authority*) to enter into *obligations,* which are legally binding agreements with suppliers of goods or services or with a beneficiary. When those obligations come due, the Treasury Department issues a

payment. The amount of payments, called *outlays,* over an accounting period called the fiscal year (running from October 1 to September 30) equals federal expenditures for that fiscal year. Federal spending (outlays) in any given year, therefore, results from the spending authority (budget authority) granted by Congress in the current and in prior fiscal years.[3]

Legislators are particularly sensitive to budget authority figures, for these — rather than the outlay numbers — are the better predictors of an agency's growth or decline. Outlays, however, are reflected in each year's national deficit levels.

Authorizing, Appropriating Committees

Whether agencies receive all the budget authority they request depends in part on the recommendations of the authorizing and appropriating committees. Each chamber has authorizing committees (Agriculture, Banking, Armed Services, Energy, and many others), which have responsibilities that differ from those of the two "appropriating" committees — the House and Senate Appropriations committees. The authorizing committees are the policy-making centers on Capitol Hill. As the substantive legislative panels, they propose solutions to public problems and advocate what they feel to be the necessary level of appropriations for new and existing federal programs.

The two Appropriations committees and their 13 subcommittees have the job of recommending how much federal agencies and programs will receive in relation to available fiscal resources and economic conditions.

For each program and agency subject to the annual appropriations process, these committees have three main options: 1) provide all the funds recommended in the previously approved authorization bill; 2) propose reductions in the amounts already authorized; or 3) refuse to provide any funds.[4]

The following chart provides a brief illustration of some of the key participants who influence a particular agency's level of funding.

Federal Agency	Authorization Committees	Appropriations Committees
Park Service, U.S. Department of the Interior	House Interior and Insular Affairs; Senate Energy and Natural Resources	House Subcommittee on Interior; Senate Subcommittee on Interior. Submitted to full committee in each house and reported.

To recapitulate, Congress requires authorizations to precede appropriations to ensure that substantive and financial issues are subject to separate and independent analysis. This procedure also permits almost every member and committee to participate in Congress's constitutional power of the purse. There are, to be sure, numerous exceptions to this two-step model. *(See Exceptions to the Rules, p. 50.)*

Constitutional Underpinning

The authorization-appropriation dichotomy is not required by the Constitution. Rather, it is a process that has been institutionalized by the rules of the House and Senate and in some cases by statute. Of the two steps, the appropriations stage appears to be on firmer legal ground because it is rooted in the Constitution. An appropriations measure, which provides departments and agencies with authority to commit funds, may be approved even if the authorization bill has not been enacted. However, this situation may attest more to the weakness or flexibility of congressional rules than to the mandate of the Constitution.

Informally, Congress has employed this division of labor since the beginning of the Republic, as did the British Parliament in 1789 as well as the colonial legislatures. As U.S. Sen. William Plumer of Michigan noted in 1806: "Tis a good provision in the constitution of Maryland that prohibits their Legislature from adding any thing to an appropriation law." [5] Generally called "supply bills" in the early Congresses, appropriations measures had narrow purposes: to provide specific sums of money for fixed periods and stated objectives. Such bills were not to contain matters of policy.

There were exceptions to this informal rule even during the early days, however, but the practice of adding "riders," or extraneous policy provisos, to appropriations bills mushroomed in the 1830s. This practice often provoked sharp controversy in Congress and delayed the enactment of supply bills. "By 1835," wrote a parliamentary expert, the "delays caused by injecting legislation [policy] into these [appropriations] bills had become serious, and John Quincy Adams ... suggested that they be stripped of everything save appropriations." [6] Two years later the House adopted a rule requiring authorization bills to precede appropriations. The Senate later followed suit.

Separate Policy and Fiscal Decisions

There are several major implications that flow from Congress's efforts to separate policy from fiscal decision making:

Flexibility. The authorization-appropriations rules, like almost all congressional rules, are not self-enforcing. Either chamber can choose to waive, ignore, or circumvent them or establish precedents and practices that obviate distinctions between the two. As one scholar has written:

> The real world of the legislative process differs considerably from the idealized model of the two-step authorization-appropriation procedure. Authorization bills contain appropriations, appropriation bills contain authorizations, and the order of their enactment is sometimes reversed. The Appropriations Committees, acting through various kinds of limitations, riders, and nonstatutory controls, are able to establish policy and act in a substantive manner. Authorization committees have considerable power to force the hand of the Appropriations Committees and, in some cases, even to appropriate.[7]

Functions of Key Participants...

President	Authorizing Committees	Appropriations Committees
—Submits executive budget and current services estimates.	—Prepare views and estimates on programs within their jurisdiction.	—Report regular and supplemental appropriations bills.
—Updates budget estimates in April and July.	—Report authorizing legislation for the next fiscal year.	—After adoption of a budget resolution, allocate budget authority and outlays among their subcommittees.
—Signs or vetoes revenue, appropriations, and other budget-related legislation.	—Include CBO cost estimates in reports accompanying their legislation.	
—May propose the deferral or rescission of appropriated funds.	*Limitations:* 1. Legislation providing contract or borrowing authority is effective only as provided in appropriations.	—Provide five-year projections of outlays in reports accompanying appropriations, and compare budget authority with amounts provided in latest budget resolution.
	2. Entitlements cannot become effective before the next fiscal year.	—Can be instructed by second budget resolution to report reconciliation bill repealing new or existing budget authority.
		—Review rescission and deferrals proposed by the president.
		Limitation: After second resolution is adopted, spending cannot exceed overall amount set by Congress.

... In Congressional Budget Process

Revenue Committees	Budget Committees	Congressional Budget Office
—Submit views and estimates on budget matters in their jurisdiction.	—Report two or more concurrent resolutions on the budget each year.	—Issues reports on the annual budget.
—Can be instructed by second budget resolution to report legislation changing tax laws.	—Allocate new budget authority and outlays among the House and Senate committees.	—Estimates cost of bills reported by House and Senate committees.
Limitation: Legislation cannot cause revenues to fall below level set in the second budget resolution.	—Monitor congressional actions affecting the budget.	—Issues periodic scorekeeping reports on status of congressional consideration of the budget.
	—Advise Congress on the status of the budget.	—Assists the budget, revenue, appropriations, and other committees.
		—Issues five-year budget projections.

Source: Adapted from Allen Schick, *Congress and Money* (The Urban Institute: 1980), pp. 8-9.

In short, there is flexibility in the authorization-appropriations procedure that allows it to accommodate stresses and strains. For example, a failure to enact authorization bills does not bring the appropriations process to a halt, though on occasion it does cause serious program dislocations.

Bicameral Differences. Because the House and Senate are dissimilar, they have different rules governing the authorization-appropriations process. These differences are described in Table 3-1 and reflect each chamber's fundamental nature: The smaller Senate permits greater procedural flexibility than the larger House.

The dissimilar rules of the House and Senate affect each chamber's legislative behavior and policy deliberations. The Senate, for example, often gets off to a slower start on appropriations measures since it is customary to wait for the House to originate those bills. "I had thought we would be on . . . the supplemental appropriations bill by now," explained Senate Majority Leader Howard H. Baker, Jr., of Tennessee in July 1983, "but once again we are waiting for our friends and colleagues in the House of Representatives." [8] Moreover, the multi-stage process creates numerous opportunities to shape issues. Policy debates may be resurrected again and again in different contexts.

Exceptions to the Rules

There are many exceptions to the authorization-appropriations rules. For instance, the House rule that forbids legislation in any general appropriations bill explicitly permits such policy making if it is a retrenchment (reduction) and if it is "germane to the subject matter of the bill." The ostensible purpose of this rule (called the Holman rule after Rep. William S. Holman of Indiana, who formulated it in 1876) is to encourage economy in government. Over the years members seldom have used the Holman rule to make policy. Instead, they have relied heavily on "limitation" riders.

Legislative provisions sometimes find their way into appropriations bills notwithstanding the strictures of the rules — for instance, if no member raises a point of order against the practice.

'Limitation' Riders. Limitations are provisions in general appropriations bills or floor amendments to those measures that prohibit the spending of funds for specific purposes. Always phrased in the negative ("None of the funds provided in this Act shall be used for. . ."), limitations are based on scores of House precedents that collectively uphold the position that because the House can refuse to appropriate funds for programs that have been authorized, it also can prohibit the use of funds for any part of a program or activity.

House members and staff aides devote endless hours to carefully drafting provisions that make policy in the guise of limitations. For guidance they turn to the House rule book, which is replete with precedents that have interpreted permissible from impermissible limitations. There are three basic criteria. Limitations cannot 1) impose additional duties or burdens on

Table 3-1 Authorization-Appropriations Rules Compared

House	*Senate*
No unauthorized appropriations is permitted except for public works in progress. The Appropriations Committee generally cannot report a general appropriations bill unless there is an authorization law.	Unauthorized appropriations are not permitted. There are exceptions: if the Senate has passed an authorization during that session; if an authorization is reported by any Senate standing committee, including Appropriations; or if an authorization is requested in the president's annual budget.
No legislation (policy) is permitted in an appropriations bill.	No legislation is permitted in an appropriations bill unless it is germane to the House-passed bill.
No appropriation is permitted in an authorization bill; floor amendments that propose appropriations are not in order in authorization bills.	There is no equivalent rule. By custom, the House initiates appropriations bills and objects to Senate efforts aimed at circumventing this arrangement.

executive branch officials; 2) interfere with these officials' discretionary authority; or 3) require officials to make judgments or determinations not required by existing law.

The 1977 anti-abortion amendment is a classic example of a limitation and the impact procedure can exert on policy. The Labor-Health Education and Welfare (now Health and Human Services) appropriations bill for that year contained a limitation on the use of funds "to perform abortions except where the life of the mother would be endangered if the fetus were carried to term." A point of order was raised and sustained against that amendment on the ground that it was legislation in an appropriations bill. The limitation required officials in the executive branch to determine when the life of a pregnant woman would be endangered. The language then was amended to read: "None of the funds appropriated by this Act shall be used to pay for abortions or to promote or encourage abortions, except when a physician has certified the abortion is necessary to save the life of the mother." Again, a point of order was raised that the amendment was legislation in an appropriations bill. And again the chair ruled in favor of the parliamentary objection, this time on the ground that the federal government employed many physicians and that they would be required to make "life-deciding" judgments.

Finally, the sponsor of the proposal, Rep. Henry J. Hyde, R-Ill., said he had no choice but to offer the following language: "None of the funds appropriated under this Act shall be used to pay for abortions or to promote or encourage abortions." There was no point of order because the amendment required no judgments by executive officials. The Hyde amendment then was adopted by the House.[9]

When the Labor-HEW bill, now containing the Hyde amendment, reached the Senate, Sen. Edward W. Brooke, R-Mass. (1967-79), offered an amendment that permitted abortions "where the life of the mother would be endangered if the fetus were carried to term, or where medically necessary, or for the treatment of rape or incest." Sen. Barry Goldwater, R-Ariz., said the amendment was legislation in an appropriations bill and raised a point of order. The Senate has its own procedural devices to obviate such points of order, however, and Senator Brooke used them successfully on the abortion issue. He raised what is called a "question of germaneness" before the presiding officer had ruled on the Goldwater point of order.

Deciding Germaneness Questions. Senate rules require that amendments be germane to general appropriations bills. And once the question of germaneness is raised, those rules require that the issue be submitted to the entire membership for resolution by majority vote and without debate. If the Senate decides that the proposed amendment is germane, the point of order automatically falls. In the abortion case described above, the Senate declared Senator Brooke's amendment germane by a 74-21 vote. To be sure, in such situations senators typically vote on the policy issue and not on the procedural question. *(See also Chapter 8.)*

In recent years, the House has experienced a rapid increase in the number of limitation amendments — from 11 in 1965 to 86 in 1980.[10] Many of these dealt with so-called social issues, particularly school busing, school prayer, and abortion. These controversial issues were repeatedly bottled up in the authorizing committees, and members wanting action on them turned increasingly to limitations as a vehicle to force House consideration. Frustrated by the sharp controversies and long delays these limitations were causing, the House changed its rules in 1983 to restrict the opportunities for members to offer limitation riders to appropriations bills.[11]

The new procedure prohibits members, with some exceptions, from proposing limitation amendments on the House floor. Only if the motion to have the Committee of the Whole rise is defeated may members offer a limitation proposal. *(House floor procedures, see Chapter 6.)*

The new procedure was applied for the first time on June 2, 1983, when a clean air rider was added to a Housing and Urban Development Department appropriations bill. "This one [rider] was just intriguing to members," said Majority Whip Thomas S. Foley, D-Wash. "They obviously wanted to cast a vote on it." [12]

Committee Rivalries

Another consequence of the two-step system is that it breeds continuing conflict between the authorizing and appropriating committees. Predictably, the authorizing committees support high levels of spending for the programs they recommend and seek ways to bypass Appropriations Committee domination. The appropriating panels, on the other hand, often view themselves as "guardians of the purse." It is their job, they believe, to say "no" to many funding requests. There are occasions, however, when maximum funding also is the preferred objective of the Appropriations committees.

Loosening the Purse Strings

Tensions between the two types of committees led to procedural strategies by the authorizing committees — especially since the 1950s — that tended to erode the Appropriations committees' authority. The two major ones were 1) use of annual or short-term authorizations and 2) "backdoor" spending.

Permanent and Annual Authorizations

Until the 1950s, most federal programs were permanently authorized.[13] Permanent authorizations provide continuing statutory authority for ongoing federal programs. Unlike the present custom, authorizations in the past usually did not recommend an amount of money to be appropriated each year to operate the programs. Instead, the Appropriations committees made these funding decisions on an annual basis. The appropriating panels, as a result, exercised more influence over agency activities than did the authorizing committees. This situation began to change after World War II. The authorizing committees won enactment of laws that converted many permanent authorizations into short-term or annual authorizations. Explained one expert of the congressional budget process:

> Over the past three decades, however, the growth of annual authorizations has been dramatic. Three [new ones] were enacted during the 1950s and seven more were added during the 1960s. Despite the objections of the Joint Study Committee in 1973 and the aspirations of those who wrote the [1974] Budget Act, 15 annual authorizations made their appearance in the 1970s and several have been added since.[14]

Several factors influenced this trend, but two have been critical:

● First, the authorizing committees wanted greater control and oversight of executive and presidential activities. Annual authorizations are a "relatively effective oversight device," two political scientists have written, "allowing for increased involvement of legislative committees in policymaking and surveillance, providing increased access to agency bases of information, improving the ability of Congress to focus attention on crucial programs, and producing an increased knowledge base from which to examine agency activity." [15]

● Second, annual authorizations put pressure on the appropriating committees to fund programs at levels recommended by the authorizing panels. Under an annual cycle, appropriations bills often are "taken up only weeks after passage of the companion authorization. As a result, the authorization is likely to exert a direct influence on the subsequent appropriation. For most annual authorization bills the amount appropriated is more than 90 percent of the authorized level." [16] The funding gap is wider for programs authorized on a multiyear basis.

● A third factor in the authorizing committees' greater leverage over the appropriating panels has been through "backdoor spending." So-called backdoor authorization measures circumvent the annual appropriations process by permitting the spending of federal monies.

Types of 'Backdoor' Spending

The three basic forms of backdoor spending are borrowing authority, contract authority, and entitlements. Each is discussed below.

● Under borrowing authority, a federal agency legally is authorized to borrow a specified amount of money from the Treasury or the public, through commercial channels, to finance activities such as building low-cost houses or making student loans. Between 1932 and 1975 Congress authorized federal agencies to borrow more than $160 billion from the Treasury.[17]

During the seven-year struggle to enact a depressed areas bill (PL 87-27), backdoor financing loomed large as an issue. Senate Banking Committee member Paul H. Douglas, D-Ill. (1949-67), the chief sponsor of the measure, favored a $200 million government loan program instead of "the customary annual appropriations process" so that the Area Redevelopment Administration could "make long-range financial commitments."[18] Senator Douglas won Senate passage of the backdoor financing method, but the House Appropriations Committee, sensitive to being circumvented, balked when the bill came up for consideration in the House. The bill eventually became law, but over the strenuous objections of the members of the Appropriations panel. "What a way to run a business — any business from a peanut stand to a bank," exclaimed House Appropriations Chairman Clarence A. Cannon, D-Mo. (1923-64). "And yet that is the way we are running the greatest government on earth. Let us close the back door."[19]

● Congress also authorizes annually millions of dollars in contract authority. An example of this type of financing arrangement would be a federal agency that is statutorily permitted to enter into contractual agreements with private firms for the construction of municipal sewage treatment plants. Appropriations must be provided in the future to liquidate these contracts (honor these commitments).

● Entitlements require the federal government to make payments to all eligible beneficiaries. Social Security, Medicare, veterans' pensions, and federal retirement benefits are examples of entitlement programs. Most entitlements are funded automatically through authority granted in permanent laws. They constitute one of the fastest growing parts of the federal budget.

> From a budgetary point of view, the significance of such programs is that, at least in the short run, their costs cannot be controlled. If the Congress appropriates $2 billion to build a dam or a highway, it can be confident that no more that $2 billion may be legally spent. But when it authorizes extended unemployment benefits, or a different reimbursement formula under Medicare, it can set no limit on the money that will uitimately flow from the

Treasury, since the government is legally obligated to provide benefits to anyone who can prove that he is eligible.[20]

The escalation of entitlement expenditures has occurred in part because of demographic factors — the aging of the population, for example — and actions of Congress to ensure that payments to eligible citizens keep pace with inflation.

Prelude to Budget Reform

By 1973 less than half of federal spending was controlled by the congressional Appropriations committees. These panels gradually lost overall control of budget expenditures as the legislative, or authorizing, committees turned to backdoor financing and permanent appropriations to accomplish their policy objectives. The result was that Congress lacked a central body to coordinate budgetary decisions, relate government revenue to expenditures, or calculate the effect of individual spending actions on the national economy. Federal expenditures skyrocketed and national fiscal policy reflected whatever emerged from Congress's decentralized budget process.

Presidents, to be sure, took advantage of the piecemeal process. President Nixon, in particular, clashed with Congress over national spending priorities and frequently impounded (refused to spend) monies for programs sponsored by Democrats in Congress. During the 1972 presidential campaign, Nixon charged Congress with being spendthrift and financially irresponsible. He told a nationwide radio audience:

> But, let's face it, the Congress suffers from institutional faults when it comes to Federal spending. In our economy, the President is required by law to operate within the discipline of his budget, just as most American families must operate within the discipline of their budget.
>
> Both the President and a family must consider total income and total out-go when they take a look at some new item which would involve spending additional money. They must take into account their financial situation as they make each and every spending decision.
>
> In the Congress, however, it is vastly different. Congress not only does not consider the total financial picture when it votes on a particular spending bill, it does not even contain a mechanism to do so if it wished.[21]

Despite this partisan critique, many members of Congress recognized that excessive fragmentation epitomized the weakness of the legislative budget process. Congress appropriates for different programs, such as defense, education, housing, and so on, with little effort to operate within an overall budget or to determine priorities among programs. "[W]e are still practicing this outdated and fragmented congressional appropriations process," declared Sen. Alan Cranston, D-Calif., in 1973. "There can be no doubt of the need for a solution to this problem." [22] Further, conflict raged between the Nixon White House and Congress over the president's impoundment of appropriated funds. "Far from administrative routine," wrote a budget expert, "Nixon's impoundments in late 1972 and 1973 were designed to rewrite national policy at the expense of congressional power and intent." [23]

The erosion of Congress's control of the purse strings, budgetary clashes with presidents, sharp internal conflicts among the appropriating, authorizing, and taxing committees, and public concern about the state of the national economy provided the impetus that led to enactment of a landmark procedural measure: the Congressional Budget and Impoundment Control Act of 1974. That act established a congressional budget process that encouraged coordination and centralization. However, it did not institute this fiscal reorganization by abolishing the traditional authorization-appropriations process. Such an attempt would have pitted the most powerful committees and members against one another and jeopardized any chance of realizing substantive budgetary changes. Instead, Congress added another budget procedure to "the existing revenue and appropriations process" of the House and Senate. [24] In brief, the act was a "shotgun marriage" — an accommodation between Congress's chronic fragmentation and budgetary integration.

The 1974 Budget Act

Passage of the 1974 budget act had a major institutional and procedural impact on the legislative branch. Not unexpectedly, some of the original requirements of the act have been changed in response to new developments. First, however, it is worthwhile to describe the main features of the 1974 act and show how they were intended to operate as well as how they have operated in practice. The key participants in the budget process are listed in the box on pages 48 and 49.

The act created three new entities: the House Budget Committee, the Senate Budget Committee, and the Congressional Budget Office (CBO). The two budget committees have essentially the same functions, which include: 1) preparing annually at least two concurrent budget resolutions; 2) reviewing the impact of existing or proposed legislation on federal expenditures; 3) overseeing the Congressional Budget Office; and 4) monitoring throughout the year the revenue and spending actions of the House and Senate. The last function listed here is called "scorekeeping" and is shared with the CBO.

The two panels, however, are constituted differently. The House Budget Committee is required to have a rotating membership: most members may serve no more than six years during the same decade. The committee must be composed of members drawn mainly from other standing committees, as follows: five each from Appropriations and Ways and Means, 19 from other committees, and a leadership member from each of the two parties, who does not rotate. The chairman may be elected to serve for eight years.

By contrast, the Senate Budget Committee has no restrictions on tenure, nor are its members required to come from other designated committees. A consequence of the membership difference is that career-oriented senators have become more knowledgeable about budgetary matters than their House Budget counterparts and, therefore, are better equipped to shape conference committee deliberations to their own liking. *(Conference committees, see Chapter 9.)*

The Congressional Budget Office is Congress's principal informational and analytical resource for budget, tax, and spending proposals. With about 230 aides, CBO performs important services for the House and Senate Budget committees and other congressional panels. Explained Senate Budget Committee Chairman Pete V. Domenici, R-N.M.: "The core services which we in Congress have come to expect of CBO have been the provision of cost estimates of bills, scorekeeping reports, economic forecasts and 5-year projections, the analysis of the president's budget in its session review, alternative budget reduction strategies, and more detailed analysis of particular problems and Federal activities." [25]

In recent years, CBO has been instrumental in advising Congress about the impact of proposed reconciliation legislation. *(Reconciliation process, see pp. 62, 64, 66.)*

Procedurally, the 1974 act established a rigorous timetable for Congress and its committees to consider the annual appropriations bills. The timetable, outlined in Table 3-2, permits Congress to review the federal budget as a whole, relating revenue raising policies to spending decisions and setting budgetary priorities among competing national programs.

Concurrent Budget Resolutions

The core of Congress's annual budget process centers around the adoption of concurrent budget resolutions: the so-called first and second budget resolutions. These resolutions are formulated by the Budget committees and are composed of two basic parts. The first deals with fiscal aggregates: total federal spending (budget authority and outlays), total federal revenue, and the public debt (or surplus) for the upcoming fiscal year (October 1 through September 30). The second part subdivides the spending aggregates into 21 functional categories, such as national defense, energy, and agriculture. *(Budget terminology, see Glossary.)*

Because of their importance to congressional policy making, budget resolutions are considered in the House and Senate under special procedures that expedite their consideration. The 1974 act changed traditional Senate procedures in two fundamental ways. First, budget resolutions carry a 50-hour statutory debate limitation, which means that they cannot be filibustered to death. Second, the 1974 act imposes a germaneness (somewhat akin to a relevancy) requirement on amendments to budget resolutions. The Senate, unlike the House, has no general germaneness rule.

Budget resolutions are not submitted to the president. They are concurrent resolutions. Hence, they cannot be vetoed; nor do they carry legal effect. Presidents, of course, may veto tax or appropriations bills that follow the guidelines established in the budget resolutions. In May 1983, for example, President Reagan threatened to veto certain tax-raising and

Table 3-2 Congressional Budget Timetable

*Deadline:**	*Action to be Completed:*
November 10	President submits current services budget. (Currently, submitted to Congress along with the president's annual budget.)
15th day after Congress convenes	President submits budget to Congress.
March 15	Legislative committees submit reports to Budget committees.
April 1	Congressional Budget Office submits report to Budget committees.
April 15	Budget committees report out first concurrent resolution on the budget.
May 15	Committees report bills authorizing new budget authority.
May 15	Congress adopts first concurrent resolution on the budget.
7th day after Labor Day	Congress completes action on appropriations bills, providing budget authority and spending authority.
September 15	Congress completes action on second concurrent resolution on the budget.
September 25	Congress completes reconciliation process implementing second concurrent resolution.
October 1	Fiscal year begins.

* Congress in some years has been unable to meet these deadlines.

spending measures called for in Congress's first budget resolution for fiscal year 1984. As one account reported it:

> Reagan declared the [veto] war this week as it became likely that neither the Republican Senate nor the Democratic House would pass overall budget resolutions that he approves of.[26]

The First Resolution. The first budget resolution has a May 15 deadline. It provides Congress and its committees with nonbinding (advisory) revenue and spending targets.[27] To assemble the first resolution, the budget panels employ several sources: annual March 15 reports from the other standing committees outlining each panel's fiscal plans for programs under its jurisdiction; the president's annual budget; informal consultations with members and staff; CBO analyses; and assessments of what the national interest and the economy require.

The Democrats' budget leaders in the House employed a unique method of assembling the party's alternative federal budget for fiscal 1984. A questionnaire was sent out to rank-and-file members asking them for their views on taxes and spending on such controversial programs as defense, Medicare, and indexing of the tax code. It also asked whether the Democrats should craft a partisan or bipartisan budget. Another purpose "behind this exercise was to alleviate the frustrations of backbenchers who felt left out of the budget process, and to make them more loyal to their party's final position." [28]

In the end, the House adopted a Democratic-sponsored budget that differed sharply from President Reagan's. The House agreed to cut Reagan's proposed increase for defense by more than half, to increase taxes, and to allocate more spending for social programs. House GOP leader Robert H. Michel, Ill., dubbed the Democratic spending blueprint the "Revenge on Ronald Reagan Act of 1983." During the two previous years, the president had pushed the Democratic-controlled House to make many unwanted spending cuts in domestic programs.

When the House- and Senate-passed first budget resolutions have different aggregate and functional totals, which is normal practice, the disagreements usually have to be resolved by a conference committee. The conferees prepare a report that provides a "bank account" for the various House and Senate committees. This account distributes the total agreed-upon spending for the year among 21 functional categories.

This allocation procedure, called a "budget crosswalk," involves two steps. First, section 302 of the budget act requires the conference report to allocate the congressionally agreed-upon spending levels for all 21 functional categories among the legislative committees having jurisdiction over these categories.

In the second step in the crosswalk, the committees subdivide their spending allocations among the appropriate subcommittees or programs. As explained by a member of the House Appropriations Committee:

> Under the Budget Act we are assigned a lump sum of funds to be appropriated by the Appropriations Committee. Under section 302 we in the Appropriations Committee allocate that [lump sum] among our subcommittees, and our subcommittees have been scrupulous in staying within those section 302 limits.[29]

The crosswalk procedure is necessary because Congress chooses to employ functional category designations developed by the Office of Management and Budget (OMB). These designations do not correspond exactly to many House and Senate committees, with their overlapping jurisdictional mandates.

Until Congress adopts the first budget resolution for a fiscal year, it may not take up any spending, revenue, entitlement, or debt legislation affecting that year unless this prohibition in the 1974 act is waived by the House and the Senate. May 15 also is the deadline for the legislative committees to report their authorization bills. This requirement is suppose to prevent delays in considering appropriations bills caused by failure to enact the authorizations in a timely manner. This provision of the 1974 act also may be waived by either chamber.

Despite the May 15 deadline, Congress still finds it difficult to clear some of the authorization bills before the appropriations measures are ready for House or Senate action. When Sen. Charles H. Percy, R-Ill., pointed out that the 1983 foreign aid appropriations measure was being debated before the corresponding foreign aid authorization bill had been enacted, Senate Appropriations member Bob Kasten, R-Wis., replied: "This is not the proper process and procedure, but time once again has forced us to go this route." [30]

The Second Resolution. After the first resolution is approved, Congress takes up individual appropriations, tax, debt, and entitlement legislation. Throughout the remainder of the spring and summer, the budget committees monitor all the discrete spending and revenue decisions made by the House and Senate and assess their impact on budget totals contained in the first resolution.

Periodic "scorekeeping" reports are issued by these panels, and the reports constitute a major enforcement tool of the budget process. As one budget scholar explains it: "During the interval between the adoption of the first and second budget resolutions, budget policies are enforced chiefly through the dissemination of information and informal bargaining, rather than through procedural means." [31]

With the coming of autumn, Congress faces another critical deadline: completion by September 15 of a second budget resolution. The second resolution may affirm or revise the budgetary totals contained in the first resolution. The budget committees typically recommend revisions that reflect 1) changing economic circumstances, 2) the spending decisions made by Congress during the spring and summer, and 3) the availability of new budgetary information.

The budget aggregates in the second resolution are binding on Congress. Measures that breach these ceilings are subject to points of order on the floor of either chamber. The congressional budget process, notes a staff director of the Senate Budget Committee, "is a set of internal rules, most of which are enforced by points of order in the House or Senate against legislation which would violate them." [32]

In March 1983, for example, the Senate debated a controversial proposal to repeal the withholding of 10 percent of a person's interest and dividend income. The withholding provision was enacted in 1982 as part of a major tax increase. Sen. John Melcher, D-Mont., offered a repeal amendment to a "must" bill restructuring the Social Security system. After two days of debate the Melcher amendment was dropped when a point of order raised by Budget Committee Chairman Domenici was upheld.

Domenici made the following argument:

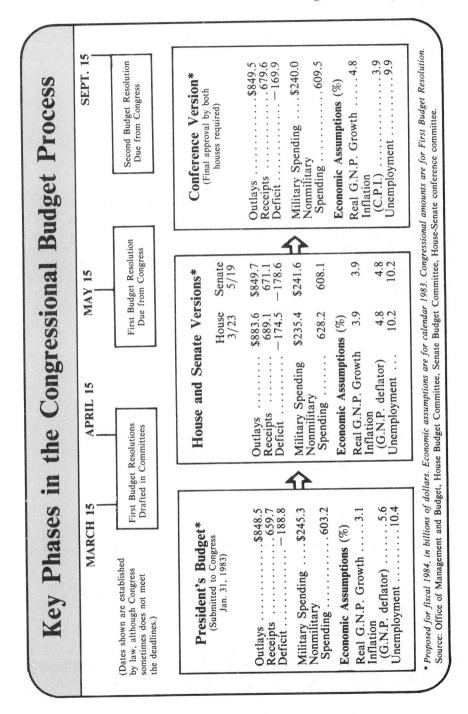

Key Phases in the Congressional Budget Process

| MARCH 15 | APRIL 15 | MAY 15 | | SEPT. 15 |

(Dates shown are established by law, although Congress sometimes does not meet the deadlines.)

First Budget Resolutions Drafted in Committees

First Budget Resolution Due from Congress

Second Budget Resolution Due from Congress

President's Budget*
(Submitted to Congress Jan. 31, 1983)

Outlays $848.5
Receipts 659.7
Deficit .... −188.8

Military Spending ... $245.3
Nonmilitary
Spending 603.2

Economic Assumptions (%)

Real G.N.P. Growth 3.1
Inflation
(G.N.P. deflator) 5.6
Unemployment 10.4

House and Senate Versions*

	House 3/23	Senate 5/19
Outlays	$883.6	$849.7
Receipts	689.1	671.1
Deficit	−174.5	−178.6
Military Spending	$235.4	$241.6
Nonmilitary Spending	628.2	608.1

Economic Assumptions (%)

Real G.N.P. Growth	3.9	3.9
Inflation (G.N.P. deflator)	4.8	4.8
Unemployment	10.2	10.2

Conference Version*
(Final approval by both houses required)

Outlays $849.5
Receipts 679.6
Deficit .... −169.9

Military Spending ... $240.0
Nonmilitary
Spending 609.5

Economic Assumptions (%)

Real G.N.P. Growth 4.8
Inflation
(C.P.I.) 3.9
Unemployment 9.9

*Proposed for fiscal 1984, in billions of dollars. Economic assumptions are for calendar 1983. Congressional amounts are for First Budget Resolution.
Source: Office of Management and Budget, House Budget Committee, Senate Budget Committee, House-Senate conference committee.

> This amendment violates section 311 [of the budget act] because it reduces revenues in fiscal year 1983. . . . There is no room at all under the [fiscal year 1983] budget resolution for a tax reduction, and that is exactly what the amendment does. It reduces revenues by $1.1 billion in fiscal year 1983.[33]

Just prior to the presiding officer's favorable ruling on the Domenici point of order, the Senate had tabled (54-43) Senator Melcher's motion to waive the budget act prohibition against his amendment.

The section 311 language, permitting points of order against bills, amendments, or conference reports that violate the budgetary totals of the second resolution, is a principal enforcement mechanism to control spending by Congress. (However, in 1982 and 1983 Congress abandoned use of a second budget resolution, postponing revisions until the following Spring.) "Delays in revising budget resolution figures, in the face of significant overruns in spending and shortfalls in revenues," and changing economic conditions, wrote a congressional budget expert, "creates an interval during which no legislation with a budgetary impact can be considered without a waiver of Section 311." [34] In conclusion, the use of waivers has diluted the force of Section 311. *(See also Accomplishments and Setbacks, pp. 66-68.)*

'Reconciliation'

"Reconciliation," another step mandated under the budget act, may be required following adoption of the second budget resolution. This procedure can force House and Senate committees to draft revisions to existing laws — those raising revenues or cutting spending, for example — so that overall federal spending is brought into conformity with the revenue and spending levels approved in the second resolution. If reconciliation is required, the 1974 act states that it must be accomplished by September 25. Six days later the new fiscal year begins.

Additional Budget Resolutions

Congress also may adopt a third budget resolution for any fiscal year (or additional ones if needed) if economic circumstances change or other developments occur, such as the election of a new president who wants action on his own fiscal agenda. For instance:

> [President Ford's] lame-duck fiscal 1978 budget was submitted just a few days before the inauguration of his successor, Jimmy Carter. Having shown that Congress could be independent of the executive, the Democratic Congress was anxious to show it could cooperate with the new Democratic president. Carter and the Budget committees moved quickly to prime the economic pump. A third concurrent resolution for fiscal 1977 was drawn up and sent to both houses calling for a jobs program on the expenditure side and a $50 individual rebate on the revenue side. The net impact was to increase the deficit by about $20 billion.[35]

Congress did not adopt the third budget resolution because President Carter withdrew some of his proposals. But Congress did revise the estimates for fiscal year 1977 when it approved the first budget resolution for fiscal 1978.

Controls on 'Backdoors' and Impoundments

The 1974 act tightened control over some types of backdoor financing methods, although the changes applied only to new backdoor schemes, not to any in effect at the time the 1974 measure was enacted. Legislation providing new contract or borrowing authority must indicate that the authority becomes effective only to the extent provided in appropriations acts. New contract and borrowing authority are, in effect, authorizations that *must* be funded later by appropriations.

Entitlement measures also are referred to the House and Senate Appropriations committees. These panels have the authority to modify proposed entitlements.

The 1974 act permits Congress to review impoundments of appropriated funds. Under the act, impoundments are divided into two categories: deferrals and rescissions.

Presidents propose deferrals if they want to delay the spending of certain funds. Unless *either* chamber passes a resolution of disapproval, the deferral is sustained.

A rescission is an executive branch recommendation to cancel congressionally approved spending for a program. Unless *both* the House and Senate approve the rescission within a specified number of days, the president must release the funds.

The 1974 act's impoundment provisions have advantages for both branches. The procedure permits Congress to review and control executive impoundments. On the other hand, presidents can employ deferrals and rescissions to achieve — even temporarily — spending objectives denied them under the regular authorization/appropriations process.[36] Congress sometimes employs the regular legislative process to deal with impoundments. It may approve or disapprove certain deferrals and rescissions in the regular or in supplemental appropriations bills.

Evolution of the Budget Process

Change is an "iron law" of congressional procedure and politics. This is certainly the case with the congressional budget process. Scores of formal and informal developments have modified the process in the few years since Congress first subjected itself to the discipline of the 1974 act. That law even contains an "elastic clause" that permits Congress to include in the first budget resolution "any other procedure which is considered appropriate to carry out the purposes of this Act."

Amendments to 1974 Law

Formally, the 1974 law has been amended only a few times and in marginal ways. The CBO, for example, is required under a 1981 change to estimate how much money state and local governments might have to expend in order to comply with certain legislation that has been reported by congressional committees. (This is separate from a rule that requires committees to include with their reports on authorization bills an estimate of how much the legislation is expected to cost.) There has been a reluctance by Congress to open the law to major revision because members believe that some of their colleagues who are unhappy with the process might attempt to dismantle the entire law.[37]

Informal Changes

Informally, the law has been changed in some fundamental ways:

● First, the scope of the budget process has been expanded to include such matters as federal credit activities. Federal credit programs, such as guaranteed loans to college students or to the Chrysler Corporation, totaled more than $200 billion for 1983 and in effect are outside the conventional budget process. Today, Congress includes in its budget resolutions advisory targets on the "total size of federal lending and loan-guarantee programs." [38] The annual budget resolutions also contain multiyear estimates of expenditures and revenues.

● Second, the first resolution rather than the second has become the major vehicle for congressional budgeting. The drafting of the second resolution, wrote a budget analyst, "has been little more than an accounting exercise. The Budget Committees have adjusted the first resolution for any changes in the economy or congressional actions that differed significantly from the assumptions on which it was based." [39] In 1982 Congress adopted an automatic triggering device allowing the first budget resolution to substitute for the second resolution if Congress did not approve the second resolution by October 1. The same procedure was followed in 1983.

● Third, the reconciliation procedure since 1980 has been associated with the first rather than the second budget resolution. Congress decided there was too little time to employ the reconciliation process after adoption of the second budget resolution. Noted Alice Rivlin, the first CBO director:

> [T]here really isn't time to go through that two-stage [budget] process. If big decisions are to be made on the budget, for example, in cutting the deficit, they have to be made early. The first budget resolution has become the place where the important decisions are made, and reconciling the parts with the whole has been moved into the first resolution. The second resolution has become unnecessary and the act might be changed to reflect that.[40]

These shifts have turned reconciliation into an effective procedure for making budgetary savings.

How 'Reconciliation' Works

Reconciliation is a two-step process designed to bring existing law into conformity with current budget plans. In practice, reconciliation has been used to reduce spending and increase revenues.

(THE AUTHORIZATION)

Public Law 97-322
97th Congress

Oct. 15, 1982
[S. 2252]

An Act

To authorize appropriations for the Coast Guard for fiscal years 1983 and 1984, and for other purposes.

Coast Guard, appropriation authorization for FY 1983 and 1984.

Be it enacted by the Senate and House of Representatives of the United States of America in Congress assembled,

Coast Guard Authorization Act of 1982.

TITLE I

Sec. 101. This title may be cited as the "Coast Guard Authorization Act of 1982".

Sec. 102. Funds are authorized to be appropriated for necessary expenses of the Coast Guard for fiscal years 1983 and 1984 as follows:

(1) For the operation and maintenance of the Coast Guard, including expenses related to the Capehart housing debt reduction, $1,800,000,000 for fiscal year 1983 and $2,000,000,000 for each such fiscal year 1984, and such additional amounts for increases in salary, pay, and other employee benefits authorized by law.

(2) For the acquisition, construction, rebuilding, and improvement of aids to navigation, shore facilities, vessels, and aircraft, including equipment related thereto, $550,000,000 for fiscal year 1983 and $650,300,000 for fiscal year 1984.

(3) For research, development, test, and evaluation, $22,000,000 for fiscal year 1983 and $32,000,000 for fiscal year 1984, of which sufficient funds shall be made available to continue in operation the Coast Guard research and development center through the end of fiscal year 1984.

(4) For the alteration or removal of bridges over navigable waters, constituting obstructions to navigation, $8,000,000, for fiscal year 1983.

(5) For retired pay including the payment of obligations therefor otherwise chargeable to lapsed appropriations for this purpose, and payments under the Retired Serviceman's Family Protection and Survivor Benefit Plans, and for payments for medical care of retired personnel and their dependents under the Dependents' Medical Care Act, such sums as may be necessary for fiscal years 1983 and 1984

(THE APPROPRIATION)

Public Law 97-369
97th Congress

Dec. 18, 1982
[H.R. 7019]

An Act

Making appropriations for the Department of Transportation and related agencies for the fiscal year ending September 30, 1983, and for other purposes.

Department of Transportation and Related Agencies Appropriation Act, 1983.

Be it enacted by the Senate and House of Representatives of the United States of America in Congress assembled, That the following sums are appropriated, out of any money in the Treasury not otherwise appropriated, for the Department of Transportation and related agencies for the fiscal year ending September 30, 1983, and for other purposes, namely:

COAST GUARD

OPERATING EXPENSES

For necessary expenses for the operation and maintenance of the Coast Guard, not otherwise provided for; purchase of not to exceed eight passenger motor vehicles for replacement only; and recreation and welfare, $1,518,963,000, of which $254,650 shall be applied to Capehart Housing debt reduction. *Provided,* That the applied ten exclusive at any one time shall not exceed two hundred of which ten exclusive at any one time shall not exceed two hundred of aircraft on hand and parts stored to meet future attrition *Provided further,* That none of the funds appropriated in this or any other Act shall be available for pay or administrative expenses in connection with shipping commissioners in the United States *Provided further,* That none of the funds provided in this Act shall be available for the expenses incurred for yacht documentation under 46 U.S.C. 103 except to the extent fees are collected from yacht owners and credited to this appropriation, and, notwithstanding any other law, the Secretary may prescribe fees to recover the expenses of yacht documentation

ACQUISITION, CONSTRUCTION, AND IMPROVEMENTS

(INCLUDING TRANSFER OF FUNDS)

For necessary expenses of acquisition, construction, rebuilding, and improvement of aids to navigation, shore facilities, vessels, and aircraft, including equipment related thereto, to remain available until September 30, 1987, $409,000,000, of which $9,000,000 shall be derived by transfer from the unobligated balances of "Pollution Fund"

ALTERATION OF BRIDGES

For necessary expenses for alteration or removal of obstructive bridges, $12,700,000, to remain available until expended

(CONCURRENT RESOLUTION ON THE BUDGET)

Aggregates

That the Congress hereby determines and declares that the Second Concurrent Resolution on the Budget for Fiscal Year 1983 is hereby revised, the First Concurrent Resolution on the Budget for Fiscal Year 1983 is hereby established, and the appropriate budgetary levels for Fiscal Years 1984 and 1985 are hereby set forth.

(a) The following budgetary levels are appropriate for the fiscal years beginning on October 1, 1981, October 1, 1982, October 1, 1983, and October 1, 1984.

(1) The recommended levels of Federal revenues are as follows:

Fiscal year 1982: $619,400,000,000
Fiscal year 1983: $665,900,000,000
Fiscal year 1984: $718,000,000,000
Fiscal year 1985: $811,400,000,000

and the amounts by which the aggregate levels of Federal revenues should be changed are as follows:

Fiscal year 1982: $500,000,000
Fiscal year 1983: +$30,900,000,000
Fiscal year 1984: +$36,000,000,000
Fiscal year 1985: +$41,400,000,000

(2) The appropriate levels of total new budget authority are as follows:

Fiscal year 1982: $777,672,000,000
Fiscal year 1983: $833,290,000,000
Fiscal year 1984: $878,474,000,000
Fiscal year 1985: $960,611,000,000

(3) The appropriate levels of total budget outlays are as follows:

Fiscal year 1982: $714,100,000,000
Fiscal year 1983: $769,818,000,000
Fiscal year 1984: $821,938,000,000
Fiscal year 1985: $881,334,000,000

(4) The amounts of the deficits in the budget which are appropriate in the light of economic conditions and all other relevant factors are as follows:

Fiscal year 1982: $105,700,000,000
Fiscal year 1983: $103,918,000,000
Fiscal year 1984: $87,938,000,000
Fiscal year 1985: $59,936,000,000

Functional Allocations for Transportation

(b) The Congress hereby determines and declares the appropriate levels of budget authority, and budget outlays, for the fiscal years 1982 through and inclusive of 1985 and the appropriate levels of new direct loan obligations, new primary loan guarantee commitments, and new secondary loan guarantee commitments for fiscal years 1982 and 1983 for each major functional category are

(8) Transportation (400)
Fiscal year 1982:
(A) New budget authority, $30,800,000,000
(B) Outlays, $21,300,000,000
(C) New direct loan obligations, $400,000,000
(D) New primary loan guarantee commitments, $750,000,000
(E) New secondary loan guarantee commitments, $2,000,000
Fiscal Year 1983:
(A) New budget authority, $21,650,000,000
(B) Outlays, $19,900,000,000
(C) New direct loan obligations, $500,000,000
(D) New primary loan guarantee commitments, $800,000,000
(E) New secondary loan guarantee commitments, $2,000,000
Fiscal Year 1984:
(A) New budget authority, $21,700,000,000
(B) Outlays, $19,700,000,000
Fiscal Year 1985:
(A) New budget authority, $22,050,000,000
(B) Outlays, $19,600,000,000

The first step calls for congressional approval of a resolution that instructs House and Senate committees to propose cuts in spending (and/or increases in revenue) on programs and agency operations by a certain date. The panels' recommended budget savings, which are suppose to meet or exceed the amounts designated for each committee in the resolution, are transmitted to the respective House and Senate Budget committees.

The second step involves the packaging of the recommendations into an omnibus reconciliation bill, followed by floor action in each chamber. The Budget committees cannot make substantive changes in the savings proposals received from each instructed committee.

In 1981 President Reagan persuaded Congress to employ reconciliation to achieve massive cuts in domestic programs (totaling about $130 billion over three years). Never before had reconciliation been employed on such a grand scale. The entire two-step process was put on a "fast track" that short-circuited regular legislative procedures. A highly charged atmosphere produced a legislative result, wrote Senate Majority Leader Baker, "that would have been impossible to achieve if each committee had reported an individual bill on subject matter solely within its jurisdiction." [41] In short, reconciliation forced numerous House and Senate committees to make unwanted cuts in programs, including entitlements, under their jurisdiction.

After enactment of the 1981 reconciliation bill, many members wondered whether Congress could reconcile itself ever again to such a drastic exercise. Rep. Richard W. Bolling, D-Mo., who at the time was the chairman of the Rules Committee, charged that exploitation of the reconciliation process "enabled the Executive to unilaterally impose its will in near totality on Congress." [42]

Senator Domenici disagreed. He noted that "it was Congress's own decision to use the reconciliation process — not the decision of the Administration." [43] Domenici also underscored reconciliation's value as Congress's most effective mechanism for achieving its budgetary goals. The controversial character of the 1981 reconciliation experience, therefore, precipitated a major introspective review of its operation and scope. [44]

Accomplishments and Setbacks

It is not easy to assess the congressional budget process. Members themselves disagree about the objectives of the original act. Some members expected the act to produce balanced budgets and spending reductions. Others wanted the new procedures to change national priorities — more for defense and less for domestic programs or vice versa. Absent agreement about the goals of the act, it is difficult to evaluate the act's performance. What is clear after a decade of experience is that the act will respond to whatever spending policies a majority in Congress wants.

The successes of the act are many. Significantly, its procedures have taken root and have been followed, albeit with some modifications, by both houses. Members, too, are better informed about the budgetary implications of their decisions and the administration's policies, the impact of the economy on the budget, and the economic assumptions that permeate any budget. Today, members are much less dependent on the White House and OMB for financial data and advice. Instead, they have adequate fiscal tools to compete with and challenge the executive branch.

Fiscal Coordination

The act has brought coherence to the congressional budget process. Members and committees now consider the budget as a whole and relate Congress's spending decisions to projected revenues and debt levels. Moreover, members believe that without the discipline of the budget process the federal deficits of the early 1980s would have been even higher. Sen. Robert Dole, R-Kan., Senate Finance Committee chairman, maintained "that without the budget process, we would be looking at even greater deficits and greater problems had we not moved in the Congress to instill some discipline within our own institution." [45] Or as another account put it, without the budget process the watchword on Capitol Hill "would again become, 'What's in it for my district?' and not, 'What will this bill do to the deficit?' " [46]

Nevertheless, the budget act is under strain in Congress. There have been missed budget deadlines, fiscal impasses, and economic forecasts that emphasize optimism over realism. Wrote Rudolph G. Penner, who succeeded Alice Rivlin as CBO director: The budget act "forces the Congress to make hard choices, and since politicians — and everyone else, for that matter — hate to make hard choices, it is not surprising that the process is so highly unpopular and may not survive in a meaningful form." [47]

Government by Continuing Resolution

Members believe the process is too complex and consumes too much of Congress's attention and energy. Substantive issues often are sidetracked in the interest of passing budget resolutions, appropriations and tax bills, omnibus reconciliation legislation, supplemental appropriations, and legislation raising the national debt ceiling. With such an agenda, it is not surprising that Congress often cannot enact all these measures in a timely fashion.

This development has led in recent years to "government by continuing resolution." Whenever Congress cannot complete action on one or more of the 13 regular appropriations bills by the start of the fiscal year, it provides temporary emergency funding for the affected federal agencies through a continuing resolution (a joint resolution).

Traditionally, continuing resolutions were employed to keep a few government agencies in operation for short periods, typically one to three months. Continuing resolutions today are major policy-making instruments of massive size and scope. They authorize *and* appropriate money each year for much of the federal government and make national policy in areas as diverse as defense, employment, public works, abortion, school busing and prayer in the schools. The surge in the use of continuing resolutions is attributed in part to Congress's inability to meet the timetable of the budget act and also to sharp legislative-executive conflicts over budget priorities.

The budget process also produces jurisdictional jealousies. The authorizing, appropriating, and taxing committees frequently resent the interference of the budget committees on their "turf." These jealousies foster conflict and undermine support for the budget process. In 1983, for instance, the chairmen of five House authorizing committees introduced legislation to dilute the authority of the Budget Committee. On the other hand, there are occasions when committee chairmen welcome the support of the Budget Committee in persuading colleagues to make painful spending decisions.

New Roles for Committees

Committees also have developed new roles and relationships under the budget process. The Appropriations committees, for example, "are no longer regarded as protectors of the purse; rather they are cast as claimants whose striving for higher spending is to be policed by budget controls." [48]

Some Appropriations members take a different view, however. According to Rep. Silvio O. Conte, R-Mass., the ranking Republican on the House Appropriations Committee, there is no need for members to maintain a "misguided concern for the integrity of a budget process which has become thoroughly corrupted and discredited by political gamesmanship and jurisdictional squabbling." [49]

Finally, the budget process has been blamed for producing results that members disapprove of. Liberal House Democrats, for example, fumed against the budget process in 1981 because it produced such startling victories for President Reagan's economic agenda. The budget act also is criticized because it compels members to make hard choices. But House Budget Chairman Jones argues that "[i]t's not the budget process that's irritating people. It's that dividing scarcer resources is not as easy as dividing growing resources." [50]

The budget process, in short, always will have its share of critics and problems. After all, it deals with one of the government's fundamental chores: the distribution or redistribution of federal resources among competing national priorities. The impending collapse of the 1974 budget act has been predicted with increasing regularity. And despite its proven usefulness, its future is far from clear. Scores of proposals have been introduced to revamp its operation, but how, when, or whether Congress can establish a consensus to fine-tune, streamline, or "reform" the act is a much more difficult matter. Without some revision, says Rep. Leon E. Panetta, D-Calif., a leading backer of the budget act, "Congress may not have the budget process to kick around anymore." [51]

Summary

Legislative changes are notable for producing mixed results and unexpected consequences. The budget act has been no exception to these conditions. Its procedures, and those applicable generally to congressional policy making, can produce whatever can attract a majority or, in some cases, an extraordinary majority. Legislative procedures, in short, define the context in which policies are made and influence the choice of strategies to advance or frustrate legislation, including budget resolutions.

Chapter 4 turns to the initial steps of the legislative process: the introduction and referral of bills to House and Senate committees and committee action on legislation. The executive branch and pressure groups usually are given most of the credit for initiating ideas that Congress eventually formulates and passes in legislative form. But Congress also initiates numerous proposals. And ideas for legislation frequently are discussed in academic circles, private associations, federal advisory committees, national commissions, citizens' groups, professional societies, and by knowledgeable individuals.

In essence, legislation "is an aggregate, not a simple production," Woodrow Wilson once wrote. "It is impossible to tell how many persons, opinions and influences have entered into its composition." [52]

Notes

1. U.S., Congress, House, *Congressional Record,* daily ed., May 25, 1982, H2789.
2. *Congressional Control of Expenditures,* House Committee on the Budget, January 1977, 6. The study was prepared by Allen Schick.
3. John William Ellwood, ed., *Reductions in U.S. Domestic Spending* (New Brunswick, N.J.: Transaction Books, 1982), 21.
4. Absent an authorization law, the Appropriations committees typically base their financial recommendations on the president's budget requests.
5. Everett Somerville Brown, ed., *William Plumer's Memorandum of Proceedings in the United States Senate, 1803-1807* (New York: The Macmillan Co., 1923), 490.
6. Robert Luce, *Legislative Problems* (Boston: Houghton Mifflin Co., 1935), 425-426.
7. Louis Fisher, "The Authorization-Appropriation Process in Congress: Formal Rules and Informal Practices," *Catholic University Law Review,* Fall 1979, 53.
8. U.S., Congress, Senate, *Congressional Record,* daily ed., July 29, 1983, S11150. Supplemental appropriations are designed primarily to meet new or unexpected financial contingencies.
9. Fisher,"The Authorization-Appropriation Process in Congress: Formal Rules and Informal Practices," 74-75. The House considered the issue on June 17, 1977, and the Senate on June 29, 1977. See Roger H. Davidson, "Procedures and Politics in Congress," in *The Abortion Dispute and the American System,* ed. Gilbert Y. Steiner (Washington, D.C.: The Brookings Institution, 1982), 30-46.
10. Norman J. Ornstein, et al., *Vital Statistics on Congress, 1982* (Washington, D.C.: American Enterprise Institute for Public Policy Research, 1982), 154.
11. U.S., Congress, House, *Congressional Record,* daily ed., January 3, 1983, H5-H22.
12. Joseph A. Davis and Susan Smith, "EPA Funding Raised: $54.4 Billion HUD Bill Passed After Test of New Rider Rule," *Congressional Quarterly Weekly Report,* June 4, 1983, 1125. Ironically, in the wake of the June 1983 Supreme Court decision declaring legislative vetoes unconstitutional, some representatives wanted to again revise House rules to allow use of the old procedure permitting

any member to offer limitation riders on appropriations bills. See U.S., Congress, House, *Congressional Record,* daily ed., June 28, 1983, H4504.

13. Authorizations and appropriations come in several forms: annual, multiyear, and permanent. For example, permanent authorizations "last for an indefinite period of time, until altered or terminated by Congress; multiyear authorizations last for a specified period of time, usually two to five years; and annual authorizations last for one year and must be renewed each year if the particular program is to be continued." However, "an authorization could lapse and the program continue through an unauthorized appropriation." See Michael D. Margeson, "The Use of Annual Authorizations, 94th-96th Congresses," Paper Prepared by the Congressional Budget Office, March 25, 1982, 2. Today, appropriations tend to be approved on an annual basis.

14. Louis Fisher, "Annual Authorizations: Durable Roadblocks to Biennial Budgeting," *Public Budgeting & Finance* (Spring 1983): 27. See also John Gist, "The Impact of Annual Authorizations on Military Appropriations in the U.S. Congress," *Legislative Studies Quarterly* (August 1981): 439-454.

15. Lawrence C. Dodd and Richard L. Schott, *Congress and the Administrative State* (New York: John Wiley & Sons, 1979), 236.

16. Allen Schick, *Congress and Money* (Washington, D.C.: The Urban Institute, 1980), 175.

17. *Congressional Control of Expenditures,* 103.

18. Quoted in a case study of the depressed areas bill. See John F. Bibby and Roger H. Davidson, *On Capitol Hill,* 2d ed. (Hinsdale, Ill.: The Dryden Press, 1972), 219-220.

19. Ibid., 221.

20. James Fallows, "Entitlements," *Atlantic,* November 1982, 52.

21. "Federal Spending," The President's Address on Nationwide Radio from Camp David, October 7, 1972, *Weekly Compilation of Presidential Documents,* vol. 8, no. 41, 1497-1499.

22. U.S., Congress, *Congressional Record,* February 8, 1973, 4015.

23. Schick, *Congress and Money,* 46.

24. Ibid., 59.

25. *Congressional Budget Office Oversight,* Hearing before the Senate Committee on the Budget, 97th Cong., 2d sess., February 5, 1982, 1.

26. *USA Today,* May 19, 1983, 8A.

27. The annual May 15 deadline is virtually unenforceable, and Congress has missed it several times.

28. *New York Times,* March 15, 1983, A22.

29. U.S., Congress, House, *Congressional Record,* daily ed., July 30, 1981, H5403. The budget act requires the House and Senate Appropriations committees to divide the lump sum among its subcommittees; the other standing committees do it by custom.

30. U.S., Congress, Senate, *Congressional Record,* daily ed., July 29, 1983, S11155.

31. Robert A. Keith, "Enforcement of Spending Ceilings and Revenue Floors in Budget Resolutions," *CRS Review,* July/August 1983, 18.

32. John McEvoy, "The Politics of the Budget Process: A View from the Senate," in *The Congressional Budget Process: Some Views from the Inside,* Center for the Study of American Business, Washington University, St. Louis, Mo., Formal Publication no. 32, July 1980, 3.

33. U.S., Congress, Senate, *Congressional Record,* daily ed., March 22, 1983, S3580. Senator Melcher's amendment, if adopted, would have delayed by six

months the 10 percent withholding of interest and dividend payments by savings institutions and corporations. This provision of the 1982 tax law was to have taken effect July 1, 1983, but Congress repealed the withholding requirement on July 28, 1983.

34. Keith, "Enforcement of Spending Ceilings and Revenue Floors in Budget Resolutions," 19.

35. Lance T. LeLoup, *The Fiscal Congress* (Westport, Conn.: Greenwood Press, 1980), 42-43.

36. Because of the June 23, 1983, decision of the Supreme Court declaring legislative vetoes unconstitutional, it is at this juncture unclear how the decision will affect the impoundment provisions of the budget act.

37. There is even a bipartisan lobbying group, the Committee for a Responsible Federal Budget, that seeks to protect the budget process from changes that would weaken it. The group is composed largely of former members of Congress.

38. Ross Evans, "Special Report: The Credit Budget," *Congressional Quarterly Weekly Report,* October 23, 1982, 2721.

39. Stanley E. Collender, *The Guide to the Federal Budget, Fiscal 1984 Edition* (Washington, D.C.: The Urban Institute Press, 1983), 18.

40. *Washington Post,* July 10, 1983, G3.

41. Howard H. Baker, Jr., "Essay, An Introduction to the Politics of Reconciliation," *Harvard Journal on Legislation* (Winter 1983): 2.

42. *Review of the Congressional Budget and Impoundment Control Act of 1974,* Hearings before the Senate Committee on Governmental Affairs, 97th Cong., 1st sess. (Washington, D.C.: U.S. Government Printing Office, 1982), 8.

43. Ibid., 42.

44. See John William Ellwood, "Congress Cuts the Budget: The Omnibus Reconciliation Act of 1981," *Public Budgeting and Finance* (Spring 1982): 50-64; Allen Schick, *Reconciliation and the Congressional Budget Process* (Washington, D.C.: American Enterprise Institute for Public Policy Research, 1982); Robert A. Keith, "Budget Reconciliation in 1981," *Public Budgeting and Finance* (Winter 1981): 37-47; James A. Miller and James D. Range, "Reconciling an Irreconcilable Budget: The New Politics of the Budget Process," *Harvard Journal on Legislation* (Winter 1983): 4-30; Steven S. Smith, "Budget Battles of 1981: The Role of the Majority Party Leadership," in *American Politics and Public Policy,* ed. Allan P. Sindler (Washington, D.C.: CQ Press, 1982), 43-78; and Lance T. LeLoup, "After the Blitz: Reagan and the U.S. Congressional Budget Process," in *Legislative Studies Quarterly* (August 1982): 321-339.

45. *Review of the Congressional Budget and Impoundment Control Act of 1974,* 107.

46. *Newsweek,* May 30, 1983, 40.

47. *Los Angeles Times,* part IV, June 26, 1983, 2.

48. Allen Schick, "The Three-Ring Budget Process: The Appropriations, Tax, and Budget Committees in Congress," in *The New Congress,* ed. Thomas E. Mann and Norman J. Ornstein (Washington, D.C.: American Enterprise Institute for Public Policy Research, 1981), 313.

49. U.S., Congress, House, *Congressional Record,* daily ed., June 16, 1982, H3495.

50. *New York Times,* October 3, 1982, 34.

51. *Washington Post,* July 7, 1982, A2. See *The Congressional Budget Process After Five Years,* ed. Rudolph G. Penner (Washington, D.C.: American Enterprise Institute for Public Policy Research, 1981); Dennis S. Ippolito, *Congressional Spending* (Ithaca, N.Y.: Cornell University Press, 1981); and Louis

Fisher, "The Budgetary Process: How Far Have We Progressed?" in *Improving the Accountability and Performance of Government*, ed. Bruce L. R. Smith and James D. Carroll (Washington, D.C.: The Brookings Institution, 1982), 75-91. On August 4, 1983, Sen. Barry Goldwater, R-Ariz., introduced legislation (S 1783) to abolish the congressional budget process.
52. Woodrow Wilson, *Congressional Government* (Boston: Houghton Mifflin, 1885), 320.

4

Preliminary Legislative Action

The introduction of a bill in the House or Senate is a simple procedure. In the House, members just drop their bills into the "hopper," a mahogany box near the clerk's desk at the front of the chamber. In the Senate, members usually submit their proposals and accompanying statements to clerks, or they may introduce their bills from the floor. Measures may be introduced only when the chamber is in session. All House and Senate bills are printed and are made available to members and the public.

The simple act of introducing a bill sets off a complex and variable chain of events that may or may not result in the final passage of a bill by Congress. Most bills follow a path in which the various steps, governed by rules and convention, are fairly predictable, but the outcome usually is uncertain. This chapter considers some of the factors that affect the probable route a bill will take and focuses on the early stages in the life of a bill: its referral to committee and, of utmost importance, its consideration in committee.

Although thousands of pieces of legislation are introduced in every Congress, a relatively small number become law. Table 4-1 shows that of the 13,000 to 29,000 measures that have been introduced in each Congress since 1965, the number emerging from committee in any one Congress never exceeded 4,200, and the number that became law never exceeded 810. Committees clearly are the primary graveyard for most bills that die in Congress. Stated positively, committees select from the vast number of bills introduced those that they feel merit further consideration.

Categories of Legislation

The winnowing process that occurs in committee suggests that the thousands of bills introduced in each Congress may be broken down roughly into three categories: bills having so little support that they are ignored and die in committee; uncontroversial bills that are expedited through Congress; and finally, major bills that are generally so controversial that they occupy the major portion of Congress's time.

Table 4-1 Bills and Public Laws

Congress	Measures Introduced	Reported From Committee	Public Laws
89th (1965-67)	26,566	4,200	810
90th (1967-69)	29,133	3,657	640
91st (1969-71)	29,041	3,250	695
92nd (1971-73)	25,354	2,703	607
93rd (1973-75)	26,222	2,787	649
94th (1975-77)	24,283	2,870	588
95th (1977-79)	22,313	2,968	633
96th (1979-81)	14,594	2,494	613
97th (1981-83)	13,240	1,877	473

Source: Final Daily Digest of the appropriate *Congressional Record*. Refers to all public bills and resolutions introduced in each Congress.

Bills Lacking Wide Support

Bills having little support usually are introduced with no expectation that they will be enacted into law. Members introduce such bills for a variety of reasons: to go on record in support of a given proposal, to satisfy individual constituents or interest groups from the member's district or state, to publicize an issue, to attract media attention, or to fend off criticism during political campaigns. Once a member has introduced a bill, he or she can claim "action" on the issue and can blame the committee to which the bill has been referred for its failure to win enactment. These bills make up a majority of the large number introduced in each Congress.

Uncontroversial Bills

Uncontroversial bills make up another large segment of the measures introduced. Examples of such legislation are bills that authorize construction of statues of public figures, establish university programs in the memory of a senator, rename a national park, or name federal buildings after former members of Congress. Committees in both chambers have developed rapid procedures for dealing with such measures. As shown in Chapters 6 and 8, these bills generally are passed on the floor without debate in a matter of minutes.

Major Legislation

Bills taking up the largest percentage of a committee's time have some or all of the following characteristics: They are prepared and drafted by executive agencies or by major pressure groups; they are introduced by committee chairmen or other influential members of Congress; they are supported by the majority party leadership; or they deal with issues on which a significant segment of public opinion and the membership of Congress believe some sort of legislation is necessary.

Bills having such characteristics do not necessarily become law; nor is there any assurance that they will become law in the form in which they originally were introduced. Indeed, sentiment may be so sharply divided that they do not even emerge from committee. Nevertheless, these are the major bills before Congress each year. They may affect the wage earner's paycheck (taxes and Social Security) and the consumer's pocketbook (health insurance and natural gas deregulation); they may be brought up repeatedly at presidential news conferences and covered in the electronic and print media. In short, they are the bills on which Congress devotes the largest portion of its committee and floor time. These bills account for perhaps only a hundred or so of the thousands introduced in each Congress.

Executive Branch Bills. The president's leadership in the initial stages of the legislative process is pronounced. The administration's major legislative proposals are outlined in the president's annual State of the Union address, nowadays televised nationally and delivered before a joint session of Congress. In the weeks and months following the address, the president sends to Congress special messages detailing his proposals in specific areas, such as energy, welfare, and health. Bills containing the administration's programs are drafted in the executive agencies, and members of Congress, usually committee chairmen, are asked to introduce them simultaneously as "companion" bills in both chambers. Only representatives and senators, not the president or executive officials, may introduce legislation in Congress.

Influential Members' Bills. Bills supported by influential members stand a good chance of receiving attention in committee. During 1981-1983, for example, the House and Senate on several occasions debated immigration reform bills. Because of the mounting public concern about the flood of illegal aliens into the country, two key members, Sen. Alan K. Simpson, R-Wyo., and Rep. Romano L. Mazzoli, D-Ky., sponsored companion bills to revamp the nation's immigration laws. Simpson and Mazzoli each chaired his chamber's Judiciary subcommittee that handled immigration measures. Because of their strategic leadership posts, the two members were successful in advancing the legislation to the House and Senate floor during the '97th and 98th Congresses. Both members also worked diligently to develop trade-offs and compromises among liberal and conservative colleagues to enhance the measure's prospects for passage.

'Must' Legislation. As legislators, members of Congress may not want to deal with controversial "no-win" public issues such as abortion or gun control. As politicians answering constituent mail, responding to inquiring journalists, and, of course, facing reelection, they may not be able to ignore them. Hence, it frequently occurs that members are in basic agreement that legislation must be enacted to deal with a given problem but are in sharp disagreement over the solution. Under these circumstances, most members work hard to compromise their differences because they realize that some type of legislation is desirable or unavoidable.

Many of the factors determining the probable route a bill will take are apparent, therefore, by the time the legislation is introduced. Bills having little support will be buried in committee; uncontroversial legislation will move quickly through Congress; major bills may or may not become law but in any case will command the greatest portion of Congress's time.

Bill Referral Procedure

Once a bill is introduced it receives an identifying number. Measures introduced in the House are identified by the letters "HR" and an accompanying number; Senate bills are identified by the letter "S" and a number. Usually, bills are assigned numbers according to the sequence in which they are introduced. Occasionally, however, members will request the bill clerk to reserve a particular number. During consideration of statehood for Alaska and Hawaii, various bills were introduced as S 49 or HR 50, representing the new states. Bill numbers also may be assigned for political and symbolic purposes. To highlight legislative concern for women's rights, Speaker Thomas P. O'Neill, Jr., D-Mass., on the first day of the 1983 session declared: "House Joint Resolution 1 this year will be ERA, the equal rights amendment." [1] Some measures are assigned the same number for several Congresses. This is done to avoid confusion among legislators and the public who have grown accustomed to referring to a proposal by its bill number. Informally, many bills also come to be known by the names of their sponsors, such as the Kemp-Roth bill, introduced by Rep. Jack F. Kemp, R-N.Y., and Sen. William V. Roth, Jr., R-Del.

With few exceptions, bills are referred to the appropriate standing committees. [2] The job of referral formally is the responsibility of the Speaker of the House and the presiding officer of the Senate, [3] but usually this task is carried out on their behalf by the parliamentarians of the House and Senate. [4] Precedent, public laws, and the jurisdictional mandates of the committees as set forth in the rules of the House and Senate determine which committees receive what kinds of bills. The jurisdiction of the House Education and Labor Committee is listed in Table 4-2.

The vast majority of referrals are routine. Bills dealing with farm crops are sent to the House Agriculture Committee and the Senate Agriculture, Nutrition and Forestry Committee; tax bills are sent to the House Ways and Means Committee and the Senate Finance Committee; and bills dealing with veterans' benefits are sent to the Veterans' Affairs committees of each chamber. [5] Thus, referrals generally are cut-and-dried decisions. (House and Senate standing committees are listed in the box on page 79.)

In the House, a member is not permitted to appeal referral decisions to the entire membership except in rare instances of erroneous referral. In the Senate, the rules do permit an appeal to the full Senate by majority vote, but in practice such appeals do not take place. Disputes over referral in the Senate are resolved informally through negotiation prior to the introduction of the bill in question.

Table 4-2 Jurisdiction of House Committee on Education and Labor

1. Measures relating to education and labor generally.
2. Child labor.
3. Columbia Institution for the Deaf, Dumb, and Blind; Howard University; Freedmen's Hospital [Institutions in the District of Columbia].
4. Convict labor and the entry of goods made by convicts into interstate commerce.
5. Labor standards.
6. Labor statistics.
7. Mediation and arbitration of labor disputes.
8. Regulation or prevention of importation of foreign laborers under contract.
9. Food programs for children in schools.
10. United States Employees' Compensation Commission.
11. Vocational rehabilitation.
12. Wages and hours of labor.
13. Welfare of miners.
14. Work incentive programs.

Source: *The Constitution, Jefferson's Manual and Rules of the House of Representatives*, H. Doc. No. 97-271, 97th Cong., 2d sess., 344-345.

Occasionally, a bill's sponsors may have the opportunity to draft legislation in such a fashion that it will be referred to a committee likely to act favorably on it rather than one where members are known to be less sympathetic. One technique is to draft the measure ambiguously so it can legitimately fall within the jurisdiction of more than one committee, thus presenting the Speaker or the presiding officer with some options in making the referral. The classic example of this involved the 1963 civil rights bill, which was drafted somewhat differently for each chamber so it could be referred to the Judiciary Committee in the House and the Commerce Committee in the Senate. The two committees were chaired respectively by Rep. Emanuel Celler, D-N.Y. (1923-73), and Sen. Warren G. Magnuson, D-Wash. (1944-81), strong proponents of the legislation. Opposed to the legislation were Rep. Oren Harris, D-Ark. (1941-66), and Sen. James O. Eastland, D-Miss. (1941, 1943-78), chairmen respectively of the House Interstate and Foreign Commerce Committee and the Senate Judiciary Committee. Careful drafting, therefore, coupled with favorable referral decisions in the House and Senate prevented the bill from being bogged down in hostile committees.

A more recent example occurred in 1977. Sen. Pete V. Domenici, R-N.M., sought legislation imposing fees on barge operators who ship freight on the nation's canals and rivers. These operators had never paid any waterway charges for using the national network of federally built and maintained locks, dams, and channels. Traditionally, proposals similar to Domenici's had been designated as "tax" measures and were referred to the Senate Finance Committee, which has jurisdiction over revenue-raising legislation. In that committee, such measures encountered strong opposition and had never won approval. In an effort to bypass the Finance Committee, Domenici designated his proposal an "inland waterways charge;" as a result, the bill was referred jointly to the Senate Public Works and Commerce committees.[6] Domenici, a member of the Public Works subcommittee that had jurisdiction of the waterways measure (the Commerce Committee deferred to the Public Works panel), won Senate passage of the measure in June 1977.

Another drafting technique by members is to introduce legislation that amends statutes over which their committees have jurisdiction. Noted Rep. Bob Eckhardt, D-Texas (1967-81):

> You can phrase your new bill as an amendment to some Act that the Committee has previously dealt with, and then the bill will go to that Committee. For instance, I had the Open Beaches Bill. I had a strong interest in it. By phrasing it as an amendment to certain legislation involving estuarine matters, I could get my bill referred to Merchant Marine and Fisheries, because that Committee had previously processed the statute my bill amended. Had I amended certain bills dealing with land use, I could have got it referred to the Interior Committee.[7]

Other examples of bill drafting that resulted in a favorable referral could be cited. Nevertheless, it is important to understand that these are the exceptions and not the rule. Committees guard their jurisdictional turfs closely, and the parliamentarians know and follow the precedents. Only instances of genuine jurisdictional ambiguity provide opportunities for the legislative draftsman and referral options for the Speaker and the presiding officer of the Senate to bypass one committee in favor of another.

Referral to Several Committees

Many bills obviously cut across the jurisdiction of several committees so that it sometimes is difficult for the Speaker or the presiding officer of the Senate to decide where to refer a bill. Particular sections of a bill, for example, may fall outside the main jurisdiction of the committee. And committees sometimes will assert their jurisdiction over bills, refusing to be bypassed on referrals. For example, in 1982 the chairman of the Ways and Means Committee's Trade Subcommittee, Sam Gibbons, D-Fla., claimed jurisdiction over legislation dealing with the "domestic content" of automobiles (requiring domestic and foreign cars to be made with a high percentage of U.S. labor and parts) that had been referred solely to the Energy Committee. In response, Speaker O'Neill then referred the bill sequentially to Ways and Means for eight days. The next year it was apparent that the Speaker had become sensitive to the trade implications of such legislation when he referred a comparable bill upon its introduction as follows:

> [R]eferred to the Committee on Energy and Commerce, and concurrently to the Committee on Ways and Means for a period ending not later than 30 calendar days following the date on which the Committee on Energy and Commerce files its report in the House.

Standing Committees of Congress

Senate

Agriculture, Nutrition and Forestry
Appropriations
Armed Services
Banking, Housing and Urban Affairs
Budget
Commerce, Science and Transportation
Energy and Natural Resources
Environment and Public Works

Finance
Foreign Relations
Governmental Affairs
Labor and Human Resources
Judiciary
Rules and Administration
Small Business
Veterans' Affairs

House

Agriculture
Appropriations
Armed Services
Banking, Finance and Urban Affairs
Budget
District of Columbia
Education and Labor
Energy and Commerce
Foreign Affairs
Government Operations
House Administration

Judiciary
Merchant Marine and Fisheries
Post Office and Civil Service
Public Works and Transportation
Rules
Science and Technology
Small Business
Standards of Official Conduct
Veterans' Affairs
Ways and Means

Responding to the jurisdictional complexities that often are encountered, the Senate has long permitted the practice of multiple referral, referring legislation to two or more committees. There are three types of multiple referral: joint referral of a bill concurrently to two or more committees; sequential referral of a bill successively to one committee, then a second, and so on; and split referral of various parts of a bill to different committees for consideration.

In the Senate, multiple referral can be implemented either by unanimous consent or upon a joint motion made by the majority and minority leaders (to date never employed). A recent example of the former method occurred on May 25, 1983, upon a request made by the majority leader:

> Mr. President, I ask unanimous consent that S. 1110, a bill to establish a national commission on monetary policy and its relation to fiscal policy, be sequentially referred to the Committee on Banking, Housing, and Urban Affairs for 30 calendar days after it is reported to the Senate by the Committee on Governmental Affairs.

No senator objected to this request. Such requests normally are granted by the Senate because senators who offer them usually have worked out an agreement previously with all interested parties — committee chairmen, party leaders, and other members concerned about the bill. By the time the bill is introduced the appropriate bases have been touched; thus no senator is likely to object to the multiple referral.

In the House, the precedents until 1975 dictated that the Speaker could refer a bill to only one committee. That year, flexibility was injected into the bill referral process by two changes in the rules. First, the Speaker was permitted to refer a bill to more than one committee through joint, sequential, or split referral. Second, the Speaker, subject to approval of the House, was permitted to create *ad hoc* committees to consider measures that overlap the jurisdictions of several committees.

Speaker O'Neill exercised this *ad hoc* committee option in 1977 by creating an Ad Hoc Energy Committee to expedite action on the Carter administration's complex energy proposals. The *ad hoc* committee was composed of members selected from the five committees to which various parts of the energy proposal initially had been referred.[8] In the Senate, the administration's 1977 energy proposals were referred to the Finance Committee and the Energy and Natural Resources Committee. There is no Senate provision for the creation of *ad hoc* committees by party leaders.

In 1977 House rules were amended to permit the Speaker to impose committee reporting deadlines during the initial referral of measures. Further, the Speaker announced on January 3, 1983, his intention "in particular situations to designate a primary committee among those to whom a bill may be jointly referred, and may impose time limits on committees having a secondary interest following the report of the primary committee."

Several observations may be made about multiple referral. First, contemporary problems tend to have repercussions in many areas; thus more and more of the major bills coming before Congress — particularly those in new problem areas — will be candidates for multiple referral. Second, to the extent that multiple referral is chosen as an option, the decentralized nature of congressional decision making is reinforced. Third, every time another committee is added to the legislative process there is one more hurdle for a bill to overcome and additional opportunities for delay, negotiation, compromise, and bargaining. Fourth, multiple referrals may promote effective problem-solving as several committees bring their expertise to bear on complex issues.

Consideration in Committee

Once a bill has been referred to a committee, the committee has several options. It may consider and report (approve) the bill, with or without amendments, and send it to the House or Senate. It may rewrite the bill entirely, reject it, or simply refuse to consider it. Failure of a committee to act on a bill usually is equivalent to killing it. When a committee does report a bill, the House or Senate generally accept its main thrust even when they amend the bill on the floor.

There are several reasons for this deference to the decisions of the committee, a practice one scholar has referred to as the "sanctity of committee decisions." [9] Committee members and their staffs have a high degree of expertise on the subjects within their jurisdiction, and it is at the committee stage that a bill comes under its sharpest congressional scrutiny. It is understandable, therefore, that a bill that has survived the scrutiny of the experts will be given serious consideration on the floor by the generalists of the House and Senate.

Exclaimed Sen. William Proxmire, D-Wis., to his colleagues on August 3, 1983: "I think the Senate ought to act on the basis of a record. That is what our hearings are all about. That is what our committees are for."

It is equally true that a committee's decision not to report a bill generally will be respected by the chamber as a whole. After all, if the experts have decided not to approve a bill, why should their decision be second-guessed? Furthermore, since all members of Congress are members of committees, and do not wish the decisions of their own committees to be overturned, they normally will reciprocate by not questioning the actions of another committee. Finally, the general impact of the rules in both chambers — particularly those of the House — is to "protect the power and prerogatives of the . . . committees . . . by making it very difficult for a bill that does not have committee approval to come to the floor." [10]

There are procedures, to be examined in Chapters 4 and 8, for overturning committee decisions or even bypassing committees, but these procedures are employed infrequently and rarely are successful.

When a committee decides to take up a major bill, it may be considered immediately by the full committee, but more often the committee chairman assigns the bill to a subcommittee for study and hearings. (Subcommittees of the House Energy and Commerce Committee are listed in the box on page 82.)

The subcommittee usually schedules public hearings on the measure, inviting testimony from interested public and private witnesses. Or the subcommittee may decide not to schedule hearings if there is strong opposition from executive branch officials or interest groups. After the hearings have concluded, the subcommittee meets to "mark up" the bill — that is, to consider line by line and section by section the specific language of the legislation before sending the bill to the full committee. The subcommittee may approve the bill unaltered, amend it, rewrite it, or block it altogether. It then reports its recommendations to the full committee.

When the full committee receives the bill, it may repeat the subcommittee's procedures, in whole or in part, or it may simply ratify the action of the subcommittee. If the committee decides to send the bill to the House or Senate, it justifies its actions in a written statement called a report, which must accompany the bill. [11]

On a major legislative proposal the entire committee process may stretch over several Congresses, with a new bill (containing identical or similar provisions) introduced at the beginning of each Congress. For

---

House Energy and Commerce Committee

Subcommittees:

Oversight and Investigations
Energy Conservation and Power
Health and the Environment
Telecommunications, Consumer Protection, and Finance
Fossil and Synthetic Fuels
Commerce, Transportation, and Tourism

---

example, an account of the struggle to enact the aforementioned immigration reform measure noted: "Proposals of such magnitude as the Simpson-Mazzoli bill may indeed require three or four years of legislative work." [12] Indeed, decades may pass before some bills become public law.

On the other hand, the process can be compressed into a very short period of time. The House acted with uncharacteristic speed in 1983 when it passed a controversial bill to revise the Social Security system and to provide funds for unemployment compensation and jobs programs. "Before adjourning March 25 for its Easter vacation," wrote a legislative analyst, "Congress cleared two major pieces of legislation and made progress on several others." [13] The start of a new Congress usually is marked by a slow legislative pace while committee and party leaders attend to matters such as filling vacancies on the committees.

The remainder of this chapter will focus on the key steps in committee consideration of a major bill: hearings, the markup and the report. To simplify the discussion, assume, as sometimes happens, that the committee chairman is also the chairman of the subcommittee to which the bill is referred, and assume further that the full committee merely ratifies the subcommittee decisions. Because the committee chairman is a central figure in the legislative process, it is first necessary to focus on the chairman's role.

Committee Chairman's Role

To a large extent, the options available to a committee in dealing with a bill are exercised by the chairman, who has wide discretion in establishing the legislative priorities of the committee. The sources of the chairman's authority are many. They include: 1) control of the committee's legislative agenda, 2) control over referral of legislation to the subcommittees, 3) management of committee funds, and 4) control of the committee staff.

The chairman usually has had a long period of service on the committee and is likely to be better informed than most other members on the myriad of issues coming before the committee. The chairman often is privy to the leadership's plans and policies, especially the Speaker's or the Senate majority leader's legislative objectives. Chairmen can use these and other resources to delay, expedite, or modify legislation.

A chairman who opposes a bill may simply refuse to schedule hearings on it until it is too late to finish action on the bill during the session. The same result can be achieved by allowing the hearings to drag on interminably. A chairman having strong negative feelings about a bill can instruct the committee staff to "stack" the witnesses testifying on it. He may, for example, ask witnesses holding favorable views to submit statements rather than appear in person.[14] Committee members who are likely to raise dilatory questions or employ obstructive tactics may be recognized before others. And through his control of committee funds and the power to hire and fire most committee staffers, the chairman can effectively block action on a bill by directing the staff to disregard it.[15]

A chairman who favors a bill can give it top priority by mobilizing staff resources, compressing the time for hearings and markups, and, in general, encouraging expeditious action by committee members. In sum, chairmen are the chief "agenda setters" of committees and employ this prerogative to powerfully influence the form in which bills are reported to the House or Senate as well as the timing of floor action on their bills.

Recent Restraints on Chairmen

The general picture of a committee chairman as an almost omnipotent figure underwent modification during the 1970s. Until then, the chairmen were the central figures in the legislative process, holding power equalled by only a few party leaders of great influence such as House Speaker Sam Rayburn, D-Texas (1913-61; Speaker 1940-47, 1949-53, 1955-61), or Senate Majority Leader Lyndon B. Johnson, D-Texas (1937-61; majority leader 1955-61). Beginning about 1970, however, the chairmen's power was gradually trimmed under pressure from newly elected members and from some senior members who wanted to equalize the distribution of power. During that decade, Congress approved several fundamental changes that ended the nearly absolute authority enjoyed by committee chairmen.

The most significant change in the status of chairmen came when both parties modified the seniority system, specifically the practice of automatically selecting as the committee chairman the member of the majority party with the longest continuous service on the committee. Seniority meant that chairmen normally came from safe congressional districts, were repeatedly reelected, and served until their retirement or death. Because many safe districts during the 1950s and 1960s were in the conservative Democratic South, chairmen often were sharply at odds with Democratic presidents, congressional leaders, and northern Democrats. Nevertheless, as seniority then was practiced the chairmen could not be removed. They were able to use their entrenched positions to block civil rights and social welfare legislation proposed by Democratic administrations.

House Changes in Seniority. In 1971 the minority party in the House, the Republicans, made the first assault on the old order when they adopted a policy declaration stating that seniority need not be followed in making committee assignments and requiring a secret ballot to elect the ranking minority member of the committee. The ranking member is the most influential member of the minority party in a Senate or House committee. This member's powers include appointment of minority members to sub-committees and control of the committee's minority funds and staff. Generally, under seniority the ranking minority member became committee chairman when there was a shift in party control of the chamber, as occurred in 1981 when the GOP took control of the Senate for the first time in 26 years.

Democrats in 1971 also established the policy that seniority need not be followed in naming committee chairmen, permitting party members to challenge any nominee for chairman through a separate ballot in their party caucus (the party organization of House Democrats). This change drama-tized the accountability of the chairmen to the caucus. Democrats also adopted a party rule specifying that no member of a committee could head more than one subcommittee. This provision was designed to create additional committee leadership opportunities for relatively junior mem-bers. Another change guaranteed subcommittee chairmen at least one staff aide.

House Democrats adopted a subcommittee "bill of rights" in 1973. Powers that had been exercised exclusively by committee chairmen were assigned to all Democrats on committees. Thus all Democrats were given power to select subcommittee chairmen, determine subcommittee jurisdic-tions, ensure that each subcommittee had an adequate budget, and guaran-tee each Democrat at least one major subcommittee assignment. Chairmen also were required to refer legislation to subcommittees within two weeks of receiving it unless the full committee determined otherwise.

In 1975 House Democrats further democratized their procedures for appointing committee chairmen. They required all committee chairmen, and even the subcommittee chairmen of the powerful Appropriations Committee, to be elected by secret ballot. In a dramatic move, the Democrats deposed three incumbent committee chairmen. This act demonstrated that chairmen who lost the support of their party colleagues risked losing their coveted posts. Two years later, Democrats voted to oust the incumbent chairman of the House Appropriations Committee's Military Construction Subcommit-tee.

Senate Changes in Seniority. Reforms since 1970 also reduced the authority of Senate committee chairmen. While there were no dramatic dismissals of sitting Democratic or Republican chairmen, as occurred in the House, both parties dropped the rigid adherence to seniority as a basis for automatically determining committee chairmen. In 1975 the Democrats, then the majority party, adopted a rule (which took effect in 1977) requiring a secret ballot on any nominee for a chairmanship if one-fifth of the party members in the Senate requested it. In 1973 the Republicans (then the minority party) had adopted a rule authorizing Republican members of each committee to elect their "ranking member" subject to ratification by all Senate Republicans.

In other important changes in committee practices since 1970, the Senate, or each of the parties individually through their own conferences, generally restricted the opportunities for senior members to monopolize key positions. In 1970 members were limited to service on only one of the four so-called elite committees: Appropriations, Armed Services, Finance, and Foreign Relations. In 1971 the Republicans adopted a party rule permitting a GOP senator to be a ranking minority member of only one committee. And in 1977 the Senate adopted a rule prohibiting a committee chairman from serving as chairman of more than one subcommittee of any committee.

These changes were designed to give junior members an opportunity to obtain leadership positions on important subcommittees. And they reinforced a characteristic of the Senate that was stressed in Chapter 1: Power always has been more evenly distributed in the Senate than in the House. The institutional trends of the 1970s and 1980s reflected a further diffusion of power from committee chairmen to subcommittees and to individual members of the Senate. "It's every man for himself," said one member. "Every senator is a baron. He has his own principality. Once you adopt that as a means of doing business, it's hard to establish any cohesion." [16]

The Chairman in Perspective

Changes in the structure of congressional committees in the 1970s have clearly chipped away at the power base of both House and Senate committee chairmen. By and large, one-person rule is being replaced increasingly by bargaining and negotiation between the chairman and the other members of his committee, particularly the subcommittee chairmen. In short, "subcommittee government" rather than "committee government," more accurately characterizes the contemporary House (and the Senate to a lesser extent). This shift in the locus of decision making limits the chairmen's prerogatives. Subcommittees were "originally creatures of the full committees, dependent upon the chairmen for their membership, powers, and staff," wrote one political scientist. "Now, as a result of a series of [party caucus] actions, subcommittees acquired a life of their own." [17]

Nevertheless, committee chairmen remain crucial figures in the legislative process. It is true that congressional decision making has become increasingly decentralized within the committee structure. But as long as Congress functions primarily through its committees the person who heads one has considerable influence over the advancement or defeat of legislation. For example, Chairman John D. Dingell, D-Mich., of the House Energy and Commerce Committee, is recognized as one of the most powerful chairmen on Capitol Hill. Called "Big John" by members, Dingell is known for the skill, intensity, and determination he brings to issues. A GOP committee colleague, Edward R. Madigan, Ill., has identified some of the sources of Dingell's authority:

Sometimes I think he is an arbitrary and capricious [person], and other times I think he is a great parliamentarian. At all times I'd much rather have him on my side than against me. Dingell is formidable not because he has more friends than anyone else, nor because he is more skilled — there are others as skilled as he is. His strength comes because he takes the skill he has and combines it with good staff work, a thorough knowledge of the issues and bulldog determination not to let go. He is the most tenacious member of Congress.[18]

Hearings

Ostensibly, hearings are important primarily as fact-finding instruments. Witnesses from the executive branch, concerned members of Congress, interest group spokesmen, academic experts, and knowledgeable citizens appear before the committee to give it their opinions as to the merits or pitfalls of a given piece of legislation. From this encounter the committee members gather the information needed to act as informed lawmakers. (A typical witness list at a committee hearing appears on page 89.)

Much of this information, however, is available to committee members long before the hearings take place. Major bills have been the subject of public debate and coverage in the media. The positions of the administration and the special interest groups are well known, and, in all likelihood, executive branch officials and pressure group lobbyists have already presented their views to committee members well in advance of the hearings. The members themselves often have strong partisan positions on the legislation and thus may have little interest in whatever additional information emerges from the hearings.[19] Hearings often are poorly attended by committee members, and interruptions are common because of floor votes or quorum calls.

Hearings Format

Staff research and preparatory work precede committee hearings. Committee aides, for example, may interview witnesses in advance of hearings, compile research and documentary materials, and prepare notebooks for committee members to use at the hearings. These notebooks may list questions — and the answers — used in probing the witnesses. Explained a committee staff director:

We write the question. Under the question we write the answer. This is the answer we expect to get on the basis of the staff research that has gone before. The Member who asks the question knows what the witness has told us in the weeks and weeks of preparation; and he knows he should get the same information. If he does not get that information, then he has the answer in front of him and he can ad lib the questions that solicit that information or refute it.[20]

Hearings can be perfunctory, particularly where similar legislation has been before the committee for several years in succession. Witnesses usually read from prepared texts, while the committee members present often feign interest or simply look bored until the statement has been read. Once the formal testimony is completed, each committee member, usually in order of seniority, will ask the witness questions. House rules allot at least five minutes per member to question witnesses. Senate rules have no such provision. Instead, each committee establishes its own rules governing internal procedures. For example, the rules of the Senate Energy and Natural Resources Committee give each member five minutes to question witnesses until all members have had an opportunity to ask questions.

The traditional format for questioning witnesses in the House and Senate does not lend itself to opportunities for extended exchanges between members and witnesses, for analysis of different points of view, or for in-depth probing of one witness's views by another. However, this is changing as numerous committees today structure their hearings to ensure that conflicting viewpoints are heard. Committees often hold panel sessions where members and witnesses of different persuasions sit in roundtable fashion to discuss the merits of particular policies.

Purposes of Hearings

Despite their limitations, hearings remain an integral part of the legislative process. They provide a permanent public record of the position of committee members and the various interested groups on a legislative proposal. Preparation of congressional testimony is regarded as an important function by executive agencies and interest groups. Above all, hearings are important because members of Congress believe them to be important. The decision to hold hearings is a critical point in the life of a bill. Seldom is a measure considered on the floor without first being the subject of hearings. The sanctity of the committee stage is based on the assumption that the experts — the committee members — carefully scrutinize a proposal, and hearings provide a demonstrable record of that scrutiny.

"Hearings can really count," declared a representative.[21] They are part of any overall strategy to get bills enacted into law. Committee members and staff typically plan with care who should testify, when, and on what issues. Ralph Nader's testimony before several congressional committees on his 1965 best-selling book, *Unsafe at Any Speed,* led to passage of the Traffic Safety Act of 1966.

Committees, in brief, often want witnesses who will provide a broad coalition of endorsements for their predetermined position and promote political and public support for this course of action. For instance, Rep. Henry A. Waxman, D-Calif., who chairs the Energy and Commerce Committee's Health and the Environment Subcommittee, successfully opposed a weakening of the Clean Air Act during the 97th Congress. In September 1981,

> Waxman assembled his subcommittee to hear testimony on the Clean Air
> Act and public opinion from pollster Lou Harris. The message was
> unequivocal. "Never in my career," said Harris, "have I seen such strong
> opinion on one side of an issue." Harris told the members it would be

political suicide to change the Clean Air Act. Waxman and others believe his testimony had a deep impact, not just on the subcommittee but on congressmen generally.[22]

Hearings serve other functions as well. They may be used to assess the intensity of support or opposition to a bill, to gauge the capabilities of an executive agency official, to publicize the role of politically ambitious committee chairmen and members, to allow citizens to express their views to their representatives, and to investigate problems and issues.

Investigation is a key power of Congress. Investigative hearings serve several purposes. They promote efficient program administration, secure information needed to legislate, and inform public opinion. Millions of American households watched on television the unfolding drama of the 1954 Army-McCarthy hearings, the 1957 hearings into corruption of the Teamsters union, the Senate Foreign Relations Committee's hearings during the 1960s on the Vietnam War, and the Watergate hearings of the 1970s. These investigative hearings often prompted the drafting of legislation to deal with the problems that were uncovered and subsequently led to more hearings on the legislation itself. On occasion, individual members conduct *ad hoc*, or "informal," investigative hearings of their own.

Importance of Timing

The chairman's control over the timing and duration of the hearings is an important factor in deciding the fate of a bill. Postponing or dragging out hearings is an obvious ploy if the chairman is opposed to a bill or wants it extensively modified. There are times, too, when a delay in the hearings will help the bill's chances. This might be true if sentiment in favor of the bill is much stronger in the other chamber than in the chairman's. Or a chairman may have time to convene an "extra" hearing. The House Small Business Committee, for instance, convened a new hearing in May 1982 to refute some other panels' criticisms of a small business research bill — "an unusual move considering the [Small Business] committee approved the bill in a 40-0 vote" the previous October. [23]

Another possibility is that both House and Senate chairmen supporting a bill may want to expedite hearings because of time pressures. For example, House Education Subcommittee Chairman John Brademas, D-Ind. (1959-81), moved quickly in 1970 to hold hearings on an environmental education measure. Hearings began in March and were completed by the end of May. However, that left only six months to pass the bill in the House, get it through the Senate, into a conference committee, back to each chamber for final approval, and then to the president for his signature, all in a busy election year.

Representative Brademas' key supporter in the Senate was Sen. Gaylord Nelson, D-Wis. (1963-81), who sponsored the legislation there and conducted hearings on it. Their strategy "called for a maximum of cooperation between [them] and their staffs to allow them to take advantage of all the opportunities that might become available to speed the passage of the

Committee Witnesses

The following list was selected from a roster of witnesses who testified in April 1983 during hearings by the Senate Finance Committee on the economic development proposals (S 267) in President Ronald Reagan's Caribbean basin initiative program.

Sen. Lawton Chiles, D-Fla.
Resident Commissioner Baltasar Corrada, New Prog.-Puerto Rico
Delegate Ron de Lugo, D-Virgin Islands
George P. Shultz, secretary of state
William E. Brock, United States trade representative
John E. Chapoton, assistant secretary of the Treasury for tax policy
Juan Luis, governor of the Virgin Islands
Charlotte Amalie, Washington, D.C.
Philip G. Kuehn, New Orleans Cold Storage and Warehouse Co., New Orleans
Gladstone Cooper, Geyco Corporation, Miami, Fla.
Robert A. Pastor, University of Maryland, College Park, Md.
Calmon Cohen, Emergency Committee for American Trade, Washington, D.C.
Stephen Koplan, representing the AFL-CIO, Washington, D.C.
Joseph Pelkzman, George Washington University, Washington, D.C.
Robert F. McKown, Florida Citrus Mutual, Lakeland, Fla.

bill." [24] Representative Brademas held 13 days of hearings on the measure and developed an extensive public record. Thus there was no need to duplicate these hearings in the Senate, and Senator Nelson conducted only two days of hearings in his committee. The result of this cooperative effort by the two chairmen was final passage of the Environmental Education Act of 1970 one month before the November elections.

In short, committee chairmen take into account a variety of factors when scheduling hearings. Among the more important are the positions of the White House, pressure groups, executive agencies, the other chamber, and key legislators; the climate of public opinion; the intensity of feeling of the principal participants; and the mix of witnesses that can create momentum and support for legislation.

The Markup

Sometime after the conclusion of the hearings, the committee or subcommittee meets to "mark up" the bill. Here committee members decide whether the legislation should be rewritten, either in whole or in part. The chairman's task is to keep the committee moving, getting unanimous agreement on as many sections of the bill as possible, trying to resolve differences through compromise, and sensing when to delay or expedite matters. Because the chairman is likely to be responsible for managing the bill on the floor, he or she will try throughout the markup to gather as much support within the committee as possible. A sharp split among the committee members of the same party will seriously damage chances of passing the bill in the House or Senate.

Chairmen may schedule pre-markup sessions to discuss possible revisions of the legislation and to develop a consensus on the bill. On the Clean Air Act, for instance, Sen. Robert T. Stafford, R-Vt., chairman of the Environment and Public Works Committee, "scheduled several seminars prior to formal markup, to educate the members on the major issues and to try to develop a consensus among the members on the issues." [25] The chairmen also usually decide which vehicle will be used for markup purposes: the bill as introduced, a related proposal drafted by the chair, or the administration's plan. Tactically, it often is easier to retain something already in a bill than to add it by amendment.

The markup, then, is where committee members redraft portions of the bill, attempt to insert new provisions and delete others, bargain over final language, and generally determine the final committee product. With the movement in the 1970s to open to the public more committee meetings, most markups today are conducted in open session. However, this edict can sometimes be ignored in practice. A journalist once recounted:

> There was a sizable audience on hand for the mark-up, but nobody heard the discussion of the bill. Although the Senate in 1976 had adopted rules requiring that mark-ups be open to the public; neither [Senator] Domenici nor [Senator] Gravel liked that idea very much. "Hell," Domenici said, "you can't negotiate in a fishbowl." So the two Senators simply ignored the rule. They huddled quietly with their aides, backs to the audience, talking over the bill in soft tones. When everything was decided, the Senators turned around, Domenici made a single motion incorporating all their agreements, and the "open" mark-up was over. [26]

Strategies During Markup

Members use various strategies during the markup. One ploy, sometimes used by opponents of a bill, is to add amendments to strengthen the measure. During markup of a gun control measure by the House Judiciary Committee in the mid-1970s, the National Rifle Association, the major lobbying group opposed to gun control, told its supporters in Congress that it would be easier to defeat a strong firearms proposal. "The way we look at it," said an NRA lobbyist, "the stronger the bill that comes out of committee, the less chance it has of passing on the floor." [27] Conversely, proponents of a strong bill might try to weaken it in committee so that it stands a better chance of winning majority support on the floor. Supporters then can try to persuade the other chamber or the House-Senate conference committee to strengthen the measure.

Another approach used by a bill's opponent is to offer a flurry of amendments to make a bill complicated, confusing and unworkable for the executive branch agencies that will have responsibility for administering the law. Moreover, offering scores of amendments may stall the markup and grant opponents additional time to lobby against the legislation. During markup of a coal slurry pipeline bill in 1982, Sen. Wendell H. Ford, D-Ky., proposed numerous "hare amendments" — which he said "breed like rabbits overnight." [28]

To win over opponents or skeptics, chairmen often willingly accept numerous amendments from their committee colleagues. In this way, these members develop a stake in the legislation and may stand united behind it on the House or Senate floor. When the Senate Energy and Natural Resources Committee was marking up a synthetic fuels bill in 1980, the chairman added to it solar energy, conservation, gasohol, and other energy programs. These additions made the bill "politically palatable," said Sen. J. Bennett Johnston, D-La. "Many of our members were just not that interested in synthetic fuels." [29]

The reverse strategy is to load down a bill with scores of "add-ons" so the legislation might sink of its own weight. For instance, Senate Finance Committee Chairman Robert Dole, R-Kan., in 1983 strongly opposed repeal of a newly enacted tax withholding law. However, because of substantial support in the Senate for repeal, Dole's panel voted to report a bill repealing the law. But during the markup, the committee also attached numerous controversial provisions to it. "I've seen bills killed around here before, even though there were the votes [to pass them] . . . , by loading them down," observed Sen. Russell B. Long of Louisiana, the ranking Democrat on the committee.[30]

An important factor affecting markup strategies in the Senate is that the rules permit legislation that has been blocked in committee to be considered on the floor. Senators can offer to pending legislation nongermane amendments that embody bills pigeonholed in committee. The opportunity to offer such amendments on the Senate floor indicates a significant difference between House and Senate committee procedures: Efforts to block legislation in committee are less successful in the Senate than in the House. Senate floor procedures provide various ways to bypass committees if they refuse to report measures. *(Senate floor procedures, see Chapter 8.)*

Nevertheless, bypassing a Senate committee occurs infrequently. All senators have an interest in seeing that the prerogatives of their own committees are respected. Thus they will make every effort to resolve their differences within the committee.

Compromise during the committee markup — indeed, at any stage of the legislative process — is more likely when the members recognize that some sort of legislation is necessary. Strip mining proposals, for example, had been defeated five times prior to 1977, twice by presidential veto. By

1977, however, it was clear to everyone — members, environmental and energy lobbyists, and the administration — that some kind of strip mining bill had to be enacted. As a result, the markup was expedited. "Now industry has recognized that there is going to be a bill," said Rep. Morris K. Udall, D-Ariz., chairman of the Interior and Insular Affairs Committee. "They'll have to live with it, so they're trying to make it a workable bill." [31]

Table 4-3 lists several major House-Senate differences regarding the introduction, referral, and committee consideration of legislation.

The Report

Assuming that major differences have been ironed out in the markup, the committee then meets to vote on reporting the bill out of committee. House and Senate rules require a committee majority to be present for this purpose; otherwise, a point of order may be made on the floor that will force the bill to be returned to committee. Bills voted out of committee unanimously stand a good chance on the floor. A sharply divided committee vote presages an equally sharp dispute on the floor. A bill is rejected if the committee vote is a tie.

Committees have several options when they vote to report, or approve, a bill. They may report the bill without any changes or with various amendments, or they may approve a "clean bill." A committee that has extensively amended a bill may instruct the chairman to incorporate the modifications in a new measure, known as a "clean bill." This bill will be re-introduced, assigned a new bill number, referred back to the committee, and reported by the panel. Only the full House or Senate, of course, can amend legislation; committees formally recommend revisions to measures.

The clean bill procedure is employed for various reasons, such as expediting floor consideration of legislation. Another factor involves germaneness. Provisions already in a bill are *ipso facto* considered to be germane; hence they are protected against points of order (germaneness rules apply to proposed floor amendments and not to provisions in the bill itself). Finally, a clean bill may reflect negotiated agreements between key committee members and executive officials.

Committees may take other actions besides favorably reporting a bill. They may report out a bill adversely (unfavorably), recommending that the bill not be passed by the full chamber, or they may report legislation without a formal recommendation, allowing the chamber to decide the bill's merits. In either case, though, the bill may be sent to the full chamber and scheduled for floor action. Committees adamantly opposed to a measure may decide, of course, not to take any action at all, thus blocking further consideration except through special procedures. *(See Chapters 5 and 7.)*

After the bill is reported favorably, or unfavorably, the chairman instructs the staff to prepare a written report. The report will describe the purposes and scope of the bill, explain the committee revisions, note proposed changes in existing law, and, usually, include the views of the executive branch agencies consulted. Committee members opposing the bill

The House bill (center), hearings testimony (l) and the committee report (r) for an emergency agricultural measure.

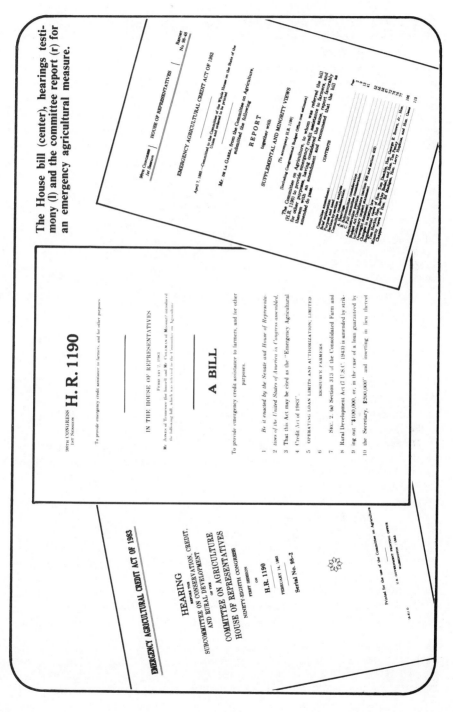

Table 4-3 Procedural Differences at Preliminary Stages

House	*Senate*
Bills must be introduced before committee or floor action can proceed.	Bills may originate from the floor.
No effective way to challenge the Speaker's (parliamentarian's) referral decisions.	Referrals are subject to appeals from the floor.
The Speaker is granted authority by House rules to refer bills to more than one committee.	Multiple referrals occur by unanimous consent, although the majority leader and minority leader can jointly offer a motion to that effect.
The Speaker is authorized, subject to House approval, to create *ad hoc* panels to consider legislation.	Neither the majority leader nor the presiding officer has authority to create *ad hoc* panels to process legislation.
Difficult to bypass committee consideration of measures.	Bypassing committee consideration of measures occurs more easily.
Floor action is less important for policy making than committees.	Floor action is as important as committee action in decision making.

often will submit dissenting, or minority, views. Any committee member may file minority, supplemental, or additional views, which are printed in the committee report. A report may be more than 1,000 pages long.

Reports are directed primarily at members of the House and Senate and seek to persuade the membership to endorse the committee's recommendations when it comes up for a vote on the floor.[32] For some members, or their staff aides, the report is the only document they read before deciding how to vote on an issue. The report, therefore, is the principal official means of communicating a committee decision to the entire chamber.

Reports are numbered, by Congress and chamber, in the order in which they are filed with the clerk of the House or Senate. (Thus, in the 98th Congress the first House report was designated H Rept 98-1 and the first Senate report as S Rept 98-1.) Both the committee-reported bill and its accompanying report are then assigned to the appropriate House or Senate calendar to await scheduling for floor action. Chapters 5 and 7 discuss the House and Senate calendars and scheduling legislation for floor action in each chamber.

Summary

Of the thousands of bills introduced in each Congress, the vast majority have little support and provoke little controversy. Congress routinely either ignores these measures or rushes them through the legislative process, reserving the bulk of its time for the relatively small number of bills that deal with the nation's major problems and programs.

Once a bill is introduced, it usually is referred to a single committee, the one having jurisdiction over its subject area. In cases of overlapping jurisdiction, a bill may be referred to several committees.

In committee the critical decision is made either to ignore, expedite, or carefully examine a legislative proposal. Since committee members and their staffs have more expertise on matters within their jurisdiction than members of Congress as a whole, the "sanctity of the committee decision" generally will be accepted. The rules and precedents of both chambers reinforce committee prerogatives. Exceptions to these rules exist, but members of Congress generally are reluctant to see the committee system weakened by frequent recourse to extraordinary procedures. Hence, members are encouraged to resolve their differences within the committees.

The key stages in committee consideration of a bill are hearings, the markup, voting, and the report. This process is controlled largely by the subcommittee and committee chairmen, who have many resources at their disposal to expedite, delay, or modify legislation. Chairmen choose tactics on the basis of their assessment of the many political and legislative factors present and their long-range objectives for the bill. Opportunities for a chairman to act arbitrarily have been trimmed somewhat by recent procedural reforms, particularly the abandonment of seniority as an automatic system for choosing chairmen.

When a bill has been reported from committee, it is ready to be scheduled for floor action. Like the winnowing process that occurs in committee, scheduling involves the budgeting of congressional time. Important political choices must be made in determining the order in which bills will be considered on the floor, how much time will be devoted to each measure, and to what extent the full chamber will be permitted to reexamine a committee decision. House scheduling of legislation is discussed in the next chapter and Senate scheduling in Chapter 7.

Notes

1. U.S., Congress, House, *Congressional Record,* daily ed., January 3, 1983, H4.
2. On rare occasions a member introducing a bill may ask unanimous consent that it be passed. Unanimous consent is more likely to be granted in the Senate than in the House and only on a noncontroversial measure or one on which all members agree that immediate action is required.
3. Article I, Section 3, of the Constitution provides that the vice president is president of the Senate, but he infrequently presides over that body. The Constitution also provides for a president pro tempore, a largely honorary position elected by the majority party. By custom, that position nowadays is held by the most senior member of the majority party. Usually, however, junior members designated by the majority leader preside over the daily sessions of the Senate.

4. Each chamber has a parliamentarian, who is an expert on rules of procedure. During a session, the parliamentarians or one of their assistants always are present to advise the chair on all points of order and parliamentary inquiries. They also provide technical assistance to members in drafting bills or motions.

5. Committee structure and jurisdiction are not identical in the House and Senate. There are 22 standing (permanent) committees in the House and 16 in the Senate.

6. See T. R. Reid, *Congressional Odyssey* (San Francisco: W. H. Freeman & Co., 1980).

7. Bob Eckhardt and Charles L. Black, Jr., *The Tides of Power* (New Haven, Conn.: Yale University Press, 1976), 146.

8. See Bruce I. Oppenheimer, "Policy Effects of U.S. House Reform: Decentralization and the Capacity to Resolve Energy Issues," *Legislative Studies Quarterly* (February 1980): 5-30; and David J. Vogler, "Ad Hoc Committees in the House of Representatives and Purposive Models of Legislative Behavior," *Polity* (Fall 1981): 89-109.

9. Randall B. Ripley, *Congress: Process and Policy* (New York: W. W. Norton & Co., 1975), 75. Also see the third edition (1983) of this book.

10. Ibid.

11. There is no formal requirement in the Senate for written reports to accompany legislation voted out of committee.

12. *New York Times,* May 22, 1983, 4E.

13. Andy Plattner, "Congress Off to Flying Start Despite Quarrels in Senate," *Congressional Quarterly Weekly Report,* March 26, 1983, 595.

14. "Stacking" was modified somewhat by the Legislative Reorganization Act of 1970, which gives the minority party on a committee at least one day in which to call witnesses. However, on issues where the committee members of both parties share similar views, the opportunities to testify for witnesses who oppose those views is limited.

15. Members of Congress rely heavily on committee staff for assistance in organizing hearings, selecting witnesses, drafting bills and for many other key support functions. The chairman's control of committee staff therefore is an important resource in his control of the legislative process.

16. Alan Ehrenhalt, "Special Report: The Individualist Senate," *Congressional Quarterly Weekly Report,* September 4, 1982, 2181. The comment was by former Sen. James B. Pearson, R-Kan. (1962-78). Pearson and former Sen. Abraham A. Ribicoff, D-Conn. (1963-81), were appointed by the bipartisan Senate leadership to constitute a study group to recommend revisions of Senate procedure and organization. The Senate Rules and Administration Committee began hearings on May 9, 1983, on the study group's 18 major reform proposals.

17. Roger H. Davidson, "Subcommittee Government: New Channels for Policy Making," in *The New Congress*, ed. Thomas E. Mann and Norman J. Ornstein (Washington, D.C.: American Enterprise Institute for Public Policy Research, 1981), 107-108.

18. *Washington Post,* May 15, 1983, A14.

19. Members unable to attend a committee session frequently assign committee staffers to attend the meeting and brief them later. Staff aides can ask questions of witnesses if authorized by committee rules or by the chairman.

20. *Workshop on Congressional Oversight and Investigations,* H. Doc. No. 96-217, 96th Cong., 1st sess., 25.

21. *The Listener,* August 26, 1976, 232.

22. *Washington Post,* December 14, 1982, A27.
23. Diane Granat, "Critics Snare Small Business Research Bill," *Congressional Quarterly Weekly Report,* May 8, 1982, 1067.
24. Dennis W. Brezina and Allen Overmyer, *Congress in Action* (New York: The Free Press, 1974), 65.
25. *State Government News,* April 1982, 4.
26. Reid, *Congressional Odyssey,* 36. Also see Bob Eckhardt, "The Presumption of Committee Openness Under House Rules," *Harvard Journal on Legislation* (February 1974): 279-302.
27. *Washington Post,* February 6, 1976, A6.
28. Joseph A. Davis, "Senate Committee Blocked: House Committee Approves Coal Slurry Pipeline Measure," *Congressional Quarterly Weekly Report,* July 31, 1982, 1867.
29. Ann Pelham, "Synthetic Fuels Bill Nearly Ready for Carter," *Congressional Quarterly Weekly Report,* June 21, 1980, 1691.
30. Pamela Fessler, " 'Christmas Tree' Ornaments?" *Congressional Quarterly Weekly Report,* May 28, 1983, 1068.
31. *Congressional Quarterly Weekly Report,* April 2, 1977, 608-609.
32. Reports also provide the courts and executive agencies with a detailed explanation of the legislative history and intent of a bill. The explanation gives the courts and agencies some guidance once a bill is enacted into law and becomes the subject of litigation before the courts or of interpretation by federal agencies.

5

Scheduling Legislation in the House

Scheduling legislation for floor debate in the House may be simple or complex. As we have seen, relatively few bills are reported from committee. For those that are, priorities for floor consideration are established by the majority leadership (the Speaker, the majority leader and majority whip), sometimes in consultation with the minority leader. Numerous factors influence their decisions: House rules, the timetable required by the 1974 Congressional Budget and Impoundment Control Act, the pressure of national and international events, the administration's programs, the leadership's policy and political preferences, and the actions of the Rules Committee. All these elements interact as legislators, pressure groups, and executive agencies maneuver to get favored legislation on the floor.

Scheduling involves many considerations: advance planning of annual recesses and adjournments, coordinating committee and floor action, providing a steady and predictable weekly agenda of business, and regulating the flow of bills to the floor during slack or peak periods. The procedures for managing the flow of bills to the floor have evolved throughout the history of Congress and still undergo frequent change. At first glance, they may appear needlessly complex and cumbersome, but they have an internal logic and over the years have served the needs of the House.

The focus in this chapter is on how bills reach the floor through one of three basic scheduling procedures: 1) special calendar days for speedy action on minor and noncontroversial legislation; 2) privileges (facilitated access to the floor) for certain categories of important legislation; and 3) actions of the Rules Committee, which is charged with the responsibility of scheduling most major legislation.

The House Legislative Calendars

Measures reported from committee are assigned by the clerk of the House to one of four regularly used "calendars." These list bills in the chronological order in which they are reported from the various committees. The calendars are: Union, House, Consent, and Private.

Legislation dealing with raising, authorizing, or spending money is assigned to the *Union Calendar*. Non-money measures of major importance are put on the *House Calendar*. Noncontroversial measures are assigned to the *Consent Calendar*. Bills of a private nature, those not of general application and usually dealing with individuals or small groups, are assigned to the *Private Calendar*.

In addition, there is a *Discharge Calendar*, which lists bills removed from committees through special, and infrequently successful, procedures. All of these are discussed below.

Minor and Noncontroversial Bills

Legislation on the Consent and Private Calendars is in order only during special calendar days. The House also processes noncontroversial measures that are on the Union, House, or Consent calendars under procedures that grant them privileged access to the floor during certain designated days of the month. These include bills dealing with the District of Columbia and measures brought to the floor under the suspension of the rules procedure. Each of these expedited procedures for processing relatively minor legislation also is discussed in this chapter.

When the House is in session, members receive a daily document, the *Calendars of the United States House of Representatives and History of Legislation,* shown on page 102, which lists all House as well as Senate measures that have been reported from committee.[1] The document is a handy reference source, but not every measure it lists is called up and considered by the House.

The Consent Calendar

Noncontroversial measures, such as the provision of a staff assistant for the chief justice of the United States, are assigned to the Consent Calendar. A bill assigned to the House or Union calendars also may be placed on the Consent Calendar at the request of the member who introduced it. The first and third Mondays of the month are Consent Calendar days. Measures must be entered on the Consent Calendar at least three days before they can be considered by the House. Bills brought up from the Consent Calendar by unanimous consent almost invariably are passed without debate or further amendment. The first time a bill is called, a single objection prevents its consideration. In such cases, the bill is returned to the Consent Calendar for possible consideration the next time such legislation is in order. If three or more members object when the bill is called a second time, the bill is stricken from the Consent Calendar for the rest of the congressional session. If members anticipate that objections will be made, they may secure unanimous consent that the bill be "passed over without prejudice" and remain on the Consent Calendar.

The Consent Calendar is supervised by six official "objectors," three members from each party, appointed by the majority and minority leaders.

As a matter of policy, the objectors will prevent consideration of bills from the Consent Calendar if they violate these criteria: 1) they involve expenditures of more than $1 million; 2) they make changes in domestic or international policy; or 3) they appear to be sufficiently controversial or substantive enough to provoke floor debate. Sponsors of Consent Calendar bills are asked to contact the objectors at least 24 hours before Consent Day to clear up any questions the objectors may have and to expedite the legislation.[2]

Suspension of the Rules

Another legislative short cut, which may be used for both important and minor public bills, is through suspension of the rules. By a two-thirds majority vote, the House may suspend its regular procedures for any bill.

A vote to suspend the rules is simultaneously a vote to pass the measure in question. Before the vote, debate is limited to 40 minutes, evenly divided between proponents and opponents. The motion to suspend the rules and pass a bill may include committee amendments, if they are stipulated in the motion, but floor amendments are not permitted. Bills that fail to gain the necessary two-thirds support may be considered again under regular House procedures. The House rules that govern legislation considered under the Consent Calendar and suspension procedure are listed in Table 5-1.

By and large, the suspension method is used for relatively minor measures, but for awhile in the mid-1970s it was employed rather frequently for important, and sometimes controversial, bills.

Until the 94th Congress (1975-77), motions to suspend the rules were in order only during the first and third Mondays of the month (following the call of the Consent Calendar) and during the last six days of a session when the backlog of bills awaiting floor debate is heavy. In 1975 the number of days for suspension of the rules was doubled by adding the first and third Tuesdays. In addition, the House instituted "cluster" voting to save more time. Under the most recent version of the "cluster" voting rule, the Speaker announces that recorded votes on a group of bills considered under the suspension procedure will be postponed until later that day or until sometime within the next two days. The bills then are brought up in sequence and disposed of without further debate. On the first clustered vote in a series, members have a minimum of 15 minutes in which to vote; on the remaining votes the Speaker may reduce the time on each one to a minimum of five minutes.

In 1977 the suspension rule was changed again — over the objections of many Republicans — to permit the Speaker to entertain motions to suspend the rules every Monday and Tuesday. The Republican minority saw this as an effort by Democrats to steamroll legislation through the House. Rep. Bill Frenzel, R-Minn., a senior GOP member with considerable expertise in procedural matters, declared that numerous bills, some important and controversial, were being hastily scheduled "under these abnormal, unnecessary, and high-risk procedures."[3]

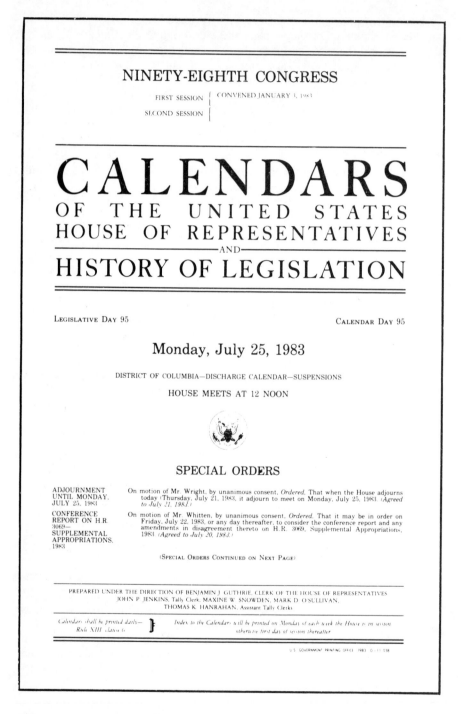

NINETY-EIGHTH CONGRESS

FIRST SESSION | CONVENED JANUARY 3, 1983

SECOND SESSION |

CALENDARS
OF THE UNITED STATES
HOUSE OF REPRESENTATIVES
—AND—
HISTORY OF LEGISLATION

LEGISLATIVE DAY 95   CALENDAR DAY 95

Monday, July 25, 1983

DISTRICT OF COLUMBIA—DISCHARGE CALENDAR—SUSPENSIONS

HOUSE MEETS AT 12 NOON

SPECIAL ORDERS

ADJOURNMENT UNTIL MONDAY, JULY 25, 1983

On motion of Mr. Wright, by unanimous consent, *Ordered,* That when the House adjourns today (Thursday, July 21, 1983, it adjourn to meet on Monday, July 25, 1983. *(Agreed to July 21, 1983.)*

CONFERENCE REPORT ON H.R. 3069—SUPPLEMENTAL APPROPRIATIONS, 1983

On motion of Mr. Whitten, by unanimous consent, *Ordered,* That it may be in order on Friday, July 22, 1983, or any day thereafter, to consider the conference report and any amendments in disagreement thereto on H.R. 3069, Supplemental Appropriations, 1983. *(Agreed to July 20, 1983.)*

(SPECIAL ORDERS CONTINUED ON NEXT PAGE)

PREPARED UNDER THE DIRECTION OF BENJAMIN J. GUTHRIE, CLERK OF THE HOUSE OF REPRESENTATIVES
JOHN P. JENKINS, Tally Clerk, MAXINE W. SNOWDEN, MARK D. O'SULLIVAN,
THOMAS K. HANRAHAN, Assistant Tally Clerks

Calendars shall be printed daily—
Rule XIII, clause 6
}
Index to the Calendars will be printed on Monday of each week the House is in session
otherwise first day of session thereafter

U.S. GOVERNMENT PRINTING OFFICE 1983 O—11-038

Majority Leader Jim Wright of Texas replied that the change made "it possible for the business of the House to be facilitated." [4] Democrats, to be sure, were also interested in limiting the ability of the minority party to obstruct the flow of legislation. The 1977 change is still in effect.

The Speaker is in complete charge of the measures considered under the suspension procedure. Committee chairmen, usually with the concurrence of their ranking minority colleagues, write the Speaker requesting that certain bills be taken up via the suspension route. Typically, these are bills that have not been reported by committee. But any measure — reported or not, previously introduced or not — can be brought to the floor under suspension of the rules if the Speaker chooses to recognize the representative offering the suspension motion.

In 1979 the Democratic Caucus adopted guidelines governing the consideration of measures under the suspension method. The Speaker, for instance, is directed not to schedule measures if they exceed $100 million in any fiscal year unless authorized to do so by the Democratic Steering and Policy Committee, the party caucus' executive committee, which the Speaker chairs.

The suspension procedure enables the House to bypass normal floor procedures and quickly pass legislation that can attract an overwhelming voting majority. Committee chairmen generally support the suspension of the rules because they can bring measures to the floor under a procedure that protects their bills from floor amendments and points of order. Republicans, as the minority, often view things differently, however. "I offered an amendment in the Commerce Committee," a GOP representative noted. "It did not carry by a majority, but it enjoyed substantial support." He added: "Therefore, I believe on the floor we would be making a mistake to permit this measure to pass under suspension. It should come up under the orderly process of the House where Members would have an opportunity of offering an amendment." [5]

During the hectic last days of a congressional session, suspension of the rules is used more frequently than merely on Mondays and Tuesdays. The parliamentary situation also is somewhat different during this period. Members who at an earlier time in the session might vote against a bill brought up under suspension because they had no opportunity to offer amendments to it or because it was a major bill, might vote for the legislation during the end-of-the-session crunch on the argument that it was that version or nothing.

In summary, it should be noted that the great bulk of legislation that comes before the House is passed by means of either the Consent Calendar or the suspension procedure.

District of Columbia Legislation

The federal capital is a unique governmental unit. Residents of the District of Columbia have no voting representation in Congress. (They have a nonvoting delegate in the House and no representation in the Senate.)

Table 5-1 The Consent Calendar and Suspension of the Rules

Consent Calendar	Suspension of the Rules
First and third Mondays	Every Monday and Tuesday, and during the last six days of the session
Bills must be placed on Consent Calendar three days before House consideration	No deadline
Bills may be amended	No floor amendments; 40 minutes of debate
Official party objectors	No objectors
Ground rules on types of bills allowed	No restrictions on substance of bills ($100 million limit established by Democratic Caucus)
Unanimous consent required for passage	Two-thirds of the members voting, a quorum being present, is required for passage

Despite "home rule" for the capital, the House exercises control over the District principally through its standing Committee on the District of Columbia and the Appropriations Committee's Subcommittee on the District of Columbia. House rules set aside the second and fourth Mondays of each month for legislation reported by the District of Columbia Committee. However, appropriations bills for the District do not come up during those special days. Instead, they are considered under the privilege given all bills reported by the Appropriations Committee. *(Details, see pp. 105-106.)*

The Private Calendar

Private bills cover a range of purposes, such as authorizing reimbursement to the family of a CIA agent who died while testing LSD for the agency, waiving immigration requirements so a Philadelphia woman could marry a Greek man, and granting citizenship to a 111-year-old Albanian woman so she could vote in one free election before she died. Under House procedures, the Speaker is required to call private bills on the first Tuesday of each month (unless the rule is dispensed with by a two-thirds vote or unanimous consent is obtained to transfer the call to some other day of the month) and, at his discretion, on the third Tuesday as well.

Few members have the time to review carefully all the private bills reported in each session. That job is done by a committee of "official objectors" composed of three members from each party appointed by the majority and minority leaders (but note that these are not the same objectors who review the Consent Calendar). Bills must be placed on the Private Calendar seven days before being called up to give the objectors time to screen them for controversial provisions. The objectors attend House sessions on Private Calendar days to answer any questions about the pending measures. If two or more members of the House object to a bill on the first Tuesday, it automatically is sent back to the committee that reported it, although at the request of a member it may at this time be "passed over without prejudice" for later consideration.

Private bills that are not opposed are considered in "the House as in Committee of the Whole." This is a special forum into which the House transforms itself to consider private bills and some public bills. Here, general debate on legislation is not permitted and amendments are considered under expedited procedures.

On the third Tuesday of the month, the Speaker gives preference to omnibus bills — those containing several previously rejected private measures. These measures are in order even if they were objected to earlier. Omnibus bills also are considered in "the House as in Committee of the Whole," but under tighter restrictions than when they first were considered. As Rep. Edward P. Boland, D-Mass., a longtime member of the Private Calendar objectors, has pointed out:

> Such omnibus bills are read by paragraph, and no amendments are entertained except to strike out or reduce amounts or provide limitations. Matter so stricken out shall not be again included in an omnibus bill during that session. Debate is limited to motions allowable under the rule and does not admit motions to strike out the last word *[see Chapter 6]* or reservations of objections. The rules prohibit the Speaker from recognizing Members for statements or for requests for unanimous consent for debate.[6]

Immigration matters constitute the bulk of the private bills. These are referred to the Judiciary Committee of each chamber for consideration and possible action.

'Privileged' Legislation

Under House rules, six standing committees have direct access to the floor for selected bills. The committees and the types of legislation eligible to be called up for immediate debate are listed in Table 5-2. Despite this privilege, most of these bills must observe a waiting period of at least three days to give members time to read the committee reports. Special rules from the Rules Committee, however, must lay over only one day, while reports on budget resolutions must be available to members for 10 days before those resolutions can come to the floor. *('Rules' reported by the Rules Committee, see p. 111.)*

Privileged measures are matters of special import to the House as an institution or to the federal government. The Appropriations, Ways and Means, and Budget panels report measures to finance the operations of the government; the Standards of Official Conduct Committee is concerned with matters involving the public reputation of the House; the House Administration panel handles necessary housekeeping proposals; and the Rules Commit-

Table 5-2 Committees With Direct Access to the Floor for Selected Legislation

Committee	Legislation
Appropriations	General appropriations bills; continuing appropriations resolutions if reported after Sept. 15.
Budget	Budget resolutions under the Congressional Budget and Impoundment Control Act of 1974.
House Administration	Printing resolutions and expenditures of the House contingent fund.
Rules	Rules and the order of business.
Standards of Official Conduct	Resolutions recommending action with respect to the conduct of a member, officer or employee of the House.
Ways and Means*	Revenue-raising bills.

* House precedents appear to indicate that the Ways and Means Committee has less privilege than the other committees because of an ambiguity in House rules. See the commentary that follows House Rule XVI, clause nine, of the rules of the House of Representatives in H. Doc. No. 97-271.

tee plays a major role in determining which measures the House considers.

Before 1974, the Interior and Insular Affairs, Public Works, and Veterans' Affairs committees also had privileged access to the floor. This was eliminated as part of changes in committee procedures adopted that year. The purpose was to narrow the range of bills with a "green light" to the floor.

Even privileged measures are subject to points of order (parliamentary objections that any member may raise at an appropriate time) on the ground that they violate certain rules of the House. If upheld, such points of order may return the measure to the committee that considered it. Frequently, therefore, committees with privileged access will ask the Rules Committee to waive points of order against their bills. The Appropriations Committee, for example, occasionally violates the House rule banning policy language (authorization legislation) in general appropriations bills and protects such language from points of order by persuading the Rules Committee to issue waivers.

Major Legislation

Most major bills, particularly controversial ones, do not go directly from committee to a calendar and then to the floor of the House. Instead, such measures are given special treatment by the Rules Committee.

The Rules Committee is among the oldest of House panels. The First Congress in April 1789 appointed an 11-member rules body to draw up its procedures. With a few early exceptions, each succeeding Congress has done the same, although for nearly a century the Rules panel was a select (temporary) committee that prepared procedures for the incoming Congress and then went out of existence.

In 1858 the Speaker became a member of the Rules Committee and, shortly thereafter, chairman of the panel. In 1880 the Rules Committee became a standing (permanent) committee, and in 1883 it initiated the practice of reporting special orders, or rules, which, when agreed to by majority votes of the House, controlled the amount of time allowed for debate on major bills and the extent to which they could be amended from the floor.

From 1858 to 1910 the Speaker determined which bills reached the House floor. He also appointed the other members of the Rules Committee and thus ensured a favorable attitude toward his policy preferences. Speakers during this period permitted the Rules Committee to acquire overwhelming authority over the House's agenda and the order of business. Speaker Joseph G. Cannon, a Republican from Illinois who was Speaker from 1903 to 1911, abused these and other powers, with the result that the House "revolted" in 1910 and removed the Speaker from the Rules Committee. The House leadership, however, retained — and still retains, in cooperation with the Rules Committee — considerable control over the flow of legislation reaching the floor.

The power of the Rules Committee lies in its scheduling responsibilities: its "traffic cop" role. As public bills are reported out of committee, they are entered in chronological order on one of two calendars, the Union Calendar (technically, the Calendar of the Committee of the Whole House on the State of the Union) or the House Calendar. On the former are placed all revenue bills, general appropriations bills, and measures that directly or indirectly appropriate money or property (including all authorization measures); all remaining public bills, which generally deal with administrative and procedural matters, go on the latter.

If all measures had to be taken up in the order in which they were listed on the calendars, as was the practice in the early nineteenth century, many major bills would not reach the House floor before Congress adjourned. Instead, major legislation reaches the floor in most instances by being granted precedence through a special order (rule) obtained from the Rules Committee. A rule is really a simple resolution (H Res). A request for a rule usually is made by the chairman of the committee reporting the bill. An example appears on page 108.

The Rules Committee holds a hearing on the request and debates it in the same manner other committees consider legislative matters. The rule, if granted, then is considered on the House floor and voted on in the same fashion as regular bills.

A Chairman Requests a Hearing on a 'Rule'

MR. DINGELL. Mr. Speaker, pursuant to the rules for the Democratic Caucus, notice is hereby given that the Committee on Energy and Commerce is seeking a rule which would limit germane amendments to the bill H.R. 6995, which was reported from the committee on September 15, 1982:

Committee on Energy and Commerce,
Washington, D.C., September 13, 1982.

Hon. Richard Bolling,
Chairman, Committee on Rules, House of Representatives, H-312,
The Capitol, Washington, D.C.

Dear Mr. Chairman: The following bill has been favorably reported by the Committee on Energy and Commerce:

H.R. 6995—To authorize appropriations for the Federal Trade Commission for fiscal years 1983 thru 1985, and for other purposes.

A copy of the bill is enclosed. The report on this bill is expected to be filed tomorrow.

It would be greatly appreciated if you would schedule a hearing before the Rules Committee on this bill as soon as possible. It is requested that a one-hour modified open rule be granted, making in order the following three amendments:

1. An amendment which would conform to the text of H.R. 3722 as introduced on May 28, 1981, by Mr. Luken and Mr. Lee;

2. An amendment in the nature of a substitute for #1 above to be offered by Mr. Florio and Mr. Broyhill; and

3. An amendment to be offered by Mr. Madigan regarding the establishment of information disclosure and certification requirements applicable to the sale of used motor vehicles.

Because it was not possible to report the bill until after May 15, I also request a waiver of Section 402(a) of the Budget Act.

This request only represents the views of the Committee on Energy and Commerce. The bill has been jointly referred to the Committee on Rules, which has some concerns that it may wish to address. We fully expect that any rule granted will reflect those concerns.

With kind regards.

Sincerely,

JOHN D. DINGELL,
Chairman.

Source: U.S., Congress, House, *Congressional Record,* daily ed., September 15, 1982, H7081-H7082.

A rule serves two principal purposes:

- It "bumps" a bill up the ladder of precedence, eliminating the waiting time that would be necessary if chronological order were observed.
- It governs the length of debate permitted once the bill reaches the floor

and the extent to which a measure can be amended. The Rules Committee, in effect, shuffles the Union and House calendars by holding back rules for some bills and reporting them for others. The Rules Committee has "clout," explained Rules member Gillis W. Long, D-La., "because it can sift through legislation coming from the other committees, decide which bills will have the right-of-way for consideration on the Floor, and determine the order in which legislation will be considered." [7]

In blocking or delaying legislation from reaching the floor, the Rules Committee is not necessarily playing an obstructionist role. It actually may be drawing fire away from the leadership, certain committees, and individual members. It is not uncommon for representatives to request the Rules Committee to prevent unwanted bills from reaching the floor. House Speaker Thomas P. O'Neill, Jr., D-Mass., a former member of the committee, once said, "It takes the heat for the rest of the Congress, there is no question about that." [8]

The committee also acts as an informal arbiter of disputes among other House committees. Because of overlapping jurisdictions, one committee may report a measure that trespasses on the authority of another. In such a case, the Rules Committee may resolve the dispute by authorizing the second committee to offer amendments or by refusing to waive points of order on the floor, thus giving members of the second committee an opportunity to attempt to delete the offending matter.

Role of the Rules Committee

As the previous discussion demonstrates, few pieces of major legislation would reach the House floor without a rule. Thus, action, or lack of it, by the Rules Committee generally determines whether a bill is considered at all. The chairman of the committee has wide discretion in scheduling the panel's order of business. By not setting a hearing on a rule for a particular bill, the chairman can, in most cases, kill the measure.

Once hearings are under way, two common delaying techniques sometimes are used:

● preventing quorums in the committee;
● scheduling a parade of witnesses to testify against issuing a rule for the bill.

House rules require committees to have a specific number of members present (a quorum) before they officially can conduct business. One-third of a committee's membership constitutes a quorum for the purpose of marking up legislation; however, a majority of the committee must be present when the panel votes on reporting a bill to the House.

The first technique involves manipulation of the rules governing a quorum. Opponents of a bill may persuade sympathetic Rules Committee members not to attend committee meetings on the bill. The Rules chairman also may either strictly observe or ignore the rules for a quorum. Strict observance of the rules can be an effective delaying tactic. For example, in 1971 Rules Chairman William M. Colmer, D-Miss. (1933-73), and several Republican members opposed a Civil Service pay bill. During a committee meeting on the bill, committee member Ray Madden, D-Ind. (1943-77), left the session briefly to greet a visiting constituent. A Republican member observed that a quorum was not present. Chairman Colmer did not send for Madden, "who was within voice range in the adjoining hallway," but "promptly adjourned the meeting for lack of a quorum." [9]

In the second strategy, opponents of a bill line up a series of witnesses to testify against it. Executive agency officials and pressure group witnesses do not testify at hearings of the Rules Committee that involve the granting of rules. The witness list is confined to legislators interested in the measure, usually the chairman and members of the committee reporting the bill, legislators opposing it, and members who desire to offer certain amendments during floor consideration. Committee rules state that all members "will be provided a reasonable opportunity to testify." This provision, when honored to the extreme, can open the way to a time-consuming flood of testimony. In 1974 two weeks of hearings were required before the Rules Committee finally granted a rule to a committee reorganization plan. Rules hearings also function as a "dress rehearsal" — previewing in advance for a bill's proponents and opponents the issues and amendments that will be raised during the House debate. [10]

After holding hearings, the Rules Committee can refuse to grant a rule, thus preventing the measure from reaching the floor. A 1981 agriculture bill initially failed to receive a rule, thus encountering delays in reaching the floor, because Rules members were dissatisfied with the procedures that were requested for considering floor amendments to the measure. "The Agriculture Committee didn't have its act together," said the Rules Committee chairman. "The bill has a range of problems, but it was impossible to structure a rule that would have been fair to all under the procedures proposed by Agriculture." [11] In short, bills may be kept from the floor that are poorly conceived, technically deficient, inimical to majority party interests, or whose jurisdiction is hotly contested by several committees.

Even on the vote to approve a rule, there is room for maneuver. The chairman may unexpectedly schedule the vote when certain committee members cannot attend. The Consumer Protection Act of 1970 failed to obtain a rule on a 7-7 tie because Rep. Richard W. Bolling, D-Mo. (1949-83), a supporter of the measure, was out of town. The vote was scheduled on only one day's notice, leaving little or no time for Bolling to return. The vote killed further action on consumer legislation in the 91st Congress, and there was a two-year delay before the House finally passed the consumer agency bill.

In 1968 the Rules Committee set a specific cutoff date after which no requests for rules would be heard. The policy was initiated by Rules Chairman Colmer and has been followed by successive committee chairman. Its purpose is to prevent logjams at the end of each session, albeit not with much success. Emergency and procedural measures, such as stopgap funding bills, are excluded from the cutoff dictum.

Types of Special Rules

The Rules Committee grants three basic kinds of rules: open, closed, and modified. The distinction between them goes solely to the question of the amendment process. All three types almost always provide a fixed number of hours for general debate. In addition, any of these types also may contain waivers of points of order. A typical rule from the Rules Committee is reproduced on page 127.

Open Rule. The majority of bills are considered under an open rule. Of the 152 rules granted during the 97th Congress, 90 were open. Under an open rule, any germane amendment may be offered from the floor. Amendments may be simple or complex. For example, an amendment may simply extend the funding of a program from two to four years or it may rewrite whole sections of a bill.

Closed Rule. A closed rule prohibits floor amendments, but rarely are such "pure" closed rules reported by the Rules Committee. Instead, closed rules in the contemporary House forbid floor amendments except those offered by the reporting committee or committees. Only 10 were reported during the 97th Congress. Critics say closed rules (also called "gag" rules) hamper the legislative process and violate democratic norms. Supporters of closed rules say they are necessary in the case of very complex measures subject to intense lobbying. In addition, national emergency legislation sometimes needs to be expedited by the closed rule procedure.

Tax bills provide a good illustration of the pressures surrounding closed rules. For decades the House considered tax measures under closed rules, agreeing with the argument of Wilbur D. Mills, D-Ark. (1939-77), chairman of the Ways and Means Committee from 1959 to 1974, that tax legislation was too complex and technical to be tampered with on the floor. If unlimited floor amendments were allowed, Mills argued, the internal revenue code soon would be in shambles and at the mercy of pressure groups.

For years House members trusted the judgment of the Ways and Means Committee, but in the 1970s disenchantment began to set in. In 1973 the Democratic Caucus approved a change in committee procedures requiring a chairman to give advance notice in the *Congressional Record* of his intention to request a closed rule. After such notice is made, a party caucus may be called at the request of 50 House Democrats. The caucus discusses the support in the party for particular amendments to the bill and may instruct Democrats on the Rules Committee to make those amendments "in order" in the House debate on the legislation.[12]

Modified Rule. A third category of special orders is the modified rule. These rules typically impose a rigorous structure on the amendment process. Modified rules may specify which parts of a bill are open to amendment, when amendments may be offered, the exact order in which they may be proposed, and who may offer them, even naming the representatives in the rule itself. Modified rules may mandate that only certain amendments will be in order and require that they be printed in the *Congressional Record* in advance of floor debate. Such rules sometimes allow amendments that normally could not be offered under regular parliamentary procedures, for example, permitting scores of amendments, including major substitutes, to be pending simultaneously on the floor in violation of House rules that limit the number of pending amendments. *(Limits on the amending process, see Chapter 6 illustration, p. 137.)*

In short, the variety of modified rules has become bewildering in their multiple types, reflecting the procedural ingenuity of the Rules Committee.

In recent years, the Rules Committee has employed complicated modified rules with increasing frequency.[13] This development reflects new procedural trends — such as the wider use of multiple referrals — with the consequence that several committees' requirements for floor amendments and longer debate time must be accommodated. Use of complicated rules also has been the result of skillful use of the amendment process by House Republicans to delay or frustrate Democratic floor strategy. Angry Democrats even circulated a letter in 1979 urging the Speaker and the Rules Committee to bring more modified rules to the floor, "allowing only a limited number of pre-selected amendments." [14]

Two years later, in the aftermath of the House Democratic leadership's unhappiness surrounding enactment of the 1981 budget reconciliation bill backed by the Reagan administration, Rules Committee Chairman Bolling outlined new procedures he intended to follow for "rules" on complex measures.

> I will seek to insure that not only the basic bill or resolution to be considered by the House be available in printed form but also that all amendments of any kind will be officially printed in their final form in a timely fashion before the Rules Committee orders reported a "rule" on the matter in question. Exceptions would be made for technical amendments to be offered by the Member designated by the appropriate legislative committee.[15]

A fundamental purpose of the advance notice procedure, and modified rules in general, explained Bolling, is to devise floor procedures that give the members of the House "the right to deal with the major elements of the conflicts before them" in systematic and rational fashion.[16]

Waiver Rules. Finally, there are rules waiving points of order. Under these rules, which appear in open, closed, and modified rules, specific House procedures may be temporarily set aside. Without such waivers, measures in technical violation of House procedures could not be dealt with rapidly, and important parts of bills could be deleted for technical reasons during floor debate. Waivers frequently are granted to the Appropriations Committee because funding bills sometimes touch on the jurisdiction of other committees, in violation of House rules. Waivers permit timely floor action on those measures. Waivers are not granted indiscriminately, however. Generally, they are confined to temporary exemptions from specific House rules and procedures. Committee chairmen, noted a Rules member, must "indicate any matter that they want a waiver on that may be subject to a point of order."[17]

House Appropriations Committee Chairman Jamie L. Whitten, D-Miss., has highlighted the value of the waiver prerogative.

> I think perhaps the saving grace is that the rules [of the House] provide that the Committee on Rules in proper cases can waive other rules. It is the supreme rule. We could not run this Government without this Committee on Rules exercising that authority in proper cases.[18]

Adoption of the Rule

All rules must be approved by a majority of the House. Rules are reported to the House by the Rules Committee and are debated for a maximum of one hour, with the time equally divided by custom between the Rules chairman, or his designee, and the ranking minority member of the committee, or a designee. The "hour rule" is the basic rule of floor debate in the House. Theoretically, it permits each member one hour of debate on any question, including the rules approved by the Rules Committee. The hour rule is never followed in practice, however. A member who controls the debate time under the hour rule, in this case the Rules chairman or his designee, always moves the "previous question" at the end of this hour (or before the full hour is used if no member seeks time for debate). Adoption of this motion by majority vote stops all debate, prevents the offering of amendments, and brings the House to an immediate vote on the main question, the rule itself in this context.

The main strategy, then, for a member wishing to amend a rule is to defeat the previous question. "I am urging my colleagues to vote against the previous question on this rule so that we can offer a substitute rule," declared Minority Whip Trent Lott, R-Miss., during a 1982 debate.[19] Under House precedents, the member who led the fight against approval of the previous question is recognized by the Speaker to propose a substitute rule. In short, the key vote here often is not on adoption of the rule but on approval of the previous question.

If there is no controversy, rules are adopted routinely by voice vote after a brief discussion.

The House seldom rejects a rule proposed by the Rules Committee. Speaker O'Neill once remarked, "Defeat of the rule on the House floor is considered an affront both to the [Rules] Committee and to the Speaker." [20] The Rules Committee generally understands the conditions the House will accept for debating and amending important bills. Only one of the 152 rules requested during the 97th Congress was rejected. Under a 1977 procedural change, the Speaker may postpone votes on rules and permit them to be voted on at five-minute intervals later in the day or anytime within the next two days. The procedure is similar to cluster voting under suspension of the rules. *(See p. 101.)*

Recent Rules Committee Changes

The Rules Committee is "specifically designed to function as the responsible agent of the majority party, using its great discretionary authority over pending legislation to facilitate the consideration and adoption of the majority party's program," Representative Bolling asserted many years before he became the committee's chairman.[21] As the agent of the majority party, the committee today generally is under the influence of the Speaker of the House.

It has not always worked that way, however. There have been "maverick" Rules chairmen. One of the best known was Rep. Howard W. Smith, D-Va. (1931-67), who presided over the committee with an iron hand from 1955 to 1967. Smith was no "traffic cop" simply regulating the flow of bills to the floor. He firmly believed the committee should "consider the substance and merits of the bills," and he often blocked measures he disapproved of and advanced those he favored, sometimes thwarting the will of the majority.[22]

The Rules Committee lacks authority to amend bills, but it can bargain for changes in return for granting rules. Smith frequently did this. In an attempt to lessen the power of the conservative coalition of southern Democrats and Republicans that controlled the committee from the mid-1930s to the early 1960s, House liberals succeeded in adopting a series of rules changes beginning in the late 1940s. These included several versions of the "21-day rule." But the independent power of the chairman was not effectively curbed until the membership of the committee was expanded in 1961.[23] The committee's present composition is nine Democrats and four Republicans. Traditionally, the panel has had a disproportionate party ratio to ensure majority control.

Since the early 1970s, the House Democratic leadership has relied on the Rules Committee to deal with the recent changes that have affected the House as an institution, such as wider use of multiple referrals of legislation and the rise of subcommittee government. Today, this committee is one of the few centralizing panels in a greatly decentralized House. Hence the importance of its rule-writing responsibilities. Noted Representative Long, a senior Democrat on the committee:

> I want to point out that the guiding principle of the Rules Committee, certainly for the past decade, has been to assure the orderly flow of legislation to the floor, and to assure that each Member — regardless of his position on a committee or his length of service — has a fair opportunity to present his case in the debate on the House floor.[24]

The Rules Committee also demonstrated its substantive responsibilities during this period. It reported out such major measures as the Legislative Reorganization Act of 1970, the Congressional Budget and Impoundment Control Act of 1974, and resolutions providing for the creation of a permanent Select Intelligence Committee and the televising of House floor sessions. Further, the committee established two permanent subcommittees and significantly increased its budget and staff resources.

The Speaker and the Rules Committee

By the 95th Congress, the Rules Committee had become closely linked to the Speaker and the Democratic Caucus. Dormant for decades, the Democratic Caucus began to stir at the end of the 1960s. Beginning in 1971, the caucus initiated procedures for using secret ballots to elect committee chairmen, including the chairman of the Rules Committee. In 1975 the Speaker was authorized to appoint, subject to caucus ratification, the majority party members of the Rules Committee. *(Re-emergence of the Democratic Caucus, see p. 37.)*

The institutional changes adopted in the 1970s reduced the Rules panel's independence. The committee can still oppose the Speaker, but this seldom happens. One exception did occur in 1977 when several Democrats on the committee opposed parts of an ethics proposal favored by O'Neill. According to some observers, he handled the challenge as follows:

O'Neill invited the Rules Committee Democrats to breakfast, at which he pounded the table, demanding their cooperation. They were not convinced. Next day, O'Neill got tougher. They were all his personal friends, O'Neill said, but by God they would find themselves on the District of Columbia Committee next year if they failed him on this one.[25]

Although the Rules Committee ultimately granted the rule requested by the Speaker in this case, the power of the committee should not be underestimated. The Speaker cannot track every major and minor bill. The caucus cannot convene every week to issue instructions to the committee. The history of the Rules Committee is "one of the committee's accommodating the leadership on the one hand and seeking independent status on the other." [26] For the time being, at least, the emphasis is on sharing power with the Speaker, the leadership, and the chairmen of the other committees.

In summary, the Rules Committee performs the critical task of assuring the orderly consideration of legislation. Although it generally works in harmony with the majority leadership today, the committee can and sometimes does act contrary to the leadership's wishes and to the will of the House. Its actions in preventing or delaying certain bills from reaching the floor, or in negotiating changes in legislation in return for a rule, led to periodic efforts, particularly in the 1950s and 1960s, to curb the committee's power. But the House is unlikely to endorse another mechanism to perform its functions. As recently as 1974 the House refused to give the Speaker authority to recognize committee chairmen to propose their own rules for bills their committees reported, a proposal that would have circumvented the Rules Committee.

Legislation Blocked in Committee

What happens when a standing committee refuses to report a bill that many members support, or when the Rules Committee fails to grant a rule to legislation with substantial support in the House? Several procedures are available to bring to the floor legislation that has been stalled in a standing committee.

Which procedure to use depends on the nature of the legislation. Suspension of the rules, discussed earlier, is appropriate if the measure is relatively uncontroversial or minor. If a major bill is being blocked by a standing committee or the Rules Committee, there are extraordinary procedures that can be employed to "spring" the bill from committee. These procedures are difficult to implement, but if the House is determined, committees can be compelled to yield legislation.

The Discharge Petition

The discharge procedure, adopted in 1910, provides that if a bill has been before a standing committee for 30 days, any member can introduce a motion to relieve the panel of the measure. A clerk of the House then prepares a discharge petition, which is made available for members to sign when the House is in session. The names are not disclosed until the required 218 signatures (a majority of the 435-member House) are obtained. The names then are published in the *Congressional Record*. A member may withdraw his or her signature until a majority is secured.

When 218 members have signed the petition, the motion to discharge is put on the Discharge Calendar. After seven days on the calendar, it becomes privileged business on the second and fourth Mondays of the month (but not during the last six days of a session). Any member who signed the petition may be recognized to offer the discharge motion. When the motion is called up, debate is limited to 20 minutes, divided between proponents and opponents. If the discharge motion is rejected, the bill is not eligible again for discharge during that session. If the discharge motion prevails, any member who signed the petition can make a motion to call up the bill for immediate consideration. It then becomes the business of the House until it is disposed of. A vote against immediate consideration assigns the bill to the appropriate calendar, with the same rights as any bill reported from committee.

Few measures are ever discharged from committee. From 1937 through 1982 (approximately the period during which the modern version of the rule has been in effect), 371 discharge petitions were filed; but only 19 measures actually were discharged.[27] Of those, 15 were passed by the House, but only two of these became law: the Fair Labor Standards Act of 1938 and the Federal Pay Raise Act of 1960. Several factors account for this. Members are reluctant to second-guess a committee's right to consider a bill. The discharge rule violates normal legislative routine, and even members who support a bill blocked in committee may refuse to sign a discharge petition for this reason.

Legislators also are reluctant to write legislation on the floor of the House, without the guidance and information provided in committee hearings and reports. Particularly in the case of complicated legislation, many members feel the need for committee interpretation. Then, too, it is not easy to obtain 218 signatures. Attempts to reduce the present requirement occasionally are made, but none has been successful.[28] Finally, members are hesitant to employ a procedure that one day may be used against committees on which they serve.

For all its limitations, the discharge rule serves important purposes. It focuses attention on particular legislative issues, and the threat of using it may stimulate a committee to hold hearings or report a bill. In May 1983 the Ways and Means Committee voted to report a controversial measure repealing a law requiring the withholding of taxes on dividend and interest income. The committee had sought to bottle up the bill but was forced to send it to the floor when 218 members signed a discharge petition. To signal its displeasure, the committee decided to report the repeal bill "without recommendation." Nonetheless, it was passed by the House.

Rules Committee's Extraction Power

The Rules Committee has an extraordinary authority that it rarely exercises: It can introduce rules for bills that the committee of jurisdiction does not want to report. The power of extraction is based on an 1895 precedent, which the committee has invoked only four times in the past three decades. Extraction is a highly controversial procedure and evokes charges of usurpation of other committees' rights. One of the rare occasions when it was used occurred on February 9, 1972. The Education and Labor Committee refused to approve a dock strike measure, but the Rules Committee went ahead and reported a rule for floor action on the bill. Despite Speaker Carl Albert's, D-Okla. (1947-77), vigorous opposition, the House adopted the rule by a 203-170 vote, thus springing the bill from the committee. The House then proceeded to pass the bill.

The threat of extraction by the Rules panel in itself can break legislative logjams. In 1967 the Judiciary Committee balked at reporting an anti-riot bill. Rules Chairman Colmer announced that his committee would soon hold hearings on a rule for the bill. This was enough to prompt the Judiciary Committee to report the bill.[29]

Discharging the Rules Committee

The discharge rule, with several variations, also applies to the Rules Committee, with one significant difference: A motion to discharge the committee is in order seven days, rather than 30 days, after a measure has been before that panel. Any member may enter the motion, which is handled like any other discharge petition in the House.

Since the Rules Committee reports "rules" as a matter of original jurisdiction, members who wish to discharge a rule must introduce one of their own so there will be something to discharge. For example, on July 12, 1982, Rep. Barber Conable, Jr., R-N.Y., filed "a petition to discharge from the Rules Committee, House Resolution 450, which will provide 10 hours of debate and consideration" of a constitutional amendment to balance the federal budget. House Resolution 450 was the rule introduced earlier by Representative Conable and referred to the Rules Committee.

Once a rule has been pending before the Rules Committee for seven legislative days, House precedents state, it is in order to bring before the House "a measure pending before a standing committee for 30 legislative days." In the example discussed above, the House Judiciary Committee had refused to take action on a constitutional balanced budget amendment for more than a year.

Proponents of the constitutional amendment worked diligently to obtain the 218 signatures for the White House-backed measure, which already had been passed by the Senate.

> As the petition neared the required number of signatures, the Democratic leadership persuaded some members to remove their names. So amendment backers and Republicans devised a new strategy. They worked intensely to gather the last 13 needed. Once they had them, the group marched en masse onto the House floor, signed the petition, and put it over the top. So organized was the "coup" that Vice President George Bush was on hand to greet the 13 in a Capitol meeting room.[30]

In the end, the required two-thirds of the House failed to support the proposed constitutional amendment. Until 1982, the last time the discharge procedure had been used successfully against the Rules Committee was in 1965.

In summation, when the Rules panel is discharged from a special rule, the bill to which it applies automatically is discharged from the legislative committee that is blocking it.

Calendar Wednesday

Under House procedures, every Wednesday is reserved for standing committees to call up measures (except privileged bills) that have been reported but not granted rules by the Rules Committee. The Speaker calls the roll of standing committees in alphabetical order. Each chairmen (or designated committee member) either passes or brings up for House debate a measure pending on the House or Union calendar. The rule may be dispensed with by unanimous consent, that is, without objection, or by a two-thirds vote of the House. The Rules Committee may not report a rule setting aside Calendar Wednesday.

The Calendar Wednesday rule was adopted in 1909 in an attempt to circumvent Speaker Cannon's control of the legislative agenda. Today it is rarely employed and usually is dispensed with by unanimous consent. On September 21, 1982, however, several Republicans objected to dispensing with Calendar Wednesday proceedings and tried to use the procedure to force consideration of measures such as abortion, school prayer, and school busing, on which the Democratic Party-controlled committees had failed to act. "Many of these bills have been bottled up very purposely by either chairmen of the committees, by the Rules Committee, or by [the Speaker],"

THOMAS S. FOLEY
WASHINGTON
MAJORITY WHIP

Congress of the United States
House of Representatives
Office of the Majority Whip
Washington, D.C. 20515

WHIP NOTICE INFORMATION
Legislative Program — 51600
Floor Information — 57400
Whip Information — 55604

My dear Colleague:

The program for the House of Representatives for the Week of July 25, 1983, is as follows:

MONDAY
July 25

HOUSE MEETS AT NOON
ALL RECORDED VOTES WILL BE POSTPONED UNTIL TUESDAY, JULY 26

District (3 Bills)

1. H.R. 3369 — D.C. Parole Board
2. H.R. 3425 — R.F.K. Stadium
3. H.R. 3547 — Capital Borrowing Authority

Suspensions (5 Bills)

1. H.R. 3497 — Defer Proposed Amendments to Federal Rules of Civil and Criminal Procedure
2. H.R. 2727 — Codify Recent Laws Related to Money and Finance
3. H.Con. Res 39 — Year of the Disabled
4. H.R. 622 — Death Benefits for Law Enforcement Officers and Firefighters
5. H.R. 2498 — To Establish a Congressional Advisory Commission on Boxing

H.R. 2350 — Health Research Extension Act (NIH Authorization)
(OPEN RULE, ONE HOUR)
(RULE ALREADY ADOPTED)
(GENERAL DEBATE ONLY)

H.R. 2957 — International Recovery and Financial Stability Act (IMF)
(OPEN RULE, TWO HOURS)
(RULE ALREADY ADOPTED)
(GENERAL DEBATE ONLY)

TUESDAY
July 26

HOUSE MEETS AT NOON
Suspensions (No Bills)
RECORDED VOTES ON BILLS DEBATED MONDAY, JULY 25

H.R. 2760 — Amend Intelligence Act of 1983
(CONTINUE CONSIDERATION)

WEDNESDAY and the
BALANCE of the WEEK
July 27, 28, 29

HOUSE MEETS AT NOON on
WEDNESDAY and 10 a.m.
BALANCE of the WEEK

H.R. 2760 — Amend Intelligence Act of 1983
(COMPLETE CONSIDERATION)
H.R. 3021 — Health Insurance for the Unemployed
(MODIFIED RULE, TWO HOURS)
H.R. 2957 — International Recovery and Financial Stability Act (IMF)
(COMPLETE CONSIDERATION)
H.R. 2867 — Hazardous Waste Control and Enforcement Act of 1983
(OPEN RULE, ONE HOUR)
H.R. 2350 — Health Research Extension Act (NIH Authorization)
(COMPLETE CONSIDERATION)

* * * * * * * * * * * *

THE HOUSE WILL ADJOURN BY 3 p.m. ON FRIDAY. ADJOURNMENT TIMES ON ALL OTHER
DAYS WILL BE ANNOUNCED DAILY. CONFERENCE REPORTS MAY BE BROUGHT UP AT ANY
TIME, AND ANY FURTHER PROGRAM WILL BE ANNOUNCED LATER.

Sincerely,

Thomas S. Foley

Thomas S. Foley
Majority Whip

declared Rep. Robert S. Walker, R-Pa.[31] But the Democrats foiled the GOP attempt when two-thirds of the House voted to dispense with Calendar Wednesday.

Calendar Wednesday has been successful only twice: on the 1950 Fair Employment Practices Act and the 1960 Area Redevelopment Act. Four factors account for the limited use of this procedure: 1) Only two hours of debate are permitted, one for proponents and one for opponents. This may not be enough to debate complex bills. 2) A committee far down in the alphabet may have to wait weeks before its turn is reached. 3) A bill that is not completed on one Wednesday is not in order the following Wednesday, unless two-thirds of the members agree. 4) The procedure is subject to dilatory tactics precisely because the House must complete action on the same day.

Final Scheduling Steps

After a bill has been granted a rule, the final decision on when the measure is to be debated is made by the majority party leaders. The leadership prepares daily and weekly schedules of floor business and adjusts them according to shifting legislative situations and demands. A bill the majority has scheduled for consideration may be withdrawn if it appears to lack sufficient support. Or measures may be put on a "fast track" by the leadership. In 1981 House Democrats developed a specific timetable for consideration of President Reagan's economic agenda. Explained Majority Leader Jim Wright of Texas:

> I should like to report to our colleagues an unprecedented agreement reached yesterday by leaders of the majority and minority, under the Speaker's guidance and upon his initiative, to develop a specific timetable for the consideration of the President's program and its various components.
>
> Never before, to my recollection, have the majority and minority leaders of the House, the chairmen and ranking minority members of the Committees on Budget, Appropriations, Rules, and Ways and Means, sat down together and established definite target dates for each step in the process — the budget resolution, the reconciliation bill, and such tax reductions as the Congress in its wisdom may approve.[32]

Nothing in the House rules requires the majority leadership to provide advance notice of the daily or weekly legislative program. This is done as a matter of long-standing custom in two principal ways. Announcements about floor action are made by majority party leaders, often in response to a query from the minority leader. The legislative program for the following day for both chambers also is printed in each issue of the *Congressional Record*, in a section called the Daily Digest. The Friday Record contains a section called the Congressional Program Ahead, which lists the following week's legislative agenda and the dates on which floor action has been scheduled.

The majority leadership also sends "whip notices" to its members at the end of each week, or more frequently, if necessary. The whip notices contain information concerning the daily program for the following week. Although sent under the majority whip's signature, they are prepared mainly by the Speaker and majority leader. The schedule often is changed in response to unforeseen events or new circumstances. A whip notice is reproduced on page 119.

The majority (and minority) whip's office has several phone recordings that announce the daily and weekly programs, legislative actions taken on the floor, and changes in the schedule. Democratic and Republican members obtain similar information from their respective cloakrooms (located just off the chamber floor). The majority whip prepares one-page summaries of pending bills, called "Whip Advisories," and publishes "Whip Issues Papers," which describes activities of the House on one or more major issues. The minority whip prepares a weekly notice of floor business for all members. The GOP party conference publishes each week summaries of bills to be considered on the floor, and the minority leader prepares "Legislative Alerts" for party colleagues that highlight measures reported from the committees.

Summary

Scheduling is a party function that the House majority leadership shares with the Rules Committee. Bills reported from committees are assigned to one of several calendars. If they are not brought up under the suspension of the rules procedure, most bills must receive a special rule, granted by the Rules Committee, giving the bill a green light to the floor and specifying the conditions under which it will be considered.

Although they are seldom employed, there are special procedures to dislodge bills that are stalled either in a standing committee or the Rules Committee.

Outside events and pressures often influence the timing of floor action on a particular bill. Upcoming congressional elections can be a critical factor in scheduling controversial bills. And the congressional work load must be taken into account.

Bargaining and compromise are necessary at each stage of the scheduling process. Members, pressure groups, and executive officials all try to influence the shaping of the House agenda. Their efforts are directed principally at the Rules Committee and the majority leadership. Once an important proposal is granted a rule and placed on the House schedule by the Speaker, the focus shifts to the intricacies of floor procedure.

Notes

1. *Calendars of the United States House of Representatives and History of Legislation* also contains short summaries of bills, the titles of measures that have become public law, bills pending in as well as those approved by House-Senate conference committees, and measures that have been vetoed by the president.
2. The objectors' criteria can be found in the U.S., Congress, House, *Congressional*

Record, daily ed., April 19, 1983, H2122.
3. U.S., Congress, House, *Congressional Record,* September 20, 1976, 31281.
4. U.S., Congress, House, *Congressional Record,* January 4, 1977, 66.
5. U.S., Congress, House, *Congressional Record,* daily ed., May 23, 1983, H3178. The measure did pass under the suspension of the rules procedure.
6. U.S., Congress, House, *Congressional Record,* daily ed., May 3, 1983, H2585. For a list of the Private Calendar Objectors, see the *Congressional Record,* daily ed., of March 22, 1983, H1468. For a statement of procedure and policy on private immigration bills, see the *Congressional Record,* daily ed., of March 2, 1983, E730-E732.
7. Rep. Gillis W. Long, D-La., "A Newsletter to Louisiana's 8th District," March 1980, 4.
8. Spark M. Matsunaga and Ping Chen, *Rulemakers of the House* (Urbana, Ill.: University of Illinois Press, 1976), 21.
9. Ibid., 98.
10. Bruce I. Oppenheimer, "The Rules Committee: New Arm of Leadership in a Decentralized House," in *Congress Reconsidered,* ed. Lawrence C. Dodd and Bruce I. Oppenheimer (New York: Praeger Publishers, 1977), 105-113.
11. *Washington Post,* October 1, 1981, A4.
12. For an example of the use of this party procedure, see Catherine E. Rudder, "Committee Reform and the Revenue Process," in *Congress Reconsidered,* 126-128.
13. See Stanley Bach, "The Structure of Choice in the House of Representatives: The Impact of Complex Special Rules," *Harvard Journal on Legislation* (Summer 1981): 553-602.
14. *Washington Star,* August 5, 1979, A3.
15. Letter from Rules Committee Chairman Richard W. Bolling, D-Mo., to all House members, July 9, 1981. Six days later, the Republican leadership wrote to all House members and expressed concern that "this policy could be used to shut out floor amendments if adequate safeguards are not built in."
16. U.S., Congress, House, *Congressional Record,* daily ed., February 9, 1982, H263. There is no consensus regarding the definition of modified rules, which limit the offering of amendments. Some are called "modified open" rules; others are dubbed "modified closed" rules. See *Procedure in the U.S. House of Representatives,* 97th Cong., "A Summary of the Modern Precedents and Practices of the House," 328-331.
17. U.S., Congress, House, *Congressional Record,* June 26, 1973, 21323. Implicitly, all special rules waive certain House rules and therefore potential points of order under them, such as the daily order of business rule. Explicitly, waivers are generally of two kinds: those waiving points of order that would prevent consideration of a bill and those waiving points of order against specific provisions in a bill or amendments to the bill that otherwise might be ruled out of order.
18. U.S., Congress, House, *Congressional Record,* daily ed., May 25, 1983, H3310.
19. U.S., Congress, House, *Congressional Record,* daily ed., August 13, 1982, H5893. A majority of his House colleagues voted with Rep. Trent Lott, R-Miss., to defeat the previous question. Lott then offered a substitute rule, but a Democratic member of the Rules Committee offered a successful motion to refer the rule to the Rules Committee.
20. *Congressional Quarterly Weekly Report,* February 14, 1976, 313.
21. Richard W. Bolling, "The House Rules Committee," *Business and Government*

Review, University of Missouri (September-October 1961): 39.

22. *Nation's Business,* February 1956, 103.

23. See, for example, James A. Robinson, *The House Rules Committee* (Indianapolis: Bobbs-Merrill Co., 1963); Charles O. Jones, "Joseph G. Cannon and Howard W. Smith: An Essay on the Limits of Leadership in the House of Representatives," *Journal of Politics* (September 1968): 617-646; and Robert L. Peabody, "The Enlarged Rules Committee," in *New Perspectives on the House of Representatives,* 2d ed., ed. Robert L. Peabody and Nelson W. Polsby (Chicago: Rand McNally, 1969).

24. U.S., Congress, House, *Congressional Record,* daily ed., May 4, 1983, H2607.

25. *Washington Post,* March 8, 1977, A1.

26. Matsunaga and Chen, *Rulemakers of the House,* 143. Also see *A History of the Committee on Rules,* 97th Cong., 2d sess. (Washington, D.C.: U.S. Government Printing Office, 1983); and Alan Ehrenhalt, "The Unfashionable House Rules Committee," *Congressional Quarterly Weekly Report,* January 15, 1983, 151.

27. Figures were made available to the author by Richard Beth, Government Division, Congressional Research Service, Library of Congress.

28. Prior to the start of the 98th Congress on January 3, 1983, Democrats, with an increased majority, considered amending the House rules to require a two-thirds majority of the membership, rather than a simple majority, to sign the petition to discharge from committee a proposed constitutional amendment. Because of the controversial nature of the recommendation, however, Democratic leaders decided to drop the idea.

29. Matsunaga and Chen, *Rulemakers of the House,* 25.

30. *Christian Science Monitor,* October 4, 1982, 4.

31. *Washington Times,* September 23, 1983, 3A.

32. U.S., Congress, House, *Congressional Record,* daily ed., March 11, 1981, H867.

6

House Floor Procedure

To a casual observer, the House floor may appear hopelessly disorganized. Legislators talk in small groups or read newspapers while a colleague drones on. People come and go in an endless stream. Motions are offered, amendments proposed, points of order raised — all evoking little apparent interest from the members present. The scene may not make much sense to visitors in the gallery.

If the visitors are there to see their representatives in action, they are likely to be disappointed. Attendance is often sparse during floor debates. Members may be in committee sessions, meeting with constituents, or attending to numerous other tasks. Members can reach the floor quickly, however, to respond to quorum calls, participate in debate, or vote.

The House chamber has two levels. Above the floor itself are the galleries for visitors, diplomats, the media, and other observers. Visitors sit on either side or facing the Speaker's rostrum; the press sits above and behind it. Unlike senators, representatives have no desks in the chamber. Their seats, which are unassigned, are arranged in semicircular rows in front of the Speaker. Aisles divide groups of seats, and a broad center aisle divides the majority and minority parties. Traditionally, the Democrats sit to the Speaker's right, the Republicans to the left. When a majority of the 435 members are present, for a recorded vote, for instance, the floor becomes alive with activity.

Normally, the House convenes daily at noon.[1] Buzzers ring in committee rooms, members' offices, and in the Capitol, summoning representatives to the floor. Rules and informal practices set the daily order of business: an opening prayer, approval of the *Journal* (a record of the previous day's proceedings), receipt of messages from the Senate or the president, one-minute speeches and insertions in the *Congressional Record*, and other routine business.

Under the rules, a majority of the House (218 members) must be present for business to be conducted. Whether or not a quorum has been established, it is assumed to be present unless officially discovered otherwise. A member may ask for a quorum call provided he or she is recognized for that purpose by the Speaker. Any member, however, may make a point of no quorum whenever a vote is pending. Informally, the House frequently operates with far fewer members.

The House usually is in session Monday through Friday. Mondays are reserved mainly for routine legislation. The workload on Fridays generally is light because many members want to return to their home districts on weekends. Most major proposals are taken up between Tuesday and Thursday.

The previous chapter outlined the normal procedure by which major legislation reported by standing committees is routed to the House floor through the Rules Committee, as well as certain legislative shortcuts to the floor, such as the Consent Calendar, Private Calendar, and suspension of the rules. This chapter will focus on major bills and the most common route by which they reach the House floor — via a "rule" granted by the Rules Committee. It will also examine basic floor procedures in the Committee of the Whole.

The basic steps in floor consideration of major bills are:

- adoption of the rule granted by the Rules Committee;
- the act of resolving the House into the Committee of the Whole;
- general debate;
- the amending process;
- final action by the full House.

Along the way we shall examine some of the strategies used by proponents of bills to secure passage of legislation and by opponents to defeat or modify bills, as well as examples of how the rules can be used to delay or expedite the proceedings.

Adoption of the 'Rule'

As was noted in Chapter 5, the first step in bringing a major bill to the floor is to adopt the special rule issued by the Rules Committee. A rule, or special order, sets the conditions under which the measure is to be considered, decreeing whether floor amendments will be permitted and how much debate will be allowed.

Rules rarely are rejected by the House, although attempts occasionally are made to do so. Challenging the Rules Committee is an uninviting task; House members realize that at some future time they will need a rule from the committee for their own bills. Rejection of a rule usually reflects sharp divisions in the House; heavy lobbying by pressure groups, the president, or federal agency officials; or general agreement that the reporting committee did a poor job of drafting the bill.

Voting down a rule is a "procedural kill." Opponents of a controversial 1974 committee reorganization proposal tried to defeat the plan by rejecting the special rule from the Rules Committee. They argued that "everybody against any part of . . . [the resolution] must stand together and vote against the rule." [2] The strategy was unsuccessful, but the example shows how

IV

House Calendar No. 31

98TH CONGRESS
1ST SESSION

H. RES. 201

[Report No. 98–204]

Providing for the consideration of the bill (H.R. 1398) to promote energy conservation by providing for daylight saving time on an expanded basis, and for other purposes.

IN THE HOUSE OF REPRESENTATIVES

MAY 18, 1983

Mr. WHEAT, from the Committee on Rules, reported the following resolution; which was referred to the House Calendar and ordered to be printed

RESOLUTION

Providing for the consideration of the bill (H.R. 1398) to promote energy conservation by providing for daylight saving time on an expanded basis, and for other purposes.

1   *Resolved,* That at any time after the adoption of this
2 resolution the Speaker may, pursuant to clause 1(b) of rule
3 XXIII, declare the House resolved into the Committee of the
4 Whole House on the State of the Union for the consideration
5 of the bill (H.R. 1398) to promote energy conservation by
6 providing for daylight saving time on an expanded basis, and
7 for other purposes, and the first reading of the bill shall be
1 dispensed with. After general debate, which shall be confined
2 to the bill and shall continue not to exceed one hour, to be
3 equally divided and controlled by the chairman and ranking
4 minority member of the Committee on Energy and Com-
5 merce, the bill shall be considered for amendment under the
6 five-minute rule. At the conclusion of the consideration of the
7 bill for amendment, the Committee shall rise and report the
8 bill to the House with such amendments as may have been
9 adopted, and the previous question shall be considered as or-
10 dered on the bill and amendments thereto to final passage
11 without intervening motion except one motion to recommit.

procedural matters can have a critical impact on the legislative process.

A typical rule from the Rules Committee is reproduced on page 127. This is an open rule for a bill dealing with daylight-saving time. The decision-making process it outlines is used in the House for most major bills.

After the House votes to adopt the rule, the Speaker declares the House resolved into the Committee of the Whole. Under most rules, there is an hour of general debate, after which the bill is open to amendment under the five-minute rule. In other instances, a rule may permit more debate, restrict amendments, waive points of order, or grant priority to committee or certain members' amendments. After all amendments are dealt with, the Committee of the Whole is directed to report the bill back to the House. There, after voting on any amendments reported (adopted) by the Committee of the Whole and on engrossment (printing the bill as revised by any changes made during floor consideration) and third reading (by title only), the House turns to a motion to recommit — returning the bill to the legislative committee that handled it, with or without instructions to revise the measure. Finally, the bill is voted on in its entirety. If the bill is passed, there also occurs an automatic *pro forma* motion to reconsider, which invariably is rejected ("laid on the table").

In the rule for the daylight-saving bill, the five principal procedural steps governing House consideration of major legislation are spelled out. These are:

- resolving the House into the Committee of the Whole;
- general debate;
- consideration of amendments under the five-minute rule;
- a recommittal motion;
- vote on final passage.

Roadblocks usually occur during the amending stage in the Committee of the Whole.

Committee of the Whole

The Committee of the Whole is simply the House in another form. Every legislator is a member. House rules require all revenue raising or appropriations bills to be considered first in the Committee of the Whole. Technically, there are two such bodies. One is the "Committee of the Whole House," which debates private bills. The other and more important is the "Committee of the Whole House on the State of the Union," commonly shortened to Committee of the Whole, which considers public measures. (Further references to the Committee of the Whole in this chapter are to its meaning as the Committee of the Whole on the State of the Union.)

The rules used in the Committee of the Whole are designed to speed up floor action. Four rules or customs distinguish the conduct of business in the Committee of the Whole from proceedings in the full House.

First, a quorum is only 100 members in the Committee of the Whole (218 constitute a quorum in the House). Second, the Speaker does not preside over the Committee of the Whole but appoints a colleague, who is a member of his own party, to chair it. Third, it is in order to close or limit debate on sections of the bill by unanimous consent or majority vote of the members present. The "previous question" motion is not permitted in the Committee of the Whole. Finally, amendments to bills are introduced and debated under the five-minute rule (discussed in this chapter on pages 132-134 in connection with the amending process) rather than under the hour rule.[3]

From the beginning, the House has observed the English precedent: The Speaker does not chair the Committee of the Whole. Instead, he selects a majority party member to preside. His role is to keep order, recognize members, and rule on points of order. The Speaker is permitted to remain in the chamber and take part in debate, but he rarely participates except to make closing remarks on closely contested major bills. By tradition, the Speaker seldom votes, except to break a tie.

Visitors in the gallery can tell whether the House is in the Committee of the Whole by noting the position of the mace, a 46-inch column of ebony rods bound together by silver and topped by a silver eagle. The mace, symbol of the Sergeant at Arms' authority, is carried by him, if called upon, to enforce order on the floor. It rests on a pedestal on a table at the right of the Speaker's podium. It is taken down from the table when the Speaker hands the gavel to the chairman of the Committee of the Whole. When the committee rises and the Speaker resumes the chair, the mace is returned to its place.[4]

General Debate

The first order of business in the Committee of the Whole is general debate on the entire bill under consideration.[5] One hour of debate usually is allowed, equally divided between the minority and majority parties. In the rule on the daylight-saving bill, one hour was authorized; for very complex legislation, as many as 10 hours may be scheduled.

Each party has a floor manager from the committee of original jurisdiction who controls time, allotting segments to supporters or opponents, as the case may be. Almost without exception, the floor manager for the majority party is the spokesman for the bill. Sometimes both sides favor passage of a bill, and both floor managers rise in support. During debate on controversial legislation, both floor managers may declare their support for the bill's aims, but reflect differences of opinion on specific parts. They also, by custom, allocate time to opponents of the bill.

The term "general debate" can be misleading, as most members deliver set speeches and engage in a minimum of give-and-take. Because committees and subcommittees shape the fundamental character of most legislation, only a limited number of representatives actually participate in debate, and those who do usually are members of the committee that drafted the legislation. Yet general debate has an intrinsic value that is recognized by most House members and experts on the legislative process.

Purposes of General Debate

General debate is both symbolic and practical. It assures both legislators and the public that the House makes its decisions in a democratic fashion, with due respect for majority and minority opinion. General debate forces members to come to grips with the issues at hand; difficult and controversial sections of the bill are explained; constituents and interest groups are alerted to a measure's purpose through press coverage of the debate; member sentiment can be assessed by the floor leaders; a public record, or legislative history, for administrative agencies and the courts is built, revealing the intentions of proponents and opponents alike; legislators may take positions for reelection purposes; and, occasionally, fence-sitters may be influenced.

Not all legislators agree on the last point. Some doubt that debate can really change views or affect the outcome of a vote. But debate, especially by party leaders just before a key vote, can change opinion. "Some votes are always changed by debate," Majority Leader Jim Wright, D-Texas, has written.[6] Those who tell you "that debate is worthless are just cynical," former New York Rep. Bella S. Abzug, D (1971-77), has said.[7] Certainly the remarks of influential members can sway votes. Speaker Sam Rayburn's "entire speech [on a bill] took only 44 words," a member once recounted, "but it turned the tide." [8] Who speaks is sometimes more important than what is said.

In sum, reasoned deliberation is important in decision making. Lawmaking consists of more than log rolling, compromises, or power plays. General debate enables members to gain a better understanding of complex issues, and it may influence the collective decisions of the House. The dilemma members often face, explained Rep. Morris K. Udall, D-Ariz., "is to know what is right, and to make the right decisions" based upon skimpy, incomplete, or unavailable information.[9]

Floor Managers' Role

Longstanding customs govern much of the action on the floor. But the floor managers direct the course of debate on each bill. The manager for the majority side often is the chairman of the committee that reported the bill, or an appointed committee colleague. The ranking minority committee member, or an appointed surrogate, usually is the floor manager for the minority party. Many committees routinely name subcommittee chairmen to manage the bills reported from their subcommittees. The floor managers are centrally located during debate at long tables near the center of the chamber, with the main aisle separating the Democratic from the Republican side.

The floor managers guide their bills through final disposition by the House. Their duties are varied. They must:

● Plan strategy and parliamentary maneuvers to meet changing floor situations.

- Respond to points of order.
- Attempt to protect the bill from amendments the majority considers undesirable.
- Alert supporters to be on the floor to vote for or against closely contested amendments.
- Advise colleagues on the meaning and importance of the amendments.
- Judge when amendments of committee members should be offered or deferred.
- Inform party leaders of member sentiment and the mood of the House toward their bill.
- Control the time for general debate and, if necessary, act to limit debate on amendments, sections or titles of the bill, or on the entire measure.

The fate of much legislation depends on the skill of the floor managers. Mistakes can kill, delay, or weaken legislation before the House. For example, on May 19, 1977, the House suspended debate on a bill to revise the Hatch Act, which limits political activity by federal employees. The bill's floor manager inadvertently had permitted adoption of an amendment that, among other provisions, prohibited the use of union dues for any political purpose. The amendment passed, with substantial support from Democrats, who had overlooked the sweeping implications of the antiunion clause. After the vote, supporters of the bill realized the implications of the amendment and quickly withdrew the bill from further consideration. Three weeks later, after the Democratic leadership had circulated the word on the amendment, debate on the bill was reopened. The controversial clause was rescinded, and the Hatch Act revisions were approved.

Conversely, effective floor management increases the chances for smooth passage of legislation. The enactment of the landmark Congressional Budget and Impoundment Control Act of 1974 was credited in large part to its skillful floor manager, Rep. Richard W. Bolling, D-Mo. (1949-83).

Floor managers are given several advantages over their colleagues. They customarily lead off debate in the Committee of the Whole and have the first opportunity to appeal for support. During debate they receive priority recognition from the chair. A floor manager may take the floor at critical moments ahead of other legislators to defend or rebut attacks on the bill, or they may offer amendments to coalesce support for the measure. The floor manager also is entitled, by custom, to close the debate on an amendment, thus having the last chance to influence sentiment.

Floor managers generally can count on support from their party leadership. They also are permitted to have up to five of their committee's staff members on the floor during debate, ready to research rules and precedents, draft amendments, answer technical questions about the bill, or prepare statements. Finally, as a result of committee hearings, discussion, and markup, the managers have a reservoir of knowledge about the technical details of a measure and are in a good position to judge which amendments to accept and reject, and the best arguments to employ for or against them.

Delaying Tactics

Despite the generally tighter rules on debate in the House than in the Senate, there are many ways to prolong or delay proceedings. Members may raise numerous points of order, make scores of parliamentary inquiries, or offer trivial amendments. They may demand recorded votes on every amendment, ask unanimous consent to speak for additional minutes on each amendment, make certain that all time for general debate is used, or, if the chair declares their amendments nongermane, appeal the ruling and demand recorded votes on each appeal.

Until a 1971 rules change, a reading of the *Journal* was used as a delaying tactic. The reading could be dispensed with only by unanimous consent or by a motion to suspend the rules, requiring a two-thirds vote. Since then, the Speaker has been authorized to examine the *Journal*, although a vote may be demanded on its approval. Rules changes in 1974 and 1977 greatly reduced demands for quorum calls as a dilatory device.

The purpose of delaying tactics is to stall action on a measure in order to allow more time to gather support (if those using such tactics favor the bill) or to kill it (if they are opposed). Sometimes delay is intended to force action and at other times to prevent it. For example, on October 8-9, 1968, Republican members kept the House in continuous session for 32 hours by employing a variety of delaying tactics. The Republicans claimed they were trying to force the reluctant Democratic leadership to bring to the floor two stalled measures: a campaign spending control bill and a legislative reorganization proposal. Democrats said the Republicans were trying to prevent House consideration of a pending bill authorizing television debates between the two major 1968 presidential candidates. In the end, none of the three bills in question was passed by Congress.

The Amending Process

The amending process is the heart of decision making on the floor. Under an open rule, amendments determine the final shape of bills passed by the House. At times, amendments become more important or controversial than the bills themselves. A good example is the 1974 Jackson-Vanik amendment — named for its sponsors, Sen. Henry M. Jackson, D-Wash. (1953-83), and Rep. Charles A. Vanik, D-Ohio (1955-81). The amendment was tacked on to a trade act after prolonged controversy in each house. It limited trade with the Soviet Union until that country lifted its restrictions on Jewish emigration.

The Five-Minute Rule

House rules require all bills and joint resolutions to be "read" three times to give members every opportunity to become familiar with the measures they are considering. In practice, bills are not read word for word. Verbatim readings generally are dispensed with by unanimous consent, although a member may insist, as a delaying tactic, on a full reading of the title or section under consideration.

The first "reading" occurs when a measure is introduced and referred to committee. The bill is not read aloud; the bill's number and title are printed in the *Congressional Record*. The second reading occurs in the Committee of the Whole. The third occurs by title (the name of the bill only) just before the vote on final passage.

Bills are considered, or "read," as specified in the rule from the Rules Committee, usually section by section. The Rules Committee might specify a reading by title rather than by section, to permit larger, interrelated parts of the measure to be open to amendment.

At the end of general debate, a bill is "read" for amendment under the five-minute rule. Under this rule, "any Member shall be allowed five minutes to explain any amendment he may offer, after which the Member who shall first obtain the floor shall be allowed to speak five minutes in opposition to it, and there shall be no further debate thereon." [10]

Actual practice differs from the rule. Amendments are regularly debated for more than the 10 minutes allowed. Members gain the floor by offering *pro forma* amendments, moving "to strike the last word," or "to strike the requisite number of words." Technically, these also are amendments, although no alteration of the bill is contemplated by the sponsors; their purpose is to extend the debate. (*Pro forma* amendments are not in order under a "closed" rule.) In addition, members may ask unanimous consent to speak longer than five minutes, and may yield part of their time to other legislators. Debate on amendments cannot extend forever, however, since the floor manager can move that discussion be terminated at a specified time. Motions to close or limit debate seldom are rejected.

Amendments are in order as soon as the section to which they apply has been read, but they must be proposed before the clerk starts to read the next section. If the clerk has passed on to a succeeding section, a member must be granted unanimous consent to offer an amendment to the previous section. In addition to being timely, amendments must be germane to the bill and section under consideration. Reading by section or title helps structure rational consideration of complex bills, but on noncontroversial measures it is common for the floor manager to ask unanimous consent that the entire bill be considered as read. In that case, the entire measure is open to amendment at any point.

The reading stage can be used to delay or prolong proceedings. Any member can object to a unanimous consent request to dispense with the reading of sections, titles, or amendments. Opponents of a bill may draft lengthy amendments, not with the expectation that they will be adopted, but to cause delays by having them read in their entirety.

During floor debate on a bill to amend the Clean Air Act, Rep. Henry A. Waxman, D-Calif., objected repeatedly to requests that sections be considered as read, claiming that the reading was necessary "because the chairman of the subcommittee [that considered the bill] is not here right at the moment. . . ." [11] Such delaying tactics usually are sparingly employed, as they invite retribution by other members. "There is not anything we can do about prolonging the reading of the [Clean Air Act]," Rep. Gene Snyder, R-Ky., observed, "but when other big bills come up" requiring expeditious action, various legislators "can object to dispensing with the reading and can require that they be read." [12] Both the rules of the game and the expectation of retaliation in kind encourage moderation in the use of dilatory tactics.

Rationale for Amendments

Amendments serve diverse objectives. Some are offered in deference to pressure groups, executive branch officials, or constituents; others are designed to attract public notice, to stall the legislative process, to demonstrate concern for an issue, or to test sentiment for or against a bill. Some amendments are more technical than substantive; they may renumber sections of a bill or correct typographical errors. One common strategy is to load down a bill with so many objectionable amendments that it will sink of its on weight. Declared Majority Leader Wright to proponents of an amendment he strongly opposed: "If that is your goal, if you just want to find a cynical way to burden down the committee bill and make it unpassable, then you might want to vote for this [amendment]." [13] Committee members themselves may vote against a bill they originally reported if objectionable or "irresistible," but inappropriate, amendments are added on the floor.

Four types of amendments are worthy of special attention: committee amendments, "riders," substitutes, and "previously noticed" amendments.

Committee and Floor Amendments. House precedents grant priority to amendments recommended by the reporting committee(s). "Committee amendments to a pending section," these precedents state, "are normally considered prior to amendments offered from the floor." [14] This condition is another example of the parliamentary advantage accorded committees by House rules and precedents. Recall, for instance, that committees receive nearly every bill introduced in the House, influence the kind of "rule" their bills receive from the Rules Committee, and control general debate on the floor.

In the past, the House was inclined to defer to the committees' recommendations.[15] That may be changing. "When I came here ... [in 1965]," reflected Rep. Thomas S. Foley, D-Wash., "most of the Members would follow the committee. Now partly because of the [Vietnam] war and the breakdown of the legitimacy of leadership, the committee's 'aye' or 'nay' isn't enough." [16] There also are certain House committees whose legislation is regularly revised on the floor because of its controversial nature, sharp splits among the committee's members, or other factors.

Riders. Riders are amendments that are extraneous to the subject matter of the bill. They are more common in the Senate because House rules, in theory at least, require amendments to be germane or relevant to the bill itself. Any member can question the relevance of a proposed amendment by raising a point of order, on which the chair must rule. Such questions are not always raised, however. The rule from the Rules Committee may waive them, the amendments may be overlooked, or members may be in general agreement with the provision. "I don't make points of order on all [riders]," a member once observed, "because some may be necessary due to changing conditions."[17] In short, House rules are not self-enforcing.

Riders often encompass proposals that are less likely to become law on their own merits (as separate bills), either because of resistance in the Senate or the probability of a presidential veto. The strategy on such issues is to draft them as riders to important legislation — "must" bills that are almost certain to be enacted — such as appropriations measures funding the federal government or bills to raise the federal debt ceiling. If the House is tenacious enough in clinging to its rider, the chances are good that it will be accepted — grudgingly — by the Senate and the president.

Substitute Amendments. There are two kinds of substitutes: a "substitute amendment" and "an amendment in the nature of a substitute." The first type is an amendment that deals with *part* of a bill. When there is a proposal to change a section of a bill, a substitute amendment offers alternative language for that pending proposal. The second kind recommends new language for the *entire bill*. Amendments in the nature of substitutes have increased in importance in recent years, in part because of the complexity of contemporary issues and also because of the greater use of multiple referrals.

For example, committees that consider the same bill may report dissimilar versions of it. Sometimes, such differences are resolved through inter-committee cooperation. Members and staff from each panel might blend their products into a consensus bill that will be offered on the House floor as an amendment in the nature of a substitute for the bill as originally introduced. Usually, the Rules Committee will accommodate the committees, giving such an amendment special status by making it the vehicle for House debate and amendment rather than the original bill.

'Previously Noticed' Amendments. All amendments must be offered from the floor, but in the House there is no requirement that they be submitted in advance ("previously noticed") to all members. Most amendments are in printed form when they are offered, but they need not be distributed ahead of time for review by members or staff. However, the Legislative Reorganization Act of 1970 provided that amendments printed in the *Congressional Record* at least one day prior to their consideration in the Committee of the Whole are guaranteed 10 minutes of debate time, regardless of any House agreements to end debate on the bill. The objective is to prevent arbitrary closing of debate when important amendments are pending, but the rule can be used also as a stalling device. For example, a member once sponsored 682 pre-noticed amendments to signal his dissatisfaction with an endangered species act. If each had been considered, more than two weeks of the House's time would have been consumed. On another occasion, members who opposed a military draft registration measure introduced pre-noticed amendments to require coal-fired attack submarines, solar-powered cruise missiles, and transcendental meditation courses for armed forces personnel. And Rep. James Weaver, D-Ore., engaged in a one-man delaying action against legislation he opposed by offering numerous pre-noticed amendments. "It was a filibuster, plain and simple," he said.[18]

Degrees of Amendments

A basic parliamentary principle permits only two degrees of amendments: an amendment and the amendment to it. Any further motion to amend is a third-degree proposal (an amendment to an amendment to an amendment) and is out of order. "The line must be drawn somewhere," Thomas Jefferson wrote, "and usage has drawn it after the amendment to the amendment." [19]

When a bill is open to revision in the House, typically only four forms of amendments are pending simultaneously. The four forms are:

- an amendment to the bill itself;
- an amendment to the first amendment;
- a substitute amendment;
- an amendment to the substitute amendment.

Once an amendment to a bill has been offered (the first degree), either an amendment to that amendment (the second degree), or a substitute amendment (another first degree proposal under House rules) is in order.[20] Assuming that an amendment to the original amendment is offered, then members still may offer a substitute as well as an amendment to the substitute (second degree). A substitute amendment does not seek merely to modify the original first degree amendment but to substitute entirely new language for it. If a substitute is adopted, it in effect replaces the language of the original first degree proposal and the second degree amendment to it, if one has been adopted.

The four amendments, with the degrees that are permissible and the order of voting on each, are shown in the illustration on page 137.

The voting sequence reveals that second degree amendments are voted on first, and that the second degree amendment to the original amendment to the bill is voted on before the second degree amendment to the substitute. After consideration of the second degree amendments, members then face a choice between two policy alternatives, with voting occurring first on the perfected substitute and then on the perfected original amendment. (Perfected amendments in this context are amendments that themselves have been amended by the second degree proposals.) The final vote occurs on the original amendment as modified by any of the subsequent amendments.

Strategically, the amendment procedure can be critical to policy formulation. Either side of an issue may be aided by the voting sequence: whether the amendment — a policy alternative — is voted upon first or last. During House consideration of a nuclear freeze proposal in 1983, the proponents wanted the House to vote first on their policy recommendation. As a result, they waited for opponents to offer a first-degree amendment before they countered with a second-degree amendment to their liking. This

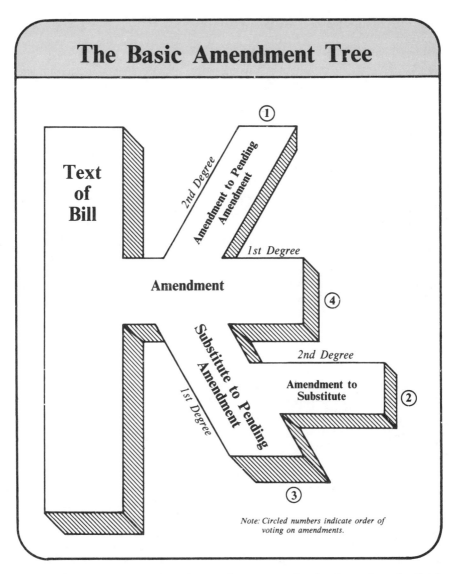

The Basic Amendment Tree

Text of Bill

① 2nd Degree — Amendment to Pending Amendment

1st Degree

Amendment

④

2nd Degree

Amendment to Substitute ②

① 1st Degree — Substitute to Pending Amendment

③

Note: Circled numbers indicate order of voting on amendments.

approach gave backers of the freeze the opportunity "to formulate the final version of any amendment." [21] The first vote, therefore, was on the freeze backers' alternative amendment to the opponents' amendment revising the text of the freeze resolution.

Maneuvering for Advantage: Common Tactics

Proponents and opponents of bills constantly seek to advance their policy objectives through the amending process. Skillful use of various motions, dilatory tactics, or shrewd drafting of the wording of amendments can influence which side carries the day. Customarily, the minority party has self-appointed "floor watchdogs" who seek to protect party interests and stymie majority steamrollers by raising points of order or making parliamentary inquiries. Timing, too, is all important to the success of many floor maneuvers, especially preferential motions and amendments to "sweeten" bills.

'Strike the Enacting Clause.' Certain motions from the floor take preference over other House business. One is the motion to "strike the enacting clause." This clause is the opening phrase of every House and Senate bill and makes it an operative law once the bill is approved by Congress and signed by the president: "Be it enacted by the Senate and House of Representatives of the United States of America in Congress assembled, . . ." Under House rules, approval of a motion to strike the enacting clause is equivalent to rejecting the measure. A motion to strike the clause is in order at any time during the amending process. It is a privileged motion that must be disposed of before the House takes up any further business on the bill. The motion is in order only once, unless the bill is materially changed by adoption of major amendments, an interpretation made by the chair if a point of order is raised against a second motion to strike.

A motion to strike the enacting clause may cause considerable excitement in the chamber, and it may be used for psychological purposes either by opponents or proponents of a measure.[22] In 1974, for example, Representative Bolling, floor manager of the bitterly contested House committee reorganization bill, surprised foes of the plan by inviting them to offer a motion to strike the enacting clause. Bolling's plan was to defeat such a motion so resoundingly that it would be clear to all members that the so-called committee reform was going to be considered in its entirety and adopted by the House.

Bolling gained an immediate psychological advantage when Rep. Joe D. Waggonner, D-La., (1961-79), one of the opposition leaders, observed that his side did not have the votes to pass the motion. It might be made, he said, "at a point in time when we think there is a chance for it to succeed." Ironically, a supporter of committee reorganization, disappointed by the course of the debate on the floor, later offered a motion to strike. It was turned down overwhelmingly because most members did not want the measure abruptly killed.

'Sweeteners.' Measures considered unpalatable can be made more acceptable, or "sweetened," by proposing changes to attract broader support. These might include amendments granting members more staff or additional office allowances, or "pork barrel" provisions providing for construction of dams, highways, port facilities, airports, and the like, in various congressional districts. In 1974 many Republican legislators were won over to a compromise committee reorganization scheme by an amendment granting a staff aide to each ranking minority member of a subcommittee. "I recognize a pot sweetener when I see one," declared Bolling, who opposed the amendment. It nevertheless was adopted, 218-180, with the support of 63 GOP members.[23]

Pot-sweetening is the opposite of a technique mentioned earlier, loading down a bill with enough unattractive amendments to kill it. There also are amendments that political scientists call "saving" and "killer" amendments. The first is essentially a compromise amendment that, if adopted, enhances prospects for the measure's enactment. The second type deliberately strengthens a bill too much and turns a majority against the legislation.[24] Adoption of an amendment to include primaries in a congressional public financing bill, for example, is almost certain to kill the legislation because many House incumbents, particularly those from safe and one-party districts, would oppose any measure that aided party challengers.

Importance of the Amending Process

Attempts are almost always made to amend controversial bills when they are considered in the Committee of the Whole. The amending process is a critical stage for any bill and, as has been seen, quite complex. Some of the main features of the process are noted below:

• Amendments in the Committee of the Whole usually are offered section-by-section under the five-minute rule.

• All amendments must be offered from the floor and are nearly always in written form.

• Amendments may not be repetitious. When an amendment is rejected, a member may not offer exactly the same proposal later.

• Any amendment may be challenged on a point of order before debate on the amendment has begun.

• Committee amendments are considered before those introduced on the floor by members.

• *Pro forma* amendments enable members to discuss the legislation under consideration for five minutes, even though no change in the bill actually is intended.

• Amendments must be germane to the subject under consideration. Occasionally, nongermane amendments may slip by, either because members generally are agreed on their intent or because the Rules Committee has barred points of order against them.

Voting in Committee of the Whole

Until 1971 there were three methods of voting in the Committee of the Whole: voice, standing (division), and teller. *Voice* voting is based on the volume of sound of members responding yea or nay. If the chair is in doubt about the result, or if any member requests it, a *standing* vote may be held. First those in favor and then those opposed are asked to stand while a head count is taken.

Any member dissatisfied with the result as announced by the chair may say, "Mr. Chairman, I demand tellers." To hold a *teller* vote, the member's demand has to be supported by one-fifth of a quorum (20 members). If that requirement is met, the chair then appoints members, usually one from each side of the question, to act as tellers (vote counters). Members file up the center aisle toward the rear of the House — the yeas first, followed by the nays — between the two tellers, who count them. Tellers then report their results to the chair, for example: "200 for and 100 against."

None of these three methods provides a public record of who voted, how they voted, or even whether they voted. Often crucial amendments were adopted in the Committee of the Whole before 1971 without recorded votes. Traditional arguments for this procedure were that it facilitated compromise and permitted members to vote the national interest against regional or local interests. Secrecy was not absolute since reporters often monitored the voting, but newsmen found it difficult to identify members whose backs were turned as they passed between the two tellers.

Many members, nonetheless, supported the addition of recorded teller voting in the Committee of the Whole. Secret voting, they argued, had enabled legislators to duck issues or vote contrary to publicly stated positions. Constituents could not trace their representatives' voting records and hold them accountable. "A member can vote for any number of amendments which may cripple a water pollution bill or render ineffective a civil rights bill or fail to provide adequate funding for hospital construction or programs for the elderly," Rep. David R. Obey, D-Wis., had noted, "and then he can turn around on final passage and vote for the bill he has just voted to emasculate by amendment." [25] (Unlike voting in the Committee of the Whole, votes on passage of major bills usually were recorded.)

Change to Recorded Teller Votes

Frustration with secret voting in the Committee of the Whole mounted in the late 1960s. Some members felt they were coming under increasing pressure from committee chairmen and party leaders to vote the party's position, whereas with recorded voting they could argue that their reelection depended on voting as their constituents wished. In 1970 the movement for instituting *recorded teller* votes succeeded.

Members of the Democratic Study Group (DSG), the largest *ad hoc* group in the House with about 235 moderate and liberal members by the late 1970s, were the driving force in the campaign to revise the teller voting procedure. Attendance by members of the DSG during Committee of the Whole proceedings had been poor. The DSG reasoned that if votes were recorded publicly attendance would improve markedly since excessive absences could be used against legislators in future reelection campaigns.

To avoid a partisan label, the DSG joined forces with reform-minded Republicans and developed a bipartisan package of amendments to a proposed legislative reorganization act. The coalition developed an anti-secrecy strategy to build public support for allowing teller votes to be recorded. Thousands of letters were mailed to newspaper editors. Editorials soon began appearing across the nation in support of recorded teller voting. Public attention helped persuade formerly hostile members to support the change.

The campaign was helped — perhaps inadvertently — by the activities of "gallery spotters," observers, often members of Vietnam antiwar groups in the late 1960s, who sat in the visitors' gallery trying to recognize and record members as they walked up the center aisle to cast their teller votes on war-related issues. The information was shared with newsmen and others. Sometimes the spotters made mistakes, provoking protests from members who were identified in news reports as voting one way when they had actually voted another. Through a confluence of factors — public pressure, members' dissatisfaction with the spotting system, and bipartisan backing — an amendment was added to the Legislative Reorganization Act of 1970 permitting votes to be recorded in the Committee of the Whole.

Recorded teller voting compelled members to take public stands on controversial issues. Under the new procedure, which took effect at the beginning of the 1971 session, members had to sign and deposit green or red cards, signifying yea or nay, in ballot boxes in full view of the House and the galleries. That simple procedure was thought by many observers to have changed the outcome almost immediately on many controversial issues, including a bill providing for federal financing of a commercial supersonic transport (SST). For months before the vote on the plane, environmental groups had been generating strong opposition to the SST, and public opinion appeared to be swinging to their position. In Congress, however, sentiment seemingly leaned toward approval of the plane. Then, on March 18, 1971, Rep. Sidney R. Yates, D-Ill., stood and said, "Mr. Chairman, I demand tellers with clerks" (now called a recorded vote by clerks). Knowing that their votes would be recorded in the *Congressional Record* and widely publicized, members voted 217-204 to cut off funds for the proposed SST.

Electronic Voting. Electronic voting, also authorized by the 1970 Legislative Reorganization Act, began in 1973, largely superseding the recorded teller voting procedure. Members insert a personalized card about the size of a credit card into one of the more than 40 voting stations located on the House floor, and press one of three buttons: Yea, Nay, or Present. Each member's vote is displayed on panels above the Speaker's desk and also on the walls of the House behind the press gallery. The system also is used to establish quorums. If electronic voting malfunctions, traditional methods are used.

New Recorded Vote Requirement. Beginning in 1979, the number of members needed to obtain a recorded vote in the Committee of the Whole was increased to one-fourth of a quorum (25) instead of one-fifth. (The one-fifth requirement was kept for recorded votes during non-Committee of the Whole sessions of the House.)

The following chart shows the impact that recorded teller votes and the electronic voting procedure has had on House voting since 1971.

Year	Number of House Recorded Votes	Year	Number of House Recorded Votes
1970	266	1976	661
1971 (Recorded teller voting first used)	320	1977	706
		1978	834
1972	329	1979	672
1973 (Electronic voting first used)	541	1980	604
1974	537	1981	353
1975	612	1982	459

The increase in the number of recorded votes caused scheduling conflicts and kept legislators running from committee meetings to the House floor to cast their votes. Many members complained that too many recorded votes were being taken on frivolous or unnecessary amendments.

In recent years there has been a downward trend in the number of recorded votes. This development reflects such factors as greater use of omnibus bills (combining separate measures into one big package) and divided control of Congress. Split party control no doubt has accentuated bicameral conflicts on policy priorities. The "paralysis of a divided Congress," has contributed to the slower pace of recent Congresses, according to Representative Udall.[26]

The voting changes placed additional pressures on the floor managers. Electronic voting cut balloting time in half, from about 30 minutes under the traditional roll-call method, to no less than 15 minutes. Further, recent changes in the rules have permitted the Speaker to postpone votes and schedule votes in clusters on matters such as passing bills or agreeing to suspension of the rules motions. The time allowed for each vote in this procedure may be reduced to five minutes by the Speaker.

Managers today have less time to coordinate floor activities during a vote. Members can enter the chamber through numerous doors, insert their cards and vote, and leave before the leadership has a chance to talk to them. As a result, both parties station monitors at all the doors to advise their colleagues when they enter and urge them to support the position of the floor manager or the party leadership.

From the floor managers' standpoint, there are advantages and disadvantages to the new system. Managers have computer display terminals that show a continuous and changing record of the progress of a vote. However, there is less time to evaluate opposition to proposals and line up votes. Thus, floor managers today must work harder to build support before bills reach the floor. On the other hand, problems such as the absence of a member or the unexpected switch on a vote by another can be spotted quickly on the computer consoles. Absent members can be summoned to the floor, and vote-switchers can be approached by persuasive members of the party.

Vote Switching. In 1976 the Speaker announced a new policy to minimize vote switching. Previously, members could change their vote until the Speaker announced the result.

> The rules were changed, however, and House members seeking to switch in the last five minutes of a vote must now wait until the end of a vote and walk to the well of the chamber. The Speaker then asks, "Are there any members in the chamber who wish to change their votes?" and the members' changes are announced by the clerk and [an explanation that they have switched] appear[s] in the *Congressional Record*. The rules change was intended to discourage switching and assist the leadership in counting noses.[27]

The only change the electronic voting machine will accept during the last five minutes is a switch from "present" to "aye" or "nay." On politically sensitive issues, to be sure, many members will hold off voting until the last minute or two to see whether their vote is needed to put their party's position over the top; if it is not, they may decide to vote the other way if it is politically more advantageous back home.

'Pairs' in Committee of the Whole. One other voting change is worth noting. On January 14, 1975, the House amended its rules to permit "pairs" in the Committee of the Whole. "Pairing" previously was limited to the House. Pairing is a voluntary arrangement between any two representatives on opposite sides of an issue. Wrote a noted House parliamentarian:

> A pair is essentially a "gentlemen's agreement," and the construction and interpretation of the terms, provisions, and conditions of a pair rests exclusively with the contracting Members. The rules do not specifically authorize them and the House does not interpret or construe them or consider questions or complaints arising out of their violation. Such questions must be determined by the interested Members themselves individually.[28]

Pairs are not counted in tabulating the final results of recorded votes.

Pairs take three forms:

● A *general* pair means that two members are listed without any indication as to how either might have voted.

● A *specific* pair indicates how the two absent legislators would have voted, one for and the other against.

● A *live* pair matches two members, one present and one absent.

In a live pair, the member in attendance casts a vote, but then withdraws it and votes "present," announcing that he or she has a live pair with a colleague and identifying how each would have voted on the issue. A live pair subtracts one vote, yea or nay, from the final tally and can influence the outcome of closely contested issues. Both parties have pair clerks to help arrange these informal agreements.

Factors in Voting

On any given day, legislators may be required to vote on measures ranging from foreign aid to abortion, from maritime subsidies to tax reform.

It is nearly impossible for a member to be fully informed on every issue before the House. Noted Rep. Dick Cheney, R-Wyo., "The sheer volume of votes is so great that there's no way you can weigh each and every issue." [29] As a result, many lawmakers rely on "cue-givers" for guidance on matters beyond their special competence. These may be committee or party leaders, members of the state congressional delegation, trusted colleagues, staff aides, or floor managers.[30] Party loyalty, constituency interests, and individual conscience are primary factors in determining a member's vote on any issue, but they are not the only factors. It is not unusual for members to vote for proposals they actually oppose in order to prevent enactment of something worse, or in the expectation that somewhere along the line the proposal will go down to defeat.

Some votes simply are cast in error. "With 500 votes or more each year in the House, I'm sure there are some times when I've met myself coming and going," said Rep. Abner J. Mikva, D-Ill. (1969-73, 1975-79).[31] Members, too, might vote one way on an authorization bill and another on the corresponding appropriations measure.

Other votes are carefully timed for impact. In 1977 the Democratic leadership attempted to defeat an amendment to repeal a 29 percent pay increase for members. The leaders "instructed congressmen who . . . found it politically impossible to support the $12,900 [annual] boost . . . to lay back and vote on it as late as possible so they wouldn't scare off others the leadership had convinced to vote for the raise." [32] During the first several minutes of the vote, there was substantial opposition to the repeal amendment, which created the needed "steamroller" effect to defeat the proposal. Later votes in support of the amendment were largely for public consumption. The reverse strategy applied during a suspense-filled vote on the 1982 tax increase. "We'll vote early to send a signal. The key is to push people onto the board in an early surge," said a House Democratic leader.[33]

Finally, the voting records of members can become a campaign issue. Representatives who miss numerous votes might find their congressional attendance record an issue during the next campaign. Moreover, many interest groups contribute campaign funds to legislators whose votes are in accord with the groups' views.

When voting on all amendments has been concluded, the Committee of the Whole "rises" (dissolves) and reports the bill back to the full House. The chairman of the Committee of the Whole hands the gavel back to the Speaker, who resumes his place at the podium. The mace is returned to its pedestal on the table next to the podium, and a quorum becomes 218 members (a majority of the House). As prescribed in the rule, there is a standard sequence of events that takes place prior to the vote on final passage of a bill.

Final Procedural Steps

After taking the chair, the Speaker announces that "under the rule, the previous question is ordered." This means that no further debate is permitted on the measure or on amendments, no amendments other than those reported by the Committee of the Whole may be considered, and previously adopted amendments are not subject to further amendment. Then, members, sitting as the House, consider the decisions taken in the Committee of the Whole. The Speaker asks all the members to identify amendments on which they want separate recorded ballots. The remaining amendments are decided *en bloc* by voice vote, after which the contested amendments are voted on individually. Except for motions to send a measure back to the reporting committee with instructions, only amendments adopted in the Committee of the Whole can now be considered. Separate recorded votes are not usually requested on amendments previously adopted in the Committee of the Whole unless the earlier votes were very close and the amendments highly controversial.

After all floor amendments are disposed of, there are two more steps before the final vote on passage. The first is *engrossment* and *third reading*. "The question is on engrossment and third reading of the bill," the Speaker declares. This is a *pro forma* question, which is approved automatically by unanimous consent. House rules provide that the bill be read by its title. (Before 1965 any legislator could demand that the bill be read in full, but the rules were changed to prevent this dilatory tactic.)

Engrossment is the preparation of a final and accurate version of the bill by an enrolling clerk for transmission to the Senate. This can be a complicated process, particularly if numerous amendments were adopted.

The second step is the *recommittal motion*, provided for in the rule from the Rules Committee. This is a privileged motion, protected and guaranteed by the rules, that gives the opponents one last chance to obtain a recorded vote on their own proposals. Recommittal is a motion to return the bill to the committee that reported it; it is always made by a member opposed to the bill. Customarily, the Speaker recognizes a member of the minority party, usually the senior minority committee member, and specifically asks if that member opposes the bill. Recommittal is in order only in the House, not in the Committee of the Whole. The motion may be a simple, or "straight," motion to recommit, or it may contain instructions to the reporting committee.

A simple motion to recommit the bill to committee, if adopted, in effect kills the bill, although technically it may be returned to the House floor later in the session. No debate is permitted on the simple recommittal motion.

Instructions in recommittal motions often embody amendments that were defeated in the Committee of the Whole. This is the only way amendments rejected earlier in the debate can be brought before the full House. Until 1970 no debate was permitted on a recommittal motion. The Legislative Reorganization Act of that year authorized 10 minutes of debate on recommittal motions with instructions. On occasion, a rule from the Rules Committee will authorize longer debate on recommittal motions with instructions.

Recommittal motions with instructions commonly provide that the committee report "forthwith." If the recommittal motion is adopted, the committee chairman immediately reports back to the House in conformity with the instructions, and the bill, as modified by the instructions, is automatically before the House again. The committee chairman states: "Mr. Speaker, pursuant to the instructions of the House on the motion to recommit, I report the bill, H.R. 1234, back to the House with an amendment." The House votes separately on this amendment, then again on the *pro forma* engrossment and third reading questions, and finally on passage of the bill.

Recommittal motions seldom are successful, but much depends on the size of the minority party in the House. Moreover, since recorded votes in the Committee of the Whole now permit the minority party to express its views openly on amendments, recommittal motions have become less important. On August 5, 1977, however, Rep. William A. Steiger, R-Wis. (1967-78), offered a recommittal motion to reject a tax on domestic crude oil — a key component of President Carter's national energy plan. The rule drafted by the Rules Committee prohibited a direct vote in the Committee of the Whole on whether such a tax should be imposed. Steiger's motion permitted a vote on an amendment to kill the tax. It was cleverly drafted to attract bipartisan support and almost carried the day, losing by only 203-219. It provided a forum for Republicans to put their views on record.

If the recommittal motion is rejected, the Speaker moves to the final vote on the whole bill. "The question is on the passage of the bill," he says.[34] Normally, final passage is by a recorded vote. If the outcome is obvious, and the members are anxious to be done with it, the measure may be passed by voice vote. When the result of the final vote has been announced, a *pro forma* motion to reconsider is made and laid on the table (postponed indefinitely) to prevent the bill from being reconsidered later. House rules state that a final vote is conclusive only if there has been an opportunity to reconsider it on the same or the succeeding day.

Summary

Although the House decision-making process may appear to be quite complex, it accommodates varied institutional interests and members' needs. There are numerous restraints on what legislators can and cannot do. Success often depends on one side gaining an advantage through use of the rules. Infinite variations are possible within the process, but basic House procedures are the same on almost all important bills:

- a "rule" reported by the Rules Committee;
- adoption of the rule by the House;
- consideration of the bill in the Committee of the Whole;
- general debate;
- consideration of amendments under the five-minute rule;
- recorded votes on major amendments;
- reporting the bill to the House once floor action is completed in the

Committee of the Whole;

● separate recorded votes, if requested, on any amendment adopted in the Committee of the Whole;

● a recommittal motion, with or without instructions;

● final passage vote.

The intensity of debate may vary; the complexity of the special "rule" may change; and a host of other factors may differ from issue to issue, but the pattern of decision making is the same regardless of the range or scope of the legislation.

After it is passed by the House, the bill moves to the Senate. There, the legislative process is quite different. If the House is characterized by devotion to rules and parliamentary procedures, the Senate is much more informal, often transacting its business by "gentlemen's agreements," with the rules ignored or set aside. Chapter 4 covered the introduction of a bill, referral, and committee action. The following chapter begins with a bill that has been reported by a Senate committee and discusses the scheduling procedure for moving a bill to the Senate floor.

Notes

1. During the 95th Congress, the House developed a regular system of scheduling floor sessions. This was done in response to the desires of members, committees, and party leaders. Members complained about problems in arranging their personal schedules and their inability to make firm commitments for meetings in their districts; committees wanted more time early in the session to work on legislation without being interrupted by floor meetings; and party leaders wished to better synchronize committee and floor action and utilize the time in session more effectively. As a result, the House by standing order varies its starting time: noon on Mondays and Tuesdays, 3 p.m. on Wednesdays, 11 a.m. on Thursdays and the balance of the week until May 15, when the convening time for Wednesdays through the balance of the week, including Saturdays if the House is in session, is advanced to 10 a.m. for the remainder of the session.

2. Roger H. Davidson and Walter J. Oleszek, *Congress against Itself* (Bloomington, Ind.: Indiana University Press, 1977), 193-194.

3. In the House sitting as the House, an hour is permitted for debate on amendments. "No member," the rule states, "shall occupy more than one hour in debate on any question in the House." Technically, then, all matters could be debated for 440 hours — one hour each for the 435 representatives, four delegates (from the District of Columbia, the Virgin Islands, American Samoa, and Guam), and one resident commissioner (from Puerto Rico). In practice, measures are debated for only one hour in total and then are voted on.

4. For a description of the seventeenth-century English origins of the Committee of the Whole, see DeAlva Stanwood Alexander, *History and Procedure of the House of Representatives* (Boston: Houghton Mifflin, 1916), 257-258.

5. Technically, the first order of business in the Committee of the Whole is the reading of the bill. This usually is dispensed with either by unanimous consent or by the terms of the "rule," which is the ordinary practice today.

6. Jim Wright, *You and Your Congressman* (New York: Coward-McCann, 1965), 153.

7. Bella S. Abzug, *Bella* (New York: Saturday Review Press, 1972), 11.
8. Wright, *You and Your Congressman,* 153.
9. U.S., Congress, House, *Congressional Record,* daily ed., May 24, 1983, H3257.
10. *Constitution, Jefferson's Manual and Rules of the House of Representatives,* 97th Cong., 2d sess., H. Doc. No. 97-271, 585-586.
11. U.S., Congress, House, *Congressional Record,* May 26, 1977, 16965.
12. Ibid., 16969.
13. U.S., Congress, House, *Congressional Record,* daily ed., May 25, 1982, H2824. The amendment was not adopted.
14. *Procedure in the U.S. House of Representatives,* 97th Cong., 4th ed. (Washington, D.C.: U.S. Government Printing Office, 1982), 526.
15. Randall B. Ripley, *Congress, Process and Policy* (New York: W. W. Norton, 1975), 116-118.
16. Michael J. Malbin, "House Democrats Are Playing With A Strong Leadership Lineup," *National Journal,* June 18, 1977, 946. See also John F. Bibby, ed., *Congress Off the Record* (Washington, D.C.: American Enterprise Institute for Public Policy Research, 1983), 23-24.
17. Richard F. Fenno, Jr., *The Power of the Purse* (Boston: Little, Brown, 1966), 74.
18. Andy Plattner, "Pacific Northwest Power Bill Cleared After House Breaks One-Man 'Filibuster,' " *Congressional Quarterly Weekly Report,* November 22, 1980, 3410. For the previous two examples, see *Washington Post,* August 15, 1979, A10, and June 20, 1978, A1.
19. *Constitution, Jefferson's Manual and Rules of the House of Representatives,* H. Doc. No. 97-271, 212.
20. When amendments in the nature of substitutes are offered first, it is possible to have as many as eight amendments pending simultaneously on the House floor. Seldom does this situation occur because confusion is all too often the result.
21. Pat Towell, "After 42 Hours of Debate: Nuclear Freeze Resolution Finally Wins House Approval," *Congressional Quarterly Weekly Report,* May 7, 1983, 869.
22. Customarily, the motion to strike also is used by members to obtain five more minutes of debate time.
23. Davidson and Oleszek, *Congress against Itself,* 239.
24. See James M. Enelow and David H. Koehler, "The Amendment in Legislative Strategy: Sophisticated Voting in the U.S. Congress," *Journal of Politics* (May 1980): 396-413; and James M. Enelow, "Saving Amendments, Killer Amendments, and an Expected Utility Theory of Sophisticated Voting," *Journal of Politics,* (November 1981): 1062-1089.
25. *Congressional Quarterly Weekly Report,* January 22, 1972, 153.
26. *Washington Post,* June 20, 1982, A4. See also Dale Tate, "Special Report: Governing by Omnibus," *Congressional Quarterly Weekly Report,* September 25, 1982, 2379-2383.
27. *New York Times,* September 22, 1982, A24.
28. *Cannon's Procedure in the House of Representatives,* H. Doc. No. 86-122, 233. Cannon further notes: "It is obviously impossible for all Members to be present at every roll call, and in cases of unavoidable absence the privilege of pairing is invaluable in preserving the rights of Members and the representation of constituencies." 231.
29. *New York Times,* June 29, 1983, A14.
30. On factors influencing votes, see, for example, John W. Kingdon, *Congressmen's Voting Decisions* (New York: Harper & Row, 1973); and Donald P. Matthews and James A. Stimson, *Yeas and Nays* (New York: John Wiley & Sons, 1975).

31. *Chicago Tribune,* April 4, 1976, 24.
32. *Washington Star,* June 30, 1977, D8.
33. *New York Times,* August 20, 1982, D14.
34. To summarize: There are several ways of voting in the House. These are: voice, standing (division), unrecorded teller, recorded vote by clerks, and electronic (recorded vote by electronic device). There are three ways to demand a recorded vote in the House that do not apply in the Committee of the Whole. First, a member may obtain a recorded vote if his request is supported by one-fifth of a quorum (44 members). Second, there is the constitutional yeas and nays (required in Article I, Section 5). Finally, House rules permit "automatic" recorded votes. A member who both objects and makes a point of order that a quorum is not present is automatically entitled to a recorded vote if the chair indicates that a quorum in fact is not present.

7

Scheduling Legislation in the Senate

The pace of activity on Capitol Hill places enormous demands on the time of legislators. Representatives and senators work long days, not only on the floor and in committee but also in meetings with executive branch officials, constituents, pressure groups, and the media. They also must stay in contact with the diplomatic community, party leaders, and state and local officials. It is not uncommon for a representative or senator to average 11 or more working hours a day while in Washington. To that must be added periodic trips home to attend important political functions or merely to "press the flesh" with constituents.

Of the two branches of Congress, it is probably in the Senate that legislators lead the more harried existence. There are fewer senators (100 compared with 435 House members), and in most cases senators represent a larger number of constituents. Senators are more in the public eye and are called upon more frequently to comment on national and international policy. The legislative and committee workload is as heavy in the Senate as in the House, but it must be carried out by fewer lawmakers. During the 97th Congress, the Senate was in session 2,156 hours; the House, 1,419 hours. The Senate averages an estimated 2,700 committee and subcommittee meetings a year and interviews more than 8,000 witnesses.[1]

The workload is heaviest for senators from the larger states, not only because of the greater number of constituents who need assistance, but also because of the multiplicity of political and economic interests in those states. "I don't see how senators from big states like New York and California, Illinois and Pennsylvania do it [all]," Majority Leader Mike Mansfield, D-Mont. (1953-77), once stated.[2] A typical schedule *(box, p. 152)* for Sen. George J. Mitchell, a Democrat from Maine, a medium-sized state, shows the varied and often conflicting demands that arise on any given day. As is true of all his colleagues, Senator Mitchell frequently is expected to be in two or more places at the same time. In such a situation, a senator must select the top priority event to attend in person, and delegate staff members to cover the rest or, as a last resort, rely on a fellow senator to fill him in on what took place.

Schedule for Sen. George J. Mitchell

(Tuesday, March 1, 1983)

8:15 A.M.   Breakfast with Sen. Jim Sasser, D-Tenn. — senators' dining room.

9:30 A.M.   Meeting with representatives from the Maine County Commissioners Association: Jean Bailey, head of the delegation; Robert Barter, Jim Gallagher and Rupert Stevens, Lincoln County; Jack Jordan and Eugene Churchill, Hancock County; Norm Ferguson, Leo McDonald and Albert Carey, Oxford County — Russell Senate Office Bldg.

12:00 Noon   Senate Democratic Conference luncheon.

2:00 P.M.   Meeting with Ken Clark and John O'Brien, Metal Trades Council, Portsmouth Shipyard. Social Security and federal employees.

3:00 P.M.   Meeting with Neil Michaud, Portland diocese director; Merton Bessey, director of finance for the diocese; Roy Green, coordinator for the diocese. Human relations.

3:30 P.M.   Meeting of Senate Finance Committee Democrats at Sen. Russell B. Long's, D-La., request, on President Ronald Reagan's nominations of Margaret M. Heckler and John A. Svahn.

3:30 P.M.   Senate Veterans' Committee hearing on Veterans Administration budget.

6:30 P.M.   Reception cosponsored by Senator Mitchell for environmental groups. Brief remarks at 6:30 p.m.

7:30 P.M.   Remarks at reception for state housing agencies, Hyatt Regency Hotel.

"It's absurd when you get a computer readout from your staff and it shows that you have four meetings at the same time," Sen. Alan K. Simpson, R-Wyo., once exclaimed. "And that happens more often than you would imagine."[3]

Flexible Scheduling System

In response to the manifold pressures on members, the Senate has evolved a highly flexible legislative scheduling system that responds to the individual member's, as well as to institutional, needs. The system bears little resemblance to what the formal rules specify and rests largely on usage and informal practice. Unlike House members, all senators have an opportunity to participate in scheduling legislation for floor action. Minor or noncontroversial bills are expedited to save time for major and controversial measures. Insofar as possible, action on important bills is scheduled to suit the convenience of members and to reduce to a minimum conflicts with legislative activity that takes place off the Senate floor. "The Senate operates largely on the basis of unanimous-consent agreements, comity, courtesy, and understanding," Democratic Leader Robert C. Byrd of West Virginia has noted.[4]

The Senate's system for classifying measures to be debated on the floor is simpler and more informal than the system used by the House. In contrast to the House with its five calendars, the Senate has only two: the *Calendar of General Orders* and the *Executive Calendar*. All legislation, major or minor, controversial or noncontroversial, is placed on the former; treaties and nominations under the Senate's "advice and consent" authority are placed on the latter.[5]

The Senate, by motion or unanimous consent, resolves into "executive session" to consider treaties or nominations. Within the course of a single day, the Senate may consider measures on both the Executive and General Orders calendars. It may go from executive session to legislative session before finishing the pending item on the Executive Calendar. It did this, for example, when it temporarily suspended debate on the Panama Canal treaties (executive session) in 1978 to take up an emergency farm bill (legislative session).

As discussed in Chapter 5, relatively noncontroversial legislation in the House comes up under the Consent Calendar, suspension of the rules, or the Private Calendar. Even specific days of the month are designated for consideration of such legislation. The Senate has no comparable procedure. Senate rules for calling up legislation — both major and minor — are cumbersome and consequently are generally ignored. One of these rules, for example, requires a daily calendar call, with the measures required to be brought up and debated in the order in which they appear on the calendar. Were the Senate to follow that rule, it would lose virtually all flexibility in processing its workload.

Noncontroversial Bills

Practically all noncontroversial measures are "called up by unanimous consent and enacted without debate," observes Democratic Leader Byrd. "In this regard, I have reference to private bills, most nominations on the Executive Calendar — which run into the thousands — and bills that are not of general interest." [6] The leaders and staff aides in both parties check with senators to clear minor or noncontroversial legislation before such measures reach the floor. A single dissent will hold up floor action until the roadblock is cleared away. But once cleared, minor and noncontroversial bills generally take only several seconds or a few minutes to pass. "Locomotive velocity may develop at this point, as bills come up and pass through with no objection," Byrd explains.[7] The box on page 155 illustrates how noncontroversial legislation typically is handled in the Senate.

The Senate's small size, flexibility, and tradition of cooperation means that the majority and minority leaders frequently can schedule noncontroversial legislation on a daily basis. Through informal floor discussions or colloquies, each examines the calendar to be sure the noncontroversial bills have been cleared by interested senators on their side. The measures then are passed quickly by voice votes.

Minor and noncontroversial measures also may reach the Senate floor on a motion of any senator. However, the majority and minority leaders normally try to reach agreement in advance on the floor schedule and are likely to oppose action that will bring bills to the floor without prior clearance from them. For example, Sen. J. Bennett Johnston, D-La., indicated he wanted to bring a private bill to the floor during the final days of the 94th Congress. "I will be constrained to move to table [kill] any motion that has not been cleared with me," declared Senator Byrd, who at that time was the majority whip.[8] (Johnston never offered the motion to bring his bill to the floor.)

Major Legislation

Once major Senate bills are reported from committee there are two main avenues by which they may be brought to the floor: through unanimous consent or by motion. Before they get there, however, the legislation may be subject to the one-day rule, the three-day rule, or "holds."

One-day and Three-day Rules

The one-day rule states that bills and reports must lie over on the calendar for one *legislative* day before they are eligible for floor consideration. This rule is seldom enforced and commonly is waived by unanimous consent. To speed up action, the majority leader states, "I ask unanimous consent that [these bills] be considered as having been on the calendar 1 legislative day for the purpose of the rules of the Senate." [9] There rarely is an objection to the request.

The three-day rule requires that the printed committee reports accompanying the legislation be available to members for at least three *calendar* days before the measures are eligible for floor action. (Chapter 8 explains the difference between legislative and calendar days.) This rule, too, may be waived by unanimous consent or by joint motion of the majority and minority leaders. However, it is common for the Senate to observe this rule.

Clearance of Noncontroversial Measures

Mr. [HOWARD H.] BAKER, [JR.], Mr. President, there are a number of items on the Calendar of General Orders that might be dealt with. I shall not propose to do all of them tonight, but let me list a few that I hope the minority leader might be in a position to consider — not today, but perhaps tomorrow or the end of the week. I shall supply the minority leader with a copy of the list I am about to read from.

Mr. President, I especially hope this week to be able to deal, perhaps on a unanimous-consent basis or, in any event, under a brief time agreement, with the following bills:

Calendar No. 101, S. 1195. Inter-American Development Bank, from the Committee on Foreign Relations;

Calendar No. 102, S. 923, Pretrial Services, from the Judiciary Committee;

Calendar No. 103, S. 816, the so-called Pfizer antitrust bill, from the Judiciary Committee;

Calendar No. 139, S. 1205, Environmental Research and Development, from the Committee on Environment and Public Works;

Calandar No. 148, S. 1095, the Water Resources Planning Act, from the Committee on Environment and Public Works;

Calendar No. 156, S. 823, chemical Tris bill from the Judiciary Committee; and

Calendar No. 165, S. 255, the patent bill, from the Judiciary Committee.

Mr. President, I hope that the distinguished minority leader might consider whether clearance can be obtained on his side of the aisle to deal with these matters, either by unanimous consent or with a brief time limitation.

Mr. ROBERT C. BYRD. Mr. President, the Democratic policy staff, under my direction, is exploring the possibility of proceeding by unanimous consent with action on the bills that the distinguished Senator has named and, overnight, the staff will continue to do that. Perhaps by tomorrow, we can have at least some of them cleared. I hope so.

Mr. BAKER. Mr. President, I thank the minority leader. I am very grateful for that. As all Senators know, and the distinguished minority leader knows in particular, it is sometimes difficult to get clearances on both sides in time to do measures on a particular day in question. For instance, today, the distinguished chairman of the Committee on the Judiciary had hoped to clear a bill that has not yet been fully cleared. I hope now, from time to time, to be able to suggest bills that are cleared on our side that the minority might consider for unanimous-consent action and also to give Senators some advance notice of those matters that the leadership might proceed to consider.

Source: U.S., Congress, Senate, *Congressional Record,* June 16, 1981, S6320.

"I have never liked the 3-day rule," Senator Byrd once explained, because it can delay the scheduling of necessary legislation.[10]

'Holds'

Finally, any senator or group of senators may place "holds" on measures, treaties, or nominations. This is an informal practice, honored by the party leaders, that effectively delays Senate action on the legislation. In 1983 the bipartisan leadership agreed to restrict the use of holds on bills and nominations. Majority Leader Howard H. Baker, Jr., R-Tenn., and Minority Leader Byrd "agreed that senators placing holds in the future will be given the courtesy of being told when the legislation or appointment will come to the Senate floor." [11] In summary, holds no longer stay in effect indefinitely.

Unanimous Consent Requests

If the Senate strictly observed every rule, it would become mired in a bog of parliamentary complications. As a result, the Senate expedites its business by setting aside the rules with the unanimous consent of the members present. Any senator can object to a unanimous consent agreement, but this seldom occurs because all members may participate in formulating these agreements, and usually they concur in the need to keep legislation moving.

By longstanding tradition, the business of the Senate is "largely transacted through unanimous-consent agreements," Massachusetts Republican Sen. Henry Cabot Lodge said in 1913, and "not only the important unanimous-consent agreements which are reached often with much difficulty on large and generally contested measures, but constantly on all the small business of the Senate we depend on unanimous consent to enable us to transact the public business." [12] That statement holds true today. Once accepted, unanimous consent agreements are as binding on the Senate as any standing rule and may be set aside or modified only by unanimous consent.

There are two types of unanimous consent requests: simple and complex.

● Simple requests are made from the floor by any senator; these almost always deal with routine business or noncontroversial actions. They are made orally and normally are accepted without objection. For example, senators regularly ask permission for staff members to be present on the floor during a debate. Committees may not meet after the first two hours of a Senate session except by unanimous consent or unless special leave is obtained from the majority and minority leaders. Simple unanimous consent agreements also may rescind quorum calls, add senators as cosponsors of bills, insert material in the *Congressional Record,* or limit the length of time members have to be recorded on roll-call votes. Some Senate rules even contain built-in unanimous consent provisions. One of these requires the full reading of the *Journal* of the previous day's proceedings at the beginning of each session. The same rule permits the reading to be dispensed with by unanimous consent. Objections seldom are raised to such motions.

. ● Complex agreements usually set the guidelines for floor consideration of specific major bills. They are proposed orally — usually by the leadership — often after protracted negotiations among party leaders and key senators.[13] Once agreed to, they are formally recorded. Such agreements may establish the sequential order in which measures will be taken up, pinpoint the time when measures are to reach the floor, and set rules for debate, including time limitations and, frequently, a requirement that all amendments be germane to the bill under consideration.

Before 1975 most unanimous consent agreements were worked out openly during the floor debate on the bill. They were offered to extricate the Senate from a difficult or confusing parliamentary situation. Today, such agreements are regularly worked out in advance of floor debate and then approved by the Senate and transmitted in printed form to all senators.

An example of a unanimous consent agreement (also called a "time-limitation agreement") is shown on page 179. In addition to identifying the bills involved, such agreements indicate each bill's position (Order No.) in relation to all other measures on the General Orders Calendar.

The fundamental objective of unanimous consent agreements is to limit the time it takes to dispose of controversial issues in an institution noted for unlimited debate. These agreements, therefore, expedite action on legislation and structure floor deliberation. Typically, agreements impose time limitations on every debatable — and thus delaying — motion, including amendments and final passage, points of order, or appeals from the rulings of the presiding officer. These agreements, however, usually allow an unlimited number of amendments to be offered, thus permitting what GOP Whip Ted Stevens of Alaska once dubbed a "time agreement filibuster."

Other usual features of these agreements specify the senators who are to control the time for debate on the bill and all amendments, and provide that the time is to be controlled by senators on opposing sides of the issue. Common, too, is the requirement that amendments be germane. Senate rules do permit nongermane floor amendments, but unanimous consent agreements often prohibit them to prevent extraneous issues from being taken up. Some agreements also set the date and time for the vote on final passage of the measure.

The Track System

Another device used to move legislation to the floor is of relatively recent origin. The track system was instituted in the early 1970s by Majority Leader Mansfield, with the concurrence of the minority leadership and other senators. It permits the Senate to have several pieces of legislation pending on the floor simultaneously by designating specific periods during the day when each proposal will be considered. The system is particularly beneficial when there are many important bills awaiting floor action or when there is protracted floor conflict on a particular bill.

Before the initiation of the track system, legislative business came to an abrupt halt during filibusters. The "two-track system enables the Senate to circumvent that barrier," noted Democratic Whip Alan Cranston, Calif. The Senate "can now continue to work on all other legislation on one 'track' while a filibuster against a particular piece of legislation is . . . in progress on the other 'track.' " [14]

Use of the track system on certain legislation is implemented by the majority leadership after obtaining the unanimous consent of the Senate. For example, Majority Leader Baker informed the Senate in 1982 that he hoped "to gain unanimous consent" to use the double-track procedure "to take up the criminal code bill or the nuclear waste bill." [15] He was not successful in that instance, however.

The use of unanimous consent agreements and the track system impose a measure of discipline on the Senate. Formerly, senators could arrive in the midst of a debate on a banking bill, for example, obtain recognition from the chair, and launch into a lengthy discussion of the wheat harvest prospects. Today, complex agreements and the track system prevent that from happening. Now, senators generally know what measure will be considered on a specific day and at what time, when they are scheduled to speak on that bill, and how long they will have the floor.

Scheduling Procedures Compared

As is probably clear to the reader by now, the Senate has nothing that compares with the scheduling function of the House Rules Committee.[16] That panel, as described in Chapter 5, regulates the flow of major bills to the floor, specifies the time for general debate, stipulates whether amendments can be offered, and decides if points of order are to be waived. The legislative route in the House is clearly marked by firm rules and precedents, but that is not so in the Senate. "Rules are never observed in this body," one president pro tempore once observed, "they are only made to be broken." [17]

Nonetheless, unanimous consent agreements and the special rules drafted by the Rules Committee are similar in several respects. Each waives the rules of the respective chamber to permit timely consideration of important measures and amendments. Each must be approved by the members of the chamber — in the Senate by unanimous consent of senators present on the floor and in the House by majority vote of the representatives. Each effectively sets the conditions for debate on the legislation in question and on all proposed amendments. And rules and unanimous consent agreements are formulated with the involvement of party leaders, although such participation in the House is generally limited to the majority party leaders. And the House leadership generally plays a significant part only for rules on particularly crucial or controversial measures.

Among the more important differences between rules and unanimous consent agreements are that rules are drafted in public session by a standing committee, while unanimous consent agreements usually are negotiated privately by senators and staff aides. Measures given a rule in the House

Table 7-1   Comparison of House Rules and Senate Unanimous
Consent Agreements

House *Special Rule*	*Senate* *Unanimous Consent Agreement*
Specifies time for general debate.	Specifies time for debating the bill and amendments offered to the bill.
Permits or prohibits amendments.	Usually restricts the offering of nongermane amendments only.
Formulated by Rules Committee in public session.	Formulated by party leaders informally in private sessions; occasionally on the Senate floor.
Approved by majority vote of the House.	Agreed to by unanimous consent of senators present on the floor.
Adoption generally results in immediate floor action on the bill.	Adoption geared more to prospective floor action.
Covers more aspects of floor procedure.	Geared primarily to debate restrictions on amendments and final passsge.
Does not specify date and exact time for vote on final passage.	May set date and exact time for vote on final passage.
Effect is to waive House rules.	Effect is to waive Senate rules.

commonly are taken up almost immediately, but unanimous consent agreements generally involve prospective action on bills.

The amendment process in each house also makes for important differences. Rules from the Rules Committee may limit the number of permissible amendments or prohibit them altogether. Senate unanimous consent agreements, except those prohibiting nongermane amendments, do not usually limit or forbid floor amendments. Interestingly, Senate practices regard an amendment as germane if it is specifically enumerated in the unanimous consent agreement, even if it really is not germane at all. Of course, all senators must be willing to waive the germaneness rule when the agreement is drawn up.

Finally, a special House rule specifies almost every significant floor procedure that will affect consideration of the bill. Complex agreements focus on two points in particular: 1) setting limits on the debate time to be allowed for amendments, motions, points of order and appeals from the rulings of the chair; and 2) setting limits on debate on final passage of the bill. In general, procedural experimentation is easier to accomplish in the smaller Senate than in the 435-member House. Table 7-1 *(above)* briefly summarizes the principal characteristics of rules drafted by the Rules Committee and Senate unanimous consent agreements.

Table 7-2 Trends in the Use of Complex Unanimous Consent Agreements, 1950-1977

	1950	1955	1959	1965	1970	1975	1976	1977
Number of agreements	40	20	20	41	50	66	54	67
Number of measures affected	29	9	14	25	24	62	53	63
Number of days in session	203	105	140	177	208	178	142	170
Average number of lines per agreement	11.4	7.5	7.7	10.0	10.0	17.1	17.2	16.9

Source: Data compiled by Robert Keith of the Congressional Research Service from the Senate Calendar of Business and made available to the author.

Senate Leadership and Unanimous Consent

Complex unanimous consent agreements are formulated through informal negotiations between party leaders and interested senators. Bargains or informal understandings sometimes are struck on the Senate floor to win approval of unanimous consent agreements. An example of the intricate negotiations that sometimes are necessary appears on page 166.

The job of the leadership is to ensure that the interests of all senators are protected, a difficult assignment given the heightened individualism and openness of the contemporary Senate. One scholar has written: "Because the system of unanimous consent would collapse if even one senator were habitually mistreated, Senate leaders strive to identify those senators interested in a given measure and to give them ample opportunity to express their interest." [18]

If members were ever to lose confidence in the unanimous consent procedure, the Senate would be in danger of reverting to hidebound observance of cumbersome rules. It would almost certainly lose the informality and flexibility that sets it apart from the more rules-conscious House. Informal norms such as courtesy and fairness to all senators buttress trust in the wide use of unanimous consent agreements. The party leaders who negotiate complex unanimous consent agreements hold the key to the continued smooth operation of the Senate.

Two recent majority leaders — Democrats Mike Mansfield, who held the post longer than any other senator (1961-1977), and Robert C. Byrd (1977-81) — are largely responsible for refining and extending the use of unanimous consent agreements. Each had his own style. Mansfield was a mild-mannered leader who viewed himself as only "one among my peers." Byrd was an activist, who worked diligently to control all procedural phases of floor action. The two approached negotiations on consent agreements in differing fashion, but each was successful in achieving agreements, even in the face of fierce opposition to particular bills. Table 7-2 indicates that complex unanimous consent agreements were used more frequently during the 1970s than in earlier years. They also became more complicated during this period and governed floor action on a larger number of measures.

During Howard Baker's tenure as majority leader (1981-85), he, too, relied heavily on unanimous consent agreements to schedule legislation. Three considerations affecting their use during this period are worth noting, however. First, there were fewer major bills subject to such agreements, reflecting, in part, the public mood against the launching of new federal domestic programs. Further, the Republican-controlled committees generally opposed reporting new legislative initiatives.

Second, 1981 began the expanded use of the budget reconciliation procedure *(see Chapter 3)*. Numerous pieces of legislation that previously would have been brought up independently under unanimous consent agreements were incorporated in an omnibus reconciliation bill. It is interesting to note that the Senate's procedure for considering reconciliation

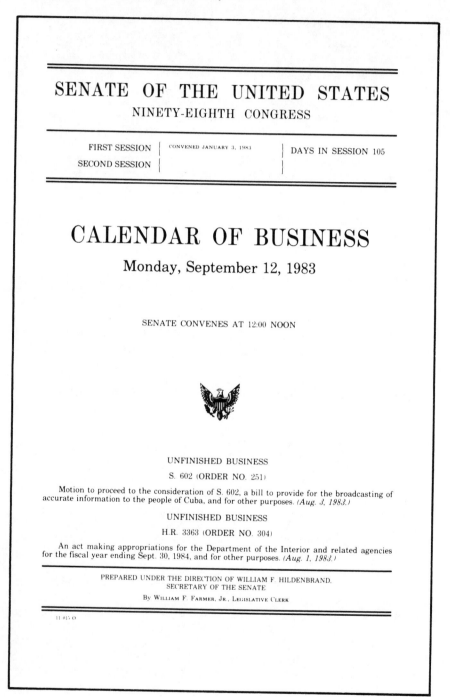

SENATE OF THE UNITED STATES
NINETY-EIGHTH CONGRESS

| FIRST SESSION | CONVENED JANUARY 3, 1983 | DAYS IN SESSION 105 |
| SECOND SESSION | | |

CALENDAR OF BUSINESS
Monday, September 12, 1983

SENATE CONVENES AT 12:00 NOON

UNFINISHED BUSINESS

S. 602 (ORDER NO. 251)

Motion to proceed to the consideration of S. 602, a bill to provide for the broadcasting of accurate information to the people of Cuba, and for other purposes. *(Aug. 3, 1983.)*

UNFINISHED BUSINESS

H.R. 3363 (ORDER NO. 304)

An act making appropriations for the Department of the Interior and related agencies for the fiscal year ending Sept. 30, 1984, and for other purposes. *(Aug. 1, 1983.)*

PREPARED UNDER THE DIRECTION OF WILLIAM F. HILDENBRAND,
SECRETARY OF THE SENATE

By WILLIAM F. FARMER, JR., LEGISLATIVE CLERK

11-015-O

bills (incorporated in the 1974 budget act) is modeled after a standard unanimous consent agreement. A consent-like procedure, reconciliation was used to avoid the need to obtain agreements on a bill-by-bill basis.

Third, Senator Baker, especially during the early part of his leadership, brought measures to the floor without first obtaining comprehensive agreements. In many cases this was because he was unable to attract the unanimous approval of the Senate. With the Senate and White House in GOP hands, the Democrats were reluctant to enter into broad agreements restricting their floor options since they had no idea what amendments might surface. Thus, narrower agreements often were negotiated on the floor, typically regulating the consideration of a particular amendment or series of amendments.[19]

The majority leader generally has an important ally in the minority leader. In contrast to the House, where scheduling is the sole prerogative of the majority leadership, Senate scheduling traditionally has been a bipartisan effort. The Senate system involves not merely a question of equity, but of necessity, because Senate rules confer on each individual member formidable power to frustrate the legislative process, including the right to object to any unanimous consent request. The late Sen. James B. Allen, D-Ala. (1969-78), once dubbed a "one-man wrecking crew" in the press, frequently employed his mastery of Senate rules to stymie the leadership's wishes.

The majority and minority leaders constantly consult with one another and with their top assistants, other senators, party colleagues, and key staff members on legislative scheduling. They also seek scheduling advice from committee leaders and "others who are going to manage the particular bills" on the floor.[20]

Outside groups also lobby party leaders to bring favored legislation to the floor. We mounted a "widespread campaign to write [Majority Leader] Baker, urging him to bring the [antiunion] matter to the floor," said the director of the National Right to Work Committee.[21] Or a few senators might threaten to vote against so-called "must" legislation unless proposals of great interest to them are scheduled for Senate consideration. In 1982, for instance, 36 senators

> sent a letter to Majority Leader Howard H. Baker, Jr., ... asking that the [balanced budget constitutional amendment] be brought to a vote immediately before the legislation to increase the debt ceiling limit. Many Republicans ... have threatened to vote against the debt ceiling measure unless they can vote first for the amendment.[22]

Baker successfully urged the Senate to first pass the debt measure "in order to provide for the orderly functioning of the Government." But he also told the Senate that it was his "intention after we return [from a July 4 recess] to turn to the consideration of a constitutional amendment dealing with a balanced budget." [23]

In short, scheduling involves numerous considerations. Party leaders must balance their interest in planning the Senate's business on a daily, weekly, and annual basis with 1) the needs of committees, which require concentrated periods of time, particularly early in the session, to process legislation assigned to them, and 2) the needs of senators, who prefer some degree of predictability and certainty in the legislative agenda so they can schedule their time most efficiently. This often means that no matter how carefully Senate leaders plan the legislative agenda — the times and dates measures will be scheduled, and in what order they will be considered on the floor — they still must juggle bills to satisfy senators, take account of external events and political circumstances, and, where possible, influence policy outcomes in the interests of their own party.

Breakdowns in Scheduling

There are times when intense divisions and strong feelings make unanimous consent agreements impossible to reach. "[W]hen you cannot get an agreement through, there is . . . but one thing to do and that is just to put your head down and plow through," explained Majority Leader Baker.[24] When unanimous consent on scheduling cannot be reached, legislation is at the mercy of opponents, who have a vast array of obstructionist tactics — including the filibuster — at their disposal.

A failure to reach an agreement delays bringing the legislation at issue to the floor. Two examples illustrate this point. The first involves the emotional and discordant issue of abortion. On April 27, 1976, Robert C. Byrd, who at that time was the majority whip, made a unanimous consent request on a proposed constitutional amendment guaranteeing unborn children the right to life. Objections were raised to his request, even though the leadership, according to Majority Leader Mansfield, "thought it had cleared the way with the parties most interested in this legislation." [25] Taken aback, concerned senators continued private negotiations to reach an agreement. An attempt later in the day to secure unanimous consent again was blocked.

Negotiations went on during the evening of April 27 and continued until the Senate convened the next day. A compromise finally was reached, under which Sen. Birch Bayh, D-Ind. (1963-81), a strong opponent of the amendment, asked and received unanimous consent that Sen. Jesse Helms, R-N.C., author of the abortion constitutional amendment, be recognized to make a motion to call up his proposal. The agreement limited debate on Helms' motion and provided for an intervening motion to table (kill) it before there could be a direct vote on adopting the Helms' motion. The compromise satisfied both sides. Proponents of the amendment for the first time were able to secure a debate, however limited, on an antiabortion amendment. Opponents were given the opportunity to vote the proposal down on procedural, rather than substantive, grounds. On April 28 the motion to table was adopted, 47-40.

In the second example, from 1977, there was a much longer delay. "For about five months," said Sen. Gaylord Nelson, D-Wis. (1963-81), the Legal Services Corporation Act "has been on the Senate Calendar awaiting consideration of the full Senate." It was not called up during that time because it faced a certain filibuster by several senators. The threat of a filibuster gave opponents leverage to force several important changes in the proposed legislation; after lengthy bargaining a compromise was reached. The bill was brought to the floor and approved on October 12 by a vote of 77-15. Party leaders sometimes will oppose bringing controversial bills to the floor unless their proponents can guarantee the necessary votes to cut off any filibusters.

Unlike the House, where failure to secure a rule from the Rules Committee usually spells certain defeat for important bills, the Senate, with its greater flexibility, has a variety of ways to secure action on legislation. Any senator can move to take measures off the General Orders Calendar. (Normally, however, such motions are made by the majority leader.) If such a move has the backing of party and committee leaders and a majority of the Senate, the proposal almost certainly will reach the floor. In situations in which a bill has been blocked by the leadership, a senator has the option of offering it in the form of a nongermane floor amendment to another bill. Finally, a senator can resort to the threat of a filibuster or object to all unanimous consent requests until the leadership yields and schedules his measure for floor action.

Keeping Senators Informed

At the end of each day, the majority leader announces the program for the next day or subsequent days. Periodically, he indicates what the legislative agenda looks like for longer periods of time. Senators are kept informed of the legislative program through a variety of means, such as weekly "whip" notices (issued more frequently as needed by each party) listing the measures to be considered each day. Floor proceedings are broadcast to senators' offices over the Senate's loudspeaker system. Senators and staff aides may listen to floor debate while working in their offices. Both parties maintain a "hotline" (automatic telephone connection) to their members' offices to keep them abreast of impending floor developments. For example, during a typical session, a member of the GOP leadership announced that the hotline had "notified Senators on this side of the aisle [that] if we have not finished the bill by normal recess or adjournment hour ... we will continue late into the evening." [26]

Senators and staff aides also monitor the *Congressional Record*, committee calendars, the daily Calendar of Business, newspapers and other publications. Most Senate offices (like House offices) have computer terminals with access to an assortment of legislative information banks. These video terminals can call up summaries of bills describing key provisions and listing when the measures were introduced, their sponsors, the committees to which they were referred, and actions taken, such as hearings, markups, and floor action. Legislative support agencies, such as the Congressional Research Service, continually prepare reports for members, committees, and staff aides on current and prospective legislative activities. Interest groups, too, monitor the legislative process and keep members informed of lawmaking activities.

Winning a Unanimous Consent Agreement

Mr. [HOWARD H.] BAKER, [JR.]. Mr. President, I am about to state a unanimous-consent request in respect to the consideration of H.R. 6590, the so-called tobacco bill, which I believe has been cleared with all the principal parties at interest, and which I will state now for the consideration of all Senators.

The PRESIDING OFFICER. Is there objection?

Mr. [DAN] QUAYLE. Mr. President, reserving the right to object, I do not have any problem, except with the last part — that the agreement be in the usual form.*

As the majority leader knows, I have been looking for a vehicle to discuss a sugar amendment that I have offered. Looking at the legislative agenda ahead and having been foreclosed on the short debt limit bill last night, with the understanding that we would find another vehicle, this certainly looks like an appropriate vehicle to discuss the sugar amendment.

If the last part can be accommodated to discuss the sugar amendment, I will not have any objection, or perhaps we can work out something else.

Mr. BAKER. I admire the tenacity of the Senator from Indiana.

Mr. QUAYLE. Mr. President, I have reserved the right to object to the unanimous-consent request propounded by the distinguished majority leader. I will not object, but I do want to state for the record that, after consultation with the majority leader, the distinguished chairman of the Agriculture Committee, and the distinguished ranking member of the Agriculture Committee and myself, we will proceed with this under the unanimous-consent arrangement.

Furthermore, it was understood that we would work together to accommodate the request of the Senator from Indiana to find a viable vehicle to have a debate on the floor of the U.S. Senate and a vote on the sugar amendment that the Senator from Massachusetts, Senator TSONGAS, and I have proposed. I accept that, though I would prefer to do it, perhaps, on this bill, because I know the urgency and the nature of it and I am also certain that it is going to go somewhere and it is going to be concluded.

But I do not want to be disruptive. I am willing to recede to the desires of the chairman and the majority leader with the understanding that the accommodation will be forthcoming. I will be working with the Senators to meet that understanding in the future. I withdraw the reservation of objection.

The PRESIDING OFFICER. Is there objection to the unanimous consent request? Without objection, it is so ordered.

* An agreement in the "usual form" means that only germane amendments will be in order to the legislation.

Source: Extracted from U.S., Congress, Senate, *Congressional Record,* daily ed., June 24, 1982, S7466-S7480.

Table 7-3   House and Senate Scheduling Compared

House	Senate
Important role for the Rules Committee.	No equivalent body.
Majority party leaders are the predominant force in scheduling, but on occasion they confront a Rules Committee that opposes their decisions.	Majority party leaders control the flow of legislation to the floor in close consultation with minority party leaders.
More formal process.	Less formal process.
Only key members are consulted in scheduling measures.	Every reasonable effort is made to accommodate the scheduling requests of all senators.
Elaborate system of calendars and special days for calling up measures.	Heavy reliance on informal practice in scheduling.
Party leaders can plan a rather firm schedule of daily and weekly business.	Party leaders regularly juggle several measures to suit events and senators.

Summary

The informality of the unanimous consent process does not mean that Senate procedure is less complex than that of the House. On the contrary, unanimous consent requests are unique to each bill and are arrived at only after careful, patient, and often difficult negotiations. The differences between House and Senate scheduling procedures are summarized in Table 7-3.

Similarities in scheduling between the two chambers also are worth noting. Scheduling is essentially a party function in both the House and Senate. As in the House, privileged legislation, such as conference reports, bills vetoed by the president, or Senate bills with House amendments, can be brought to the floor at almost any time on the motion of any member.[27] But in the Senate, to a greater degree than in the House, party leaders decide when such motions will be made.

Standing committees provide the legislation considered by both chambers. Although party leaders largely set the agenda, they are dependent on committees to process the legislation. "I have said to the press time and time again this week that it was my intention to bring [an assistance bill for Southeast Asia] up once it reached the calendar and before we recessed," Majority Leader Mansfield once said during a 1975 Senate session. "Now it is too late. It is not on the calendar." [28] There are occasions, too, when majority leaders ask the committee chairmen to stop reporting out controversial legislation because there is insufficient time remaining in a session to consider such measures.

As in the House, there are a number of ways in the Senate to bring up

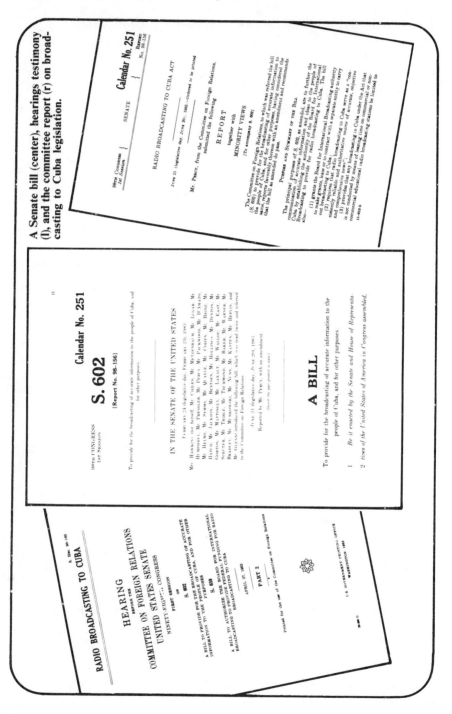

A Senate bill (center), hearings testimony (l), and the committee report (r) on broadcasting to Cuba legislation.

stalled bills, including measures never considered in committee. Senate rules provide for discharging committees, suspending rules, placing measures directly on the General Orders Calendar, and offering nongermane amendments on the floor. These are discussed in Chapter 8, Senate Floor Procedure.

In the Senate, the extent of the support for or opposition to a bill is the critical factor in getting the bill to the floor. If a voting bloc is large enough, and intensely committed to a bill, it usually can overcome the resistance of even the most intransigent committee chairman.

When there is a strong political consensus, bills may sail smoothly through the Senate. In the absence of such a consensus, the rules of that body can be applied to bring virtually any measure to a screeching halt. The art of legislating in the Senate requires an understanding of the procedural dynamics of floor action. The interplay of issues, rules, and personalities affect floor strategy and the eventual outcome of all bills.

Notes

1. *Legislative Activity Sourcebook: United States Senate,* Prepared for the Commission on the Operation of the Senate, 94th Cong., 2d sess. (1976), 1-49. By comparison, during 1981-82 there were about 7,000 House committee and subcommittee meetings. See *Los Angeles Times,* part I, August 7, 1983, 30.
2. *U.S. News and World Report,* August 16, 1976, 28.
3. *Christian Science Monitor,* August 2, 1983, 13.
4. U.S., Congress, Senate, *Congressional Record,* daily ed., March 21, 1980, S2789.
5. Each calendar is printed separately. There also are separate executive and legislative *Journals.* The General Orders Calendar is found in the Senate *Calendar of Business,* which is printed each day the Senate is in session. Measures on the calendar are assigned a calendar order number. The Senate *Executive Calendar* appears whenever there is executive business on it.
6. U.S., Congress, Senate, *Congressional Record,* January 26, 1973, 2301. Byrd at the time was majority whip. It should be noted that according to Senate rules: "Any rule may be suspended without advance notice by unanimous consent of the Senate. . . ."
7. U.S., Congress, Senate, *Congressional Record,* daily ed., April 8, 1981, S3618.
8. U.S., Congress, Senate, *Congressional Record,* September 30, 1976, 33820.
9. U.S., Congress, Senate, *Congressional Record,* daily ed., December 10, 1982, S14345.
10. U.S., Congress, Senate, *Congressional Record,* daily ed., June 22, 1983, S8914.
11. *Washington Times,* February 25, 1983, 3A. See also Majority Leader Howard H. Baker's, Jr., remarks on "holds" in U.S., Congress, Senate, *Congressional Record,* daily ed., December 6, 1982, S13901.
12. U.S., Congress, Senate, *Congressional Record,* January 11, 1913, 1388.
13. Unlike simple requests, which are formulated orally, complex unanimous consent agreements are formalized in writing and reported to senators by means of the *Congressional Record,* the front page of the daily *Calendar of Business,* and in party whip notices.
14. U.S., Congress, Senate, *Congressional Record,* January 21, 1975, 928.

15. U.S., Congress, Senate, *Congressional Record,* daily ed., April 20, 1982, S3691.
16. The Senate's Rules and Administration Committee has jurisdiction over internal Senate matters but is not involved in scheduling bills for floor debate.
17. See Floyd M. Riddick, *Congressional Procedures* (Boston: Chapman & Grimes, 1941), 322.
18. Robert Keith, "The Use of Unanimous Consent in the Senate," *Committees and Senate Procedures,* A Compilation of Papers Prepared for the Commission on the Operation of the Senate, 94th Cong., 2d sess., 161. This excellent study covers the history, trends, and contemporary use of unanimous consent agreements. Much of the information on unanimous consent agreements was developed by Mr. Keith and is used here with his permission.
19. The information on Senate Majority Leader Baker's use of unanimous consent agreements was made available to the author by Martin Gold, formerly counsel to the majority leader. In 1983 Senator Baker announced he would not seek reelection to the Senate.
20. U.S., Congress, Senate, *Congressional Record,* daily ed., April 18, 1980, S3924.
21. *Washington Times,* September 23, 1982, 4A.
22. Michael J. Malbin, "Huge Budget Deficit Projections Fuel Drive for Balanced Budget Amendment," *National Journal,* May 1, 1982, 757.
23. U.S., Congress, Senate, *Congressional Record,* daily ed., June 23, 1982, S7374. On August 4, 1982, the Senate approved a balanced budget constitutional amendment (it subsequently was rejected by the House). See Nadine Cohodas, "Special Report: Balanced Budget Amendment," *Congressional Quarterly Weekly Report,* August 7, 1982, 1887-1893.
24. U.S., Congress, Senate, *Congressional Record,* daily ed., May 25, 1983, S7494.
25. U.S., Congress, Senate, *Congressional Record,* April 27, 1976, 11351.
26. U.S., Congress, Senate, *Congressional Record,* daily ed., August 11, 1982, S10154.
27. In general, privileged matter in the Senate means that such propositions are not subject to unlimited debate (the filibuster) on the motion to call them up for consideration; they are not referred to committee; they are in order at almost any time a senator can gain recognition from the presiding officer; they do not displace the pending business but rather suspend consideration of that measure temporarily; and they are not subject to the one-day layover rule.
28. U.S., Congress, Senate, *Congressional Record,* March 21, 1975, 7982.

8

Senate Floor Procedure

A visitor who moves from the House gallery to the Senate gallery immediately is struck by the contrast in atmosphere. The Senate chamber is more sedate, it is quieter, and business is conducted at a more relaxed pace. The chamber is smaller and more intimate. With fewer members milling about, senators are more easily recognizable than their House counterparts. Typically, only a handful of senators are present on the floor. The remainder are busy in committee meetings or occupied with constituent or other legislative business. All senators, however, generally arrive on the floor quickly in response to buzzers announcing roll-call votes or quorum calls.

There are four semicircular tiers of desks in the Senate. Each of the 100 senators has an assigned desk, complete with snuffbox and open inkwell. There are no electronic voting machines in the Senate; each senator responds aloud as his name is reached during a roll call. Both the Senate and the House employ microphones on the floor, but, unlike the House, each senator has his or her own microphone.

The chamber is ringed by an upper level of galleries for the press, visitors, and dignitaries. On the floor, a broad aisle separates the Republicans, sitting on the right (facing the podium), from the Democrats, on the left. Depending on the makeup of the Senate, there may be more desks on one side than the other.

The senators face a raised platform. One of several persons may occupy the chair and preside over the session. When he is in attendance, the constitutional president of the Senate — the vice president of the United States — sits there. He may vote only to break a tie. Usually, of course, the vice president is not present.

The Constitution also provides for a Senate president pro tempore, elected by that body, to preside in the vice president's absence. The president pro tem usually is the most senior senator of the majority party. In practice, each day's session is chaired by several temporary presiding officers — senators chosen by the president pro tem to serve for a particular period of time.

Neither the president pro tem nor the presiding officer is analogous to the Speaker of the House, in part because neither possesses the political resources to exert such wide-ranging influence in the Senate. For example, the president pro tempore "has never been able to establish his authority as a party leader to the extent of the Majority Leader," Democratic Leader Robert C. Byrd, W. Va., has observed. "This is partly the result of the President pro tempore's irregular appointments and uncertain tenure over the years while serving in the absence of the Vice President." [1]

The principal elective leaders of the Senate are to be found at the front two desks on the center aisle, those assigned to the majority and minority leaders. To the left of the majority leader and the right of the minority leader sit the party whips, second in command in the Senate party hierarchy. These party leaders, or their designees, remain on the floor at all times to protect their party's interests.

There is frequent contact between the leadership and individual senators. To a much greater extent than in the House, each member has the power to influence the course of the legislative process on a daily basis. Any senator can disrupt the Senate's consideration of a bill more easily and with more telling effect than any one representative in the House. A senator, declared former Majority Leader Mike Mansfield, D-Mont. (1953-77), "if he wants to exercise his power, can tie up the Senate for days, and if he allies himself with a few other senators, he can tie up the Senate for weeks." [2] That this does not occur on a regular basis is a tribute to the operation of the Senate's system of unanimous consent, the skill of party leaders, the long tradition of trust, accommodation, and reciprocal courtesy among members, which have survived periodic lapses into hard-line partisanship and confrontation.

Because it is smaller and can operate more flexibly, the Senate normally functions by setting aside many of its own time-consuming rules in order to process legislation efficiently. This chapter describes how the Senate processes legislation once it is readied for floor action. Four main topics are discussed: 1) the daily order of floor business, 2) consideration of major bills under a unanimous consent agreement, 3) consideration of bills without a unanimous consent agreement, and 4) special floor procedures that are used to bypass Senate committees.

Throughout this chapter various procedural devices used to delay or expedite legislation are examined, and comparisons with House procedure are highlighted. First, it is worthwhile to note what a "day" means in the Senate.

'Legislative' and 'Calendar' Days

The Senate, unlike the House, regularly distinguishes between a "calendar" and a "legislative" day.[3] The former is the commonly understood notion of what constitutes a day. The latter refers not to a day when the Senate is in session but to the period between a *recess* and an *adjournment* of the Senate. Recesses and adjournments, in short, determine the sequence of legislative days and calendar days. If the Senate adjourns at the end of a daily session, the legislative day ends with that calendar day. If, however, it chooses to recess, the legislative day is carried over to the next calendar day. Democratic leader Byrd once provided this illustration:

> The Senate has been recessing this year from day to day since January 3. There has not been an adjournment of the Senate since January 3. It has recessed over every day. So although today is calendar day Friday, March 28, 1980, we are still in the legislative day of January 3, 1980, because the Senate has never adjourned since it came in on January 3.

> If we should adjourn today until Tuesday ... then, on Tuesday, the legislative day would have caught up with the calendar day, because we then would be in a new legislative day.[4]

The longest legislative day on record ran from April 20 through August 2, 1922, a total of 105 calendar days, when the Senate was considering the Fordney-McCumber Tariff Act. Once the Senate adjourns after a series of recesses, the legislative day and calendar day become the same. Hence, the legislative day leaped forward by more than three months when the Senate met for the first time after August 2, 1922.

The distinction between the types of days is important because many of the Senate's rules are tied to the legislative day. For instance, a Senate rule requires that the "proceedings of the Senate shall be briefly and accurately stated in the Journal," which "shall be read" at the commencement of each new legislative day. However, it is not necessary to read the *Journal* at the beginning of a session following a recess because the Senate is still in the same legislative day.

The decision to adjourn or recess is made either by unanimous consent or by majority vote on a motion made by the majority leader. If a quorum cannot be obtained, the Senate must adjourn. Adjournment favors senators trying to delay business since it may trigger a series of time-consuming tactics when the Senate next convenes. The majority leader's decision to ask for a recess or an adjournment therefore can have a significant effect on controversial legislation in the Senate. Party leaders generally prefer recesses to adjournments. Recesses grant the leadership greater flexibility in shaping the Senate's daily agenda. Senate rules prescribe a daily order of business, but it can be followed only when the Senate begins a new legislative day.

To reduce the potential for time-consuming procedural steps that can follow an adjournment, the leadership typically employs unanimous consent. The majority leader obtains unanimous consent each day following a recess to approve that day's *Journal,* so that at the beginning of the next legislative day any senators intending to wage a filibuster will not have the opportunity to waste time by requiring the reading of a lengthy *Journal* entry.

Daily Order of Business

Under resolutions adopted at the start of each Congress, the Senate generally convenes each day at noon. The leadership, by a unanimous consent request, may modify the time on a day-to-day basis to stay abreast of the Senate's workload. In the spring of 1978, having lost time debating the Panama Canal treaties, and facing a filibuster on a labor bill, the leadership frequently convened the Senate at 10 a.m. Near the end of a session, in particular, and sometimes in the middle of the year, the majority leader frequently brings in the Senate even earlier, perhaps at 8:30 a.m. To regularize the daily agenda, it has been Majority Leader Howard H. Baker, Jr's., R-Tenn., policy:

> to target for a 6 o'clock recess or adjournment time, except on Thursdays, and if a late session of the Senate is necessary, Thursday will be chosen as the night when Members should be on notice of that possibility. Every effort will be made, absent extraordinary circumstances, to convene the Senate at a reasonable hour and to complete our business by 6 or 6:30 p.m. on days other than Thursdays.[5]

The regular order of business in the Senate, as in the House, begins with a prayer and the reading of the *Journal* of the previous day's activities. The *Journal* reading is almost always dispensed with by unanimous consent, except when a member wishes to use the reading as a delaying tactic.[6] Then there is a brief period reserved for remarks by the majority and minority leaders and, if it is the beginning of a new legislative day, the "morning hour" follows. This period technically runs for a maximum of two hours. "Morning business" is conducted during this time, including the receipt of messages, reports, and communications from the president, the House, and heads of executive branch departments. Bills and resolutions are introduced and referred to committee, committee reports filed, statements inserted in the *Congressional Record,* and brief speeches delivered.

Senators may speak during morning business only by unanimous consent. That is why the party leaders usually ask unanimous consent that there be a period for the transaction of routine morning business and that senators be allowed to speak therein for up to two minutes, or up to five minutes, and so on.[7] Under the rules, bills and resolutions must be read twice — each reading on a different legislative day — before they can be referred to committee. But rarely is this rule invoked; unanimous consent is obtained to dispense with it. When morning business is concluded, the Senate considers "unobjected to measures" on the General Orders Calendar.

The leadership may restrict or change the "morning hour" by unanimous consent. Majority Leader Mansfield once announced, "There will be no morning hour tomorrow for the conduct of morning business, unless it occurs late in the afternoon." [8] A nondebatable motion to proceed to any item on the calendar also is in order during the morning hour. Rarely is such a motion made during this period, however.

Following morning hour, the leadership may schedule "special orders" for up to 15 minutes. Under special orders, members are given permission to speak for a limited time on any subject. The Senate then proceeds to "unfinished business" — legislation pending from a previous day.

If there is no unfinished business, the majority leader or another senator offers a motion to take up a new measure that the leadership, after consultation with the minority leader and other interested senators, has scheduled for floor action. This may be a critical juncture in the proceedings, for it is at this point that opponents of the bill in question might begin delaying tactics, such as a filibuster to prevent the bill from being considered.

This sequence of activities is subject to change by unanimous consent. It also may be affected by the method by which the previous daily session was ended — by recess or by adjournment. The distinction is important at this stage. If the Senate had recessed, it can resume consideration of unfinished business, with no intervening activity, such as morning business. If it had adjourned, it normally must begin its session with morning business, following the prayer and approval of the *Journal.*

Debate in the Modern Senate

In the early Congresses, the Senate was characterized by protracted debates and great orators: Daniel Webster, John Calhoun and Stephen Douglas on slavery, and later by Henry Cabot Lodge and others on the League of Nations. Today, senators are so busy, and the legislative agenda so crowded, that extended deliberation is the exception, rather than the rule. On occasion, debate still serves to publicize issues, build constituencies, and influence Senate votes. After one spirited floor session, Sen. Spark M. Matsunaga, D-Hawaii, declared, "I was really undecided on the pending amendment, but Senator [Gary] Hart so ably presented his case that I will join him" in opposing the amendment.[9]

Then, too, there still are "great debates" that capture national attention and mobilize national sentiment on critical issues such as civil rights, arms control, the nuclear freeze, Social Security, and the Panama Canal treaties. During the 1978 debate over the treaties, the Senate for the first time allowed live national radio coverage.[10]

Debate in the modern Senate consists primarily of prepared speeches, perfunctorily read or inserted in the *Congressional Record* without having been formally delivered.[11] When intense debate does occur, it is often among only a handful of senators with special interest in the legislation. Sen. Ernest F. Hollings, D-S.C., has been critical of this situation: "We get in here working hot and heavy in debate, but there is no one here to listen." [12] As in the House — even though only a scattering of members are on the floor — a quorum technically is present until a member suggests otherwise.

Any senator may suggest the absence of a quorum. When this occurs the presiding officer is obligated to direct the clerk to call the roll of members. In contrast to House practice, the presiding officer may not first count the senators present to determine whether a quorum in fact exists, except during post-cloture proceedings. The calling of the roll is mandatory unless it is dispensed with by unanimous consent.

Quorum calls, however, are commonly employed to give senators time to work out procedural arrangements, such as a unanimous consent agreement, or to give a member scheduled to speak time to reach the floor. Once this is done, further calling of the roll to establish a quorum is dispensed with by unanimous consent. When Lyndon Johnson was majority leader, he "would ask for a quorum call and wait, sometimes for close to an hour, while the reading clerk droned slowly through the names. Then, when Johnson was ready for the Senate to resume, he would suspend the calling of the roll." [13] A good description of how quorum calls are used appears in the box on page 177.

Quorum calls to delay proceedings temporarily are to be distinguished from "live" quorums. Here a senator insists that at least a majority of the members come to the chamber and answer to their names. This can be a time-consuming process. Recalling that Sen. Strom Thurmond, R-S.C., once demanded a "live" quorum, a Senate colleague observed, "It took almost one hour to round up fifty-one Senators to respond to their names." [14] The two types of quorum calls are distinguished by the different number of bells that ring in members' offices and Senate committee rooms.

If the Senate officially discovers that it lacks a quorum, it has two options: 1) it must adjourn (recess if there is a previous order to that effect), or 2) it may instruct the sergeant-at-arms to request (compel) the attendance of senators.

Floor Manager's Role

Floor managers have the major responsibility for guiding legislation to final passage. "I lean on the manager of the bill and the ranking [committee] members to carry the load" on the floor, Democratic leader Byrd observed when he was Senate majority leader. [15] The skill of the floor manager often determines the fate of legislation.

Senate floor managers, like their House counterparts, have varied responsibilities. They may offer amendments to strengthen their bills or win more support as well as to counter proposed weakening amendments; they have to respond to points of order when they are raised against language in the legislation; and they must alert proponents when their support is needed.

Strategic calculations are a manager's stock in trade. For example, Sen. John C. Culver, D-Iowa (1975-81), the floor manager, once was able to persuade Sen. William L. Scott, R-Va. (1973-79), to offer a troublesome amendment at the most advantageous time from Culver's standpoint.

> The theory behind having Scott bring up the amendment now is that it is better to have such a proposal come up in the morning — a time when many senators are in committee meetings or in their offices and are more distracted than usual from the business that is taking place on the floor. Also, Culver figures that most of his colleagues will assume that at this point, especially after a long day of taking up amendments — and major ones — yesterday, only routine "housekeeping" amendments are being considered, and that they will pay less attention to the issue, be less eager to join the fray, than they might be later on. [16]

By informal custom, floor managers are accorded priority of recognition by the presiding officer. Explained Senator Byrd: "The manager of a bill also

Using Quorum Calls to Draft Amendments

Those who care for the law and sausage, the saying goes, may be well advised not to watch either being made.

Theorists who regard legislating as a precise and formal discipline could have been startled by events on the Senate floor Monday when Senator Edward M. Kennedy of Massachusetts persuaded the Republican majority to preserve the "meals on wheels" program for elderly shut-ins.

Customarily, amendments to Senate bills are submitted on the floor in printed form, or at least typewritten. Because it was improvised in a volatile political situation, the Kennedy amendment was handwritten, by at least four different agents of varying legibility.

Most Senate amendments are debated and then voted up or down. But Senator Kennedy's amendment, to preserve separate identity and funding for "meals on wheels," was scarcely debated at all; instead it was discussed in a series of private huddles and repeatedly rewritten on the floor.

To accommodate these negotiations, the Senate invoked its favorite stalling device: the quorum call. When a member suggests there is not a quorum of 51 members on the floor — there almost never is except when it's time to vote — all action ceases while the clerk calls the roll.

Rewriting the Kennedy amendment eventually required three quorum calls. In each of them the Massachusetts Democrat gathered in the aisle with Republican Senators Jeremiah Denton of Alabama, Bob Dole of Kansas and John Heinz of Pennsylvania, each flanked by a staff aide. . . .

At one point, Mr. Kennedy agreed that states need not spend the same dollar amounts for "meals on wheels" but only the same share of their budgets for nutrition for the elderly. His aide, Lawrence Horowitz, scratched "amount" out of the amendment, wrote "%" over it and scribbled "percentage of funds" in the margin.

Later Senator Kennedy agreed that states could be freed of this requirement if they put a "significant" burden on their nutrition programs, instead of an "unreasonable" one, and the amendment was rewritten again.

So successful had these impromptu negotiations been that the Kennedy amendment was adopted 72 to 0, despite strong administration resistance. . . .

Source: Excerpted from Warren Weaver, Jr., "Reading the Handwriting on the Bill," *New York Times,* November 5, 1981, A24.

is entitled to preferential recognition — not ahead of the [majority leader and minority leader], but following in line, and is accorded that recognition generally by the Chair." [17]

Staff aides often assist floor managers. Senators rely more heavily on staff assistance during floor debate than do House members. Aides draft amendments and arguments and negotiate with aides of other senators to marshal support for legislation being considered.

Bills Considered by Unanimous Consent

The importance of unanimous consent agreements to the efficient operation of the legislative process in the Senate has already been cited. A typical example of a unanimous consent agreement is shown on page 179.

This complex agreement, like most others controlling major legislation, reflects standard operating procedure for the Senate: No day is specified when the bill will be taken up; nongermane amendments are prohibited with exceptions noted in the agreement; debate on each designated amendment is limited to one hour with 30 minutes stipulated for any other amendments; 30 minutes debate is permitted on any debatable motion, appeal, or point of order; and there are provisions regulating the division of time on amendments and other motions. There are two interesting features, however, which are seldom in most unanimous consent agreements. First, the agreement specifies the exact date and time when the Senate is to proceed to consideration of the measure. Second, it limits debate on the entire bill, including amendments, to 13 hours.

As noted in the previous chapter, unanimous consent agreements are printed in the *Congressional Record,* the daily Senate *Calendar of Business* (illustrated on page 162), and party whip notices. Senators check with party leaders, committee members, and staff to learn when bills are to be considered. The next day's or the next week's legislative program also is announced by the majority leadership at the close of each daily session.

Measures governed by unanimous consent agreements may be called up by the majority leader at the conclusion of the period for 15-minute special order speeches. Customarily, the presiding officer briefly summarizes the terms of the agreement, then recognizes the bill's floor manager, usually the chairman of the committee or subcommittee that handled the bill, for a short description of the legislation and its intent. The floor manager is followed by the ranking minority committee or subcommittee member, who presents similarly brief opening remarks. The Senate then is ready to debate and consider amendments to the bill.

The Amending Process

Unlike the House, the Senate has no five-minute rule for debating amendments. There are no "closed" rules in the Senate. Any measure is open to virtually an unlimited number of amendments unless a unanimous consent agreement specifies otherwise. On occasion, a floor manager may ask that a measure pass without amendments. Opponents still are likely to offer amendments, but if the floor manager has sufficient support they are likely to be voted down.

Senators, unlike House members in the Committee of the Whole, can modify their own amendments without the need for unanimous consent or

Unanimous Consent Agreement

S 66 (ORDER NO. 106)

Ordered. That at 1:00 p.m. on Monday, June 13, 1983, the Senate proceed to the consideration of S. 66 (Order No. 106), a bill to amend the Communication Act of 1934, and that there be 13 hours of consideration thereon, including debate on any amendments, debatable motion, appeals, or points of order which are submitted or on which the Chair entertains debate, with the time to be equally divided and controlled by the Senator from Oregon (Mr. Packwood) and the Senator from West Virginia (Mr. Byrd), or their designees.

Ordered further, That no amendment that is not germane to the provisions of the said bill shall be received, with the following exceptions: a Commerce Committee modification to the committee amendment; an amendment to be offered by the Senator from Oregon (Mr. Packwood) dealing with telecommunications; an amendment to be offered by the Senator from South Dakota (Mr. Abdnor) dealing with deleting the "two-way" grade communication; and an amendment to be offered by the Senator from South Dakota (Mr. Abdnor) dealing with insuring that all providers of telecommunications services share in the obligation of providing universal service: *Provided,* That there be 1 hour debate on each of the above amendments, with the time to be equally divided and controlled by the mover of such and the manager of the bill.

Ordered further, That there be 30 minutes debate on any other amendment, debatable motion, appeal, or point of order if submitted to the Senate, with the time to be equally divided and controlled by the mover of such and the manager of the bill.

Ordered further, That at the conclusion of the debate, the Senate proceed to vote on passage of S. 66. *(May 18, 1983)*

the majority approval of the chamber. A senator, for example, might propose an amendment that the floor manager will support if the language is discretionary rather than mandatory. The senator can make the change on his own authority and facilitate the amendment's chances of being adopted by the Senate. These modifications are permissible until the Senate takes some action on the amendment, such as agreeing to take a vote on it or arranging a unanimous consent agreement limiting debate time. Senators sometimes quickly ask for action on their amendments because even though they lose the right to modify them they gain the right to offer amendments to their own amendments, should the need arise.

Senators must be recognized by the presiding officer before they can offer amendments. Officially reported committee amendments take precedence over those offered by other members from the floor. Committee amendments, however, are subject to further amendment from the floor.

Senators can propose amendments at any time to any section of a bill. This approach differs from the more orderly routine followed by the House, where the rules specify that each part of a measure be considered in sequential order, usually section-by-section. Senate custom gives individual senators greater flexibility in amending legislation. Amendments must be read by the Senate clerk, but this usually is dispensed with by unanimous consent unless an attempt is being made to delay the bill.

Principle of 'Precedence'

An important concept that shapes the amending process in the Senate is "precedence." While both the House and Senate have a rule specifying that only amendments in the first and second degree are permitted, there are basic differences in how each chamber interprets first and second degree amendments. This, in turn, affects the number of amendments that can be pending to a bill at the same time. In the Senate, even third degree amendments occasionally are made in order by unanimous consent.

Both chambers also operate under the rule that so-called second degree amendments are voted on before first degree amendments, but because of differing traditions over what constitute first and second degree amendments, the order of voting on amendments may differ.

The principle of precedence determines which amendments (perfecting or substitute) may be offered when others are pending and the order in which those amendments are voted on. A perfecting amendment is one that simply alters language, either to the bill or to a pending amendment, but does not seek to substitute new text for the pending proposal. Perfecting amendments have precedence over substitutes. Thus, if senator A offers a perfecting amendment to a bill (a first degree amendment), and senator B then proposes a second degree perfecting amendment to it, no other amendments are in order until the second degree proposal is disposed of. And if the latter is adopted, other second degree amendments — perfecting or substitute —may be offered until the entire text of the first degree amendment has been disposed of.

Alternatively, senator B may offer a second degree substitute for senator A's amendment to the bill. Then senator C, under the Senate's principle of precedence, can introduce a second degree perfecting amendment to senator A's amendment, which would be voted upon before the substitute. These steps in the Senate amendment process differ from those permitted in the House. *(Comparison, see Chapter 6, p. 136.)*

To recapitulate, policy decisions often are affected by the Senate's precedence principle, which determines 1) the number of amendments that may be pending simultaneously to a bill, and 2) the order of voting on them. A good example of their impact occurred in 1980. Democratic leader Byrd used his privilege of being recognized ahead of other senators to offer a nongermane strip mining amendment (first degree, perfecting) to a maritime cargo bill. Majority Leader Baker, who supported Byrd's move, asked for the yeas and nays (a roll-call vote) on Byrd's amendment. Then Byrd offered a second degree perfecting proposal to his own amendment.

This parliamentary maneuver, which shut off further floor amendments to Byrd's original amendment, angered Sen. Howard M. Metzenbaum, D-Ohio, who opposed the effort to modify the strip mining reclamation law. When you "have access to the floor," he said to Byrd, "and offer a perfecting amendment and then an amendment to that perfecting amendment, you are in a position to foreclose the right of other Members of the Senate to offer their amendments." [18] Senators Metzenbaum and John Melcher, D-Mont., "were ready to introduce 272 amendments to delay debate on the Byrd proposals." [19] Senator Byrd's tactic prevented them from offering their amendments. In the end, the Senate approved the Byrd amendments.

The order of voting on amendments can be of strategic importance, too. Senators may introduce amendments following the precedence principle in order to obtain an early test vote on their policy alternatives. One purpose would be to identify defecting senators who might be kept in line through personal persuasion. Or members might want their amendment to be voted on last, on the assumption that they have enough support to defeat all damaging amendments and thus can demonstrate to opponents that the choice is between the pending amendment or nothing at all.

Strategic Uses of Amendments

Timing, strategy, lobbying, and skillful drafting are important parts of the amending process. Party leaders often try to get unanimous consent to arrange the order in which senators call up their amendments. On important measures, senators regularly jockey for position in offering amendments. Whether an amendment is accepted or rejected sometimes depends on its purpose, and its purpose may not always be to amend the bill under consideration. Two examples will illustrate the point.

Defeating Legislation. One strategy of opponents of a bill is to load the legislation down with controversial amendments, possibly sparking a filibuster and jeopardizing Senate passage. Or the bill may be recommitted to the committee that reported it — sometimes a fatal blow. "All I know," Sen. Russell B. Long, D-La., has observed, "is that when you get the package too big, what happens is that the whole package goes under." [20]

There are other, more subtle, ways to defeat measures through amendments. In 1964 an opponent of the proposed Medicare insurance program offered an amendment to provide *higher* cash payments to Social Security recipients. It was an appealing proposal, particularly in an election year, but it would have required additional payroll taxes to fund the increase. As former Sen. Clinton P. Anderson, D-N.M. (1949-73), noted, the proposal contained an "ambush. . . . [I]f such an amendment was approved, it would make the levying of still more taxes for Medicare all but impossible." [21]

Medicare supporters, meeting in the majority leader's office, developed a counterstrategy. They drafted an amendment that combined *lower* cash payments for retirees with a program of hospital insurance for the aged through Social Security. This revised amendment was passed by the Senate, the first time either house had approved a Medicare proposal.

Defusing Controversial Issues. A timely amendment can prevent potential embarrassment to committees, members, and even presidents. In 1977 President Jimmy Carter announced that U.S. troops gradually would be withdrawn from South Korea. Subsequently, the Senate Foreign Relations Committee endorsed the withdrawal plan in a provision to a bill authorizing State Department operations. Republican leader Baker, who opposed the plan, said he would offer an amendment on the floor to delete the language supporting a troop withdrawal.

Senator Byrd sensed that there was strong opposition to Carter's withdrawal plan and that Baker's amendment might receive strong support, thus embarrassing the new president. He asked the bill's floor manager, Sen. George S. McGovern, D-S.D. (1963-81), to yield to him soon after debate began. Then Byrd proposed an amendment emphasizing the impact of a troop withdrawal on other Asian countries (the first degree amendment). Byrd immediately followed up with an amendment specifying the need for regular consultation with and reporting to Congress by the president on troop withdrawal policy (a second degree amendment) to forestall Senator Baker's proposal. For three hours, Byrd "fought a holding action against any conservatives who objected that the language implicitly endorsed the Carter plan." [22] After Byrd had agreed to modify his amendment seven times to meet floor objections, the Senate finally adopted the modest declaration "that U.S. policy toward Korea should be arrived at by joint decision of the president and the Congress." [23] An effort was made to recommit the whole bill to the Foreign Relations Committee, but Byrd successfully moved to table (kill) the recommittal motion.

Voting on Amendments

The Senate has three types of voting: voice, division (standing) and roll call. Voice and division voting are similar to House procedures, but there is nothing comparable to the recorded teller vote or the electronic voting procedures of the House. The system of buzzers that summons senators to the floor is much like that of the House. During a roll call members respond "yea" or "nay" as their names are called alphabetically.

The Senate establishes the length of time for roll-call votes at the start of each Congress. When the 98th Congress convened on January 3, 1983, the Senate agreed by unanimous consent:

> [T]hat, for the duration of the 98th Congress, there be a limitation of 15 minutes each on any roll call vote with [a] warning signal to be sounded at the midway point, beginning at the last 7 minutes, and when roll call votes are of 10-minutes duration, the warning signal [is to] be sounded at the beginning of the last 7 minutes.

When votes are grouped back-to-back (referred to in the Senate as "stacking"), the second and succeeding votes occur, by unanimous consent, at 10-minute intervals.[24]

Voting times, too, are arranged to accommodate senators. On one occasion, for example, the Senate unanimously agreed to a request from the majority leader to set a one-hour and 15-minute roll-call vote.[25]

Party leaders and floor managers make every effort to assure that their supporters are on the floor when needed for a vote. "My experience convinces me," commented Senator Byrd, that voting "is the most critical step in the legislative process. . . . [The leaders and the floor managers must] "have the right members at the right place and at the right time." [26]

Party leaders give advance notice of impending votes in whip notices and announcements from the floor. Occasionally, complex unanimous consent agreements specify the exact date and time for votes on final passage of a bill. On the other hand, the times for votes on amendments sometimes are agreed to by unanimous consent without elaborate negotiations during the debate on the bill.

Recorded votes in the Senate usually can be obtained quite easily; only a "sufficient second" — one-fifth of the senators present — is needed, with a minimum of 11 required by the Constitution. If the minimum number is not on the floor at the time the request is made, a senator can summon other colleagues through a quorum call, try to get their support, and then renew the request for a roll-call vote. Most roll calls occur on amendments.

Increase in Voting. Over the years there has been a gradual increase in the number of roll-call votes, although some drop-off is evident in recent years. The increase may have occurred for several reasons: pride of authorship, evidence of having taken a position on critical and controversial issues, and demonstration of Senate support for a measure that may end up in a conference committee to resolve differences with the House. The following figures show the trend in voting since 1971:

Year	Number of Roll Calls	Year	Number of Roll Calls
1971	423	1977	636
1972	532	1978	516
1973	594	1979	497
1974	544	1980	531
1975	611	1981	483
1976	700	1982	469

'Cue-givers.' Senators, like representatives, rely on numerous "cue-givers" for guidance on voting because of the range and complexity of legislation. "When it comes to voting," Sen. James L. Buckley, C/R-N.Y. (1971-77), once wrote, "an individual senator will rely heavily not only on the judgment of staff, his own and his committee's, but also on a select number of senators whose knowledge he has come to respect and whose general perspectives he shares." [27] The position of the reporting committee is an important factor to many senators. "A lot of members of the Senate," commented Sen. Edmund S. Muskie, D-Maine (1959-80), "will arrive on the floor, and there's an amendment up that they really haven't had a chance to look at, and they'll just come up and ask, 'What's the committee position?' " [28]

Casting Procedural Votes. On controversial amendments, members often maneuver for procedural, rather than substantive, votes. A vote to table (kill) amendments or other motions is a classic procedural ploy to avoid being recorded directly on politically sensitive policy issues. Senator Byrd has explained the difference:

> A motion to table is a procedural motion. It obfuscates the issue, and it makes possible an explanation by a Senator to his constituents, if he wishes to do so, that his vote was not on the merits of the issue. He can claim that he might have voted this way or he might have voted that way, if the Senate had voted up or down on the issue itself. But on a procedural motion, he can state he voted to table the amendment, and he can assign any number of reasons therefore, one of which would be that he did so in order that the Senate would get on with its work or about its business. [29]

Therefore, if a procedural vote can be arranged to kill or delay a bill, it is more likely to win the support of senators, who may prefer to duck the substantive issue.

Like the House, the Senate permits vote "pairing," either "live" or "dead" pairs. In a live pair, one senator is present on the floor during the vote. The practice is for the senator to cast his vote, yea or nay, then withdraw it and announce, "I have a pair with the senator from [naming the state]. If he were present and voting, he would vote [yea or nay]. If I were at liberty to vote, I would vote [yea or nay]." In a dead pair, both senators are absent from the floor. Their positions are printed after each roll call in the *Congressional Record.* Live and dead pairs are not tabulated on roll-call votes, but a live pair can affect the outcome of a vote. Explained Senator Byrd:

> The arranging of pairs has been decisive from time to time on very close votes, because it is possible to pair off enough present Senators to affect the outcome of the vote and perhaps make a difference of 1 or 2 votes which, had the Senators present not been paired, would have decided the issue opposite to the outcome that resulted.
>
> However, Senators generally will not agree to give a "live" pair except on the condition that the outcome is not changed by virtue of the pair given. [30]

Final Action on a Bill

"When no Senator seeks recognition," Senator Byrd further explained, "the Chair automatically puts the question of adoption of amendments and passage of bills." [31] Thus, once the amending process is completed the Senate proceeds to a vote on final passage, unless a unanimous consent agreement has been made setting a later date and time for the final vote. The floor manager announces that there are no further amendments. He then requests a third, and final, reading of the bill. The presiding officer orders the bill engrossed — put in the precise form in which it emerged from the Senate's amending process — and "read" a third time (the title of the bill only), a procedure that takes only a few seconds.

The final vote is not over until the chair announces the outcome. Senators, like House members, may change their vote during the regular 15-minute voting period, which in the Senate is a minimum and not the maximum time allowed. For example, during an unusually lengthy Senate roll call in 1982 dozens of senators switched their votes and defeated a proposal offered by Sen. Dale Bumpers, D-Ark. "I just want to announce that Dr. Cary's in his office for everyone whose arm is out of socket," exclaimed the senator from Arkansas.[32] (Dr. Freeman Cary is the Senate physician.)

After the result of the final vote on the bill has been announced, there is still one more parliamentary step required before Senate action is complete. This step is available only to the side that prevailed on the final vote. If the bill has been passed, a senator who voted for the bill, or who did not vote, makes a motion to reconsider the vote. (On a voice or standing vote, any senator can offer the motion.) Immediately thereafter, another proponent of the bill moves to table (kill) the motion to reconsider. By this procedural device Senate rules protect the bill from further consideration. Rarely does the motion to table fail.[33] This procedure also is used after votes on amendments. The House procedure, described in Chapter 6, is identical.

To summarize, the usual Senate floor procedure for major legislation is as follows: First, a unanimous consent agreement is negotiated; second, the bill is called up by the floor manager after being scheduled by the joint majority and minority leadership; third, the bill is considered for amendment, with the debate time regulated by the unanimous consent agreement; fourth, there is a final vote (voice vote or roll call) on final passage.

But what happens when a major bill reaches the floor in the absence of a unanimous consent agreement? By and large, the procedural sequence is much the same, but the legislation is much more vulnerable to obstructionist tactics, particularly the filibuster.

Bills Not Having Unanimous Consent

Sometimes party leaders are unable to achieve unanimous consent agreements. This may happen for a variety of reasons: intense opposition to the bill by certain senators, a general desire for unrestricted debate and amendment, commitments by some senators to protect the interests of absent colleagues, or simply personal pique of some senators against party leaders. Passage of legislation then becomes a much more difficult task. At the very least, debate will be extensive and amendments will be numerous. Operating under the Senate's rules, this can be extremely time-consuming. Moreover, if there is intense opposition to a bill on the part of one or more senators, the well-known device of the filibuster may be threatened or actually used.[34]

It is sometimes difficult to tell when "extended debate" becomes a filibuster; a senator does not make a motion to "filibuster" a bill. When a filibuster becomes evident, Senator Byrd once said, "I will be able to perceive one, because I know one when I see it." [35]

Typically, the filibuster is viewed as the last recourse, forcing an almost complete stoppage of normal floor business — a situation most senators try to avoid if at all possible. Nevertheless, it is the most distinctive feature of Senate floor procedures and deserves thorough discussion.

The Filibuster

Generally characterized in the public mind as a nonstop speech, a filibuster in the fullest sense employs every parliamentary maneuver and dilatory motion to delay, modify, or defeat legislation. Asked for filibustering pointers by a colleague, Sen. Howard M. Metzenbaum, D-Ohio, said: "If it takes unanimous consent, object. If not, you make a little speech, suggest the absence of a quorum, then . . . use parliamentary procedures . . . motions to adjourn, motions to recess." He added: "You have to have the floor protected 100 percent of the time." [36]

More has been written about "extended debate" in the Senate than any other congressional procedure. Hollywood even glamorized the filibuster in a 1930s movie, "Mr. Smith Goes to Washington," starring Jimmy Stewart.

The filibuster has been part of the Senate from its earliest days. It is a formidable weapon — particularly late in a session when time is running out — that can be used by any senator or group of senators. Defenders of the filibuster say it is needed to prevent bad bills from becoming law, protect minority rights against majority steamrollers, ensure thorough analysis of legislation, and dramatize issues for the public. Opponents argue that the filibuster thwarts majority rule, brings the Senate into disrepute, and permits small minorities to extort unwarranted concessions in bills supported by Senate majorities.

These pro and con arguments highlight a dilemma: How to strike a balance between the right to debate and the need to decide.[37] There is no easy answer. What is apparent is that the filibuster is a powerful bargaining device. Even the possibility of its use can force compromises in committee or on the floor. Senators of widely diverse viewpoints have resorted to it from time to time or have threatened to use it in order to influence legislation. There are numerous examples that can be used to illustrate the impact of the filibuster.

Civil Rights Filibusters. Before the 1970s, filibusters were most often identified with southern Democrats, who used them to defeat or delay civil rights measures. The 1957, 1960, and 1964 Civil Rights Acts were the objects of systematic filibusters by southern senators, each of whom held the floor for several hours, yielding to colleagues for long questions, while others remained in their offices or left Capitol Hill until it was their turn to talk. The southerners demanded periodic quorum calls, keeping the pressure on supporters of civil rights legislation, who had to stay near the chamber to prevent the Senate from adjourning rather than recessing.

Adjournment would have played into the hands of the senators conducting the filibusters by requiring a series of routine, but time-consuming, procedures every time the Senate was forced to convene anew. Senators supporting a filibuster certainly would refuse unanimous consent requests to dispense with any of the elements of daily procedure, thereby further delaying action on the bills being filibustered. During an extended filibuster, the Senate sometimes remains in session throughout the night, with filibuster opponents forced to remain near the Senate floor — sometimes sleeping on couches and cots — to be ever ready in the event of quorum calls.

Every bill faces two potential filibusters: the first on the motion to take up the legislation and the second on consideration of the bill itself. The 1964 civil rights filibuster consumed 16 days on the motion to take up the measure and 57 days on the legislation itself. Those filibusters were unique in that they marked the first time the Senate had ever voted to end an extended debate on a civil rights bill.

Changing Trends in Filibusters. Moderate and liberal senators traditionally had opposed use of the filibuster, but times changed. During the 1970s and early 1980s, Sens. Alan Cranston, D-Calif., Frank Church, D-Idaho (1957-81), Charles McC. Mathias, R-Md., Lowell P. Weicker, Jr., R-Conn., Robert Packwood, R-Ore., Birch Bayh, D-Ind. (1963-81), and others conducted filibusters against the Vietnam War; President Richard Nixon's nominations of Clement Haynsworth, G. Harrold Carswell, and William H. Rehnquist to the Supreme Court; a 1981 anti-busing amendment; and a 1982 anti-abortion bill.

While liberal and moderate senators had employed the filibuster in the past (on the 1948 Taft-Hartley Act, for example), the "recent obstructionism represents, in frequency alone, a significant departure from past liberal practice." [38] Conversely, senators who had unswervingly supported the filibuster, often as a matter of principle, became more flexible. In 1971 Sen. John C. Stennis, D-Miss., a traditional defender of the practice, urged his colleagues to terminate an extended debate on a draft extension bill in the name of national security.

In sum, the filibuster is a "parliamentary tool available to liberals and conservatives who wish to dramatize issues in the only forum of our national government that provides for thorough analysis and unhurried consideration of proposed public laws." [39]

Ending a Filibuster. There are two interrelated methods of ending a filibuster: by informal compromise or by cloture — a formal Senate procedure used to terminate debate. Frequently, cloture cannot be obtained unless compromises are made. Party leaders sometimes try "shuttle diplomacy" between the two sides, noted GOP Whip Ted Stevens of Alaska, to avoid full-scale filibusters.[40]

Informal Compromise—In 1982 the Senate considered a supplemental appropriations bill to which many senators hoped to add a $5.1 billion mortgage subsidy program. In the wake of high unemployment in the home building industry and high interest rates, Sen. Richard G. Lugar, R-Ind., advocated the subsidy amendment as a way to promote housing construction and home ownership. Sen. William L. Armstrong, R-Colo., opposed it and was able to employ the Senate's rules to delay final action on the legislation indefinitely. Republican leader Baker then worked out a compromise satisfactory to both senators.

> [L]ong hours of negotiation produced a complicated agreement today that helped end the filibuster led by Senator William L. Armstrong, Republican of Colorado. As his price for the agreement, Mr. Armstrong demanded that the housing measure be brought to the floor under a procedure, suspension of the rules, requiring a two-thirds vote.[41]

Subsequently, Senator Lugar won on the vote to suspend the rules (63-27), and his subsidy amendment was added to the appropriations bill. *(Senate suspension of the rules procedure, see p. 195.)*

There is a danger, however, in altering bills to placate those who filibuster against them. Senators favoring strong legislation may be unwilling to accept a weaker substitute. During a filibuster, senators may meet in the cloakroom — off the Senate floor — or in the offices of the party leaders to conduct negotiations, which can go on day and night. The process may take several days or even weeks, depending on how controversial the bill may be. If compromise fails, the odds increase that opponents of the legislation may win the battle and thus sidetrack the bill indefinitely. Alternatively, proponents may manage to invoke cloture.

Cloture—After decades of determined resistance by many senators, the Senate in 1917 adopted Rule XXII, which for the first time gave the Senate the formal means (cloture) to end extended debate. Until that time, debate could be terminated only by unanimous consent, an impossibility in the face of a filibuster.

What finally prompted the Senate to adopt Rule XXII was a filibuster that had killed a bill to arm U.S. merchant ships against attacks by German submarines. President Woodrow Wilson strongly criticized the filibuster and called a special session of the Senate, which adopted the cloture rule on March 8, 1917, five weeks before war was declared.

Under Rule XXII a cloture petition signed by 16 senators first must be filed with the presiding officer. Two days later, and one hour after the Senate convenes, the presiding officer must ascertain whether a quorum is present. That having been established, the presiding officer is obliged to ask, "Is it the sense of the Senate that the debate shall be brought to a close?" A vote immediately is held. If three-fifths of the entire Senate membership (60 of 100 members) vote in favor, cloture is invoked. Thereafter, no senator may speak for more than one hour. Before 1975, when the current three-fifths rule was adopted, a two-thirds majority of those senators present and voting was required to invoke cloture. (The two-thirds requirement still applies to proposals to amend the Senate's rules.)

Once cloture is invoked, only germane amendments may be offered, and the presiding officer may rule out of order dilatory motions. The cloture rule has helped ease some types of delaying tactics but has not effectively ended all of them, as pointed out in the discussion of the so-called "post-cloture filibusters" below.

There is no limit to the number of times cloture can be sought on a single piece of legislation. The record for cloture votes is six, which has occurred on three occasions: on the question of recognizing the winner of the disputed 1975 New Hampshire senatorial election, on a 1978 labor law revision bill, and on an anti-school busing rider to a Justice Department authorization bill in 1981.

Cloture may be tried immediately after a bill is brought to the floor, but usually senators respect and value the tradition of extended debate. Sen. George D. Aiken, R-Vt. (1941-75), once said he would refuse "to vote for cloture until discussion and debate on an important measure has been carried on for at least two weeks." [42] Occasionally, however, cloture is sought soon after a bill is called up in order to block a threatened filibuster, test sentiment for or against a measure, or expedite action on the legislation.

Cloture helps to speed up floor action on a bill because once cloture is achieved all further amendments must be germane. For instance, a cloture motion was filed on December 2, 1975, as soon as the Senate began debate on a rail services measure, and cloture was invoked two days later. Anxious for final action on the bill before the session ended, the leadership announced on December 4 that the Senate would stay in continuous session until action on the bill was completed. "Now if it means midnight, it means midnight," said Senator Byrd, then the majority whip.[43]

On the theory that even a weak bill is better than no bill, supporters of a certain measure frequently are willing to compromise with filibustering senators. Yet there are measures on which both sides are deeply divided. In these situations there is very little room for bargaining. When possible, cloture is the preferred tactic of the majority in such cases. But the relative ease of invoking cloture under the three-fifths rule has brought forth increasing reliance on yet another dilatory tactic — the post-cloture filibuster.

Post-cloture Filibuster

Filibusters are used to defeat or weaken bills by talking them to death. The post-cloture filibuster attempts to do the same thing by employing an array of parliamentary tactics to delay final action. The technique involves extensive use of roll calls, quorum calls, and reading of amendments, none of which count against the one hour of floor time allotted to each member after cloture is invoked. Before several senators' hour has been used up, weeks or months may elapse. The post-cloture filibuster is particularly effective if opponents of a bill have had the foresight to offer a large number of germane amendments before cloture is achieved. These amendments remain pending after cloture. However, no new amendments are in order after the cloture vote, except by unanimous consent.

For the most part, the post-cloture filibuster is a contemporary and innovative dilatory tactic. Senators were long aware of its availability, but they seldom employed it. Members apparently believed that it violated the spirit of fair play. Once the battle had been fought and cloture invoked by a large majority, the informal rules of the game dictated that further delaying actions be ended. The post-cloture filibuster, however, was used three times in 1976 and once in 1977. Sen. James B. Allen, D-Ala. (1969-78), is often credited with discovering this tactic.

In 1977 Sens. James G. Abourezk, D-S.D. (1973-79), and Howard M. Metzenbaum, D-Ohio, prolonged consideration of an intensely controversial natural gas deregulation bill for two weeks after cloture had been invoked. The Senate leadership even held an all-night Senate session, the first in 13 years, in an attempt to break their post-cloture filibuster. The story of the efforts of the two senators and the extraordinary countertactics employed to combat them is a classic example of the use of this form of filibuster.

Cloture Rule Loopholes. Under Senate rules, any senator who offers a germane amendment before the vote to invoke cloture occurs is eligible to call it up after cloture is agreed to. Senator Metzenbaum had introduced 212 printed amendments in one day alone. They were a mixture of substance and technicalities. He proposed numerous alternative dates for the various deadlines in the bill, alternative sums of money, redefinitions of terms, and various deletions and additions to the bill. Altogether, 508 amendments were pending when cloture was invoked.

With so many amendments pending, the two senators had plenty of ammunition with which to delay Senate proceedings. Here is how their strategy was carried out:

● Senators Abourezk and Metzenbaum called up numerous amendments and objected to unanimous consent requests to suspend the required reading. In one case, the clerk took 55 minutes to read an amendment.

● Occasionally the senators would demand two roll-call votes on a single amendment, one on the proposal itself and another on the routine motion to reconsider. In such instances, the two senators shrewdly voted with the majority to reject the amendments so that they would be eligible to offer the motions to reconsider.

● Although debate on the amendments was minimal under cloture, the two senators demanded roll-call votes on each amendment, a process requiring 15 minutes. They made repeated quorum calls to ensure that 51 senators were present on the floor. Each quorum call could take an hour or more.

These relatively simple steps enabled Abourezk and Metzenbaum to tie the Senate in knots. None of the time consumed for their procedural motions counted against the hour each controlled once cloture was invoked. Frustration and bitterness grew as the post-cloture filibuster rolled on. "In the course of the last few days," commented Sen. Baker, "we have gone through a torture that the Senate has seldom encountered, including not just an all-night session, but an all-night session that was unique and different from others, as we painfully knew, because the roll calls and quorum calls came at 15-, 30-, and 45-minute intervals." [44]

Finally, Senator Byrd, several members, and staff aides devised a counterstrategy. The aim was to rule out of order the bulk of the Abourezk-Metzenbaum amendments pending at the desk. Byrd enlisted the cooperation of Vice President Walter F. Mondale, the presiding officer of the Senate under the Constitution.

When the Senate convened on October 3, 1977, Mondale recognized Majority Leader Byrd, who made the point of order "that when the Senate is operating under cloture, the Chair is required to rule out of order all amendments which are dilatory or which on their face are out of order." Under previous Senate precedents, the chair had to wait for a point of order to be raised against each amendment before ruling whether it was dilatory.

Mondale sustained Byrd's point of order. Abourezk appealed the decision but lost on a 79-14 vote. The stage then was set for a pre-arranged plan. Reading from a typed script given him by Byrd, Mondale recognized only the majority leader (recall his priority of recognition), who called up 33 of Metzenbaum's amendments. (Technically, a senator can call up any amendment pending at the desk, even if it is not his own.) Each of the senator's amendments was quickly ruled out of order by the presiding officer, who ignored the senators who wanted to appeal the chair's ruling, a customary right of members.

Bedlam broke out on the floor. Cries of "dictatorship" and "steamroller" were heard. "The Senate of the United States has just seen an outrageous act," declared Sen. Gary Hart, D-Colo. Abourezk and Metzenbaum, feeling betrayed by the administration, ended their filibuster. With nine days of debate and 129 roll-call votes behind it, the Senate enacted the natural gas deregulation measure. Several new precedents had been set for strengthening enforcement of the cloture rule, and studies of Rule XXII were proposed.

1979 Revision of Rule XXII. On February 22, 1979, the Senate amended Rule XXII to restrict opportunities for the so-called post-cloture filibuster. Once cloture is invoked, under the change, a 100-hour cap is imposed on all post-cloture action, including the time spent reading and voting on amendments, quorum calls, and any other procedural motion. No measure, then, is to be debated beyond a total of 100 hours following a successful cloture vote. The change also provides "that no Senator shall call up more than two amendments until every other Senator has had the opportunity to call up two amendments." [45] The presiding officer is directed to give priority of recognition to another senator rather than to a member seeking to call up a third amendment. All first and second degree amendments also must be submitted prior to the cloture vote.

Collectively, these changes were designed to reduce the ability of senators to carry on post-cloture filibusters. They have had limited impact, however. Senators continue to conduct effective post-cloture filibusters.

Senators sometimes even vote against cloture to avoid the frustrations of the post-cloture filibuster. "I am voting against cloture," said Senator Byrd in 1982, "because I want to avoid a post-cloture filibuster." This dilatory technique, he added, "is an abomination to the Senate and to the legislative process." Senator Baker expressed similar sentiments. The Senate must address the post-cloture filibuster because "I think now we have made Rule XXII a nullity."[46]

Despite the 100-hour cap, post-cloture filibusters continue because any senator can use his or her hour of debate under Rule XXII for delaying purposes. A senator can call up scores of germane amendments, ask for votes on each amendment, and request numerous quorum calls. The time expended for such procedural matters now is charged against the 100-hour cap but not against the senator's hour. Senator Patrick J. Leahy, D-Vt., for example, asked the presiding officer this question in 1980, soon after the new rule had been adopted:

> If 99 senators yielded back all their time and one remaining Senator yielded back 45 minutes, then, within a matter of 10 or 15 seconds of that time, called up an amendment at the desk and asked for the yeas and nays and vote, is it correct that he might be able to string that out for 100 hours, that 15 minutes? Ninety-nine and a half hours having been yielded back so somebody might be able actually to string out 100 hours?

The presiding officer responded: "The Senator is correct. It is possible." [47]

In short, filibusters may continue even after cloture is invoked. They may be terminated through such means as expiration of the 100-hour cap, compromises between the contending sides, or mistakes that cause filibustering senators to lose the floor, such as a violation of the two-speech rule. That rule forbids members from "making a third speech on the same question in the same legislative day." [48]

Final Vote on a Bill

Once cloture is invoked, filibusters by amendment broken, and other delaying tactics ended, the Senate proceeds to a final vote on the bill under consideration. If obstructionist tactics cannot be ended, the leadership may withdraw the bill and proceed to other business.

On legislation not regulated by complex agreements and not the target of deliberate obstructionist tactics, the floor managers and party leaders try to fashion *ad hoc* agreements under which amendments can be disposed of. But because of the strong commitment in the Senate to giving every member ample opportunity to be heard, this can be a lengthy process. For example, the 1976 Tax Reform Act, which was not filibustered, consumed 25 days of debate. There were 209 amendments and motions on the bill and 129 roll-call votes. The length of time debating this legislation reflected its importance to senators and the country as well as the complexity of its provisions.

Paradoxically, while it is relatively easy to frustrate floor action, Senate rules make it difficult for committees to bottle up legislation and prevent it from reaching the floor. The means by which senators can force bills to be considered by the Senate are discussed in the following section.

Procedures to Circumvent Committees

In an earlier chapter, it was seen that the House has a number of procedures for bringing bills to the floor that are blocked in committee. These include Calendar Wednesday, the discharge petition, the power of extraction by the Rules Committee, and the suspension of the rules procedure. Except for suspension, which generally is used for relatively noncontroversial bills, these alternative House procedures are seldom employed and rarely successful.

Bypassing committees, while not an everyday occurrence in the Senate, is easier to accomplish than in the House. At least four techniques are available to senators: 1) use of nongermane amendments, also known as riders; 2) placing House-passed and Senate-introduced bills immediately on the Calendar of General Orders; 3) suspending Senate rules; and 4) implementing the discharge procedure. The first two are the most effective.

Nongermane Amendments

Unlike the House, the Senate has never had a rule requiring amendments to be germane to pending legislation. "Amendments may be made," Thomas Jefferson wrote in the parliamentary manual he prepared during his service as president of the Senate (1797-1801), "so as totally to alter the nature of the proposition." [49] A classic case occurred in 1965 when Sen. Everett McKinley Dirksen, R-Ill. (1951-69), tried to add a proposal for a constitutional amendment on legislative reapportionment to a joint resolution designating August 6 to September 6 as "National American Legion Baseball Month." Dirksen's amendment had been blocked by the Judiciary Committee. An opponent of the proposal called the senator's attempt a "foul ball."

More recently, portions of President Jimmy Carter's 1977 national energy program were attached temporarily to several House-passed private bills. Subsequently, those portions were repackaged into public bills.

Senate Prohibitions. Although the Senate does not have a general germaneness rule, there are four situations where the Senate requires germane amendments to pending legislation:

● Unanimous consent agreements as usually drawn up contain a requirement that amendments be germane.

● Amendments to general appropriations bills.

● When cloture has been invoked.

● During consideration of concurrent budget resolutions.

"The intent of the 'germaneness' restriction" in the 1974 budget act, remarked Sen. Lawton Chiles, D-Fla., "was to prevent extraneous nonbudgetary amendments from being added to budget resolutions." [50]

What germaneness means in practical circumstances is not always easy to determine. In general, noted one presiding officer, if an "amendment expands the effect of the bill or introduces new subject matter it is not germane." [51] Thus, if a farm bill dealt with five items — barley, wheat, rice, cotton, and soybeans, and a senator sought to amend the measure by adding corn to the list, a germaneness point of order could be made against the amendment.

Uses of Riders. There is little doubt that the Senate's deliberative role is strengthened because it permits senators to raise new issues on the floor through nongermane amendments. Proposals bottled up in committee that a majority favors can be offered as riders to pending measures. "Must" bills, such as debt ceiling and appropriations legislation, often are handy vehicles for this purpose.

The practice also enables members to respond with dispatch to changing circumstances. On May 6, 1982, for instance, Democrats Byrd and Daniel Patrick Moynihan, N.Y., offered amendments dealing with Social Security to a Defense Department authorization measure. They wanted to send a signal to the Reagan White House not to take any action reorganizing the system until Congress had considered the recommendations of the National Commission on Social Security Reform. Senate Armed Services Committee Chairman John Tower, R-Texas, called the amendments "politically inspired," without any relevance to the defense bill. [52]

In brief, germaneness sometimes has been a vexatious issue for the Senate. On the one hand, the lack of a general prohibition on riders permits senators to raise and debate popular and unpopular issues and lessens the opportunity for arbitrary committee action. On the other hand, some senators complain that the practice wastes the Senate's time by permitting contentious debate on matters unrelated to the fundamental purpose of a pending bill. Besides these legislative nongermane amendments, numerous "limitation" riders are added in every session to appropriations bills. *(See Chapter 3, p. 50.)*

Placing Measures on the Calendar

When measures are passed by the House and sent to the Senate, they customarily are referred to a committee. As noted earlier, all measures, including House-passed bills, must be read twice on different legislative days before they can be referred to committee. Under Senate Rule XIV, if any senator objects to the second reading the committee stage is bypassed and the House-passed bill, or Senate-introduced bill, is placed directly on the calendar.

This procedure was used by supporters of the 1957 and 1964 Civil Rights Acts (the 1960 Civil Rights Act was introduced as a nongermane amendment). Backers of those measures wanted to avoid sending the bills to the Judiciary Committee, which had an unbroken record of never reporting a civil rights bill. On October 14, 1981, Democratic leader Byrd employed the same tactic to circumvent the Judiciary Committee. He objected to referring the House-passed extension of the 1965 Voting Rights Act to that panel; thus it went directly on the calendar. Placing a bill on the calendar also gives the leadership the option of calling up either the House-passed measure or, should there be one, the version reported by the Senate committee.

Senators occasionally use the Rule XIV procedure when they introduce measures. "I ask unanimous consent to have the bill read a second time under Senate Rule XIV so that I may put the bill on the calendar," said Appropriations Committee Chairman Mark O. Hatfield, R-Ore., during a Senate debate in 1982. His measure dealt with restrictions on the federal funding of abortions. To avoid the "countless delays" in dealing with abortion riders to appropriations bills, Senator Hatfield had called for a permanent statute dealing with abortions.

> I am introducing this legislation today and objecting to its being referred to committee since extensive hearings have already been held on various pro-life measures before the Senate, and since the issue of Federal funding for abortion has been repeatedly debated and decided in this Chamber.[53]

Although effective, Rule XIV is used sparingly because of the general deference to committee prerogatives. It is sometimes used when the proponent of a bill feels intensely enough about it to flout the jurisdiction of a committee that is known to oppose it.[54] For example, in 1977 a waterway users bill was passed by the Senate and sent to the House. The House dropped an "inland waterway charge" and substituted a "fuel tax" on barge operators. When the bill returned to the Senate, it was headed for the Finance Committee, which handles all tax matters. Finance Committee Chairman Long was known to oppose the bill, sponsored by Sen. Pete V. Domenici, R-N.M. As noted in Chapter 4, when the senator originally introduced the bill, it had been drafted so as to avoid having it referred to Long's committee.

To prevent the House-passed version of the bill from being referred to the Finance Committee, Domenici used Rule XIV, and the measure was placed directly on the calendar for floor action. The result was that the Senate eventually approved a toll on the nation's barge operators.

More commonly, House-passed measures are held at the clerk's desk by unanimous consent. When the House passed President Carter's 1977 energy package, it was held at the desk until Senate leaders decided how the package was to be handled by various committees. Similarly, the 1975 House-passed bill providing financial assistance to New York City was held at the desk with the proviso that the leadership could call it up at any time. House-passed measures are also held at the desk when similar Senate bills are already pending on the calendar or are expected shortly to be reported out of committee.

Suspension of the Rules

Senate rules can be suspended, provided there is one day's notice in writing and the terms of the suspension motion are printed in the *Congressional Record*. The rules are silent on the number of votes needed to suspend

Senate rules. Precedents have required two-thirds of those present and voting to approve suspensions. The procedure is rarely used because it represents a challenge to the committee system and is open to dilatory tactics. In effect, three filibusters are possible on suspension motions: first, on the motion to suspend the rules; second, on the motion to take up the bill; and third, on the bill itself.

Suspension motions occasionally are made by senators who want to offer policy amendments to general appropriations measures. Policy amendments (legislative language) to appropriations measures are forbidden by Senate rules and can be made in order only by unanimous consent or by the suspension route.

The Discharge Procedure

Discharging a bill from a committee has taken place only 14 times in the history of the Senate. It was last employed successfully in 1964. The prevailing sentiment is that the procedure undercuts the committee system and also that the rules governing its use are cumbersome. The discharge motion can be made only during the "morning hour" and must remain at the clerk's desk for one legislative day. Thus party leaders can forestall discharge motions for days or weeks simply by recessing, thus keeping the Senate in the same legislative day. If debate on the motion is not concluded within the morning hour, the motion is placed on the calendar, where it faces the threat of a series of filibusters. A vote to discharge a committee of a bill requires a simple majority vote unless it is necessary to invoke cloture to stop a filibuster.

There is technically yet another way to bypass a Senate committee: by unanimous consent. The Senate, as has been seen in this chapter, can do almost anything it wants by unanimous consent. However, unanimous consent will not be obtained if a single member — presumably a member of the committee that would be bypassed — objects; thus this procedure is seldom attempted.

Summary

There are more differences than similarities between Senate and House floor procedures, the result primarily of the smaller size and greater opportunity for informal arrangements in the Senate. Procedures such as unanimous consent agreements, the track system, the filibuster and the cloture rule, nongermane amendments, morning business, legislative days, and executive sessions have no real counterpart in the House. Conversely, the five-minute rule, rules from the Rules Committee, recorded teller votes, and electronic voting cannot be found in the Senate.

The larger, more complex, House emphasizes formal rules and precedents. The Senate functions in a largely *ad hoc* fashion, emphasizing reciprocity and courtesy among senators. House procedure is relatively straightforward, with few detours. The Senate changes its procedures to meet new contingencies, accommodate members, and resolve unforeseen problems. The Senate occasionally observes its formal rules, but more commonly waives them by unanimous consent and modifies its debate arrangements to suit each bill.

Senate rules emphasize the influence of individual members. As Senator Byrd has observed: "The rules of the Senate are made for the convenience of those who wish to delay." [55] As a result, it is often more difficult to create winning coalitions in the Senate than in the House. The discipline imposed by House rules generally aids party leaders in forming and sustaining majorities. The Senate's informality requires leaders to negotiate new majorities constantly.

There also are more opportunities to revise legislation on the Senate floor than in the House. Senators feel freer to offer amendments to legislation coming from committees, other than their own, than do members of the House, who are somewhat more likely to defer to the committees' decisions. And to a far greater degree in the Senate than in the House, members are assured that their party leaders will make every effort to accommodate their scheduling needs.

A crucial legislative arbiter on virtually all important legislation is the conference committee. Composed of groups of legislators from each chamber, this "third house of Congress" reconciles differences between House- and Senate-passed versions of bills. The next chapter examines this important congressional institution and other ways of resolving differences in bills passed by the two houses of Congress.

Notes

1. U.S., Congress, Senate, *Congressional Record,* daily ed., May 21, 1980, S5674.
2. *Wall Street Journal,* November 11, 1977, 14.
3. On November 17, 1982, for the first time since 1793, the House operated on two legislative days in the same day. It adjourned at 1:19 p.m. (the first legislative day) and then reconvened at 4 p.m. that day (the second legislative day). Sharp partisanship stimulated the Democratic leadership to employ this rare scheduling device.
4. U.S., Congress, Senate, *Congressional Record,* daily ed., March 28, 1980, S3234.
5. U.S., Congress, Senate, *Congressional Record,* daily ed., January 25, 1982, S3.
6. Forcing the reading of the *Journal* and offering amendments or corrections to it occasionally are employed as a filibustering device. For an example, see the Senate proceedings of March 4, 1975. Also see Margo Carlisle, "Changing the Rules of the Game in the U.S. Senate," *Policy Review* (Winter 1979): 79-92.
7. U.S., Congress, Senate, *Congressional Record,* daily ed., March 28, 1980, S3234. Senators may introduce bills only during morning business. However, the informal practice is to permit senators, by unanimous consent, to introduce them at any time.
8. U.S., Congress, Senate, *Congressional Record,* February 27, 1970, 5207.
9. U.S., Congress, Senate, *Congressional Record,* June 9, 1977, 18179.
10. During his tenure as majority leader, Howard H. Baker, Jr., urged the Senate, unsuccessfully, to permit national television coverage of its floor debates. Senator

Baker's objective was to restore the Senate's role as a major national forum for debate. He said: "If the criticism of allowing cameras on the Senate floor is that Senators will be there posturing, then that's the best argument for the cameras. I want to bring the Senators back and begin national debates." See Richard Reeves, "Why Howard Baker is Leaving the Senate," *Washington Post Parade Magazine*, August 7, 1983, 10.

11. A Senate rule requires three hours of germane discussion at the beginning of each day's debate on a measure. Called the Pastore Rule after its sponsor, former Sen. John O. Pastore, D-R.I. (1950-76), its purpose is to confine debate to pending business.

12. *Wall Street Journal*, September 17, 1973, 10.

13. Rowland Evans and Robert Novak, *Lyndon B. Johnson: The Exercise of Power* (New York: The New American Library, 1966), 115.

14. Joseph S. Clark, *Congress: The Sapless Branch* (New York: Harper & Row, 1964), 247-248.

15. U.S., Congress, Senate, *Congressional Record*, October 28, 1977, 5857.

16. Elizabeth Drew, *Senator* (New York: Simon & Schuster, 1979), 173-174.

17. U.S., Congress, Senate, *Congressional Record*, daily ed., April 18, 1980, S3923. See also Stanley Bach, "Parliamentary Strategy and the Amendment Process: Rules and Case Studies of Congressional Action," *Polity* (Summer 1983): 573-592.

18. U.S., Congress, Senate, *Congressional Record*, daily ed., August 19, 1980, S11212.

19. Kathy Koch, "Senate Votes to Weaken Strip Mining Law," *Congressional Quarterly Weekly Report*, August 23, 1980, 2453.

20. U.S., Congress, Senate, *Congressional Record*, September 29, 1976, 33269.

21. Clinton P. Anderson, *Outsider in the Senate* (New York: The World Publishing Co., 1970), 283.

22. *Congressional Quarterly Weekly Report*, June 18, 1977, 1204. See also U.S., Congress, Senate, *Congressional Record*, June 16, 1977, 19441-19468.

23. Ibid.

24. Party leaders have expressed reservations about stacking votes. See U.S., Congress, Senate, *Congressional Record*, daily ed., June 10, 1983, S8219-S8220, S8222-S8223.

25. See U.S., Congress, Senate, *Congressional Record*, daily ed., September 13, 1983, S13227.

26. U.S., Congress, Senate, *Congressional Record*, January 26, 1973, 2301.

27. James L. Buckley, *If Men Were Angels* (New York: G. P. Putnam's Sons, 1975), 129.

28. Bernard Asbell, *The Senate Nobody Knows* (Garden City, New York: Doubleday & Co., 1978), 267.

29. U.S., Congress, Senate, *Congressional Record*, September 23, 1975, 29814.

30. U.S., Congress, Senate, *Congressional Record*, daily ed., April 8, 1981, S3618.

31. U.S., Congress, Senate, *Congressional Record*, daily ed., July 22, 1983, S10701.

32. *New York Times*, December 21, 1982, D29.

33. On May 24, 1976, the Senate voted against the confirmation of an individual for a seat on the Consumer Product Safety Commission. Opponents of the nomination, however, failed to offer the motion to reconsider so that it could be tabled. Two days later, the Senate agreed to a motion to reconsider and then approved the nomination. The motion is in order within two calendar days after the vote is taken.

34. The word derives from the Dutch word *Vrijbuiter,* meaning freebooter. Passing into Spanish as *filibustero,* it was used to describe military adventurers from the United States who in the mid-1800s fomented insurrections against various Latin American governments. For an account of William Walker, filibusterer of the 1850s, see *Smithsonian,* June 1981, 117-128. The first legislative use of the word is said to have occurred in the House in 1853, when a representative accused his opponents of "filibustering against the United States." By 1863 the word filibuster had come to mean delaying action on the floor, but the term did not gain wide currency until the 1880s.

35. U.S., Congress, Senate, *Congressional Record,* daily ed., July 18, 1983, S10216.

36. *New York Times,* December 12, 1982, 4E.

37. The longest speech in the history of the Senate was made by Strom Thurmond, D-S.C., during a filibuster against passage of the Civil Rights Act of 1957. He spoke for 24 hours and 18 minutes in a round-the-clock session, August 28-29, 1957.

38. Allan L. Damon, "Filibuster," *American Heritage,* December 1975, 97.

39. U.S., Congress, Senate, *Congressional Record,* February 26, 1979, 3232.

40. *Washington Post,* June 11, 1982, A11.

41. *New York Times,* May 28, 1982, A16. See also Harrison Donnelly, "Veto Expected: Senate Approves $5.1 Billion For Mortgage Subsidies In Fiscal '82 Spending Bill," *Congressional Quarterly Weekly Report,* May 29, 1982, 1246.

42. George D. Aiken, *Aiken: Senate Diary* (Brattleboro, Vt.: Stephen Greene Press, 1975), 325.

43. U.S., Congress, Senate, *Congressional Record,* December 4, 1975, 38442. For a useful history of the cloture rule, see Sen. Robert C. Byrd's, D-W. Va., commentary in U.S., Congress, Senate, *Congressional Record,* daily ed., March 10, 1981, S1928-S1937. For the past several years, Senator Byrd periodically has addressed the Senate on its history, rules, and traditions. His statements will be compiled in a Senate volume.

44. *Congressional Quarterly Weekly Report,* October 1, 1977, 2070.

45. U.S., Congress, Senate, *Congressional Record,* daily ed., March 10, 1981, S1934.

46. U.S., Congress, Senate, *Congressional Record,* daily ed., September 22, 1982, S11939-S11940.

47. U.S., Congress, Senate, *Congressional Record,* daily ed., June 10, 1980, S6525.

48. U.S., Congress, Senate, *Congressional Record,* daily ed., December 20, 1982, S15748.

49. *Constitution, Jefferson's Manual and Rules of the House of Representatives,* 97th Cong., 2d sess., H. Doc. No. 97-271, 235.

50. *Washington Post,* May 18, 1982, A23.

51. U.S., Congress, Senate, *Congressional Record,* daily ed., February 9, 1982, S599.

52. U.S., Congress, Senate, *Congressional Record,* daily ed., May 6, 1982, S4643-S4644.

53. U.S., Congress, Senate, *Congressional Record,* daily ed., April 15, 1982, S3557-S3558.

54. For a discussion of the leadership's concern about overuse of Rule XIV, see U.S., Congress, Senate, *Congressional Record,* daily ed., September 27, 1983, S12971.

55. U.S., Congress, Senate, *Congressional Record,* August 31, 1976, 28607.

9

Resolving House-Senate Differences

Before legislation can be sent to the president for his consideration, it must be passed by both houses in identical form. House- and Senate-passed versions of the same bill frequently differ, sometimes only slightly but often on critical points. The two versions must be reconciled by mutual agreement. Whenever possible, this is done informally. However, a fair percentage of all bills passed by both chambers require action by a House-Senate conference committee — an *ad hoc* joint committee composed of members selected by each chamber to resolve differences on a particular bill in disagreement.[1]

> Over one-quarter of all public bills enacted during the 96th Congress (1979-81) — including all of the annual appropriations bills — were products of conference deliberations. Many other bills that were not enacted also ended up in conference committees.[2]

Almost all major or controversial legislation requires conference committee action.

Obscurity of the Process

The conference committee process is older than Congress itself. State legislatures used conference committees before 1789 to reconcile differences between the chambers of their bicameral legislatures. The conference committee system was taken for granted when the first Congress convened, and it has been in use ever since.[3] Nevertheless, for many citizens the conference committee is little known or understood, compared to the other aspects of the legislative process.

The relative obscurity of the conference process is explained by the fact that until the mid-1970s, conference committees almost always met in secret sessions with no published record of their proceedings. The conference committees produced a conference committee report that showed the results of the secret negotiations, but the bargaining and deliberations that led to those results were not formally disclosed.

In one of the most significant reforms of congressional procedure of the past decade, both chambers in 1975 adopted rules requiring open conference committee meetings unless a majority of the conference members (called conferees or managers) from either chamber voted in public to hold secret sessions. In 1977 the House went a step further, adopting a rule requiring the full House to vote to close a conference. This occurs usually on legislation dealing with national security.

A Critical Juncture

The conference committee is one of the most critical points in the legislative process. For several reasons, however, members of Congress may try to avoid this stage and resolve House-Senate differences on legislation without recourse to the conference committee process. For one thing, there is pressure to approve the legislation quickly. For another, there may be concern in one house that conferees of the other chamber will try to weaken the legislation. And third, there always is the possibility that a conference committee will become deadlocked — particularly in the weeks and days before the final adjournment of Congress.

Failure of the conferees to reach agreement before the end of a Congress means that the bill dies. For example, the controversial 1980 Alaskan lands bill, called the conservation issue of the century by President Jimmy Carter, never went to conference because its House sponsors realized that with time running out it had to accept the Senate's version of the legislation or there would be no bill at all. *(See box, p. 203.)*

This chapter first discusses how House-Senate differences on a bill are resolved without a conference. It then explores the complexities of the conference committee process. Finally, the chapter examines the last steps of the legislative process — final House and Senate approval of legislation (of the conference compromise for bills sent to conference committees) and presidential approval or veto, with subsequent action by Congress on vetoed bills. *(An example of a conference report appears on p. 215, a public law on p. 220.)*

Agreement Without a Conference

There are two principal methods of resolving House-Senate differences without a conference. First, there is verbatim adoption of one chamber's version of a bill by the other. This is a common occurrence and may involve informal consultation before or after passage of the bill by one chamber. Second, the two houses may send measures back and forth several times, amending each other's amendments, before they agree to identical language on all provisions of the legislation.

It is usual for House and Senate committee staff to communicate regularly on legislation of mutual interest. Drafts of measures are exchanged for comment and consistency, companion bills are studied, and strategies are devised to facilitate passage in each chamber. Executive branch officials and pressure groups often participate in these informal strategy sessions. This kind of prior consultation frequently helps clear away obstacles to passage — allowing legislation to be approved by both houses in identical form, thus avoiding the need for a conference.

Avoiding a Conference to Clear a Bill

The only hope for an Alaska lands bill this session lies in a Senate package close enough to the House version that a conference on the differences can be avoided, a key senator in the debate said yesterday.

Sen. Paul E. Tsongas, D-Mass., said a conference would be vulnerable to "pre-conference, mid-conference and end-conference filibusters" from the two Alaska senators, who oppose what the Senate has done so far.

The measure, which would place more than 100 million acres of wild Alaskan territory in varying categories of environmental protection, has been under discussion off the Senate floor since a week ago yesterday, when debate broke down.

Tsongas was the environmentalist champion in the floor debate, proposing amendments to strengthen an Energy Committee bill offered by Sen. Henry M. Jackson, D-Wash. But in closed-door negotiations designed to win Jackson's agreement, he has forged a compromise package that has come dangerously close to alienating not only the Alaska senators but also the Alaska coalition of 32 environmental groups.

A meeting with coalition leaders Tuesday, Tsongas told reporters, provided "no particular wear and tear on the grin muscles." Beth Johnson of the coalition confirmed that the group is still reserving judgment on what she called "the Tsongas-Jackson agreement."

Tsongas said Reps. Morris K. Udall, D-Ariz., and John F. Seiberling, D-Ohio, key House members on the issue, had joined the ongoing talks. The question, he said, is reaching an accommodation "without everyone jumping ship. . . . The middle ground on this issue is very narrow."

Sen. Ted Stevens, R-Alaska, reiterated his position that although concessions to his viewpoint may have satisfied Jackson, they will not satisfy him. He said he would continue to push for the original committee provisions.

Source: Joanne Omang, "Alaska Lands Bill's Only Hope Seen in Avoiding Conference," *Washington Post,* July 31, 1980, A7.

Consultation also may take place after one or both chambers have passed a bill. A typical example occurred in 1976. In August the House had passed its version of legislation to strengthen enforcement of antitrust laws. The Senate, having previously passed another version, was expected to go to conference to resolve the differences. However, in September Sen. James B. Allen, D-Ala. (1969-78), announced his intention to filibuster both the usually routine motion to appoint conferees and the conference report itself. House and Senate staff aides met informally to discuss ways to reconcile differences between the two versions. As a result of those negotiations, a substitute for the original antitrust bill was drafted, passed by the Senate and sent to the House, thereby avoiding the filibusters by Allen. "What we're hoping," said Senate Majority Leader Mike Mansfield, D-Mont. (1953-77), "is that the House will accept what the Senate has done and send it to the President. In the short time we have left [before final congressional adjournment], any other course is suicidal." [4] The House followed Mansfield's advice and passed the Senate version without amendment. The president signed the bill into law.

Limits to Nonconference Tactics

Under the "back and forth" approach, two points are worth noting:

● There is a limit to the number of times measures may be shuffled between the chambers. In brief, the third-degree amendment prohibition, discussed in Chapters 6 and 8, also applies to amendments between the House and Senate. Each chamber gets "two shots" at amending the amendments of the other body.

● The "back and forth" alternative procedure is employed intentionally to avoid conferences and is feasible only when circumstances warrant its use. For instance, a House chairman asked the chamber to concur in the Senate amendment to the House amendment to the Senate-passed bill. House approval is "appropriate parliamentary procedure, which allows us to avoid the trouble of a conference when faced with such small [bicameral] differences." [5] Once the House, in this case, agrees to the Senate amendment, the bill is cleared for the president.

Why Conference Committees?

It is often clear from the outset that controversial measures will end up in conference. Members plan their floor strategy accordingly. They make floor statements that emphasize their unyielding commitment to their own chamber's positions. In advance of a "House-Senate conference," noted Senate Majority Leader Howard H. Baker, Jr., R-Tenn., "it is not unusual for the respective [chambers] to stake out positions for themselves and even to utter statements about their absolute intransigence, that sometimes does not always prevail when the conference convenes." [6]

Members frequently add expendable amendments to use as bargaining chips in conference. Such amendments can be traded away for other provisions considered more important. Use of such tactics has been refined to an art form by some senators. For example, Sen. Russell B. Long, D-La., "usually comes to conference with a bill loaded up with amendments added on the Senate floor. . . . Long has plenty of things he is willing to jettison to save the goodies." [7] Alternatively, one chamber may deliberately keep out of its bill something it knows the other chamber really wants. During a conference, the House conferees, for instance, may "give in" to the Senate, but only in return for Senate acceptance of something favored by the House. For these reasons it is difficult to identify the "winners" or "losers" in conference simply by counting the number of times one house appeared to give in to the other.[8]

Sometimes amendments are added to make sure that certain points of view are heard in conference. Massachusetts Sen. Edward M. Kennedy, D, once offered an amendment to a defense appropriations bill to delete $100,000 intended for the National Board for the Promotion of Rifle Practice and to abolish the authority of the secretary of defense to supply ammunition to gun clubs. Although it was clear the House was strongly opposed to Kennedy's proposals, the Senate floor manager of the bill said he was "willing to take that to conference, so that both sides of the argument can be fully developed." [9]

There are other motivations, too, for taking an amendment to conference. According to one senator:

> I have been in this body long enough to beware of the chairman of a committee who says in an enticing voice, "Let me take the amendment to conference," because I think that is frequently the parliamentary equivalent of saying, "Let me take the child into the tower and I will strangle him to death." [10]

Today, with conference committees open to the public, it sometimes is necessary to put up a fight for such amendments before dropping them.

There also are instances when members prefer that certain issues be resolved in conference, rather than on the floor. Speaker Sam Rayburn, D-Texas (1913-61), once explained:

> My position is this: I should like to see this bill in conference. I have pointed out a great many things in both bills. I think there are frailties in the House measure and also in the Senate measure, but I think we can do a better job in conference than we can here.[11]

A small group of conferees may be able to reach compromises that are impossible in the full House or Senate in the heat of floor debate on a controversial bill.

In addition, measures sometimes are sent to conference for the political convenience of members. Legislators may vote for a bill, fully aware that it contains unnecessary special interest provisions, in the expectation that conferees from the other house will kill those items that constitute a costly "raid on the Treasury" or are simply ill-advised. When one chamber "passes the buck to the other," former Sen. George D. Aiken, R-Vt. (1941-75), wrote, "the conference committees simply get together and straighten things out. Then every member of Congress can tell his constituents that he voted for the things they wanted and against the things they opposed, and they will never know the difference." [12]

Finally, House and Senate floor managers consider whether they want recorded votes on certain amendments when they are debated in their chamber. For example, Sen. John C. Culver's, D-Iowa (1975-81), strategy on an amendment he opposed was to seek a recorded vote on it in order "to beat the amendment, and beat it good, burying the issue in the Senate once and for all, and also putting him in a position to tell a Senate-House conference on the bill that the proposal was resoundingly defeated in the Senate." [13]

Alternatively, floor managers sometimes prefer not to draw attention to amendments they oppose — and thus hope to avoid taking roll-call votes — on the assumption that it then will be easier to drop them in conference.

Conference Committee Process

There are five major steps in the conference committee process: 1) requesting a conference, 2) selecting conferees, 3) conference committee bargaining, 4) the conference committee report, and, 5) final House and Senate action on the conference committee version of the bill.

Requesting a Conference

When the House passes a bill, and it then is amended by the Senate and returned, the House has several options. It may: 1) refuse to take further action, in which case the measure dies; 2) approve an entirely new version of the bill and send it to the Senate; 3) agree to the Senate's amendments, negating the need for a conference; 4) amend the Senate's amendments and return the measure once again to the Senate; or 5) request a conference.

Occasionally, the Speaker may refer the Senate amendments, especially if they are nongermane to the House-passed measure, to the standing committee having jurisdiction over the subject matter of the amendments. More commonly, though, on major legislation a member will ask and receive unanimous consent for the House to disagree to the Senate's amendments and request a conference with the Senate. The Speaker usually recognizes an appropriate committee member to offer the motion — which requires majority approval — to go to conference on the bill.

When the situation is reversed, and a Senate-passed bill is amended by the House and returned to the Senate, it is "held at the desk and almost always subsequently laid before the Senate by the Presiding Officer upon request or motion of a Senator [usually the manager of the bill.]" [14]

The House amendment or amendments may be dealt with in four ways by the Senate: 1) by adopting a motion to refer the amendment(s) to the appropriate standing committee, 2) by further amending the House amendments, 3) by agreeing to the House amendments (thus clearing the bill), or 4) by disagreeing to the House amendments, in which case a conference is requested by motion or unanimous consent.

In short, both chambers vote themselves into a state of disagreement before going to conference.

Selecting Conferees

The selection of conferees is governed in both chambers by rules and precedent. On each occasion in which a bill is sent to conference, the House Speaker and the presiding officer of the Senate formally appoint the respective conferees. In fact, both chambers rely on the chairman and ranking minority member of the committee that originally considered and reported the bill to make the selection.

The Speaker and the presiding officer almost never deviate from the list of proposed conferees given them by the committee leaders, who generally select members of their own committees. A member of another committee may be appointed when he or she has special knowledge of the subject matter or if the bill is of particular interest to the member's state or district. When a bill has been referred to several committees (multiple referral), it is common to have conferees from all the committees that handled it.

Seniority used to be a dominant criterion in the appointment of conferees. But in the wake of the procedural reforms of the 1970s, junior members, especially those with particular expertise or interest in the legislation going to conference, are now often selected. "We used to select conferees by seniority," commented a Senate chairman, but "now we try to get more balance ideologically and geographically while still including those who made the biggest contribution to the bill." [15]

Increasingly, members of the subcommittee that reported the bill are being appointed conferees, as they often are the most knowledgeable about the legislation. Rules of several House committees, in fact, require conferees to be named from the appropriate subcommittees.

Party ratios on conference committees generally reflect the party membership in the House and Senate. In the nineteenth century it was common for each chamber to select three conferees — two majority party members and one member of the minority. Today the number of conferees usually ranges from seven to 11, but there is no limit.

The trend in recent years has been to increase the size of conference delegations, particularly for energy and spending legislation. Members want to be where the action is. On the natural gas portion of President Carter's massive 1977 energy package, for example, the Senate included all 18 members of the Energy and Natural Resources Committee as conferees along with 10 other senators. The House appointed 25 conferees (17 Democrats and eight Republicans).

The largest conference in congressional history involved the 1981 omnibus budget reconciliation bill. "Over 250 Senators and Congressmen met in 58 [subconferences] to consider nearly 300 issues" in disagreement, noted Senator Baker.[16] Larger conferences have a tendency to lengthen the bicameral bargaining process.

The conferees from each house vote as a unit, with a majority vote deciding each issue. The House and Senate have, in effect, one vote each. Bargaining and compromises are enhanced by this feature of the conference process.

Rules and precedents require that a majority of conferees must have "generally supported" the bill. "The child is not to be put to a nurse that cares not for it," wrote Thomas Jefferson.[17] And in 1960 Sen. Richard B. Russell, D-Ga. (1933-71), expressed a view that is still strongly held by most members:

> When I go to a conference as a representative of the Senate, I represent the Senate viewpoint as vigorously as possible, even though it may not be in accord with the vote or votes I cast on the floor of the Senate. I conceive that to be the duty of the conferee.[18]

Selecting conferees according to this criterion is not always easy, particularly in the case of highly controversial bills that have passed one or the other chamber by narrow margins. One of the stumbling blocks on the 1977 natural gas bill was that both the Senate and House conference delegations were divided among themselves on whether to deregulate or continue price controls on natural gas.

Usually, a member's vote on final passage is taken as evidence of an overall position on a measure for purposes of selection to a conference committee. Yet a member who votes for the final version may have voted against critical amendments that were adopted during floor debate or for amendments intended to cripple the bill. House rules address this knotty issue by directing the Speaker to name no less than a majority of conferees who generally supported the House position "as determined by the Speaker."

In case of a conflict of interest or views, conferees are permitted to resign from conference committees. That step once was taken by Sen. Robert C. Byrd, D-W.Va., when he was majority whip. He explained:

> I was named as a Senate conferee. I do not feel — after thinking overnight about the matter — that I can conscientiously serve as a conferee on that amendment. Although there is no rule that would bind me to support the Senate position on the amendment. I would not wish to go to the conference and oppose the Senate position, because in so doing I would be putting myself and my will above the Senate and the majority will of the Senate.[19]

Senator Byrd's remarks illustrate another important point about conferees: The House or Senate may adopt motions instructing their conferees to sustain the majority position of the chamber on a particular amendment or provision of a bill. This places additional political and moral pressure on the conferees and normally hardens their position in conference committee bargaining. "We need to give the House conferees some backbone to stand up to the Senate on this issue," declared a House member in support of a motion to instruct conferees.[20] However, instructions adopted by either chamber are not binding. Conferees may disregard them, particularly when they feel the need for room to maneuver or compromise. Of course, the full House and Senate still have an opportunity to accept or reject the conference committee report on the bill, and a new conference may be requested if either house feels that its conferees have grossly violated their instructions.

The House and Senate seldom reject the list of conferees designated by the Speaker or the presiding officer. The House requires unanimous consent to change the Speaker's choices. The Senate's rules provide several ways to overrule the presiding officer. Senators may offer substitute motions naming conferees other than those appointed by the presiding officer. Senators also are free to filibuster or threaten to filibuster the motion to appoint conferees in an effort to change the list. Finally, a senator may challenge the conferees at the time they actually are appointed. These procedures are rarely invoked, however. Challenging the presiding officer's decision is tantamount to questioning the basic prerogative of committee leaders to select the conferees since the presiding officer only *formally* appoints the conference delegation.

Challenging conferees is even more difficult in the House, where the Speaker not only endorses the nominees of the committee chairmen but also is the leader of the majority party.

Who gets named a conferee (or who is passed over) sometimes can be critical to conference outcomes. *(See box, p. 210.)* In 1983, for instance, freshman Rep. Bob Wise, D-W.Va., persuaded the House to delete funding for a dam in his district. The Senate restored the funding for the project, and the matter went to conference. Wise was not selected as a conferee. West Virginia's Senator Byrd, a strong proponent of the dam, was a member of the conference. "I'll be a conferee," he said. "I'm not going to take anything lying down." [21] Byrd personally telephoned over 120 House members to praise the dam. In the end, the two chambers voted to support Byrd's position rather than Representative Wise's. (Of course, there was no guarantee that a majority of the House conferees would have accepted Wise's position on the dam even if he had been named a conferee.)

Bargaining in Conference

Conferees usually convene in the Capitol building itself rather than in one of the Senate or House office buildings. A conference chairman is selected in *ad hoc* fashion, as there are no congressional rules governing the procedure. On recurring measures that go to conference annually, such as appropriations and revenue bills, the chairmanship often rotates between the two houses. Despite the informal nature of the selection process, the chairman plays an important role in the conference negotiations, arranging the time and place of meetings, the agenda, and the order in which the disagreements are negotiated. The chairman sets the pace of conference bargaining, proposes compromises, and recommends tentative agreements.

The staff, too, play an important role in conference deliberations. They draft compromise amendments, negotiate agreements, provide advice to members, and prepare the conference reports. Aides played a particularly important role during the complex conference on the 1981 omnibus reconciliation bill. According to the executive director of the House Budget Committee:

> The role of the staff has been not only to explore where there may be areas of agreement, but also to make the deal. How else are you going to get hundreds of issues resolved in a couple of weeks unless you give the staff some kind of license? [22]

Conference committee bargaining, like bargaining throughout the legislative process, is subject to outside pressure. Even before the 1975 "sun-

---

The Importance of Conferee Selection

One of the central figures in the backroom House-Senate budget negotiations was the most junior House conferee: William H. Gray III, a liberal Democrat from Philadelphia.

Gray made it known that he could influence about 40 votes in the House: 19 from the Congressional Black Caucus and another 20 or so urban liberals sympathetic to the caucus' budget priorities.

Knowing how slim a margin they would be working with when they brought the conference report back to the House floor, House budget leaders paid close attention to Gray's arguments for higher domestic spending.

A likable, diligent champion of social spending, Gray pushed for more money for job training programs, health care for the unemployed, human services and education.

Gray was important in developing the special reserve fund that set aside about $8.5 billion for "recession relief" programs that have not been enacted into law.

Much of Gray's persuasion took place in private, such as at a Friday evening meeting June 17 with the three major conferees — House Budget Committee Chairman James R. Jones, D-Okla., Senate Budget Committee Chairman Pete V. Domenici, R-N.M., and ranking Senate Budget Democrat Lawton Chiles, D-Fla. — and Sen. Howard M. Metzenbaum, D-Ohio., a liberal conferee.

Domestic priorities vs. defense spending were discussed at the meeting. "Gray was a key in pulling things together," said a House Budget Committee aide.

"He was instrumental in producing agreement," said a Senate Budget Committee aide. "He was helpful in making the reserve fund work. He dealt with it in a very realistic, very pragmatic way, with a good overview of the process."

Gray returned this year for his second go-round on the Budget Committee. He first joined the panel as a freshman in 1979, but he left in 1981 to become a member of the Appropriations Committee. He now holds one of the Budget slots set aside for Appropriations members.

The two prior years of experience were helpful in the budget conference, said Gray, a 41-year-old Baptist minister. "I didn't have to start from scratch because I'm familiar with the process," he said.

Source: Adapted from Diane Granat, "Rep. Gray: Junior Conferee at Center Stage," *Congressional Quarterly Weekly Report,* June 25, 1983, 1271.

---

shine" rules required open conference meetings, conferees were lobbied heavily by special interest groups, executive agency officials, and even the president on occasion. On important measures, two experts on Congress observe, the president or presidential aides "write letters to conferees; . . . administration personnel show up at conference meetings; and the president freely threatens to use his veto unless conferees compromise." [23]

Bargaining Objectives. Two key objectives underlie the bargaining at conference sessions: First, conferees want to sustain the position of their respective chambers on the bill; second, they want to achieve a result acceptable both to a majority of each chamber's conferees and to a majority of the membership of both chambers. Normally, bargaining and compromise are necessary. The conferees may be able to reach compromises quickly on their differences. For example, it often is relatively painless to split the difference on bills appropriating funds for federal programs. Or logrolling may occur, with House conferees agreeing to certain Senate-passed provisions in order to gain leverage to win acceptance of House-passed provisions that are strongly supported by members of their own chamber. Offers and counter offers are part of the often exhausting conference process. *(See box, pp. 212-213.)*

One tactic sometimes used to break a deadlock is for the conferees of one chamber to threaten to break off negotiations and return to their chamber for instructions — thereby reinforcing their position when negotiations resume. A House member once described this ploy as follows:

> Last year there was a difference of about $400 million between the House and Senate versions of the foreign aid appropriations [bill]. The chairman of the House delegation in the conference took a very firm position that we had to end up with slightly less than 50 percent of the difference as a matter of prestige. It was the day we [Congress] were to adjourn. We were in conference until about 10:30 p.m., and the Senate [conferees] wouldn't give in. I think the difference between conferees was only five or ten million dollars. The Senate was fighting for its prestige, and our chairman for his. At 10:30 he started to close his book [staff papers prepared for the conference] and he got up saying he would get instructions from the House. All the rest of our [House] conferees did the same. That prospect was too much for the senators. They capitulated.[24]

This example illustrates a number of factors in conference bargaining: the importance of timing and leadership; the influence of certain members on the negotiations; the impact of threats to convene another series of protracted meetings after one side receives instructions; the role that fatigue can play in resolving hotly contested issues; and the political and professional investment that senators and representatives have in upholding the prestige of their respective chamber and committees.

Procedural Limits on Bargaining. The conference bargaining process is carefully limited by rules and precedents. Conferees may not go beyond the scope of the bills agreed to by the House and Senate. If, for example, the House authorizes $5 million for a program and the Senate authorizes $10 million, an agreement must be sought within those limits. (However, conferees may exceed the fiscal recommendations in each house's bill if neither version contains an overall total amount.)

Equally important, conferees can consider only the points of disagreement between the two Houses; they may not reconsider provisions agreed to in identical form by both houses.

Going to Conference on a Tax Bill...

Tax bills are the stuff of which legislative legends are made. And the Tax Equity and Fiscal Responsibility Act of 1982 will stand up there with the best of them.

For starters, the bill was a total rejection of the constitutional principle that all measures raising revenues should originate in the House.

In fact, the House did not vote on the legislation until it emerged from conference. The Senate Finance Committee simply substituted the tax increase measure for the text of a minor revenue bill (HR 4961) passed by the House in 1981. House Democrats, after concluding that their safest political course was to keep their fingerprints off the revenue-raising bill, asked to go directly to conference with the Senate-passed measure.

That made the conference technically difficult, since in drafting compromise legislation conferees are not supposed to go beyond the scope of the different Senate- and House-passed bills. The House maintained that its conference position was made up of bills that had been favorably reported by the Ways and Means Committee. However, the Senate parliamentarian ruled that the scope of the conference was solely the Senate-passed bill.

In the end, this dictum was at least partially ignored. A provision that both sides found mutually beneficial — extending unemployment benefits in hard-pressed states — found its way into the measure despite the fact that nothing like it appeared in the Senate bill.

But the fact that the House had no formal legislative position generally made it more difficult for the House to press its case, and the final product looked very much like the bill the Senate approved.

Conference meetings on tax bills in recent years have tended to be held in one of several tiny, cramped rooms in the Capitol that are convenient to either the House or the Senate chamber.

This year things were different — sort of. Public meetings of the conference were held in the spacious and elegant Ways and Means hearing room in the Longworth House Office Building. There were plenty of seats for the press and for the hundreds of lobbyists, legislative analysts and the plain curious.

For some it was like old home week. One evening the former chairman of the Ways and Means Committee, Wilbur Mills, D-Ark., sat behind the press table next to former Senate Finance Committee member Carl Curtis, R-Neb. Milling around the room were former Finance member William Hathaway, D-Maine; former Ways and Means member James C. Corman, D-Calif.; and former Rep. Gerry Brown, R-Mich.

The hearing room was capacious and comfortable, but conferees' decisions were hammered out elsewhere. Typically, the proceedings went like this:

The conference committee would gather in the hearing room, and one chamber's conferees would offer its proposals on one or another part of the bill. The other side would withdraw to consider the offer privately in caucus. Finally

...To Resolve Revenue Differences

— often hours later — the conferees would troop back into the hearing room to announce their counter offer. Then the process would start again.

The cycle was repeated for more than a week. Sometimes word reached the public that House members were caucusing in the Ways and Means room in the Capitol. A long line would form outside with the hope that some snippet of information might be disclosed when members emerged. Rarely did that happen.

A Senate Finance Committee staffer revealed with evident glee that one day, while the public and press staked out the Ways and Means room, the Senate's conferees were meeting in another room near the Senate chamber and not one soul stood outside the door as the senators went in and out.

New and innovative tax conference survival techniques developed as the negotiations ran into marathon late-night sessions — one of which lasted until 8:45 in the morning.

One legislative analyst from a high-powered New York law firm came to the daily encounters with her purse filled with raisins, dried fruit, nuts and a change purse loaded down with coins to call her office from the bank of pay phones outside the hearing room.

Lobbyists brought paperback copies of long novels and made bets as to when they would finish the thousand-page tomes. Reporters did crossword puzzles, told old war stories of tax conferences past, and spoke longingly of far-off places where their families, friends and colleagues vacationed while they waited out the tax bill.

The lobbyists were identified not by their names, but by their employers. "That's Exxon," said one lobbyist. He also pointed out "Westinghouse and Marriott."

By 2 o'clock in the morning even the lobbyists' Gucci loafers, expensive navy blue suits, silk blouses and coordinated designer outfits began to look rumpled.

Finance Committee Chairman Robert Dole, R-Kan., related a story that tells much about the way tax bills are really written.

At the end of the conference it appeared that the conferees had agreed to raise $600 million more in revenues than actually were needed to meet the requirements of the budget reconciliation bill. Dole suggested that perhaps they should cut back on a provision to double the excise tax on tobacco.

Another conferee noted that they had lost the votes of members who opposed the tobacco tax anyway. Why not do something that would really help, he asked. Dole then suggested postponing the effective date of the provision requiring tax withholding on interest and dividend income. Conferees thought that was a dandy idea, and the requirement was put off until July 1983.

Source: Dale Tate, "Legislative Legend-making, Tax Bill Style, *Congressional Quarterly Weekly Report,* August 21, 1982, 2043.

Another result of the rule requiring conferees to stick to the specific matters committed to them is that they may not insert in the conference version of the bill provisions on new subjects — such as new programs or amendments to laws not already amended by the bill. This precedent was formalized in the Legislative Reorganization Act of 1970. This restriction, like many other rules and precedents, sometimes is waived or ignored and new material is in fact incorporated in the conference version.

The new congressional budget process places further constraints on conferees. Discipline and coordination have replaced the piecemeal, unco-ordinated approach of the past. The House and Senate budget committees monitor the recommendations of all committees, including those of confer-ence committees, to see that they conform to overall budget guidelines.

'Amendment in the Nature of a Substitute.' A conference committee has maximum flexibility when, during initial floor action, one of the houses takes a bill from the other and instead of passing it with amendments strikes out everything after the enacting clause and inserts a completely new version of the bill. This is an "amendment in the nature of a substitute." In such cases, the conference committee can consider the versions of both houses (in effect, two entirely separate bills) and actually draft a third version of the legislation, provided, of course, that it is a reasonable (that is, germane) modification of either the House or Senate version.

Nongermane Senate Amendments. As discussed in Chapter 8, Senate practices and greater flexibility enable it to add amendments that are considered nongermane under House rules. House conferees traditionally opposed amendments of this kind, contending that they undercut the role of House committees and enabled important and controversial issues to be adopted with minimum consideration. House rules permit only one hour of debate on conference reports.

Frequently, the House was faced with a "take it or leave it" proposition — accept the nongermane Senate amendments or lose the bill in its entirety, including the House-passed provisions, since conference reports are not open to amendment. Members of the House expressed frustration over this recurring dilemma. "I have chafed for years," declared Rules Committee Chairman William M. Colmer, D-Miss. (1933-73), in 1970, "about the other body violating the rules of this House by placing entirely foreign, extraneous, and nongermane matters in House-passed bills." [25] As a result, the House finally acted against the Senate practice in the 1970s by taking several procedural steps, including a 1972 rules change permitting separate votes on the nongermane portions of conference reports. The changes were designed to accommodate the Senate's right to offer nongermane amendments while protecting the procedural prerogatives of the House.

Any House member may make a point of order against a conference report when it is called up for final approval on the ground that it contains nongermane material. There are occasions, to be sure, when special rules are obtained from the Rules Committee to protect the conference report against such points of order. Assuming there is no rule, the Speaker sustains the

98TH CONGRESS }
1st Session }

HOUSE OF REPRESENTATIVES

{ REPORT
{ No. 98-325

INTEREST AND DIVIDENDS TAX WITHHOLDING REPEAL

JULY 27, 1983.—Ordered to be printed

Mr. ROSTENKOWSKI, from the committee of conference,
submitted the following

CONFERENCE REPORT

[To accompany H.R. 2973]

The committee of conference on the disagreeing votes of the two
Houses on the amendment of the House to the amendment of the
Senate to the bill (H.R. 2973) to repeal the withholding of tax from
interest and dividends, having met, after full and free conference,
have agreed to recommend and do recommend to their respective
Houses as follows:

That the Senate recede from its disagreement to the amendment
of the House to the amendment of the Senate and agree to the
same with amendments as follows:

In lieu of the matter proposed to be inserted by the House
amendment insert the following:

TITLE I—INTEREST AND DIVIDEND TAX COMPLIANCE

SEC. 101. SHORT TITLE: AMENDMENT OF 1954 CODE.

*(a) SHORT TITLE.—This title may be cited as the "Interest and
Dividend Tax Compliance Act of 1983".*

*(b) AMENDMENT OF 1954 CODE.—Except as otherwise expressly pro-
vided, whenever in this title an amendment is expressed in terms of
an amendment to a section or other provision, the reference shall be
considered to be made to a section or other provision of the Internal
Revenue Code of 1954.*

SEC. 102. REPEAL OF WITHHOLDING ON INTEREST AND DIVIDENDS.

*(a) IN GENERAL.—Subtitle A of title III of the Tax Equity and
Fiscal Responsibility Act of 1982 (relating to withholding of tax
from interest and dividends) is hereby repealed as of the close of
June 30, 1983.*

*(b) CONFORMING AMENDMENT.—Except as provided in this section,
the Internal Revenue Code of 1954 shall be applied and adminis-*

11-006 O

215

point of order; the representative who raised the objection on the floor then moves to reject the nongermane conference matter. Forty minutes of debate, equally divided between those who support and those who oppose the motion, is permitted under this procedure, after which the House votes on the motion to reject. If it is adopted, the nongermane material is deleted, and the question before the House is disposition of the remaining conference material minus the nongermane portion.

On the other hand, defeat of the motion permits the House to keep the nongermane matter in the conference report.

The effect of these House procedural changes was to cut back somewhat the inclusion of Senate nongermane amendments in conference reports. House conferees now are able to request that certain Senate nongermane amendments be dropped in conference, as they would be subject to points of order in the House otherwise. And during Senate floor debate, senators sometimes urge their colleagues not to offer nongermane amendments because their adoption might jeopardize enactment of the legislation itself. As Sen. Long has emphasized, "We should not add [nongermane] amendments that might prevent . . . bills from getting through the House."[26]

The Conference Report

When at least a majority of the conferees from each chamber have reached agreement, they instruct committee staff aides to prepare a report explaining their conference decisions. A majority of the conferees from each house must sign the report in order for it to be sent back to the House and Senate. Once accomplished, the conference committee has concluded its work. *(Obtaining signatures of conferees, see box, p. 217.)*

Conferees who oppose the final conference compromise may refuse to sign the report (unlike reports of standing committees of each chamber, precedent prohibits minority or additional viewpoints in conference committee reports).

Conference reports must be printed in the *Congressional Record* before they are brought before the House or Senate for final action. In addition, the 1970 Legislative Reorganization Act requires conference reports to be accompanied by a statement explaining specific changes made by conferees. This statement is prepared jointly by the conferees of both houses so that the explanation of what was decided upon would not be different in the two houses and thus subject to differing interpretations.

Floor Action on Conference Reports

Once the conference report is agreed to and filed with the House and Senate, it must be acted upon by both chambers before it is cleared for the president.

Customarily, the chamber that requests a conference acts last on the conference report, but only if the "papers" are in its possession. The papers are the official documents, such as the bill as originally introduced and the amendments added to it by the other chamber. Normally, the papers are

---

Obtaining Signatures on Conference Reports

Rep. Charles Wilson, D-Texas, has a recollection that shows how important the administration and congressional leaders considered the 1978 natural gas bill.

On August 17, before the final House and Senate signatures were obtained on the gas conference report at a White House meeting, Wilson left for Texas in the afternoon. He left behind his signature on a blank piece of paper. At the time only 10 of the necessary 13 House signatures had been obtained. Wilson says he authorized his signature to be pasted on the conference report if Rep. Joe D. Waggonner Jr., D-La., also agreed to sign. Wilson said he didn't want to be the only member from a producer state signing.

After Wilson left town, Waggonner announced he was opposed to the conference agreement and would not sign. Wilson said two other liberal opponents of the bill, Reps. James C. Corman, D-Calif., and Charles B. Rangel, D-N.Y., were induced to sign and make the necessary 13, with the assurance that Wilson had signed. Then a phone call was made from the White House to Wilson in Texas and by midnight he agreed to have his name placed on the report.

Source: Adapted from "Obtaining a Majority of Signatures on a 1978 Natural Gas Bill," in *Washington Post,* September 30, 1978, A3.

---

held by the chamber that agreed to go to conference; that house then would be the first to consider the conference report. However, the papers may be transferred to the other chamber by agreement of the conference committee.

There are occasions when policy outcomes are influenced by which chamber acts first or last on the conference report. In 1979, for example, House Government Operations Committee Chairman Jack Brooks, D-Texas, got the House to ask for a conference with the Senate on a measure creating a Department of Education. He wanted the House to act last on the conference report so that the parliamentary options available to the bill's opponents — who were more numerous in the House — would be limited.

The first chamber to act on a conference report has three options: adopt, reject, or recommit the conference report — return it to the conferees for further deliberation. When the first chamber to act adopts the conference report, however, this automatically dissolves the conference committee, and the other chamber is faced with either a yes or no vote on the conference report. Chairman Brooks' strategy worked. Through intense lobbying by the White House and various education groups, the House agreed to the conference report establishing the new department.

Conference reports are privileged and may be brought up at almost any time the House and Senate are in session. Usually, this is with the prior approval of the leadership. The senior conferee from each house's delegation normally acts as the floor manager of the conference version.

Both chambers require conference reports to be accepted or rejected in their entirety. If conferees cannot agree on certain amendments, these are submitted to each chamber individually and acted upon separately. These are called "amendments in disagreement." In such cases, the conference report is debated and agreed to first; then any amendments in disagreement are considered. Every amendment must be agreed to in identical form before congressional action on the bill is complete.

Conference reports are seldom rejected. Outright rejection of a report kills the bill and may require a repetition of the entire legislative process. This becomes particularly significant in the weeks immediately before the final adjournment of a Congress when members face the choice of 1) accepting the bill as is, 2) recommitting it to a conference committee, in all probability jeopardizing final approval, or 3) killing the bill, knowing there is no time to move a revised bill through Congress.

Conference reports also benefit from the same deference that members grant the reports of their own standing committees. The conferees are the experts on the legislation, and the sanctity of their decision generally is respected.[27]

Once the conference report is approved by both houses, the papers are delivered to the house that originated the measure. A copy of the bill as finally agreed to by Congress is prepared by an enrolling clerk. The "enrolled bill" is signed by the Speaker and presiding officer of the Senate, or by other authorized officers, and sent to the president.

Presidential Approval or Veto

Under the Constitution (Article I, section 7), the president has a qualified veto power. The president can disapprove of legislative acts, subject to the ability of Congress to override the vetoes by a two-thirds vote of the members present and voting in each house. Once an enrolled bill is sent to the White House, the president has 10 days, excluding Sundays, to sign or veto it. If no action is taken within the 10-day period, and Congress is in session, the bill automatically becomes law without the president's signature. If the final adjournment (called *sine die*) of a session of Congress takes place before the 10-day period ends, and the president does not sign the measure, the legislation dies as a "pocket veto." [28]

Woodrow Wilson wrote that the president, in using the veto power, "acts not as the executive but as a third branch of the legislature." [29] The president can use the veto, or the threat of a veto, to advance legislative and political goals. Often, the threat of a veto is itself enough to persuade Congress to change its legislative course. For instance, Sen. Jake Garn, R-Utah, explained to the Senate why a 1983 appropriations bill would not be vetoed by President Ronald Reagan.

[T]he resulting bill is acceptable to the administration. On the day of the conference, the conferees received a letter from Mr. [David A.] Stockman, [director of the Office of Management and Budget], stating that he would recommend the bill be signed if the conferees satisfactorily addressed four issues.

Each of these issues were, indeed, resolved to the administration's satisfaction.[30]

Sen. William Proxmire, D-Wis., put the matter more vividly when he told the Senate why a specific compromise on another controversial measure was agreed to by House and Senate conferees. "There is another fundamental reason we did it — that is because we faced the veto, that great, big monster of a veto."[31]

The veto is one of the president's most effective legislative weapons. Congress, particularly during periods of divided party control of the chambers, finds it very difficult to attract the two-thirds vote in each house that is required to override presidential vetoes.

The frustration is not entirely one-sided. Presidents can be tied up by adroit congressional maneuvering. Congress virtually can force the president to approve measures by attaching them as "riders" to legislation regarded as essential by the president. "Almost everyone has heard of . . . the practice indulged in by Congress," Rep. Emanuel Celler, D-N.Y. (1923-73), once said, "of coercing the President to approve a bill that he does not want by coupling it with one that is necessary or highly desirable."[32]

Presidents veto measures for a variety of reasons: they are considered unconstitutional; they believe they encroach on the chief executive's powers and duties; or they hold them to represent ill-advised and costly policies. When President Richard Nixon vetoed the 1973 War Powers Resolution (which Congress subsequently enacted by overriding his veto), he cited all three factors as the basis of his action.

Presidents may use vetoes as a political technique to gain public support for administration policies. President Franklin D. Roosevelt dramatized his disapproval of a 1935 measure by personally delivering his veto message to a joint session of Congress. Presidents Nixon and Reagan each vetoed a bill on nationwide television.

The president, to be sure, receives recommendations from many quarters during the 10-day period allowed under the Constitution to decide whether to sign or veto legislation. After the *sine die* adjournment of the 97th Congress, for example, scores of groups and officials urged President Reagan to sign — rather than pocket veto — legislation giving the pharmaceutical industry tax incentives to produce drugs for persons afflicted with rare diseases.

The legislation is backed by the medical community, by top officials in the Department of Health and Human Services and by members of the hundreds of volunteer organizations representing those afflicted by orphan diseases. Together [with many members of Congress], they have been deluging the White House with appeals for presidential support.[33]

PUBLIC LAW 98-21—APR. 20, 1983   97 STAT. 65

Public Law 98-21
98th Congress

An Act

To assure the solvency of the Social Security Trust Funds, to reform the medicare reimbursement of hospitals, to extend the Federal supplemental compensation program, and for other purposes.

Apr. 20, 1983
[H.R. 1900]

Be it enacted by the Senate and House of Representatives of the United States of America in Congress assembled,

Social Security Amendments of 1983.

SHORT TITLE

SECTION 1. This Act, with the following table of contents, may be cited as the "Social Security Amendments of 1983".

42 USC 1305 note.

TABLE OF CONTENTS

Despite advice from the Treasury and Justice departments to pocket veto the proposal, the president signed the measure into law (PL 97-414).

Veto Override Procedures

When the president vetoes a measure, the Constitution provides that "he shall return it with his objections to that House in which it shall have originated." Neither chamber is under any obligation to schedule an override attempt. And neither the Constitution nor Congress sets a deadline for overridding a veto. Party leaders may realize they have no chance to override and may not even attempt it. Because of popular support for the president's action, or for other reasons, the political environment may not be conducive to a successful override.

In 1982 House Interior Committee Chairman Morris K. Udall, D-Ariz., wanted to seek an override of President Reagan's veto of a water rights measure. He chose not to push for it because members were "in the middle of a very bitter partisan budget fight." [34]

If an override attempt fails in one chamber, the process ends and the bill dies. If it succeeds, the measure is sent to the other chamber, where a second successful override vote makes it law. The Constitution requires roll-call votes on override attempts.

Whether signed by the president or passed over a veto, the bill now becomes a public law and is sent to the General Services Administration, the government's housekeeping department, for deposit in the National Archives and publication in the *Statutes at Large*, an annual volume that compiles all bills that have been passed by Congress and signed into law, or have become law through a veto override.

Summary

Both chambers must approve identical versions of a bill before the legislation can be sent to the White House. Often, differences are resolved by informal consultation or by one house's acceptance of the other's bill without further amendment. Major legislation, however, generally contains controversial provisions on which the House and Senate differ. Resolution of these differences is achieved through the conference committee process. A conference committee is appointed, composed generally of members selected from the House and Senate standing committees that originally handled the legislation.

The conferees are expected to support their chamber's positions on the major issues in the bill regardless of their committees' or their personal views. Sometimes, their bargaining positions are reinforced by instructions from their parent chamber. Conference committee bargaining resembles bargaining elsewhere in the legislative process. It includes the traditional techniques of compromise and logrolling. There are, however, some restrictions that are unique to the conference process. Conferees are not allowed, for example, to go beyond the scope of the bills agreed to by their respective chambers.

Until the 1970s, the Senate's more flexible floor procedure permitting nongermane amendments to House-passed bills enabled the Senate to force the House to accept many provisions unrelated to the legislation at hand. House floor procedure on conference reports did not permit members to consider and vote separately on Senate nongermane amendments added to conference reports. The House responded in the early 1970s by amending its own procedures, with the result that the nongermane Senate amendment now is a somewhat less effective device for winning congressional approval of provisions that were never considered by the House.

Conference reports generally are accepted by both chambers for two important reasons: 1) members' disinclination to repeat the entire legislative process, and 2) their deference to the expertise of the conferees.

The final step of the legislative process is presidential action, but the president's veto power influences the entire legislative process. The extraordinary majority (two-thirds) required to override a veto forces Congress to consider the White House's position from the moment a bill is introduced until it is finally passed in identical form by both houses. Congress occasionally tries to achieve certain objectives by attaching "riders" opposed by the president to legislation that the administration regards as essential.

Enactment of legislation does not bring the legislative process to a close. Once a bill becomes law, it may set in motion a new federal program, redefine the role of executive branch agencies, or change the responsibilities of federal, state, and local governments in numerous program areas. All these new activities generated by a law become, in time, the subject of renewed congressional scrutiny as Congress endeavors to monitor the implementation and effects of the laws it passes. The next chapter turns to this broad area of congressional activity, usually termed "legislative oversight."

Notes

1. Ada G. McCown, *The Congressional Conference Committee* (New York: Columbia University Press, 1927), 12. Also see Gilbert Steiner, *The Congressional Conference Committee, Seventieth to Eightieth Congresses* (Urbana: University of Illinois Press, 1951); and David J. Vogler, *The Third House, Conference Committees in the United States Congress* (Evanston, Ill.: Northwestern University Press, 1971).
2. *Congressional Quarterly's Guide to Congress,* 3d ed. (Washington, D.C.: Congressional Quarterly, 1982), 434.
3. Roy Swanstrom, *The United States Senate, 1787-1801,* S. Doc. No. 64, 87th Cong., 1st sess. (Washington, D,C.: U.S. Government Printing Office, 1962), 232.
4. *Washington Post,* September 14, 1976, D8. See also *National Journal,* September 25, 1976, 1353-1355; and *Congressional Quarterly Weekly Report,* September 18, 1976, 2578-2579.
5. U.S., Congress, *Congressional Record,* March 21, 1974, 7589. See also the Record for April 10, 1974, 10569. When either chamber acts for the first time to amend the other's legislation, that change is considered to be part of the original

text. In short, it is a "free" amendment. For instance, if the House passes a measure and the Senate amends it, the Senate amendment is viewed as part of the original text. If the House then amends the Senate's change, that is a first degree amendment. A subsequent Senate amendment to the House amendment is a second degree amendment. No other inter-chamber amendments are in order because they would be in the third degree. Absent bicameral agreement at this juncture, the two chambers may decide to go to conference, or the House may concur in the Senate's amendment, or the Senate may recede from its amendment to the House amendment.

6. U.S., Congress, Senate, *Congressional Record,* daily ed., December 20, 1982, S15757.
7. *National Journal,* May 22, 1976, 694.
8. John Ferejohn, "Who Wins in Conference Committee?" *Journal of Politics* (November 1975): 1033-1046; Walter J. Oleszek, "House-Senate Relationships: Comity and Conflict," *The Annals* (January 1974): 80-81.
9. U.S., Congress, Senate, *Congressional Record,* October 2, 1972, 16549-16552.
10. Richard F. Fenno, Jr., *The Power of the Purse* (Boston: Little, Brown & Co., 1966), 610.
11. U.S., Congress, House, *Congressional Record,* July 2, 1935, 10635.
12. George D. Aiken, *Aiken: Senate Diary, January 1972-January 1975* (Brattleboro, Vt.: Stephen Greene Press, 1975), 303.
13. Elizabeth Drew, *Senator* (New York: Simon & Schuster, 1979), 174.
14. *Enactment of a Law,* S. Doc. No. 97-20, 97th Cong., 2d sess., 24.
15. *Los Angeles Times,* November 14, 1977, part I, 15.
16. U.S., Congress, Senate, *Congressional Record,* daily ed., July 29, 1981, S8711.
17. Jefferson quoted in U.S., Congress, Senate, *Congressional Record,* May 12, 1959, 7975.
18. U.S., Congress, Senate, *Congressional Record,* August 26, 1960, 17831.
19. U.S., Congress, Senate, *Congressional Record,* December 11, 1975, 21736.
20. U.S., Congress, House, *Congressional Record,* daily ed., June 23, 1983, H4435.
21. *Washington Post,* June 22, 1983, A2; and July 16, 1983, A23.
22. *New York Times,* July 23, 1981, A19. Also see Michael J. Malbin, *Unelected Representatives: Congressional Staff and the Future of Representative Government* (New York: Basic Books, 1980), Chapter 5.
23. Ted Siff and Alan Weil, *Ruling Congress* (New York: Grossman Publishers, 1975), 184.
24. Quoted in Charles L. Clapp, *The Congressman* (Washington, D.C.: The Brookings Institution, 1962), 249.
25. U.S., Congress, House, *Congressional Record,* September 15, 1970, 31842.
26. U.S., Congress, *Congressional Record,* October 1, 1976, 34518.
27. There are, however, exceptions. The 1976 clean air bill, for example, fell victim to a filibuster on the eve of the 94th Congress's final adjournment.
28. Under the Constitution, Congress does not have the opportunity to override a pocket veto. The question of whether a president can pocket veto legislation during a congressional recess or during recesses between the first and second session of a Congress became an issue in 1970 when President Richard Nixon used the veto during a six-day recess. The pocket-vetoed measure, a medical training bill, had been passed by both houses by nearly unanimous votes, indicating that a regular veto would have been overridden. Sen. Edward M. Kennedy, D-Mass., challenged Nixon's use of the pocket veto in court. The U.S. Court of Appeals for the District of Columbia upheld Kennedy's challenge and

declared that Nixon had improperly used his pocket veto power. *Kennedy v. Sampson* (511 F. 2d 430, D.C. Circuit, 1974). However, the use of pocket vetoes still is a murky area. See, for example, *New York Times,* September 29, 1982, B8; and U.S., Congress, Senate, *Congressional Record,* daily ed., August 20, 1982, S11030, S11048-S11049.

29. Woodrow Wilson, *Congressional Government* (Boston: Houghton Mifflin Co., 1885), 52. Later in his book, Wilson wrote that the "president is no greater than his prerogative of veto makes him; he is, in other words, powerful rather as a branch of the legislature than as the titular head of the Executive." 260.

30. U.S., Congress, Senate, *Congressional Record,* daily ed., June 29, 1983, S9430.

31. U.S., Congress, Senate, *Congressional Record,* daily ed., December 20, 1982, S15678.

32. U.S., Congress, House, *Congressional Record,* February 25, 1952, A1152.

33. *Los Angeles Times,* December 26, 1982, part I, 1. See also *Congressional Quarterly Weekly Report,* January 8, 1983, 14.

34. Tim Gallimore, "No Override Attempted: President Reagan's Veto of Water-Rights Measure Left Standing by Congress," *Congressional Quarterly Weekly Report,* June 12, 1982, 1404. See also Frank B. Feiget, "Congressional Response to Presidential Vetoes in Foreign and Defense Policy: Truman to Ford," in *Interaction: Foreign Policy and Public Policy,* ed. Don C. Piper and Ronald J. Terchek (Washington, D.C.: American Enterprise Institute of Public Policy Research, 1983), 35-50; and Myron A. Levine, "Tactical Constraints and Presidential Influence on Veto Overrides," *Presidential Studies Quarterly,* Fall 1983, 646-650.

10

Legislative Oversight

Congress "sometimes gets in the habit of 'pass it and forget it' lawmaking," Sen. Hubert H. Humphrey, Jr., D-Minn. (1949-64, 1971-78), once lamented.[1] Efficient government, he realized, requires careful attention by Congress to the administration of laws. A thoughtful, well-drafted law offers no guarantee that the policy intentions of legislators will be carried out.

The laws passed by Congress are general guidelines, and sometimes their wording is deliberately vague. The implementation of legislation involves the drafting of administrative regulations by the executive agencies, and day-to-day program management by agency officials. Agency regulations and rules are the subject of "legislative oversight" — the continuing review by Congress of how effectively the executive branch is carrying out congressional mandates. Or as Sen. Patrick J. Leahy, D-Vt., has put it:

> I believe that oversight is one of the Congress's most important constitutional responsibilities. We must do more than write laws and decide policies. It is also our responsibility to perform the oversight necessary to insure that the administration enforces those laws as Congress intended.[2]

Congress formalized its legislative oversight function in the Legislative Reorganization Act of 1946. That act required congressional committees to exercise "continuous watchfulness" of the agencies under their jurisdictions and implicitly divided oversight functions into three areas:

● Authorizing committees (such as Agriculture, Education and Labor, and Commerce) were required to review federal programs and agencies under their jurisdictions and propose legislation to remedy deficiencies they uncovered.

● Fiscal oversight was assigned to the Appropriations committees of each chamber, which were to scrutinize agency spending.

● Wide-ranging investigative responsibility was assigned to the House Government Operations Committee and the Senate Governmental Affairs Committee to probe for inefficiency, waste, and corruption in the federal government. To some degree, all committees perform each type of oversight.

225

Formalizing Oversight

The House and Senate always have had authority to investigate programs and agencies of the executive branch. The first congressional investigation in American history, in 1792, delved into the conduct of the government in the wars against the Indians. One of the broadest investigations was an 1861 effort "to inquire into the conduct of the present [Civil] war." Other notable probes have included investigations into the Credit Mobilier in 1872-73, the Money Trust in 1912, the Teapot Dome scandal in 1923, Stock Exchange operations in 1932-34, and defense spending during World War II.

The 1946 reorganization act stated Congress's intention to exercise its investigative authority primarily through standing committees rather than by means of specially created investigating committees. The act provided for continuous review of programs instead of sporadic hearings whenever errors, malfeasance, or injustices surfaced. The "continuous watchfulness" precept of the act implied that Congress henceforth would participate actively in administrative decision making, in line with the observation that "administration of a statute is, properly speaking, an extension of the legislative process." [3]

During the 1970s, both houses amended their rules to grant additional oversight authority to the standing committees. The Legislative Reorganization Act of 1970 rephrased in more explicit language the oversight duties of the committees and required most House and Senate panels to issue biennial reports on their oversight activities. The House Committee Reform Amendments of 1974 assigned "special oversight" responsibilities to several standing committees; the Senate adopted the same approach, called "comprehensive policy oversight," when it approved the Committee System Reorganization Amendments of 1977. Both special oversight and comprehensive policy oversight are akin to the broad review authority granted the House Government Operations Committee and the Senate Governmental Affairs Committee.

Explained Sen. Adlai E. Stevenson III, D-Ill. (1970-81), floor manager during Senate debate on the 1977 changes:

> Standing committees are directed and permitted to undertake investigations and make recommendations in broad policy areas — for example, nutrition, aging, environmental protection, or consumer affairs — even though they lack legislative jurisdiction over some aspects of the subject. Such oversight authority involves subjects that generally cut across the jurisdictions of several committees. Presently, no single committee has a comprehensive overview of these policy areas. [This rule change] corrects that. It assigns certain committees the right to undertake comprehensive review of broad policy issues. [4]

Rules Governing Oversight

Several other rules changes during this period are worth noting.
- The House directed its committees to create oversight subcommittees,

undertake future research and forecasting, prepare oversight plans, and review the impact of tax expenditures (credits, incentives, and the like) on matters that fall within their respective jurisdictions.[5]

● The Senate required each standing committee to include "regulatory impact statements" in committee reports accompanying the legislation it sends to the floor. One of these statements, for instance, might evaluate the amount of additional paperwork that would result from enactment of a proposed bill.

● Passage of the 1974 Congressional Budget and Impoundment Control Act strengthened Congress's review capabilities by directing the General Accounting Office (GAO) — a legislative support agency of Congress — to assist House and Senate committees in program evaluation and in the development of "methods for assessing and reporting actual program performance."

Congress requires these additional oversight devices because it faces an executive establishment of massive size and diffuse direction. Even with the "increasing demand for balanced Federal budgets," wrote a scholar, "we should not deceive ourselves into thinking that the Federal Government of the future will be a shrinking violet, retreating to the modest proportions it had in George Washington's or Grover Cleveland's time."[6]

Congress, in short, needs a variety of oversight techniques to hold agencies accountable because if one technique proves to be ineffective committees and members can employ others singly or in combination.

Techniques of Oversight

Congress's decentralized committee system means that oversight generally is initiated on an *ad hoc*, unsystematic basis. No single legislative agency or leadership group coordinates the numerous oversight activities of the House and Senate.

The objectives of oversight often vary from committee to committee. The focus may be on promoting administrative efficiency and economy in government, protecting and supporting favored policies and programs, airing an administration's failures or wrongdoing, or its achievements, publicizing a particular member's or a committee's goals, reasserting congressional authority vis-a-vis the executive branch, or assuaging the interests of pressure groups.

The following sections describe the most common methods by which Congress exercises its oversight responsibility.

Hearings and Investigations

The traditional method of exercising congressional oversight is through committee hearings and investigations into executive branch operations. Legislators need to know how effectively federal programs are working and how well agency officials are responding to committee directives. And they want to know the scope and intensity of public support for government programs in order to assess the need for legislative changes.[7] In 1983, for example, the Senate Armed Services Committee began a broad inquiry into the way the nation's defense institutions formulate and carry out military policy. In the wake of large Pentagon budget increases, the panel wanted "to know how [military] decisions are made, and how they could be made better." [8]

Although excessive use of hearings and investigations can bog down governmental processes, judicious use of such tools helps to maintain a more responsive bureaucracy, while supplying Congress with information needed to formulate new legislation.[9] Committee members and committee staffs may conduct oversight hearings around the country (field hearings) to watch public programs in operation and, in some cases, to take testimony from citizens and local officials.

Legislative Veto

Numerous statutes contain provisions that, while delegating authority to the executive branch, reserve to Congress the right to approve or disapprove executive actions based on that authority. This power generally is referred to as the "legislative veto." This procedure allows one or both houses, by majority vote, to veto certain executive branch initiatives, decisions, and regulations.

Since 1932, when a legislative veto provision was first used by Congress in an executive reorganization law, "more than 200 statutes, containing well in excess of 300 separate veto provisions, have subjected the implementation of executive decisions to some further form of congressional review." [10]

The legislative veto was an attractive oversight technique because, even though Congress seldom exercised its veto prerogative to overturn agency decisions, committees and members felt the practice kept federal administrators sensitive and responsive to congressional interests. It was employed in legislation dealing with both domestic and international issues.

On June 23, 1983, however, the Supreme Court declared in a historic decision, *Immigration and Naturalization Service v. Chada,* that the legislative veto is unconstitutional. In a 7-2 vote, the court majority said the device violated the separation of powers, the principle of bicameralism, and the presentation clause of the Constitution (legislation passed by both chambers must be presented to the president for his signature or veto). The decision, wrote Justice Byron R. White in a dissent, "strikes down in one fell swoop provisions in more laws enacted by Congress than the court has cumulatively invalidated in its entire history."

With the current manifestation of the legislative veto gone, Congress and the executive branch are in for a period of institutional readjustments and accommodations. Lawmakers have begun to search for replacements to the practice and to review the available techniques for controlling executive actions.[11] *(Congressional alternatives, see box, pp. 230-231.)*

Some members foresee much legislative-executive turmoil in the wake of the decision and congressional reluctance to delegate further authority to the executive branch unless it is short-term and defined in great detail.

Others hold a different perspective. Noted Rep. Joe Moakley, D-Mass.:

> [T]he decision should not be viewed as a disaster or as a victory for anyone. Congress, admittedly, has lost a tool which has, in its better applications, proved useful and efficient. But, by restraining Congress from immersing itself in every item of regulation and adjudication, the court has saved Congress from drowning in detail it lacks the institutional capacity to manage, and freed it to act within the scope of its legitimate role for shaping national policy.[12]

In short, no one can yet predict the long-run consequences of the court's decision on legislative-executive relations and congressional oversight.

Authorization Process as Oversight

Congress not only has the authority to create or abolish executive agencies and transfer functions between or among them; it also can enact "statutes authorizing the activities of the departments, prescribing their internal organization and regulating their procedures and work methods." [13] The authorization process, as noted in Chapter 3, is an important oversight tool. As a House member observed during debate on a bill to require annual congressional authorization of the Federal Communications Commission (FCC):

> Our subcommittee hearings disclosed that the FCC needs direction, needs guidance, needs legislation, and needs leadership from us in helping to establish program priorities. Regular oversight through the reauthorization process, as all of us know in Congress, is necessary, and nothing brings everybody's attention to spending more forthrightly than when we go through the reauthorization process.[14]

Congress, too, may pass laws that "deauthorize" previously approved projects, such as the construction of dams.

Appropriations Process as Oversight

Congress probably exercises its most effective oversight of agencies and programs through the appropriations process. By cutting off or reducing funds, Congress can abolish agencies or curtail programs. By increasing funds, it can build up neglected program areas. In either case, it has formidable power to shape ongoing public policies. The power is exercised mainly by the House and Senate Appropriations committees, particularly through their powerful subcommittees, whose budgetary recommendations are only infrequently changed by the full committee or by the House and Senate.

The Appropriations committees define the precise purpose for which money may be spent, they adjust funding levels, and often they attach provisos prohibiting expenditures for certain purposes. In sum, the appropriations process as an oversight technique, notes congressional budget expert Allen Schick, is comparable to a Janus-like weapon: "the stick of spending reductions in case agencies cannot satisfactorily defend their budget requests

Congress Studies Alternatives...

Congress began looking at new ways to rein in the executive branch, without using the legislative veto, during hearings the week of July 18. The ideas ranged from repealing entire laws that contain legislative vetoes to a constitutional amendment to make such vetoes legal.

With Congress bereft of the veto mechanism, which the Supreme Court found unconstitutional June 23, two House panels and a Senate subcommittee sorted through alternatives to replace it.

The legislative veto has been used in various forms over the past 50 years to allow one or both houses of Congress, or even a congressional committee, to block an executive branch regulation or order, without requiring the president's approval.

Some 200 statutes contain veto provisions. The hearings explored ways to fix those laws and write new ones while preventing a major shift of power to the executive branch.

Among the options discussed were:

● Repealing all statutes that contain unconstitutional legislative vetoes, and rewriting the laws to limit power delegated to the executive branch.

● Excising the veto from laws that include severability clauses, which would delete the offending passage while preserving the remainder of the statute.

● Requiring that before any agency regulation takes effect, it must be approved by the House and Senate in a joint resolution, which then must be signed by the president. This method was included in a Consumer Product Safety Commission bill (HR 2668) passed by the House June 29.

● Requiring a "report and wait" procedure, by which agency regulations would be submitted to Congress, where they would sit for a specific period of time. The rules would go into effect unless disapproved by Congress and the president during that period. This concept also was embodied in HR 2668, providing that a proposed rule could not take effect for 90 days, giving Congress time to enact a joint resolution of disapproval. Senators Carl Levin, D-Mich., and David L. Boren, D-Okla., introduced a similar plan (S 1650) July 20.

● Using amendments — riders — to appropriations bills to bar spending money to implement an agency regulation that Congress dislikes.

● Passing a constitutional amendment overturning the Supreme Court's decision. Such an amendment would have to be ratified by [three-fourths of] the states.

● Passing legislation that would remove the federal courts' jurisdiction over the legislative veto, or give members of Congress weight in federal appeals courts if they challenge the validity of rules that were disapproved by concurrent resolution. Rep. Charles Pashayan, Jr., R-Calif., offered these ideas.

"Whatever the range of solutions, it is clear that the Supreme Court decision will mean more problems for the executive in carrying out its functions and a much greater workload for Congress," observed Norman J. Ornstein, a Catholic Univesity professor of politics, at a July 20 hearing of the Senate Judiciary Subcommittee on Administrative Practice and Procedure.

... To the Legislative Veto

The other hearings were held in the House Judiciary Subcommittee on Administrative Law and the House Foreign Affairs Committee.

Besides the House action on the Consumer Product Safety Commission bill, there already have been several other responses to the Supreme Court's ruling.

The House Rules Committee July 12 sent a foreign aid authorization bill (HR 2992) back to the Foreign Affairs Committee because the measure contained a legislative veto. Foreign Affairs has not yet reworked the bill.

And the Senate Armed Services Committee June 27 decided to restrict the president's control over military pay raises by requiring that any presidential pay proposal that varies from his defense secretary's recommendation must be submitted as legislation.

This process replaced a plan the committee was considering before the Supreme Court ruling. That proposal would have subjected the president's alternative pay scheme to a one-house legislative veto.

The most drastic reply to the high court's ruling came from Stanley Brand, general counsel to the House, in testimony July 19 before the Foreign Affairs Committee.

Brand said Congress would be best off to discard all laws that contain legislative vetoes and then rewrite them to restrict the delegation of power to the executive branch.

But Committee Chairman Clement J. Zablocki, D-Wis., said Brand's suggestion was unworkable because it would create an excessive workload for Congress.

"It does not address the practical problems that will arise if Congress is forced to promulgate every executive regulation," Zablocki said.

Levin, in testimony July 20 before the Senate subcommittee, said he believes his proposed joint resolution veto would be constitutional because it would require approval by both the House and Senate and the president's signature.

Deputy Attorney General Edward C. Schmults said the Reagan administration will work with Congress in a "spirit of comity" to resolve problems resulting from the decision.

Schmults said only minor adjustments are needed to fix laws that now contain vetoes. In place of the veto, he said, "there are many effective and fully constitutional mechanisms whereby Congress can carry out its constitutional oversight function."

He said the administration will continue to honor existing "report and wait" provisions.

Source: Adapted from Diane Granat, "Legislative Veto Replacements Considered," *Congressional Quarterly Weekly Report,* July 23, 1983, 1501.

and past performance, and the carrot of more money if agencies produce convincing success stories or the promise of future results." [15]

Congress, too, has created statutory offices of inspectors general (IGs) in nearly 20 major federal agencies and departments. Granted wide latitude and independence by the Inspectors General Act of 1978, these officials conduct investigations and audits of their agencies to improve efficiency, end waste and fraud, and discourage mismanagement. IGs keep Congress informed about federal activities and problems through the issuance of periodic reports.

Nonstatutory, Informal Controls

There are various informal ways in which Congress can influence federal administrators. Executive officials, conscious of Congress's power over the purse strings, are attuned to the nuances of congressional language in hearings, floor debate, committee reports, and conference reports. For example, in committee reports the verbs "expects," "urges," "recommends," "desires," and "feels" display in roughly descending order how obligatory a committee comment or viewpoint is intended to be. [16] If federal administrators believe congressional directives to be unwise, they are more likely to ask for informal consultation with members and committee staff than to seek new laws or resolutions. In fact, executive officials are in frequent contact with committee members and staff. Analyzing the House Appropriations Committee's relationship with the federal bureaucracy, one scholar wrote:

> [There] is a continuing and sometimes almost daily pattern of contacts between the Committee on Appropriations and the executive branch. When Congress is not in session, communication continues by telephone or even, on occasion, by visits to the homes of members of the committee. If the full story were ever known, the record probably would disclose a complex network of relationships between members of the Committee on Appropriations and its staff and officials, particularly budget officers, in the executive branch. [17]

Such informal contacts enable the committees to exercise policy influence in areas where statutory methods might be inappropriate or ineffective.

Members sometimes urge their colleagues, administrative agencies, and the courts to exercise caution in interpreting committee reports, floor debate, and other nonstatutory devices as expressions of the intent of Congress. [18] Federal Judge Abner J. Mikva, a former House member, recounted a story about the pitfalls of interpreting the legislative history of a bill.

> I remember when Mo Udall was managing the strip-mining bill, and there had been all sorts of problems getting it through. They'd put together a very delicate coalition of support. One problem was whether the states or the feds would run the program. One member got up and asked, "Isn't it a fact that under this bill the states will continue to exercise sovereignty over strip mining?" And Mo replied, "You're absolutely right." A little later someone else got up and asked, "Now is it clear that the Federal Government will have the final say on strip mining?" And Mo replied, "You're absolutely

right." Later, in the cloakroom, I said, "Mo, they can't both be right." And Mo said. "You're absolutely right." [19]

GAO Audits

The GAO was created by the Budget and Accounting Act of 1921. Under the direction of the comptroller general, the GAO conducts audits of executive agencies and programs at the request of committees and members of Congress to make sure that public funds are properly spent. The Legislative Reorganization Act of 1970 and the Congressional Budget and Impoundment Control Act of 1974 expanded the GAO's investigative authority.[20]

The GAO is Congress's premier field investigator. The agency sends Congress some 1,000 reports annually, addressing ways to root out waste and fraud in government programs and promote program performance. GAO studies frequently lead to the introduction of legislation, congressional hearings, or cost-saving administrative changes. The head of the GAO, the comptroller general, is appointed for a single 15-year term by the president, subject to the advice and consent of the Senate. The GAO works only for Congress.

Reporting Requirements

Numerous laws require executive agencies to submit periodic reports to Congress and its committees. Approximately 4,000 such reports were sent to Capitol Hill during the 97th Congress.[21] Some reports are of minimal value because they are couched in broad language that reveals little about program implementation; others may be more specific. Generally, however, the report requirement encourages self-evaluation by the executive branch and promotes agency accountability to Congress.

Periodically, executive agencies recommend the elimination of certain reports. The Reagan administration wanted to drop 200 reports to Congress. Such recommendations are reviewed carefully by the appropriate congressional committees. The chairman of the Senate Small Business Committee, for instance, did not want two Small Business Administration reports dropped. "I believe it is essential that the Small Business Committee have access to this . . . information independently to ensure effective and efficient oversight." [22]

Ad Hoc Groups

There are numerous information groups and caucuses of Senate and House members that focus on specific issues and programs. There is, for example, a bipartisan organization of representatives and senators called Members of Congress for Peace through Law, which keeps its members informed about defense and foreign policy legislation, undertakes research, conducts discussion groups, and provides liaison with citizens' groups.[23]

Outside organizations also provide Congress with information on inadequacies in federal programs and other problems with the bureaucracy and exert pressure for more ambitious oversight. In recent years, there has been a proliferation of special interest groups, ranging from the Children's Defense Fund, to committees against steel imports or trading with Cuba. Many of these groups also employ computers "to assist them in research on such subjects as the performance of Governmental agencies." [24] "Think tanks" such as the Brookings Institution and the American Enterprise Institute periodically conduct studies of public policy issues and advise members of Congress and others on how well federal agencies and programs are working.

Senate Confirmation Process

High-ranking public officials are chosen by the president "by and with the Advice and Consent of the Senate," in accordance with the Constitution. In general, the Senate gives presidents wide latitude in selecting Cabinet members but closely scrutinizes judicial and diplomatic appointments as well as nominees to regulatory boards and commissions. Increasingly in recent years, Senate committees are probing the qualifications, independence, and policy predilections of presidential nominees, seeking information on everything from physical health to financial assets.

Nomination hearings establish a public record of the policy views of nominees, on which appointed officials can be called to account at a later time. "We all ask questions at confirmation hearings, hoping to obtain answers that affect actions," observed Sen. Carl Levin, D-Mich.[25] For example, committees try to extract pledges from nominees that they will testify at hearings when requested to do so, with the not so subtle threat that otherwise the appointee's name will not be sent to the full Senate for action.

Program Evaluation

Program evaluation is an approach to oversight that uses social science and management methodology, such as surveys, cost-benefit analyses, and efficiency studies, to assess the effectiveness of ongoing programs. It is a special type of oversight that has been specifically provided for in many agency appropriations bills since the late 1960s and in the 1974 Congressional Budget and Impoundment Control Act. The studies often are carried out by the GAO and by the executive agencies themselves.[26]

Despite the multiplicity of methods to evaluate programs, members sometimes disagree about how to measure performance. Several factors frequently account for their divergent perspectives. People may not agree on the objectives of certain programs. Public laws often are the products of conflicts and compromises, and when those compromises are translated into legislative language ambiguity about program goals may be the result. Many policies have competing objectives or produce unintended results. In addition, there may be no agreement about criteria for determining program success or failure. Finally, even if decision makers agree on objectives and criteria, they may interpret the assessments differently. Members and committees who support particular programs are unlikely to view with favor evaluations that recommend repeal or revision of those programs.

Casework

Each senator's and representative's office handles thousands of requests each year from constituents seeking help in dealing with executive agencies. The requests range from inquiries about lost Social Security checks or delayed pension payments to disaster relief assistance and complicated tax appeals to the Internal Revenue Service.

Most congressional offices employ specialists, called "case workers," to process these petitions. Depending on the importance or complexity of a case, a member himself may contact federal officials, bring up the matter in committee or even discuss the case on the floor. Casework has the positive effect of bringing quirks in the administrative machinery to members' attention. And solutions to an individual constituent's problems can suggest legislative remedies on a broader scale. "As much as 40 percent of [my staff's] time is spent in case work," said Sen. William S. Cohen, R-Maine. "We're the ones who act as a check against bureaucratic indifference."[27]

Support Agency Studies

There are three other support agencies of Congress in addition to the GAO: the Congressional Research Service (CRS), the Office of Technology Assessment (OTA), and the Congressional Budget Office (CBO). Each prepares, or contracts for, reports or studies to assist committees and members in reviewing federal agency activities, expenditures, and performance. Their analyses often spark legislation to correct shortcomings.[28]

Oversight by Individual Members

Some members conduct their own personal reviews of agency activities and develop ways to publicize what they believe to be examples of governmental waste and inefficiency. Sen. William Proxmire, D-Wis., for instance, since 1975 has periodically bestowed a "Golden Fleece Award" on agencies that, in his estimation, wastefully spend tax dollars.[29] Rep. Berkley Bedell, D-Iowa, utilizes another technique.

> One of the practices I have is to make unannounced visits to the executive branch of the Government. I simply select an agency at random, open a door, walk in, and start asking questions of the people who work in that office.[30]

On occasion, individual members will conduct *ad hoc* field oversight hearings of their own. These sessions usually permit constituents to testify about their problems with federal agencies. They usually garner favorable publicity for the legislator, too.

Oversight in the 1980s

While some legislators and scholars complain that congressional oversight is irregular and shallow, the mid-1970s saw a surge of legislative interest in the process. The bipartisan House leadership even dubbed the

96th Congress (1979-81) the "Oversight Congress." Throughout the decade there was an increase in oversight activity by the committees. Speaker Thomas P. O'Neill, Jr., concluded that "members appear to be more committed to tightening up controls on the executive branch." He released a report that "showed a 20 percent increase in committee oversight meetings in the first 11 months of 1979 compared to 1977; 39 percent of all hearings were for oversight, compared to 34 percent in 1977." [31]

Among the many factors that contributed to this surge of oversight activity, several are worth noting. They included:

● Heightened public dissatisfaction and concern about governmental waste, fraud, program mismanagement, and escalating expenditures.

● Congressional assertiveness and distrust of the executive branch in the wake of the Vietnam War, "Watergate," and revelations of abuses by such agencies as the CIA, FBI, and IRS.

● The election of representatives and senators who were skeptical about the national government's ability to resolve public problems.

● The proliferation of federal programs and regulations that touched the lives of practically every citizen, who told their elected officials about problems they encountered with federal agencies.

● A shift from the "politics of fiscal abundance" to the "politics of fiscal scarcity" compelled members and committees to scrutinize program activities and expenditures carefully.

● A rapid increase in the number of groups and trade associations that moved to Washington and pressured Congress to examine governmental actions that affected these special interests.

● The expansion of autonomous subcommittees and staff assistance on Capitol Hill, which permitted the new breed of aggressive legislators to scrutinize federal activities.

Lack of Consensus on Oversight

Despite the demonstrable increase in legislative review activities and Congress's augmentation of its staff, budget, and authority for oversight, many members and commentators still fault congressional efforts in this area. Several factors help to explain why doing more in oversight is often perceived as doing less. [32]

First, there is no clear consensus on how to measure oversight, quantitatively or qualitatively. As a result, members' anxiety about Congress's ability to review the massive federal establishment remains high. Quantitatively, no one really knows how much oversight Congress is doing. It is clear, however, that undercounting characterizes statistical analyses of oversight no matter what definition of that activity is employed. [33] Part of the problem is that legislative review is a ubiquitous activity carried out by many entities: committees, members' offices, legislative support agencies, and committee and personal staff aides. Almost any committee hearing, for example, even ones ostensibly devoted to formulating new legislation, might devote considerable attention to reviewing past policy implementation. Qualitatively, there is little agreement among members on the criteria that can be used to evaluate effective oversight.

Second, some legislators hold oversight objectives that appear impossible to meet. They would like to see Congress conduct comprehensive reviews of the entire executive establishment. In brief, they find Congress's selective and unsystematic oversight approach generally unsatisfactory, even if there is more of it. Oversight is too often a "guerrilla foray" rather than the continuous watchfulness contemplated by the Legislative Reorganization Act of 1946.

Third, many committees and individual members feel they have minimal impact on the bureaucracy. Exclaimed House Majority Leader Jim Wright, D-Texas:

> Fighting the redtape and the overregulation of bureaucratic rulemaking and guideline writing are among the most frustrating things any of us have had to do in Congress — it is almost like trying to fight a pillow. You can hit it — knock it over in the corner — and it just lies there and regroups. You feel sometimes as though you are trying to wrestle an octopus. No sooner do you get a hammerlock on one of his tentacles than the other seven are strangling you.[34]

To many members of Congress, as to the rest of us, federal agencies often seem impenetrable mazes.

Fourth, oversight may produce more questions than answers. Congress finds it easier "to highlight what's going wrong and to blame it on someone," declared Sen. Lawton Chiles, D-Fla., "than to try to determine what to do about it."[35] In short, more oversight by Congress does not mean that shortcomings or inefficiencies in federal departments and agencies necessarily will be corrected.

Fifth, Congress seeks to shape executive actions to its own objectives, not simply to conduct or commission neutral evaluation studies of departmental activities. Oversight is part of the legislative-executive tug-of-war that characterizes the American separation of powers system. According to Allen Schick:

> The key issue for Congress is not administrative performance but its ability to influence agency actions. Congress is interested in performance, but it expresses this interest by seeking dominion over agencies. The distribution of political power between the legislative and executive branches, not simply [or even mainly] the quality of programs, is at stake.[36]

In brief, a fragmented and assertive Congress is often frustrated by its inability to control and coordinate a fragmented and sophisticated bureaucracy.

Despite Congress's general interest in oversight, there are factors that limit effective performance. Legislators still have too little time to devote to their myriad tasks, including oversight. Huge investments of time, energy, and staff assistance are required to ferret out administrative inadequacies.

Some members are reluctant to support massive investigations that may only reveal that a program is working fairly well, not a determination that attracts much constituent attention or media coverage. However, many members accept the fact that much of their effort in this area is unglamorous.

The review process sometimes is inhibited by the alliances that develop between committees, agencies and clientele groups. Examples of these "subgovernments" or "iron triangles," as the alliances often are called, are the House and Senate Merchant Marine committees-Federal Maritime Commission-Maritime unions axis and the Education committees-Department of Education-National Education Association combine.[37] Each component of the alliance usually is supportive of the other. In such cases, committees are less likely to review agency programs critically. A committee staff director has observed:

> Those who are program advocates in the beginning become program protectors along the way. They may criticize here and there, cut back or defer fund authorizations as circumstances dictate, call for evaluations and reports when trouble spots appear, but they do not propose to jettison the programs they have authorized, and continue to authorize, over the years.[38]

Most committee members favor oversight and believe that the process is needed to help reveal and correct administrative problems before they reach serious proportions. But a handful may agree with the chairman who declared, "I am ready to do [oversight] whenever there is evidence [of wrongdoing], but I want an indictment first." [39]

Finally, there are members and scholars who say that Congress lacks electoral, political, and institutional incentives for oversight. As a result, legislators are "insufficiently dissatisfied with their oversight behavior to feel a strong enough stimulus to alter existing patterns." [40] However, there is sentiment in the nation that there are too many laws. "We over-legislated. There is no question about that," observed Speaker O'Neill.[41] If such sentiment is widespread, the 1980s may become a period when Congress passes fewer laws and conducts more frequent and more thorough reviews of executive agencies and programs.

Summary

To some extent, Congress's interest in oversight has been a cyclical phenomenon. Historically, oversight often has been more intense when the executive and legislative branches of government have been controlled by different parties. Recent changes in rules and procedures, which have strengthened the tools of oversight, may have evened out the cyclical curve somewhat by encouraging regular monitoring of federal programs. In the current climate, these changes, combined with the influx of activist legislators, probably mean that for the next few years at least the legislative branch will actively assert policy and oversight initiatives, regardless of which party occupies the White House.

The important issue is how to balance Congress's oversight responsibil-

ities with the executive's need for reasonable discretion in program administration. Too much congressional interference can wreak havoc with agency
routines. On the other hand, for Congress to ignore its oversight role is
tantamount to abandoning the implementation of the law — and its
interpretation — to the whims of nonelected officials.

Notes

1. U.S., Congress, Senate, *Congressional Record,* March 28, 1974, 4611.
2. U.S., Congress, Senate, *Congressional Record,* daily ed., June 21, 1983, S8822.
   For several studies on oversight, see Morris S. Ogul, *Congress Oversees the
   Bureaucracy* (Pittsburgh: University of Pittsburgh Press, 1976). Professor Ogul's
   book contains a lengthy bibliography on oversight. Joseph P. Harris, *Congressional Control of Administration* (Washington: The Brookings Institution, 1964);
   Seymour Scher, "Congressional Committee Members as Independent Agency
   Overseers: A Case Study," *American Political Science Review* (December
   1960): 911-920.
3. David B. Truman, *The Governmental Process* (New York: Alfred Knopf, 1953),
   439. The continuous watchfulness provision was retitled legislative "review" in
   the Legislative Reorganization Act of 1970. That act ·also directed House and
   Senate committees to submit biennial reports on their oversight activities.
4. U.S., Congress, *Congressional Record,* February 1, 1977, 2897.
5. Michael J. Malbin, *Unelected Representatives* (New York: Basic Books, 1979).
   See Chapter 6 for an analysis of a House oversight subcommittee in action.
6. *Workshop on Congressional Oversight and Investigations,* H. Doc. No. 96-217,
   96th Cong., 1st sess., 198. See also Louis Fisher, "Congress and the President in
   the Administrative Process: The Uneasy Alliance," in *The Illusion of Presidential Government,* ed. Hugh Heclo and Lester M. Salamon (Boulder, Colo.:
   Westview Press, 1981), 21-43.
7. Richard F. Fenno, Jr., "The Impact of PPBS on the Congressional Appropriations Process," in *Information Support, Program Budgeting, and the Congress,*
   ed. Robert L. Chartrand, Kenneth Janda, and Michael Hugo (New York:
   Spartan Books, 1968), 181-182.
8. *Christian Science Monitor,* June 27, 1983, 1.
9. Congressional requests for executive agency information may be blocked by
   executive privilege. See Bernard Schwartz, "Executive Privilege and Congressional Investigatory Power," *California Law Review* (March 1959): 3-50; Raoul
   Berger, *Executive Privilege: A Constitutional Myth* (Cambridge, Mass.: Harvard University Press, 1974); *U.S. v. Nixon,* 418 U.S. 683 (1974); and
   "Symposium: United States v. Nixon," *UCLA Law Review* (October 1974): 1-40.
   Also see the remarks of Rep. John N. Erlenborn, R-Ill., on executive privilege in
   U.S., Congress, *Congressional Record,* daily ed., July 28, 1983, E3835.
10. William West and Joseph Cooper, "The Congressional Veto and Administrative
    Rulemaking," *Political Science Quarterly* (Summer 1983): 286. The data cited
    in this study was compiled by Clark Norton of the Congressional Research
    Service, Library of Congress.
11. See, for example, Steven Pressman, "House Passes New Version: Congress
    Considers Choices in Legislative Veto Aftermath," *Congressional Quarterly
    Weekly Report,* July 2, 1983, 1327-1334; Richard E. Cohen, "Life Without the
    Legislative Veto — Will Congress Ever Learn to Like It?" *National Journal,*
    July 2, 1983, 1379-1381; and Michael Wines, "Legislative Veto Debate Threat-

ens To Hogtie FTC Reauthorization Bill," *National Journal,* September 10, 1983, 1830-1833. Also see Frederick M. Kaiser, "Congressional Action To Overturn Agency Rules: Alternatives to the 'Legislative Veto,' " *Administrative Law Review* (Fall 1980): 667-711.

12. U.S., Congress, House, *Congressional Record,* daily ed., June 29, 1983, H4825. Also see *Washington Post,* September 11, 1983, F1.

13. Harris, *Congressional Control of Administration,* 284.

14. Quoted in Louis Fisher, "Annual Authorizations: Durable Roadblocks to Biennial Budgeting," *Public Budgeting and Finance* (Spring 1983): 38.

15. *Workshop on Congressional Oversight and Investigations,* 199.

16. Michael Kirst, *Government Without Passing Laws* (Chapel Hill: University of North Carolina Press, 1969), 37. See also William Rhode, *Committee Clearance of Administrative Decisions* (East Lansing: Michigan State Press, 1959).

17. Holbert N. Carroll, *The House of Representatives and Foreign Affairs,* revised ed., (Boston: Little, Brown, 1966), 172. A good example of nonstatutory controls involves the reprogramming of funds within executive accounts. Reprogramming refers to the expenditure of funds for purposes not originally intended when Congress approved the department's budget. Agencies secure approval for reprogramming from the appropriate House and Senate committees.

18. See the remarks of Sen. William L. Armstrong, R-Colo., in U.S., Congress, Senate, *Congressional Record,* daily ed., December 21, 1982, S15912.

19. *New York Times,* May 12, 1983, B8. See also *New York Times,* October 22, 1982, A16.

20. For studies of the General Accounting Office (GAO), see Thomas D. Morgan, "The General Accounting Office: One Hope for Congress to Regain Parity of Power With the President," *North Carolina Law Review* (October 1973): 1279-1468; Richard E. Brown, *The GAO, Untapped Source of Congressional Power* (Knoxville: University of Tennessee Press, 1970); John T. Rourke, "The GAO: Auditor ... Analyst ... Advocate," *The Bureaucrat* (Spring 1981): 43-49; Erasmus H. Kloman, ed., *Cases in Accountability: The Work of the GAO* (Boulder, Colo.: Westview Press, 1979); Frederick C. Mosher, *The GAO: The Quest for Accountability in American Government* (Boulder, Colo.: Westview Press, 1979); and Joseph Pois, *Watchdog on the Potomac: A Study of the Comptroller General of the United States* (Washington, D.C.: University Press of America, 1979).

21. *Reports To Be Made To Congress,* Clerk of the U.S. House of Representatives, H. Doc. No. 98-11, 98th Cong., 1st sess., January 3, 1983. See also J. Malcolm Smith and Cornelius P. Cotter, "Administrative Accountability: Reporting to Congress," *Western Political Quarterly* (June 1957): 405-416; and John R. Johannes, "Study and Recommend: Statutory Reporting Requirements as a Technique of Legislative Initiative — A Research Note," *Western Political Quarterly* (December 1976): 589-596.

22. *New York Times,* June 16, 1982, A13. See also *Washington Post,* August 20, 1982, D8, for a review of Congress's successful effort to require the Defense Department to file quarterly reports with the House and Senate whenever weapons research and procurement costs exceed certain levels.

23. *Congressional Quarterly Weekly Report,* July 31, 1970, 1952-1956. See also Susan Webb Hammond, Arthur G. Stevens, Jr., and Daniel P. Mulhollan, "Congressional Caucuses: Legislators as Lobbyists," in *Interest Group Politics,* ed. Allan J. Cigler and Burdett A. Loomis (Washington, D.C.: CQ Press, 1983), 275-297.

24. *New York Times,* August 26, 1983, A14.
25. *New York Times,* April 14, 1983, B10.
26. See, for example, Joseph Wholey, and others, *Federal Evaluation Policy* (Washington: The Urban Institute, 1970); Joel Havemann, "Congress Tries to Break Ground Zero in Evaluating Federal Programs," *National Journal,* May 22, 1976, 706-713; "Evaluation: A Cautious Perspective," Public Policy Forum, *The Bureaucrat* (April 1976): 3-100; Robert T. Nakamura and Frank Smallwood, *The Politics of Policy Implementation* (New York: St. Martin's Press, 1980); George C. Edwards III, *Implementing Public Policy* (Washington, D.C.: CQ Press, 1980); and Harry S. Havens, "A Public Accounting, Integrating Evaluation and Budgeting," *Public Budgeting and Finance* (Summer 1983): 102-113.
27. *Washington Post,* December 16, 1982, C5. See also William Cohen and Kenneth Lasson, *Getting the Most Out of Washington: Using Congress To Move the Federal Bureaucracy* (Washington, D.C.: Facts on File, 1982); John R. Johannes, "Political Culture and Congressional Constituency Service," *Polity* (Summer 1983): 555-572; Laurily K. Epstein and Kathleen A. Frankovic, "Casework and Electoral Margins: Insurance is Prudent," *Polity* (Summer 1982): 691-700; Robert Klonoff, "The Congressman As Mediator Between Citizens and Government Agencies: Problems and Prospects," *Harvard Journal on Legislation* (Summer 1979): 701-734; John R. Johannes and John C. McAdams, "The Congressional Incumbency Effect: Is It Casework, Policy Compatibility, or Something Else?" *American Journal of Political Science* (August 1981): 512-542; Morris P. Fiorina, "Some Problems in Studying the Effects of Resource Allocation in Congressional Elections," *American Journal of Political Science* (August 1981): 543-567; and Diana Evans Yiannakis, "The Grateful Electorate: Casework and Congressional Elections," *American Journal of Political Science* (August 1981): 568-580.
28. See the panel discussion on the oversight assistance provided Congress by the congressional support agencies in *Workshop on Congressional Oversight and Investigations,* 118-130.
29. See *Christian Science Monitor,* August 5, 1982, 1.
30. U.S., Congress, House, *Congressional Record,* daily ed., June 8, 1983, H3737.
31. *National Journal,* January 5, 1980, 36. See also Joel D. Aberbach, "Changes in Congressional Oversight," *American Behavioral Scientist* (May/June 1979): 493-515; and Leon Halpert, "Legislative Oversight and the Partisan Composition of Government," *Presidential Studies Quarterly* (Fall 1981): 479-491.
32. The following several paragraphs are excerpted from the author's "Integration and Fragmentation: Key Themes of Congressional Change," *The Annals* (March 1983): 202-203.
33. See, for example, Harris, *Congressional Control of Administration,* 9; Ogul, *Congress Oversees the Bureaucracy,* 11; and Aberbach, "Changes in Congressional Oversight," 494.
34. *Workshop on Congressional Oversight and Investigations,* 5.
35. Ibid., 144.
36. Allen Schick, "Politics Through Law: Congressional Limitations on Executive Discretion," in *Both Ends of the Avenue,* ed. Anthony King (Washington, D.C.: American Enterprise Institute for Public Policy Research, 1983), 166.
37. See, for example, J. Leiper Freeman, *The Political Process: Executive Bureau-Legislative Committee Relations,* revised ed. (New York: Random House, 1965); Randall B. Ripley and Grace A. Franklin, *Congress, the Bureaucracy and Public*

Policy, rev. ed. (Homewood, Ill.: The Dorsey Press, 1980); and Timothy B. Clark, "The President Takes on the 'Iron Triangles' and So Far Holds His Own," *National Journal,* March 28, 1981, 516-518.

38. Herbert Roback, "Program Evaluation by and for the Congress," *The Bureaucrat* (April 1976): 27. See also Donald Lambro, "Congressional Oversights," *Policy Review* (Spring 1981): 115-128.
39. *Committee Organization in the House,* Hearings before the House Select Committee on Committees, 93d Cong., 1st sess., H. Doc. No. 94-187, 67. The statement was made by Willian Robert (Bob) Poage, D-Texas (1937-78), former chairman of the House Agriculture Committee.
40. Morris S. Ogul, "Congressional Oversight: Structures and Incentives," in *Congress Reconsidered,* 2d ed., ed. Lawrence C. Dodd and Bruce I. Oppenheimer (Washington, D.C.: CQ Press, 1981), 330. See also Morris P. Fiorina, "Congressional Control of Bureaucracy: A Mismatch of Incentives and Capabilities," in *Congress Reconsidered,* 2d ed., 332-348; Fiorina, *Congress: Keystone of the Washington Establishment* (New Haven: Yale University Press, 1977); and R. Douglas Arnold, *Congress and the Bureaucracy: A Theory of Influence* (New Haven: Yale University Press, 1979).
41. *Christian Science Monitor,* May 11, 1982, 15.

11

A Dynamic Process

Anyone who views lawmaking in Congress as a precise, neat process of drafting, debating, and approving legislation overlooks the dynamic forces at work on Capitol Hill. It is not a static institution.

For better or worse, the interests, pressures, perceptions, and prejudices of members of Congress change rather quickly, a result, in part, of the election cycle, but also of other pressures and influences. The demands made by the presidency and the courts, international events, business and citizen lobbying, and media disclosures are some of the ever-present forces that affect lawmaking. Congress, in short, is an institution in which procedures reflect and, in turn, perpetuate the messiness, openness, pragmatism, compromise, and deliberateness so characteristic of much American policy making. As House Energy and Commerce Committee Chairman John D. Dingell, D-Mich., puts it: "Legislation is like a chess game more than anything else. It is a seemingly endless series of moves, until ultimately somebody prevails through exhaustion, or brilliance, or because of overwhelming public sentiment for their side."[1]

Throughout this book, the point is made that at every stage of the legislative process a new winning coalition must be formed to carry a policy recommendation up the next rung of the legislative ladder; otherwise, its progress is jeopardized. And that coalition is ever changing, as the forces that mold it change. While coalitions are formed to advance legislation, others may form to tear it down. If opponents fail in one session of Congress they always can come back in the next to try again. A classic example of this was cited in an earlier chapter.

In 1982 Congress approved a major revenue bill that included a withholding tax on interest and dividend income. Barely a year later it turned around and repealed the provision. This is not a rare occurrence; occasionally, it occurs even in the same session of Congress. In 1981 Congress repealed the $122 minimum monthly Social Security benefit at the urging of the Reagan administration but later the same year voted to restore it because of adverse public reaction. The point is not whether one or the other action was wise, but rather that Congress is subject to steady and sometimes unrelenting pressure from many sides on a host of controversial and usually complicated issues. Sen. Howard H. Baker, Jr., R-Tenn., has observed that "there aren't any, or seldom [are there any], sweeping solutions for fundamental problems." [2] This general condition results, on occasion, in a spasmodic pattern of lawmaking.

Despite its built-in — and frequently beneficial — inefficiencies, Congress's policy making role is firmly grounded in the Constitution. It is true that the pre-eminent place envisioned for Congress by the authors of the Constitution has been modified by the growth of executive power in the twentieth century. But it is equally true that the constitutional separation of powers has preserved for Congress an independent role that distinguishes it from legislative bodies in most Western democracies.

This book has focused on congressional procedures and rules because the mechanics of legislating influence the policy-making process. Procedural details and nuances have a crucial policy impact, and it is impossible to understand why certain policies are adopted and others are not without an appreciation of the rules governing the process. Substance, in short, can be shaped through procedure.

The "rules of the game" are as important in illuminating the outcomes of the legislative process as they are in comprehending who wins at any competition, the presidential nominating system, for example. To use the presidential election analogy, it is difficult to appreciate electoral strategy in the general campaign without understanding the Electoral College or the campaign finance rules. Similarly, one cannot apprehend the behavior of members of Congress as participants in policy formation without a knowledge of the rules and procedures under which they operate.

Congressional rules serve many functions: they promote stability, divide responsibilities, minimize conflict in daily decision making, legitimize decisions, and distribute power. Paradoxically, because the rules do distribute power they create tensions between those whose influential positions are protected by the rules and those whose influence is limited or threatened by proposed changes in the rules.

The substantial overhaul of congressional procedures that took place during the past decade was in large part an effort by junior and newly elected members of Congress to correct perceived deficiencies and to gain more influence. When the two parties dropped seniority as the sole basis for deciding which members would head committees, they were not simply changing a selection procedure; just as important were the opportunities that were opened up for newer members to attain positions of authority.

This change, in turn, greatly affected members' relationships with interest groups and the executive branch. There are now many points of access for groups and individuals trying to influence congressional decisions. Changes in the rules can have broad impact outside Congress.

The effect of congressional rules and practices on policy outcomes has been demonstrated repeatedly in these chapters. The requirement for an extraordinary majority of the Senate to invoke cloture gives to a well-organized minority the ability to block passage of legislation desired by a majority. Civil rights legislation, perhaps the classic case, was repeatedly delayed in the 1950s and 1960s by the opponents' use of the filibuster.

On the other hand, the rules themselves may change in response to events or policy goals. Some rules are modified or ignored, while new ones come out of struggles over a particular problem. Cloture was made somewhat easier in 1975 by changing the size of the Senate majority needed to invoke it from two-thirds of those voting to three-fifths of the entire membership. In reaction, a long-ignored procedure was revived in 1976: the post-cloture filibuster. That tactic in turn led to another tightening up of the cloture rule in 1979, albeit with mixed results and some unanticipated consequences.

This book also has cited cases where an ostensibly procedural decision can be used to mask a policy objective. When members vote to table a bill, procedurally they are merely postponing consideration of it. Nevertheless, such a procedure usually sidetracks the legislation permanently, while allowing members to say they did not take a position on the measure.

Important, too, are the differences in the way the two chambers operate. Each chamber functions under rules and procedures that reflect its basic constitutional design. A close examination of the differences as well as the similarities between the two bodies is indispensable to an accurate understanding of how Congress functions.

The most significant and enduring feature of the rules is that they require bills to pass through a labyrinth of decision points before they can become law. It is generally more difficult to pass legislation than to defeat it. These multiple decision points, coupled with weak party discipline, make necessary a constant cycle of coalition building — by means of the various bargaining techniques — to move legislation past each potential roadblock. The shifting coalitions, as noted earlier, combine, dissolve, and recombine in response to the widely varying issues and needs of members. Unlike the past, when a few "barons" dominated much legislative policy making, the greater decentralization of authority in today's Congress creates an environment in which scores of members have some — and often significant — bargaining power.

Coalition building is possible primarily for two reasons. First, members of Congress, who represent diverse constituencies, are not equally concerned about every item on the legislative agenda. Second, members pursue many objectives other than the enactment of legislation. They may seek reelection, election to higher office, appointment to prestigious committees, or simply personal conveniences such as additional staff or office space. These conditions create numerous opportunities for coalition building through the three types of bargaining discussed — logrolling, compromise, and the distribution of nonlegislative favors (primarily by the congressional leadership).

Another factor determining whether a series of majority coalitions can be built is the extent to which members are in general agreement that a law is required or inevitable on a particular subject. Members may have widely divergent views on the solution to the problem, but they usually will work to compromise their differences when dealing with so-called "must" legislation.

The makeup of recent Congresses adds another dimension to coalition building, however. It would appear that a higher percentage of members today feel less bound to their party leaders and less inclined to follow the procedural customs and courtesies on Capitol Hill or the traditional ways of doing business. Moreover, a widely held belief by members of recent Congresses is that too many ambitious laws — setting up expensive but ineffective programs — were passed in the 1960s and 1970s, and that the appropriate task today is to review existing statutes rather than add new ones.

A critical factor influencing the entire congressional process is time. As the two-year cycle of a Congress runs its course, every procedural device that can be employed has a policy consequence — either delaying or speeding up the processing of legislation. Frequently, as the countdown to final adjournment occurs, the bargaining process shifts into high gear. Bills that have been deadlocked for months are moved along swiftly as logrolling and compromises "save" bills in which members have a vested interest. Deadlines and threatened or actual procedural and policy crises, in brief, frequently activate the lawmaking process. Legislation stalled by opponents dies if not enacted before adjournment.

Congressional Procedures and the Policy Process has been revised during a period when Congress and the president devoted large amounts of time and energy to budgetary issues. In the face of soaring federal deficits, one issue seemed to dominate the congressional agenda: money. Members sought answers to recurring questions. How much will the program cost? Where will the monies come from to finance it? Which programs merit spending reductions or increases?

President Ronald Reagan, to be sure, accentuated this development by his insistence on broad domestic spending cuts while demanding dramatic increases in military funding. From a procedural standpoint, legislators found that traditional lawmaking routines and the customary give-and-take that produce legislative compromises were being thrown out of kilter by the emphasis on fiscal matters. But while Congress was forced to allocate more and more of its time to federal budgetary questions, its ability to deal with the changeover from a period of resource abundance to an era of resource scarcity proved to be extremely difficult. This prompted a re-evaluation of congressional procedures, including those mandated by the 1974 Congressional Budget and Impoundment Control Act.

Such internal and external pressures often compel legislators to engage in major introspective reviews of the institution's organization and operations. A concomitant feature of the legislative process, therefore, is that Congress from time to time seeks to change its rules and procedures to remedy specific problems, become more efficient, redistribute power, or affect policy outcomes. Rules changes in the immediate future are likely to focus on revision of the budgetary process, on oversight procedures, and on the Senate's post-cloture filibuster.

And so the dynamic interplay between policy making and the rules continues. Precedents and practices are revised or abandoned and new ones established, often with great difficulty, in response to changing needs and pressures. Congress's dynamism is assured by the regular infusion of new members, changing circumstances and conditions, and the fluctuating expectations of citizens. If Congress reduces or increases its lawmaking activity, it usually is not by accident but in reaction to legislators' perceptions of what their constituents and the country want. For its part, the nation expects Congress to use its considerable powers and policy-making procedures to help resolve, or at least allay, the pressing issues facing the country as it approaches the twenty-first century.

Notes

1. *Washington Post,* June 26, 1983, A14.
2. *New York Times,* February 1, 1983, A20.

Glossary of Congressional Terms

Act—The term for legislation once it has passed both houses of Congress and has been signed by the president or passed over his veto, thus becoming law. Also used in parliamentary terminology for a bill that has been passed by one house and engrossed. *(See Law, Engrossed Bill.)*

Adjournment Sine Die—Adjournment without definitely fixing a day for reconvening; literally "adjournment without a day." Usually used to connote the final adjournment of a session of Congress. A session can continue until noon, Jan. 3, of the following year, when, under the 20th Amendment to the Constitution, it automatically terminates. Both houses must agree to a concurrent resolution for either house to adjourn for more than three days.

Adjournment to a Day Certain—Adjournment under a motion or resolution that fixes the next time of meeting. Under the Constitution, neither house can adjourn for more than three days without the concurrence of the other. A session of Congress is not ended by adjournment to a day certain.

Amendment—A proposal of a member of Congress to alter the language, provisions or stipulations in a bill or in another amendment. An amendment usually is printed, debated and voted upon in the same manner as a bill.

Amendment in the Nature of a Substitute—Usually an amendment that seeks to replace the entire text of a bill. Passage of this type of amendment strikes out everything after the enacting clause and inserts a new version of the bill. An amendment in the nature of a substitute also can refer to an amendment that replaces a large portion of the text of a bill.

Appeal—A member's challenge of a ruling or decision made by the presiding officer of the chamber. In the Senate, the senator appeals to members of the chamber to override the decision. If carried by a majority vote, the appeal nullifies the chair's ruling. In the House, the decision of the Speaker traditionally has been final; seldom are there appeals to the members to reverse the Speaker's stand. To appeal a ruling is considered an attack on the Speaker.

Appropriations Bill—A bill that gives legal authority to spend or obligate money from the Treasury. The Constitution disallows money to be drawn from the Treasury "but in Consequence of Appropriations made by Law."

It usually is the case that an appropriations bill provides the actual monies approved by authorization bills, but not necessarily the full amount permissible under the authorization measures. By congressional custom, an appropriations bill originates in the House, and it is not supposed to be considered by the full House or Senate until the related authorization measure is enacted. Under the 1974 Congressional Budget and Impoundment Control Act, general appropriations bills are supposed to be enacted by the seventh day after Labor Day before the start of the fiscal year to which they apply, but in recent years this deadline rarely has been met. In addition to general appropriations bills, there are two specialized types. *(See Continuing Resolution, Supplemental Appropriations Bill.)*

Authorization Bill—Basic, substantive legislation that establishes or continues the legal operation of a federal program or agency, either indefinitely or for a specific period of time, or which sanctions a particular type of obligation or expenditure. An authorization normally is a prerequisite for an appropriation or other kind of budget authority. Under the rules of both houses, the appropriation for a program or agency may not be considered until its authorization has been considered. An authorization also may limit the amount of budget authority to be provided or may authorize the appropriation of "such sums as may be necessary." *(See also Appropriations Bill.)*

Bills—Most legislative proposals before Congress are in the form of bills and are designated by HR in the House of Representatives or S in the Senate, according to the house in which they originate, and by a number assigned in the order in which they are introduced during the two-year period of a congressional term. "Public bills" deal with general questions and become public laws if approved by Congress and signed by the president. "Private bills" deal with individual matters such as claims against the government, immigration and naturalization cases, land titles, etc., and become private laws if approved and signed. *(See also Concurrent Resolution, Joint Resolution, Resolution.)*

Bills Introduced—In both the House and Senate, any number of members may join in introducing a single bill or resolution. The first member listed is the sponsor of the bill, and all members' names following his are the bill's cosponsors. Many bills are committee bills and are introduced under the name of the chairman of the committee or subcommittee. All appropriations bills fall into this category. A committee frequently holds hearings on a number of related bills and may agree to one of them or to an entirely new bill. When introduced, a bill is referred to the committee or committees that have jurisdiction over the subject with which the bill is concerned. Under the standing rules of the House and Senate, bills are referred by the Speaker in the House and by the presiding officer in the Senate. In practice, the House and Senate parliamentarians act for these officials and refer the vast majority of bills. *(See also Report, Clean Bill.)*

Budget Authority—Authority to enter into obligations that will result in immediate or future outlays involving federal funds. The basic forms of budget authority are appropriations, contract authority and borrowing authority. Budget authority may be classified by (1) the period of availability (one-year, multiple-year or without a time limitation), (2) the timing of congressional action (current or permanent), or (3) the manner of determining the amount available (definite or indefinite).

Calendar—An agenda or list of business awaiting possible action by each chamber. The House uses five legislative calendars. *(See Consent, Discharge, House, Private, and Union Calendar.)*

In the Senate, all legislative matters reported from committee go on one calendar. They are listed there in the order in which committees report them or the Senate places them on the calendar; they may be called up out of order by the majority leader either by obtaining unanimous consent of the Senate or by a motion to call up a bill. The Senate uses one nonlegislative calendar; this is used for treaties and nominations. *(See Executive Calendar.)*

Calendar Wednesday—In the House, committees, on Wednesdays, may be called in the order in which they appear in Rule X of the House, for the purpose of bringing up any bills from either the House or the Union Calendar, except bills that are privileged. General debate is limited to two hours. Bills called up from the Union Calendar are considered in Committee of the Whole. Calendar Wednesday is not observed during the last two weeks of a session and may be dispensed with at other times by a two-thirds vote. This procedure is rarely used and routinely is dispensed with by unanimous consent.

Call of the Calendar—Senate bills that are not brought up for debate by a motion, unanimous consent or a unanimous consent agreement are brought before the Senate for action when the calendar listing them is "called." Bills must be called in the order listed. Measures considered by this method usually are noncontroversial, and debate is limited to a total of five minutes for each senator on the bill and any amendments proposed to it.

Clean Bill—Frequently after a committee has finished a major revision of a bill, one of the committee members, usually the chairman, will assemble the changes and what is left of the original bill into a new measure and introduce it as a "clean bill." The revised measure, which is given a new number, then is referred back to the committee, which reports it to the floor for consideration. This often is a timesaver, as committee-recommended changes in a clean bill do not have to be considered and voted on by the chamber. Reporting a clean bill also protects committee amendments that might be subject to points of order concerning germaneness.

Cloture—The process by which a filibuster can be ended in the Senate other than by unanimous consent. A motion for cloture can apply to any measure before the Senate, including a proposal to change the chamber's rules. A cloture motion requires the signatures of 16 senators to be introduced, and to end a filibuster the cloture motion must obtain the votes of three-fifths of the entire Senate membership (60 if there are no vacancies), except that to end a filibuster against a proposal to amend the standing rules of the Senate a two-thirds vote of senators present and voting is required. The cloture request is put to a roll-call vote one hour after the Senate meets on the second day following introduction of the motion. If approved, cloture limits each senator to one hour of debate. The bill or amendment in question comes to a final vote after 100 hours of consideration (including debate time and the time it takes to conduct roll calls, quorum calls and other procedural motions). *(See Filibuster.)*

Committee—A division of the House or Senate that prepares legislation for action by the parent chamber or makes investigations as directed by the parent chamber. There are several types of committees. Most standing committees are divided into subcommittees, which study legislation, hold hearings and report bills, with or without amendments, to the full committee. Only the full committee can report legislation to the House or Senate.

Committee of the Whole—The working title of what is formally "The Committee of the Whole House [of Representatives] on the State of the Union." The membership is comprised of all House members sitting as a committee. Any 100 members who are present on the floor of the chamber comprise a quorum of the committee. Any legislation, however, must first have passed through the regular legislative committee or the Appropriations Committee and have been placed on the calendar.

Technically, the Committee of the Whole considers only bills directly or indirectly appropriating money, authorizing appropriations or involving taxes or charges on the public. Because the Committee of the Whole need number only 100 representatives, a quorum is more readily attained, and legislative business is expedited. Before 1971, members' positions were not individually recorded on votes taken in Committee of the Whole.

When the full House resolves itself into the Committee of the Whole, it supplants the Speaker with a "chairman." A measure is debated and amendments may be proposed, with votes on amendments as needed. When the committee completes its work on the measure, it dissolves itself by "rising." The Speaker returns, and the chairman of the Committee of the Whole reports to the House that the committee's work has been completed.

At this time members may demand a roll-call vote on any amendment adopted in the Committee of the Whole. The final vote is on passage of the legislation.

Concurrent Resolution—A concurrent resolution, designated H Con Res or S Con Res, must be adopted by both houses, but it is not sent to the president for his signature and therefore does not have the force of law. A concurrent resolution, for example, is used to fix the time for adjournment of a Congress. It also is used as the vehicle for expressing the sense of Congress on various foreign policy and domestic issues, and it serves as the vehicle for coordinated decisions on the federal budget under the 1974 Congressional Budget and Impoundment Control Act. *(See also Bills, Joint Resolution, Resolution.)*

Conference—A meeting between the representatives of the House and the Senate to reconcile differences between the two houses on provisions of a bill passed by both chambers. Members of the conference committee are appointed by the Speaker and the presiding officer of the Senate and are called "managers" for their respective chambers.

A majority of the managers for each house must reach agreement on the provisions of the bill (usually a compromise between the versions of the two chambers) before it can be considered by either chamber in the form of a "conference report." When the conference report goes to the floor, it cannot be amended, and, if it is not approved by both chambers, the bill may go back to conference under certain situations, or a new conference must be convened. Many rules and informal practices govern the conduct of conference committees.

Bills that are passed by both houses with only minor differences need not be sent to conference. Either chamber may "concur" in the other's amendments, completing action on the legislation. Sometimes leaders of the committees of jurisdiction work out an informal compromise instead of having a formal conference.

Consent Calendar—Members of the House may place on this calendar most bills on the Union or House Calendar that are considered to be noncontroversial. Bills on the Consent Calendar normally are called on the first and third Mondays of each month. On the first occasion that a bill is called in this manner, consideration may be blocked by the objection of any member. The second time, if there are three objections, the bill is stricken from the Consent Calendar. If less than three members object, the bill is given immediate consideration.

A bill on the Consent Calendar may be postponed in another way. A member may ask that the measure be passed over "without prejudice." In that case, no objection is recorded against the bill, and its status on the Consent Calendar remains unchanged. A bill stricken from the Consent Calendar remains on the Union or House Calendar.

Continuing Resolution—A joint resolution drafted by Congress "continuing appropriations" for specific ongoing activities of a government department or departments when a fiscal year begins and Congress has not yet enacted all of the regular appropriations bills for that year. The continuing resolution usually specifies a maximum rate at which the agency may incur obligations. This usually is based on the rate for the previous year, the president's budget request or an appropriation bill for that year passed by either or both houses of Congress, but not cleared.

Contract Authority—Budget authority contained in an authorization bill that permits the federal government to enter into contracts or other obligations for future payments from funds not yet appropriated by Congress. The assumption is that funds will be available for payment in a subsequent appropriations act.

Correcting Recorded Votes—Rules prohibit members from changing their votes after the result has been announced. Occasionally, some hours, days or months after a vote has been taken, a member may announce that he was "incorrectly recorded." In the Senate, a request to change one's vote almost always receives unanimous consent. In the House, members are prohibited from changing their votes if tallied by the electronic voting system. If taken by roll call, it is permissible if consent is granted.

Dilatory Motion—A motion made for the purpose of killing time and preventing action on a bill or amendment. House rules outlaw dilatory motions, but enforcement is largely within the discretion of the Speaker or chairman of the Committee of the Whole. The Senate does not have a rule banning dilatory motions, except under cloture.

Discharge a Committee—Occasionally, attempts are made to relieve a committee from jurisdiction over a measure before it. This is attempted more often in the House than in the Senate, and the procedure rarely is successful.

In the House, if a committee does not report a bill within 30 days after the measure is referred to it, any member may file a discharge motion. Once offered the motion is treated as a petition needing the signatures of 218 members (a majority of the House). After the required signatures have been obtained, there is a delay of seven days. Thereafter, on the second and fourth Mondays of each month, except during the last six days of a session, any member who has signed the petition must be recognized, if he so desires, to move that the committee be discharged. Debate on the motion to discharge is limited to 20 minutes, and, if the motion is carried, consideration of the bill becomes a matter of high privilege.

If a resolution to consider a bill is held up in the Rules Committee for more than seven legislative days, any member may enter a motion to discharge the committee. The motion is handled like any other discharge petition in the House. *(Senate procedure, see Discharge Resolution.)*

Discharge Calendar—The House calendar to which motions to discharge committees are referred when they have the required number of signatures (218) and are awaiting floor action.

Discharge Petition—*(See Discharge a Committee.)*

Discharge Resolution—In the Senate, a special motion that any senator may introduce to relieve a committee from consideration of a bill before it. The resolution can be called up for Senate approval or disapproval in the same manner as any other Senate business. *(House procedure, see Discharge a Committee.)*

Division Vote—*(See Standing Vote.)*

Enacting Clause—Key phrase in bills beginning, "Be it enacted by the Senate and House of Representatives. . . ." A successful motion to strike it from legislation kills the measure.

Engrossed Bill—The final copy of a bill as passed by one chamber, with the text as amended by floor action and certified by the clerk of the House or the secretary of the Senate.

Enrolled Bill—The final copy of a bill that has been passed in identical form by both chambers. It is certified by an officer of the house of origin (clerk of the House or secretary of the Senate) and then sent on for the signatures of the House Speaker, the Senate president pro tempore and the president of the United States. An enrolled bill is printed on parchment.

Executive Calendar—This is a nonlegislative calendar in the Senate on which presidential documents such as treaties and nominations are listed.

Executive Session—A meeting of a Senate or House committee (or occasionally of either chamber) that only its members may attend. Witnesses regularly appear at committee meetings in executive session — for example, Defense Department officials during presentations of classified defense information. The public and press are not allowed to attend.

Expenditures—The actual spending of money as distinguished from the appropriation of funds. Expenditures are made by the executive branch; appropriations are made only by Congress. The two rarely are identical in any fiscal year. In addition to some current budget authority, expenditures may represent budget authority made available one, two or more years earlier.

Filibuster—A time-delaying tactic associated with the Senate and used by a minority in an effort to prevent a vote on a bill or amendment that probably would pass if voted upon directly. The most common method is to take advantage of the Senate's rules permitting unlimited debate, but other forms of parliamentary maneuvering may be used. The stricter rules used by the House make filibusters more difficult, but delaying tactics are employed occasionally through various procedural devices allowed by House rules. *(See Cloture.)*

Five-Minute Rule—A debate-limiting rule of the House that is invoked when the House sits as the Committee of the Whole. Under the rule, a member offering an amendment is allowed to speak five minutes in its favor, and an opponent of the amendment is allowed to speak five minutes in opposition. Debate is then closed. In practice, amendments regularly are debated more than 10 minutes, with members gaining the floor by offering pro forma amendments or obtaining unanimous consent to speak longer than five minutes. *(See Strike Out the Last Word.)*

Germane—Pertaining to the subject matter of the legislation at hand. House amendments must be germane to the bill being considered. The Senate requires that amendments be germane when they are proposed to general appropriation bills, bills being considered once cloture has been adopted, or, frequently, when proceeding under a unanimous consent agreement placing a time limit on consideration of a bill. The 1974 budget act also requires that amendments to concurrent budget resolutions be germane. In the House, floor debate must be germane, and the first three hours of debate each day in the Senate must be germane to the pending business.

House Calendar—A listing for action by the House of public bills that do not directly or indirectly appropriate money or raise revenue.

Joint Resolution—A joint resolution, designated H J Res or S J Res, requires the approval of both houses and the signature of the president, just as a bill does, and has the force of law if approved. There is no practical difference between a bill and a joint resolution. A joint resolution generally is used to deal with a limited matter such as a single appropriation.

Joint resolutions also are used to propose amendments to the Constitution in Congress. They do not require a presidential signature, but become a part of the Constitution when three-fourths of the states have ratified them.

Law—An act of Congress that has been signed by the president or passed over his veto by Congress. Public bills, when signed, become public laws, and are cited by the letters PL and a hyphenated number. The two digits before the number correspond to the Congress, and the one or more digits after the hyphen refer to the numerical sequence in which the bills were signed by the president during that Congress. Private bills, when signed, become private laws.

Legislative Day—The "day" extending from the time either house meets after an adjournment until the time it next adjourns. Because the House normally adjourns from day to day, legislative days and calendar days usually coincide. But in the Senate, a legislative day may, and frequently does, extend over several calendar days. *(See Recess.)*

Legislative Veto—A procedure permitting either the House or Senate, or both chambers, to review proposed executive branch regulations or actions and to block or modify those with which they disagree. The specifics of the procedure may vary, but Congress generally provides for a legislative veto by including in a bill a provision that administrative rules or action taken to implement the law are to go into effect at the end of a designated period of time unless blocked by either or both houses of Congress. Another version of the veto provides for congressional reconsideration and rejection of regulations already in effect. The Supreme Court on June 23, 1983, restricted greatly the form and use of the legislative veto, ruling that it is an unconstitutional violation of the lawmaking procedure provided in the Constitution.

Majority Leader—The majority leader is elected by his party colleagues. In the Senate, in consultation with the minority leader and other senators, the majority leader directs the legislative schedule for the chamber. He also is his party's spokesman and chief strategist. In the House, the majority leader is second to the Speaker in the majority party's leadership and serves as his party's legislative strategist.

Majority Whip—In effect, the assistant majority leader in either the House or Senate. His job is to help marshal majority forces in support of party strategy and legislation.

Marking Up a Bill—Going through the contents of a piece of legislation in committee or subcommittee, considering its provisions in large and small portions, acting on amendments to provisions and proposed revisions to the language, inserting new sections and phraseology, etc. If the bill is extensively amended, the committee's version may be introduced as a separate bill, with a new number, before being considered by the full House or Senate. *(See Clean Bill.)*

Minority Leader—Floor leader for the minority party in each chamber.

Minority Whip—Performs duties of whip for the minority party.

Morning Hour—The time set aside at the beginning of each legislative day for the consideration of regular, routine business. The "hour" is of indefinite duration in the House, where it is rarely used.

In the Senate it is the first two hours of a session following an adjournment, as distingusihed from a recess. The morning hour can be terminated earlier if the morning business has been completed. Business includes such matters as messages from the president, communications from the heads of departments, messages from the House, the presentation of petitions, reports of standing and select committees and the introduction of bills and resolutions. During the first hour of the morning hour in the Senate, no motion to proceed to the consideration of any bill on the calendar is in order except by unanimous consent. During the second hour, motions can be made but must be decided without debate. Senate committees may meet while the Senate conducts morning hour.

Motion—In the House or Senate chamber, a request by a member to institute any one of a wide array of parliamentary actions. He "moves" for a certain procedure, the consideration of a measure, etc. The precedence of motions, and whether they are debatable, is set forth in the House and Senate manuals.

One-Minute Speeches—Addresses by House members at the beginning of a legislative day. The speeches may cover any subject, but are limited to one minute's duration.

Override a Veto—If the president disapproves a bill and sends it back to Congress with his objections, Congress may try to override his veto and enact the bill into law. Neither house is required to attempt to override a veto. The override of a veto requires a recorded vote with a two-thirds majority in each chamber. The question put to each house is: "Shall the bill pass, the objections of the president to the contrary notwithstanding?" *(See also Pocket Veto, Veto.)*

Pair—A voluntary arrangement between two lawmakers, usually on opposite sides of an issue. If passage of the measure requires a two-thirds majority vote, a pair would require two members favoring the action to one opposed to it. Pairs can take one of three forms — specific, general and live. The names of lawmakers pairing on a given vote and their stands, if known, are printed in the *Congressional Record.*
The specific pair applies to one or more votes on the same subject. On some pairs lawmakers specify how they would have voted.

Pocket Veto—The act of the president in withholding his approval of a bill after Congress has adjourned. When Congress is in session, a bill becomes law without the president's signature if he does not act upon it within 10 days, excluding Sundays, from the time he gets it. But if Congress adjourns *sine die* within that 10-day period, the bill will die even if the president does not formally veto it. *(See also Veto.)*

Point of Order—An objection raised by a member that the chamber is departing from rules governing its conduct of business. The objector cites the rule violated, the chair sustaining his objection if correctly made. Order is restored by the chair's suspending proceedings of the chamber until it conforms to the prescribed "order of business."

President of the Senate—Under the Constitution, the vice president of the United States presides over the Senate. In his absence, the president pro tempore, or a senator designated by the president pro tempore, presides over the chamber.

President Pro Tempore—The chief officer of the Senate in the absence of the vice president; literally, but loosely, the president for a time. The president pro tempore is elected by his fellow senators, and the recent practice has been to choose the senator of the majority party with the longest period of continuous service.

Previous Question—A motion for the previous question, when carried, has the effect of cutting off all debate, preventing the offering of further amendments, and forcing a vote on the pending matter. In the House, the previous question is not permitted in the Committee of the Whole. The motion for the previous question is a debate-limiting device and is not in order in the Senate.

Printed Amendment—A House rule guarantees five minutes of floor debate in support of, and five minutes in opposition to, amendments printed in the *Congressional Record* at least one day prior to the amendment's consideration in the Committee of the Whole. In the Senate, while amendments may be submitted for printing, they have no parliamentary standing or status. An amendment submitted for printing in the Senate, however, may be called up by any senator.

Private Calendar—In the House, private bills dealing with individual matters such as claims against the government, immigration, land titles, etc., are put on this calendar. The private calendar must be called on the first Tuesday of each month, and the Speaker may call it on the third Tuesday of each month as well.

When a private bill is before the chamber, two members may block its consideration, which recommits the bill to committee. Backers of a recommitted private bill have recourse.

The measure can be put into an "omnibus claims bill" — several private bills rolled into one. As with any bill, no part of an omnibus claims bill may be deleted without a vote.

Privilege—Privilege relates to the rights of members of Congress and to the relative priority of the motions and actions they may make in their respective chambers. The two are distinct. "Privileged questions" deal with legislative business. "Questions of privilege" concern members themselves.

Privileged Questions—The order in which bills, motions and other legislative measures are considered by Congress is governed by strict priorities. A motion to table, for instance, is more privileged than a motion to recommit. Thus, a motion to recommit can be superseded by a motion to table, and a vote would be forced on the latter motion only. A motion to adjourn, however, takes precedence over a tabling motion and thus is considered of the "highest privilege." *(See also Questions of Privilege.)*

Pro Forma Amendment—*(See Strike Out the Last Word.)*

Questions of Privilege—These are matters affecting members of Congress individually or collectively. Matters affecting the rights, safety, dignity and integrity of proceedings of the House or Senate as a whole are questions of privilege in both chambers.

Questions involving individual members are called questions of "personal privilege." A member rising to ask a question of personal privilege is given precedence over almost all other proceedings. An annotation in the House rules states that the privilege is derived chiefly from the Constitution, which gives him a conditional immunity from arrest and an unconditional freedom to speak in the House. *(See also Privileged Questions.)*

Quorum—The number of members whose presence is necessary for the transaction of business. In the Senate and House, it is a majority of the membership. A quorum is 100 in the Committee of the Whole House. If a point of order is made that a quorum is not present, the only business that is in order is either a motion to adjourn or a motion to direct the sergeant-at-arms to request the attendance of absentees.

Readings of Bills—Traditional parliamentary procedure required bills to be read three times before they were passed. This custom is of little modern significance. Normally a bill is considered to have its first reading when it is introduced and printed, by title, in the *Congressional Record*. In the House, its second reading comes when floor consideration begins. (This is the most likely point at which there is an actual reading of the bill, if there is any.) The second reading in the Senate is supposed to occur on the legislative day after the measure is introduced, but before it is referred to committee. The third reading (again, usually by title) takes place when floor action has been completed on amendments.

Recess—Distinguished from adjournment in that a recess does not end a legislative day and therefore does not interrupt unfinished business. The rules in each house set forth certain matters to be taken up and disposed of at the beginning of each legislative day. The House usually adjourns from day to day. The Senate often recesses, thus meeting on the same legislative day for several calendar days or even weeks at a time. *(See Adjournment.)*

Recognition—The power of recognition of a member is lodged in the Speaker of the House and the presiding officer of the Senate. The presiding officer names the member who will speak first when two or more members simultaneously request recognition.

Recommit to Committee—A motion, made on the floor after a bill has been debated, to return it to the committee that reported it. If approved, recommittal usually is considered a death blow to the bill. In the House, a motion to recommit can be made only by a member opposed to the bill, and, in recognizing a member to make the motion, the Speaker gives preference to members of the minority party over majority party members.

A motion to recommit may include instructions to the committee to report the bill again with specific amendments or by a certain date. Or, the instructions may direct that a particular study be made, with no definite deadline for further action. If the recommittal motion includes instructions to "report the bill back forthwith" and the motion is adopted, floor action on the bill continues; the committee does not actually reconsider the legislation.

Reconsider a Vote—A motion to reconsider the vote by which an action was taken has, until it is disposed of, the effect of putting the action in abeyance. In the Senate, the motion can be made only by a member who voted on the prevailing side of the original question or by a member who did not vote at all. In the House, it can be made only by a member on the prevailing side.

A common practice in the Senate after close votes on an issue is a motion to reconsider, followed by a motion to table the motion to reconsider. On this motion to table, senators vote as they voted on the original question, which allows the motion to table to prevail, assuming there are no switches. The matter then is finally closed and further motions to reconsider are not entertained. In the House, as a routine precaution, a motion to reconsider usually is made every time a measure is passed. Such a motion almost always is tabled immediately, thus shutting off the possibility of future reconsideration, except by unanimous consent. Motions to reconsider must be entered in the Senate within the next two days of actual session after the original vote has been taken. In the House they must be entered either on the same day or on the next succeeding day the House is in session.

Recorded Vote—A vote upon which each member's stand is individually made known. In the Senate, this is accomplished through a roll call of the entire membership, to which each senator on the floor must answer "yea," "nay" or, if he does not wish to vote, "present." Since January 1973, the House has used an electronic voting system for recorded votes, including yea-and-nay votes formerly taken by roll calls. When not required by the Constitution, a recorded vote can be obtained on questions in the House on the demand of one-fifth (44 members) of a quorum or one-fourth (25) of a quorum in the Committee of the Whole. *(See Yeas and Nays.)*

Report—Both a verb and a noun as a congressional term. A committee that has been examining a bill referred to it by the parent chamber "reports" its findings and recommendations to the chamber when it completes consideration and returns the measure. The process is called "reporting" a bill.

A "report" is the document setting forth the committee's explanation of its action. Senate and House reports are numbered separately and are designated S Rept or H Rept. When a committee report is not unanimous, the dissenting committee members may file a statement of their views, called minority views and referred to as a minority report. Members in disagreement with some provisions of a bill may file additional or supplementary views. Sometimes a bill is reported without a committee recommendation. Adverse reports occasionally are submitted by legislative committees. When a committee is opposed to a bill, it usually fails to report the measure at all. Some laws require that committee reports, favorable or adverse, be made.

Rescission Bill—A bill rescinding or canceling budget authority previously made available by Congress. The president may request a rescission to reduce spending or because the budget authority no longer is needed. Under the 1974 budget act, unless Congress approves a rescission within 45 days of continuous session after receipt of the proposal, the funds must be made available for obligation.

Resolution—A "simple" resolution, designated H Res or S Res, deals with matters entirely within the prerogatives of one house or the other. It requires neither passage by the other chamber nor approval by the president, and it does not have the force of law. Most resolutions deal with the rules or procedures of one house. They also are used to express the sentiments of a single house, such as condolences to the family of a deceased member, or to comment on foreign policy or executive business. A simple resolution is the vehicle for a "rule" from the House Rules Committee. *(See also Concurrent Resolution, Joint Resolution, Rules.)*

Rider—An amendment, usually not germane, which its sponsor hopes to get through more easily by including it in other legislation. Riders become law if the bills embodying them are enacted. Amendments providing legislative directives in appropriations bills are outstanding examples of riders, though technically legislation is banned from appropriations bills. The House, unlike the Senate, has a strict germaneness rule; thus, riders usually are Senate devices to get legislation enacted quickly or to bypass lengthy House consideration and, possibly, opposition.

Rules—The term has two specific congressional meanings. A rule may be a standing order governing the conduct of House or Senate business and listed among the permanent rules of either chamber. The rules deal with duties of officers, the order of business, admission to the floor, parliamentary procedures on handling amendments and voting, jurisdictions of committees, etc.

In the House, a rule also may be a resolution reported by the Rules Committee to govern the handling of a particular bill on the floor. The committee may report a "rule," also called a "special order," in the form of a simple resolution. If the resolution is adopted by the House, the temporary rule becomes as valid as any standing rule and lapses only after action has been completed on the measure to which it pertains. A rule sets the time limit on general debate. It also may waive points of order against provisions of the bill in question, such as nongermane language, or against certain amendments intended to be proposed to the bill from the floor. It may even forbid all amendments or all amendments except those proposed by the legislative committee that handled the bill. In this instance, it is known as a "closed" or "gag" rule as opposed to an "open" rule, which puts no limitation on floor amendments, thus leaving the bill completely open to alteration by the adoption of germane amendments.

Senatorial Courtesy—Sometimes referred to as "the courtesy of the Senate," it is a general practice — with no written rule — applied to consideration of executive nominations. Generally, it means that nominations from a state are not to be confirmed unless they have been approved by the senators of the president's party of that state, with other senators following their colleagues' lead in the attitude they take toward consideration of such nominations.

Speaker—The presiding officer of the House of Representatives, selected by the caucus of the party to which he belongs and formally elected by the whole House.

Standing Committee—*(See Committee.)*

Standing Vote—A nonrecorded vote used in both the House and Senate. (A standing vote also is called a division vote.) Members in favor of a proposal stand and are counted by the presiding officer. Then members opposed stand and are counted. There is no record of how individual members voted.

Strike From the Record—Remarks made on the House floor may offend some member, who moves that the offending words be "taken down" for the Speaker's cognizance, and then expunged from the debate as published in the *Congressional Record.*

Strike Out the Last Word—A motion whereby a House member is entitled to speak for five minutes on an amendment then being debated by the chamber. A member gains recognition from the chair by moving to "strike out the last word" of the amendment or section of the bill under consideration. The motion is pro forma, requires no vote and does not change the amendment being debated.

Substitute—A motion, amendment or entire bill introduced in place of the pending legislative business. Passage of a substitute measure kills the original measure by supplanting it. The substitute also may be amended. *(See also Amendment in the Nature of a Substitute.)*

Supplemental Appropriations Bill—Legislation appropriating funds after the regular annual appropriations bill for a federal department or agency has been enacted. A supplemental appropriation provides additional budget authority beyond original estimates for programs or activities, including new programs authorized after the enactment of the regular appropriations act. *(See also Appropriations Bill.)*

Suspend the Rules—Often a time-saving procedure for passing bills in the House. The wording of the motion, which may be made by any member recognized by the Speaker, is: "I move to suspend the rules and pass the bill. . . ." A favorable vote by two-thirds of those present is required for passage. Debate is limited to 40 minutes and no amendments from the floor are permitted. If a two-thirds favorable vote is not attained, the bill may be considered later under regular procedures. The suspension procedure is in order every Monday and Tuesday and is intended to be reserved for noncontroversial bills.

Table a Bill—A motion to "lay on the table" is not debatable in either house, and usually it is a method of making a final, adverse disposition of a matter. In the Senate, however, different language sometimes is used. The motion may be worded to let a bill "lie on the table," perhaps for subsequent "picking up." This motion is more flexible, keeping the bill pending for later action, if desired. Tabling motions on amendments are effective debate-ending devices in the Senate.

Teller Vote—This is a largely moribund House procedure in the Committee of the Whole. Members file past tellers and are counted as for, or against, a measure, but they are not recorded individually. In the House, tellers are ordered upon demand of one-fifth of a quorum. This is 44 in the House, 20 in the Committee of the Whole. The House also has a recorded teller vote, now largely supplanted by the electronic voting procedure. *(See Recorded Vote.)*

Treaties—Executive proposals — in the form of resolutions of ratification — which must be submitted to the Senate for approval by two-thirds of the senators present. Treaties today are normally sent to the Foreign Relations Committee for scrutiny before the Senate takes action. Foreign Relations has jurisdiction over all treaties, regardless of the subject matter.

Treaties are read three times and debated on the floor in much the same manner as legislative proposals. After approval by the Senate, treaties are formally ratified by the president. Unlike legislative documents, however, treaties do not die at the end of a Congress but remain "live" proposals until acted on by the Senate or withdrawn by the president.

Unanimous Consent—Proceedings of the House or Senate and action on legislation often take place upon the unanimous consent of the chamber, whether or not a rule of the chamber is being violated. Unanimous consent is used to expedite floor action and frequently is used in a routine fashion, for example, when a senator requests the unanimous consent of the Senate to have specified members of his staff present on the floor during debate on an amendment.

Unanimous Consent Agreement—A device used in the Senate to expedite legislation. Much of the Senate's legislative business, dealing with both minor and controversial issues, is conducted through unanimous consent or unanimous consent agreements. On major legislation, such agreements usually are printed and transmitted to all senators in advance of floor debate. Once agreed to, they are binding on all members unless the Senate, by unanimous consent, agrees to modify them. An agreement may list the order in which various bills are to be considered, specify the length of time bills and contested amendments are to be debated and when they are to be voted upon and, frequently, require that all amendments introduced be germane to the bill under consideration. In this regard, unanimous consent agreements are similar to the "rules" issued by the House Rules Committee for bills pending in the House. *(See Rules.)*

Union Calendar—Bills that directly or indirectly appropriate money or raise revenue are placed on this House calendar according to the date they are reported from committee.

Veto—Disapproval by the president of a bill or joint resolution (other than one proposing an amendment to the Constitution). When Congress is in session, the president must veto a bill within 10 days, excluding Sundays, after he has received it; otherwise, it becomes law without his signature. When the president vetoes a bill, he returns it to the house of origin along with a message stating his objections. *(See also Pocket Veto, Override a Veto.)*

Voice Vote—In either the House or Senate, members answer "aye" or "no" in chorus, and the presiding officer decides the result. The term also is used loosely to indicate action by unanimous consent or without objection.

Yeas and Nays—The Constitution requires that yea-and-nay votes be taken and recorded when requested by one-fifth of the members present. In the House, the Speaker determines whether one-fifth of the members present requested a vote. In the Senate, practice requires only 11 members. The Constitution requires the yeas and nays on a veto override attempt. *(See Recorded Vote.)*

Yielding—When a member has been recognized to speak, no other member may speak unless he obtains permission from the member recognized. This permission is called yielding and usually is requested in the form, "Will the gentleman yield to me?" While this activity occasionally is seen in the Senate, that chamber has no rule or practice to parcel out time, other than in unanimous consent agreements.

Selected Bibliography

1. Congress and Lawmaking

Berman, Daniel M. *In Congress Assembled.* New York: Macmillan, 1964.

Bibby, John, and Davidson, Roger H. *On Capitol Hill.* 2d ed. Hinsdale, Ill.: The Dryden Press, 1972.

Burnham, James. *Congress and the American Tradition.* Chicago: Henry Regnery, 1959.

Davidson, Roger H., and Oleszek, Walter J. *Congress and Its Members.* Washington, D.C.: CQ Press, 1981.

DeGrazia, Alfred, ed. *Congress: The First Branch of Government.* Washington, D.C.: The American Enterprise Institute for Public Policy Research, 1966.

Galloway, George B. *The Legislative Process in Congress.* New York: Thomas Y. Crowell, 1953.

Goehlert, Robert U., and Sayre, John R. *The United States Congress, A Bibliography.* New York: The Free Press, 1982.

Griffith, Ernest S., and Valeo, Francis R. *Congress: Its Contemporary Role.* 5th ed. New York: New York University Press, 1975.

Gross, Bertram M. *The Legislative Struggle.* New York: McGraw-Hill, 1953.

Jones, Charles O. *The United States Congress.* Homewood, Ill.: The Dorsey Press, 1982.

Keefe, William J. *Congress and the American People.* 2d ed. Englewood Cliffs, N.J.: Prentice-Hall, 1984.

Kozak, David C., and Macartney, John D., eds. *Congress and Public Policy.* Homewood, Ill.: The Dorsey Press, 1982.

Luce, Robert. *Legislative Procedures.* Boston: Houghton Mifflin, 1922.

———. *Legislative Assemblies.* Boston: Houghton Mifflin, 1924.

———. *Legislative Principles.* Boston: Houghton Mifflin, 1930.

———. *Legislative Problems.* Boston: Houghton Mifflin, 1935.

Mikva, Abner J., and Saris, Patti B. *The American Congress.* New York: Franklin Watts, 1983.

Orfield, Gary. *Congressional Power.* New York: Harcourt, Brace, Jovanovich, 1975.

Polsby, Nelson W., ed. *Congressional Behavior.* New York: Random House, 1971.

Rieselbach, Leroy N. *Congressional Politics.* New York: McGraw-Hill, 1973.

Ripley, Randall B. *Congress, Process and Policy.* 3d ed. New York: W. W. Norton, 1983.

Saloma, John S. *Congress and the New Politics.* Boston: Little, Brown & Co., 1969.

Vogler, David. *The Politics of Congress.* 4th ed. Boston: Allyn & Bacon, 1983.

Young, Roland. *The American Congress.* New York: Harper & Bros., 1958.

2. The Congressional Environment

Baker, Ross K. *Friend and Foe in the U.S. Senate.* New York: The Free Press, 1980.

Bauer, Raymond, and others. *American Business and Public Policy: The Politics of Foreign Trade.* New York: Atherton Press, 1963.

Blanchard, Robert O., ed. *Congress and the News Media.* New York: Hastings House, 1974.

Bolling, Richard. *House Out Of Order.* New York: E. P. Dutton & Co., 1965.

_____. *Power in the House.* New York: E. P. Dutton & Co., 1968.

Chamberlain, Lawrence H. *The President, Congress and Legislation.* New York: Columbia University Press, 1946.

Cigler, Allan J., and Loomis, Burdett A., eds. *Interest Group Politics.* Washington, D.C.: CQ Press, 1983.

Cohen, Richard E. "On the Run With Richard Gephardt — A Day in the Life of a House Member." *National Journal,* October 8, 1983, 2059-2063.

Cooper, Joseph, and Mackenzie, G. Calvin, eds. *The House at Work.* Austin: University of Texas Press, 1981.

Davidson, Roger H., and others. *Congress in Crisis: Politics and Congressional Reform.* Belmont, Calif.: Wadsworth Publishing Co., 1966.

Dodd, Lawrence C., and Oppenheimer, Bruce I., eds. *Congress Reconsidered.* 2d ed. Washington, D.C.: CQ Press, 1981.

Edwards, George C., III. *Presidential Influence in Congress.* San Francisco: W. H. Freeman, 1980.

Fenno, Richard F., Jr. *Home Style: House Members in Their Districts.* Boston: Little, Brown & Co., 1978.

Graber, Doris A. *Mass Media and American Politics.* Washington, D.C.: CQ Press, 1980.

Hasbrouck, Paul. *Party Government in the House of Representatives.* New York: Macmillan, 1927.

Hechler, Kenneth W. *Insurgency.* New York: Columbia University Press, 1940.

Holtzman, Abraham. *Legislative Liaison: Executive Leadership in Congress.* Chicago: Rand McNally, 1970.

Hopkins, Bruce R. "Congressional Reform: Towards A Modern Congress." *Notre Dame Lawyer,* February 1972, 442-513.

Huitt, Ralph K. "Democratic Party Leadership in the Senate." *American*

Political Science Review, June 1961, 333-344.

Jacobson, Gary C., and Kernell, Samuel. *Strategy and Choice in Congressional Elections.* New Haven, Conn.: Yale University Press, 1981.

Johannes, John. "Congress and the Initiation of Legislation." *Public Policy,* Spring 1972, 281-309.

Jones, Charles O. *The Minority Party in Congress.* Boston: Little, Brown & Co., 1970.

Kernell, Sam. "Is the Senate More Liberal Than the House?" *Journal of Politics,* May 1973, 332-366.

King, Anthony, ed. *Both Ends of the Avenue, The Presidency, the Executive Branch, and Congress in the 1980s.* Washington, D.C.: The American Enterprise Institute for Public Policy Research, 1983.

Kravitz, Walter. "Relations Between the Senate and House of Representatives: The Party Leaderships." In *Policymaking Role of Leadership in the Senate.* A Compilation of Papers Prepared for the Commission on the Operation of the Senate, 94th Cong., 2d sess., 1976, 121-138.

Moe, Ronald, and Teel, Stephen. "Congress as Policy-Maker: A Necessary Reappraisal." *Political Science Quarterly,* September 1970, 443-470.

Ornstein, Norman J., ed. *Congress in Change.* New York: Praeger Publishers, 1975.

_____, and Mann, Thomas E., eds. *The New Congress.* Washington, D.C.: The American Enterprise Institute for Public Policy Research, 1981.

Peabody, Robert L. *Leadership in Congress.* Boston: Little, Brown & Co., 1976.

_____, and others. "The United States Senate as a Presidential Incubator: Many Are Called but Few Are Chosen." *Political Science Quarterly,* Summer 1976, 236-258.

Price, David. *Who Makes the Laws?* Cambridge, Mass.: Schenkman Publishing Co., 1972.

Ripley, Randall B. *Majority Party Leadership in Congress.* Boston: Little, Brown & Co., 1969.

Schlozman, Kay Lehman, and Tierney, John T. "More of the Same: Washington Pressure Group Activity in a Decade of Change." *Journal of Politics,* May 1983, 351-377.

Sundquist, James. *Politics and Policy.* Washington, D.C.: The Brookings Institution, 1968.

Wayne, Stephen. *The Legislative Presidency.* New York: Harper & Row, 1978.

3. Congressional Budget Process

Committee for a Responsible Federal Budget. "The Congressional Budget Act and Process: How Can They Be Improved?" Compendium and proceedings of a symposium held in Arkadelphia, Ark., on January 11-13, 1982.

Research and Policy Committee. "Strengthening the Federal Budget Process: A Requirement for Effective Fiscal Control." Washington, D.C.:

Committee for Economic Development, 1983.

Ellwood, John William. "Congress Cuts the Budget: The Omnibus Reconciliation Act of 1981." *Public Budgeting and Finance*, Spring 1982, 50-64.

_____, and Thurber, James A. "The Politics of the Congressional Budget Process Re-Examined." In *Congress Reconsidered.* 2d ed., edited by Lawrence C. Dodd and Bruce I. Oppenheimer, Washington, D.C.: CQ Press, 1981, 246-271.

Fenno, Richard F., Jr. *The Power of the Purse.* Boston: Little, Brown & Co., 1966.

Fisher, Louis. "Annual Authorizations: Durable Roadblocks to Biennial Budgeting." *Public Budgeting and Finance*, Spring 1983, 23-40.

_____. "In Dubious Battle? Congress and the Budget." *Brookings Bulletin,* vol. 17., Spring 1981, 6-10.

_____. *Presidential Spending Power.* Princeton, N.J.: Princeton University Press, 1975.

_____. "The Authorization-Appropriation Process in Congress: Formal Rules and Informal Practices." *Catholic University Law Review,* Fall 1979, 51-105.

Greider, William. *The Education of David Stockman and Other Americans.* New York: E. P. Dutton, 1981.

Hartman, Robert W. "Congress and Budget-Making." *Political Science Quarterly*, Fall 1982, 381-402.

Keith, Robert A. "Budget Reconciliation in 1981." *Public Budgeting and Finance*, Winter 1981, 37-47.

Havemann, Joel. *Congress and the Budget.* Bloomington: Indiana University Press, 1978.

Ippolito, Dennis S. *Congressional Spending.* Ithaca, N.Y.: Cornell University Press, 1981.

LeLoup, Lance T. *The Fiscal Congress.* Westport, Conn.: Greenwood Press, 1980.

_____. "After the Blitz: Reagan and the U.S. Congressional Budget Process." *Legislative Studies Quarterly*, Winter 1981, 37-47.

Ott, David J., and Ott, Attiat F. *Federal Budget Policy.* 3d ed. Washington, D.C.: The Brookings Institution, 1977.

Penner, Rudolph G., ed. *The Congressional Budget Process After Five Years.* Washington, D.C.: The American Enterprise Institute for Public Policy Research, 1981.

Pfiffner, James P. *The President, the Budget, and Congress: Impoundment and the 1974 Budget Act.* Boulder, Colo.: Westview Press, 1979.

"The Reagan Budget: Redistribution of Power and Responsibilities, Five Perspectives." *PS,* American Political Science Association, vol. 14, Fall 1981.

Rivlin, Alice M. "Congress and the Budget Process." *Challenge*, March-April 1981, 31-37.

Schick, Allen. *Congress and Money.* Washington, D.C.: The Urban Institute, 1980.

_____. *Reconciliation and the Congressional Budget Process.* Washington, D.C.: The American Enterprise Institute for Public Policy Research, 1981.

_____. "The Three-Ring Budget Process: The Appropriations, Tax, and Budget Committees in Congress," edited by Thomas E. Mann and Norman J. Ornstein. In *The New Congress.* Washington, D.C.: The American Enterprise Institute for Public Policy Research, 1981, 288-328.

_____. "Congressional Control of Expenditures." Prepared for the House Budget Committee, U.S. House of Representatives. Washington, D.C.: U.S. Government Printing Office, 1977.

Wildavsky, Aaron, *The Politics of the Budgetary Process.* 4th ed. Boston: Little, Brown & Co., 1984.

Wilmerding, Lucius. *The Spending Power.* New Haven, Conn.: Yale University Press, 1943.

4. Preliminary Legislative Action

Abram, Michael, and Cooper, Joseph. "The Rise of Seniority in the House of Representatives." *Polity,* Fall 1968, 35-51.

Bowsher, Prentice. "The Speaker's Man: Lewis Deschler, House Parliamentarian." *The Washington Monthly,* April 1970, 22-27.

Cooper, Joseph. *The Origins of the Standing Committees and the Development of the Modern House*, Rice University Monograph in Political Science, vol. 56, no. 3, Summer 1970.

Davidson, Roger H., and Oleszek, Walter J. *Congress against Itself.* Bloomington: Indiana University Press, 1977.

Deering, Christopher J., and Smith, Steven S. *Committees in Congress.* Washington, D.C.: CQ Press, 1984.

Eckhardt, Bob. "The Presumption of Committee Openness Under House Rules." *Harvard Journal on Legislation,* February 1974, 279-302.

Fenno, Richard F., Jr. *Congressmen in Committees.* Boston: Little, Brown & Co., 1973.

Fox, Harrison W., Jr., and Hammond, Susan Webb. *Congressional Staffs.* New York: The Free Press, 1977.

Goodwin, George. *The Little Legislatures.* Amherst: University of Massachusetts Press, 1970.

Kofmehl, Kenneth. *Professional Staffs of Congress.* 3d ed. West Lafayette, Ind.: Purdue University Press, 1977.

Kravitz, Walter. "Evolution of the Senate's Committee System." *The Annals,* January 1974, 27-38.

Malbin, Michael J. *Unelected Representatives: Congressional Staff and the Future of Representative Government.* New York: Basic Books, 1979.

Morrow, William L. *Congressional Committees.* New York: Charles Scribner's Sons, 1969.

Price, David E. "Professionals and 'Entrepreneurs': Staff Orientations and

Policy Making on Three Senate Committees." *Journal of Politics,* May 1971, 313-336.

"Private Bills in Congress." *Harvard Law Review,* vol. 79, 1966, 1684-1706.

Shepsle, Kenneth A. *The Giant Jigsaw Puzzle: Democratic Committee Assignments in the Modern House.* Chicago: University of Chicago Press, 1978.

Van Der Slik, Jack R., and Stenger, Thomas C. "Citizen Witnesses before Congressional Committees." *Political Science Quarterly,* Fall 1977, 465-485.

Wilson, Woodrow. *Congressional Government.* Gloucester, Mass.: Peter Smith, 1885.

5. Scheduling Legislation in the House

"A History of the Committee on Rules," Committee Print, 97th Cong., 2d sess., Washington, D.C.: U.S. Government Printing Office, 1983.

Albert, Carl. *The Office and Duties of the Speaker of the House of Representatives.* H. Doc. No. 94-582, 94th Cong., 2d sess., 1976.

Chiu, Chang Wei. *The Speaker of the House of Representatives Since 1896.* New York: Columbia University Press, 1928.

Cooper, Joseph, and Brady, David W. "Institutional Context and Leadership Style: The House From Cannon to Rayburn." *American Political Science Review,* June 1981, 411-425.

Drew, Elizabeth. "A Tendency to Legislate." *New Yorker,* June 26, 1978, 80-89.

Elder, Shirley, and Clancy, Paul. *Tip.* New York: Macmillan, 1980.

Froman, Lewis A., and Ripley, Randall B. "Conditions for Party Leadership: The Case of the House Democrats." *American Political Science Review,* March 1965, 52-63.

Jones, Charles O. "Joseph G. Cannon and Howard W. Smith: An Essay on the Limits of Leadership in the House of Representatives." *Journal of Politics,* September 1968, 617-646.

Mackaman, Frank H., ed. *Understanding Congressional Leadership.* Washington, D.C.: CQ Press, 1981.

Matsunaga, Spark M., and Chen, Ping. *Rulemakers of the House.* Urbana: University of Illinois Press, 1976.

Ripley, Randall B. "Party Whip Organizations in the United States House of Representatives." *American Political Science Review,* September 1964, 561-576.

"Scheduling the Work of the House." H. Doc. No. 95-23, 95th Cong., 1st sess., January 4, 1977.

6. House Floor Procedure

Alexander, DeAlva Stanwood. *History and Procedure of the House of Representatives.* Boston: Houghton Mifflin Co., 1916.

Arieff, Irwin B. "House Floor Watchdog Role Made Famous by H. R. Gross

Has Fallen on Hard Times." *Congressional Quarterly Weekly Report,* July 24, 1982, 1775-1776.

Bach, Stanley. "The Structure of Choice in the House of Representatives: The Impact of Complex Special Rules." *Harvard Journal on Legislation,* Summer 1981, 553-602.

Clausen, Aage R. *How Congressmen Decide.* New York: St. Martin's Press, 1973.

Damon, Richard E. *The Standing Rules of the U.S. House of Representatives.* Ph.D. diss., Columbia University, 1971.

Fleisher, Richard, and Bond, Jon R. "Beyond Committee Control: Committee and Party Leader Influence on Floor Amendments in Congress." *American Politics Quarterly,* April 1983, 131-161.

Froman, Lewis A. *The Congressional Process: Strategies, Rules and Procedures.* Boston: Little, Brown & Co., 1967.

Harlow, Ralph V. *The History of Legislative Methods in the Period Before 1825.* New Haven, Conn.: Yale University Press, 1917.

House, Albert V., Jr. "The Contributions of Samuel J. Randall to the Rules of the National House of Representatives." *American Political Science Review,* October 1935, 837-841.

Kingdon, John W. *Congressmen's Voting Decisions.* New York: Harper & Row, 1973.

MacNeil, Neil. *Forge of Democracy: The House of Representatives.* New York: David McKay, 1963.

Polsby, Nelson W. "The Institutionalization of the House of Representatives." *American Political Science Review,* March 1968, 144-168.

Rhodes, John J. "Floor Procedure in the House of Representatives." In *We Propose: A Modern Congress,* edited by Mary McInnes, 201-206. New York: McGraw-Hill, 1966.

Riddick, Floyd M. *The Organization and Procedure of the United States Congress.* Manassas, Va.: National Capitol Publishers, 1949.

Robinson, William A. *Thomas B. Reed, Parliamentarian.* New York: Dodd, Mead & Co., 1930.

Siff, Todd, and Weil, Alan. *Ruling Congress: A Study on How the House and Senate Rules Govern the Legislative Process.* New York: Grossman, 1975.

Sinclair, Barbara. "The Speaker's Task Force in the Post-Reform House of Representatives." *American Political Science Review,* June 1981, 397-410.

7. Scheduling Legislation in the Senate

Asbell, Bernard. *The Senate Nobody Knows.* Garden City, N.Y.: Doubleday, 1978.

Bone, Hugh A. "An Introduction to the Senate Policy Committees." *American Political Science Review,* June 1956, 339-359.

Clark, Joseph S. *The Senate Establishment.* New York: Hill & Wang, 1963.

Cohen, William S. *Roll Call: One Year in the United States Senate.* New

York: Simon & Schuster, 1981.

Ehrenhalt, Alan. "Special Report: The Individualist Senate." *Congressional Quarterly Weekly Report,* September 4, 1982, 2175-2182.

Glass, Andrew J. "Mansfield Reforms Spark 'Quiet Revolution' in Senate." *National Journal,* March 6, 1971, 499-512.

Granat, Diane. "Inside Congress: 'Tuesday Through Thursday Club.'" *Congressional Quarterly Weekly Report,* July 16, 1983, 1427-1432.

Huitt, Ralph K. "The Internal Distribution of Influence: the Senate." In *The Congress and America's Future,* edited by David B. Truman, 91-117. Englewood Cliffs, N.J.: Prentice-Hall, 1965.

Jewell, Malcolm. "The Senate Republican Policy Committee and Foreign Policy." *Western Political Quarterly,* December 1959, 966-980.

Oleszek, Walter J. "Party Whips in the United States Senate." *Journal of Politics,* November 1971, 955-979.

Polsby, Nelson W. "Goodbye to the Inner Club." *Washington Monthly,* August 1969, 30-34.

Riddick, Floyd M. *Majority and Minority Leaders of the Senate.* S. Doc. 97-12, 97th Cong., 1st sess. Washington, D.C.: U.S. Government Printing Office, 1981.

Robinson, Donald Allen. "If the Senate Democrats Want Leadership: An Analysis of the History and Prospects of the Majority Policy Committee." In *Policymaking Role of Leadership in the Senate.* A Compilation of Papers Prepared for the Commission on the Operation of the Senate, 94th Cong., 2d sess., 1976, 40-57.

Stewart, John G. "Central Policy Organs in Congress." In *Congress Against the President,* edited by Harvey C. Mansfield, Sr., 21-33. New York: Praeger Publishers, 1975.

Walker, Jack L. "Setting the Agenda in the U.S. Senate." In *Policymaking Role of Leadership in the Senate.* A Compilation of Papers Prepared for the Commission on the Operation of the Senate, 94th Cong., 2d sess., 1976, 96-120.

Webber, Ross. "U.S. Senators: See How They Run." *Wharton Magazine,* Winter 1980-1981, 37-43.

8. Senate Floor Procedure

Bach, Stanley. "Parliamentary Strategy and the Amendment Process: Rules and Case Studies of Congressional Action." *Polity,* Summer 1983, 573-592.

Beeman, Richard R. "Unlimited Debate in the Senate: The First Phase." *Political Science Quarterly,* September 1968, 419-434.

Burdette, Franklin L. *Filibustering in the Senate.* Princeton, N.J.: Princeton University Press, 1940.

Carlisle, Margo. "Changing the Rules of the Game in the U.S. Senate." *Policy Review,* Winter 1979, 79-92.

Cohen, Richard E. "Marking an End to the Senate's Mansfield Era." *National Journal,* December 25, 1976, 1802-1809.

Dove, Robert B. *Enactment of a Law.* S. Doc. 97-20, 97th Cong., 2d sess. Washington, D.C.: U.S. Government Printing Office, 1982.

Drew, Elizabeth. *Senator.* New York: Simon & Schuster, 1979.

Evans, Rowland, and Novak, Robert. *Lyndon B. Johnson: The Exercise of Power.* New York: New American Library, 1966.

Foley, Michael. *The New Senate Liberal Influence on a 'Conservative Institution,' 1959-1972.* New Haven: Yale University Press, 1980.

Froman, Lewis A. *The Congressional Process: Strategies, Rules and Procedures.* Boston: Little, Brown & Co., 1967.

Gilfry, Henry H. *Precedents: Decisions on Points of Order With Phraseology in the United States Senate.* S. Doc. 129, 61st Cong., 1st sess. Washington, D.C.: U.S. Government Printing Office, 1909.

Harris, Joseph P. *The Advice and Consent of the Senate.* Berkeley: University of California Press, 1953.

Huitt, Ralph K. "The Outsider in the Senate: Alternative Role." *American Political Science Review,* September 1961, 566-575.

Keith, Robert. "The Use of Unanimous Consent in the Senate." In *Committees and Senate Procedures.* A Compilation of Papers Prepared for the Commission on the Operation of the Senate, 94th Cong., 2d sess., 1977, 140-168.

Keynes, Edward. "The Senate Rules and the Dirksen Amendment: A Study in Legislative Strategy and Tactics." In *The Legislative Process in the U.S. Senate,* edited by Lawrence K. Pettit and Edward Keynes, 104-149. Chicago: Rand McNally, 1969.

Lehnen, Robert G. "Behavior on the Senate Floor: An Analysis of Debate in the U.S. Senate." *Midwest Journal of Political Science,* November 1967, 505-521.

Mackenzie, G. Calvin. *The Politics of Presidential Appointments.* New York: The Free Press, 1981.

Matthews, Donald. *U.S. Senators And Their World.* Chapel Hill: University of North Carolina Press, 1960.

Peffer, William A. "The Senate's Powers and Functions: Its Rules and Methods of Doing Business." *The North American Review,* August 1898, 176-190.

Ripley, Randall B. *Power in the Senate.* New York: St. Martin's Press, 1969.

Shuman, Howard E. "Senate Rules and the Civil Rights Bill: A Case Study." *American Political Science Review,* December 1957, 955-975.

Siff, Todd, and Weil, Alan. *Ruling Congress: A Study of How the House and Senate Rules Govern the Legislative Process.* New York: Grossman, 1975.

9. Resolving House-Senate Differences

Bach, Stanley, "Germaneness Rules and Bicameral Relations in the U.S. Congress." *Legislative Studies Quarterly,* August 1982, 341-357.

Fenno, Richard F., Jr. Chap. 12 in *The Power of the Purse: Appropriations Politics in Congress.* Boston: Little, Brown & Co., 1966.

___. *The United States Senate: A Bicameral Perspective.* Washington, D.C.: The American Enterprise Institute for Public Policy Research, 1982.

Ferejohn, John. "Who Wins in Conference Committee?" *Journal of Politics,* November 1975, 1033-1046.

Gore, Albert. "The Conference Committee: Congress' Final Filter." *Washington Monthly,* June 1971, 43-48.

Horn, Stephen. *Unused Power: The Work of the Senate Committee on Appropriations.* Washington, D.C.: The Brookings Institution, 1970, 154-173.

Manley, John F. Chap. 6 in *The Politics of Finance: The House Committee on Ways and Means.* Boston: Little, Brown & Co., 1970.

McCall, Samuel W. Chap. 9 in *The Business of Congress.* New York: Columbia University Press, 1911.

McCown, Ada C. *The Congressional Conference Committee.* New York: Columbia University Press, 1927.

Oleszek, Walter J. "House-Senate Relationships: Comity and Conflict." *The Annals,* January 1974, 75-86.

Paletz, David L. *Influence in Congress: An Analysis of the Nature and Effects of Conference Committees Utilizing Case Studies of Poverty, Traffic Safety, and Congressional Redistricting Legislation.* Ph.D. diss., University of California, Los Angeles, 1970.

Pressman, Jeffrey L. *House vs. Senate: Conflict in the Appropriations Process.* New Haven, Conn.: Yale University Press, 1966.

"Reform Penetrates Conference Committees." *Congressional Quarterly Weekly Report,* February 8, 1975, 290-294.

Riggs, Richard. "Separation of Powers: Congressional Riders and the Veto Powers." *University of Michigan Journal of Law Reform,* Spring 1973, 735-759.

Rogers, Lindsay. "Conference Committee Legislation." *North American Review,* March 1922, 300-307.

Steiner, Gilbert. *The Congressional Conference Committee, Seventieth to Eightieth Congresses.* Urbana: University of Illinois Press, 1951.

Strom, Gerald S., and Rundquist, Barry S. "A Revised Theory of Winning in House-Senate Conferences." *American Political Science Review,* June 1977, 448-453.

Vogler, David J. *The Third House: Conference Committees in the U.S. Congress.* Evanston, Ill.: Northwestern University Press, 1971.

10. Legislative Oversight

Aberbach, Joel D. "Changes in Congressional Oversight." *American Behavioral Scientist,* May-June 1979, 493-515.

Dodd, Lawrence C., and Schott, Richard L. *Congress and the Administrative State.* New York: John Wiley & Sons, 1979.

Edwards, George C., III. *Implementing Public Policy.* Washington, D.C.: CQ Press, 1980.

Fisher, Louis. *The Politics of Shared Power: Congress and the Executive.*

Washington, D.C.: CQ Press, 1981.

Fitzgerald, John L. "Congressional Oversight or Congressional Foresight: Guidelines from the Founding Fathers." *Administrative Law Review,* Summer 1976, 429-445.

Freeman, J. Leiper. *The Political Process: Executive Bureau-Legislative Committee Relations.* rev. ed. Garden City, N.Y.: Doubleday & Co., 1965.

Gray, Kenneth E. "Congressional Interference in Administration." In *Cooperation and Conflict,* edited by Daniel J. Elazar and others, 521-542. Itasca, Ill.: F. E. Peacock Publishers, 1969.

Harris, Joseph P. *Congressional Control of Administration.* Washington, D.C.: The Brookings Institution, 1964.

Henderson, Thomas A. *Congressional Oversight of Executive Agencies.* Gainesville: University of Florida Press, 1970.

Immigration and Naturalization Service v. Chada, et al., no. 80-1832, June 23, 1983. Supreme Court of the United States.

Kaiser, Fred. "Oversight of Foreign Policy: The U.S. House International Relations Committee." *Legislative Studies Quarterly,* August 1977, 255-280.

Kaufman, Herbert. *Are Government Organizations Immortal?* Washington, D.C.: The Brookings Institution, 1976.

Lees, John D. "Legislatures and Oversight: A Review Article on a Neglected Area of Research." *Legislative Studies Quarterly,* May 1977, 193-208.

Ogul, Morris S. *Congress Oversees the Bureaucracy.* Pittsburgh, Pa.: University of Pittsburgh Press, 1976.

Ripley, Randall B., and Franklin, Grace A. *Congress, the Bureaucracy, and Public Policy.* rev. ed. Homewood, Ill.: The Dorsey Press, 1980.

Scher, Seymour. "Conditions for Legislative Control." *Journal of Politics,* August 1963, 526-551.

Schick, Allen. "Congress and the 'Details' of Administration." *Public Administration Review,* September/October 1976, 516-527.

Taylor, Telford. *Grand Inquest: The Story of Congressional Investigations.* New York: Simon & Schuster, 1955.

11. A Dynamic Process

Bailey, Stephen K. *Congress Makes a Law.* New York: Columbia University Press, 1950.

Berman, Daniel M. *How A Bill Becomes A Law: Congress Enacts Civil Rights Legislation.* 2d ed. New York: Macmillan, 1966.

Bibby, John F., ed. *Congress off the Record, The Candid Analyses of Seven Members.* Washington, D.C.: The American Enterprise Institute for Public Policy Research, 1983.

Brenner, Philip, *The Limits and Possibilities of Congress.* New York: St. Martin's Press, 1983.

Cleveland, Frederic N. *Congress and Urban Problems: A Casebook on the Legislative Process.* Washington, D.C.: The Brookings Institution, 1969.

Eidenberg, Eugene, and Morey, Roy D. *An Act of Congress.* New York: W. W. Norton & Co., 1969.

Ferejohn, John A. *Pork Barrel Politics.* Stanford, Calif.: Stanford University Press, 1974.

Franck, Thomas M., and Weisband, Edward. *Foreign Policy by Congress.* New York: Oxford University Press, 1979.

Hale, Dennis, ed. *The United States Congress.* New Brunswick, N.J.: Transaction Books, 1983.

Maslow, Will. "FEPC: A Case History in Parliamentary Maneuver." *The University of Chicago Law Review,* June 1946, 407-444.

Oleszek, Walter J. "Integration and Fragmentation: Key Themes of Congressional Change." *The Annals,* March 1983, 193-205.

Ornstein, Norman J., ed. *The Role of the Legislature in Western Democracies.* Washington, D.C.: The American Enterprise Institute for Public Policy Research, 1981.

Peabody, Robert L., and others. *To Enact A Law.* New York: Praeger Publishers, 1972.

Redman, Eric. *The Dance of Legislation.* New York: Simon & Schuster, 1973.

Rieselbach, Leroy N., ed. *Legislative Reform: The Policy Impact.* Lexington, Mass.: Lexington Books, 1978.

Robinson, James A. *Congress and Foreign Policy-Making.* Homewood, Ill.: The Dorsey Press, 1962.

Schlesinger, Arthur, Jr. "Congress and the Making of American Foreign Policy." *Foreign Affairs,* October 1972, 78-113.

Sundquist, James L. *The Decline and Resurgence of Congress.* Washington, D.C.: The Brookings Institution, 1981.

Index